# A New History of American and Canadian Folk Music

# A New History of American and Canadian Folk Music

Dick Weissman

BLOOMSBURY ACADEMIC
NEW YORK • LONDON • OXFORD • NEW DELHI • SYDNEY

BLOOMSBURY ACADEMIC
Bloomsbury Publishing Inc
1385 Broadway, New York, NY 10018, USA
50 Bedford Square, London, WC1B 3DP, UK

BLOOMSBURY, BLOOMSBURY ACADEMIC and the Diana logo are
trademarks of Bloomsbury Publishing Plc

First published in the United States of America 2020

Library of Congress Cataloging-in-Publication Data
Names: Weissman, Dick, author.
Title: A new history of American and Canadian folk music / Dick Weissman.
Description: New York, NY : Bloomsbury Academic, 2019. | Includes bibliographical
references and index.
Identifiers: LCCN 2019008327 (print) | LCCN 2019009949 (ebook) | ISBN 9781501344169
(ePub) | ISBN 9781501344176 (ePDF) | ISBN 9781501344145 (pbk. : alk. paper) | ISBN
9781501344152 (hardback : alk. paper)
Subjects: LCSH: Folk music–United States–History and criticism. | Folk
music–Canada–History and criticism.
Classification: LCC ML3550 (ebook) | LCC ML3550 .W45 2019 (print) |
DDC 781.62/1009–dc23
LC record available at https://lccn.loc.gov/2019008327

ISBN:    HB:    978-1-5013-4415-2
         PB:    978-1-5013-4414-5
         ePDF:  978-1-5013-4417-6
         eBook: 978-1-5013-4416-9

Typeset by Integra Software Services Pvt. Ltd.
Printed and bound in the United States of America

To find out more about our authors and books visit www.bloomsbury.com
and sign up for our newsletters.

# Contents

# Preface: A personal note

My own interest in folk music started in my home town of Philadelphia, when my older brother dragged me to see Pete Seeger perform at the 1948 Progressive Party convention. At the time I was a pre-teenager who knew nothing about the banjo or American folk music. I was captivated by the sound of the banjo. Over the next five years I bought as many recordings as I could afford by such artists as Seeger and Woody Guthrie, and I scoured discount stores for recordings of Memphis Minnie, Big Bill Broonzy, and Brownie McGhee.

When I was sixteen years old I bought a mimeographed (!) edition of Pete Seeger's banjo instruction book. I followed his instructions to search for a banjo in a pawn shop and I found a quality banjo for $25. Although I could read music and play the piano, I knew nothing about string instruments and was unable to follow Pete's directions. When I enrolled at Goddard College in Vermont, Lil Blos, my best friend's girlfriend, offered to teach me how to play.

By arrangement with Goddard, my junior year at college was spent in New York and New Mexico. I took guitar and banjo lessons from Jerry Silverman, met and played with the incredible Reverend Gary Davis in New York and a wonderful though little-known banjoist named Stu Jamieson in Albuquerque.

After college I moved to New York and became involved in the Greenwich Village folk scene doing low-paying gigs, teaching banjo and guitar, and making my first records. At the time I was a total purist, something of a "folk-Nazi," as Utah Phillips would say. Most of my folkie friends were quite surprised when I later joined a pop-folk group called *The Journeymen*. We toured extensively for three and a half years and I then returned to New York to be a studio musician, songwriter, and record producer.

I burned out on the commercial music world and moved to Colorado in 1972. Since then I have composed a great deal of instrumental music, written a number of songs, recorded albums, and written books about American roots music.

It would be fair to say that I fall somewhere between a participant and a scholarly observer of American folk music.

# Acknowledgments

This book reflects my own experiences in listening to and playing folk music, traditional, pop oriented, and experimental. Over the years my musical mentors have included guitarist-arranger-composer Dan Fox, guitarist Barry Galbraith, and musicians Stuart Jamieson and the Reverend Gary Davis. All of them have passed on, but their music is as vivid to me as it was when I first heard it.

I have benefited from conversations, discussions, and arguments with Harry Tuft in Denver; my Oregon friends Chico Schwall in Eugene; Terry Currier, Allen Jones, and Michael Kearsey in Portland; and Stephen Wade in Maryland. Thanks to Weston Kearsey for his input on freak and punk rock. Talking about songwriting with John Phillips and traditional music with Hedy West also influenced me in a variety of ways. In no way do I mean to imply that any or all of these friends are responsible for my conclusions or observations.

For their musical inspiration I want to thank Brownie McGhee, Pete Seeger, Erik Darling, Frank Hamilton, Mitch Imori, String Band, and many other musicians along the way.

This book is for Susan Planalp, whose proofreading skills and questions made it better than it would otherwise have been.

To hear the author's own music go to his website, www.dickweissman.com. To communicate with the author write to r2s@comcast.net.

Special thanks to Leah Babb-Rosenfeld, who signed this book; Amy Martin, her editorial assistant; David Campbell, the production editor; various anonymous reviewers, fact checkers, and Vidya Sundara Rajan, the copy editor.

# Introduction: A New Look at American and Canadian Folk Music

Because this book deals with a number of conflicts and controversies in the way that music has evolved and is currently performed, I would like to begin with an incident described by folklore scholar Archie Green in Glenn Ohrlin's book *The Hell-Bound Train*. Archie describes how he went to a folk music festival in Timbo, Arkansas, and eagerly awaited a performance by cowboy singer and folksong collector Glenn Ohrlin. Archie was astonished when he heard Ohrlin sing a Woody Guthrie song. After the performance, Green talked to Ohrlin and asked why he had chosen to sing a Woody Guthrie song. Ohrlin replied that at folk festivals people would rather hear protest songs than authentic cowboy ballads.

This simple statement reveals a great deal about what has transpired during the folk music revival. In this case a traditional singer who performs music for money on a regular basis has learned to adjust his repertoire to the taste of the revival audience. In the late twentieth century when this incident occurred, the music had changed from "home-made" music sung at family gatherings or in the home, to a mass-mediated music presented with the use of electronic equipment for a paying audience. Let's take a look at how this process evolved.

## The early years

Over the years numerous scholars in the fields of folklore, vernacular music, and American studies have examined the history of North American folk music and its various subspecialties. This book is an attempt to look at the history and evolution of this genre, along with an attempt to focus on many of the controversies that have enveloped the music over the years. Because folk music fans regard the music from the standpoint of a community with shared interests, these controversies represent a contrast to such feelings.

Folk music itself has existed since human beings began to sing and to play musical instruments. In the nineteenth century scholars, philosophers, and nationalists viewed folk music as an expression of agrarian culture and romanticized it as the antithesis of rapidly developed industrialization. As such, scholarship about folk music constituted a romanticized revolt against mass production in a literal sense and as popular music became mass produced, a cultural one as well.

Initially scholars focused on ballads and hypothesized that music was not composed by individual musicians but by a sort of mysterious group process. This collectivization of individual artistic efforts was also part of a scholarly fantasy world: creating a sort of alleged collective primitive artistry on the part of the folk community. This construct contrasted the nobility of the folk to the more prosaic and hum drum world of the urbanized factory worker. Francis James Child, a nineteenth-century Harvard-educated scholar, developed a numerical listing of ballads, henceforth referred to as "Child ballads," that included traditional English and Scottish ballads. This list became a landmark that was used in ensuing collections by various folklorists in the United States, Canada, and England.

Paralleling the organization of these traditional ballads was the existence of *Broadside Ballads*, songs composed by individual musicians and sold at modest prices in the street. There was also a tradition beginning in the eleventh century AD of troubadours and trouveres who were minstrels employed throughout Europe as court musicians for the entertainment of the court and its subjects. It is possible to regard these musician-entertainers as the first professional folksingers.

# John Lomax

An example of the almost saintly regard given to traditional Child ballads was the contempt with which Harvard scholars treated a young John Lomax and his early studies of American cowboy songs. To these gentlemen, cowboy songs were simply pop doggerel, unworthy of scholarly study. A variety of feuds surrounded Lomax's career, including his publication and copyright of edited versions that combined several songs into a single version. Some collectors took a dim view of this editing process, while others were critical of the notion of copywriting the work of various singers and folksong collectors under the "authorship" of a single scholar.

Another early controversy about the collection and publication of folk songs involved the question of what songs a particular collector chose to record, transcribe, and publish. When Cecil Sharp began to collect folksongs in the Southern Appalachian Mountains in 1915, he was only interested in collecting traditional ballads that originated in the UK.

Similarly, Frances Densmore, the pioneering collector of Native American music, had no interest in peyote songs or other contemporary Native American music. She only pursued songs that fit into her notion of what constituted traditional and unspoiled Native American music.

## Specialization and concentration on specific genres

The early scholars of North American folk music were largely interested in the lyrics of traditional ballads. They collected the many variations of such ballads from state to state, or province to province in Canada. Many of these collectors were folklorists as opposed to being musicians. Howard Odum and Guy Johnson, early collectors of African-American music, were sociologists or American studies scholars (before the formal existence of that term). Most folklorists did not have the musical skills that would have enabled them to transcribe and notate music. Consequently, many of the early folksong collections did not bother to include the music of the songs. This created a sort of schism that still exists today, between folklorists and ethnomusicologists. Folklorists concentrate on texts while ethnomusicologists specialize in music and musical notation. Additionally, a third faction was motivated by the desire to encourage amateur musicians to learn and sing folk songs. This last group of collections was inclined to include musical arrangements of songs suitable for semi-skilled piano players. Up until around 1955 the piano was far more popular in North America than the guitar. This was a bit ironic because most of the songs were originally performed by untrained musicians and singers who either sang without accompaniment or sang to the back-up of banjos, fiddles, mandolins, or guitars. The very people who performed these songs would have been mostly unable to learn them from such collections.

Some of the folklorists of the early–middle twentieth century began to focus on very specific musical genres or geographical areas. Collections of sea shanties, lumberjack songs, and African-American secular or religious music began to appear, alongside the more general works of scholar-collectors like John and Alan Lomax or amateur scholar Carl Sandburg.

# Performance versus participation

Early performances of folk music took place in a community where participation, not performance, was the order of the day. Many people in rural communities, black or white, sang or played such instruments as the fiddle, banjo, guitar, or mandolin. The great majority of the music was transmitted from one person to another without the use of written music. Music was played in the home, at local dances, on street corners, and in churches. Until the 1920s there was no radio, and phonograph records were a comparative rarity. There were no microphones, no amplifiers, and much traditional music developed in relatively isolated rural areas.

One common way to compare professionalization versus performance is the commonly used phrase, "it's the singer, not the song." In other words, although fine vocalists or excellent musicians were admired, traditional music was performed as a respite from hard-scrabble living. Farmers, coal miners, and cotton pickers worked long hours for modest wages, and music was played as a release from their labors at the end of the day or on the weekend.

# Professionalization

The literal definition of folk music includes the notion of songs being learned and performed within a family or a particular, usually rural, community. As radio developed, starting in the 1920s, and phonograph records began to be widely circulated, a new sort of professional class of musicians developed. Although it is a memory at best in today's world, live music on the radio used to be ubiquitous. A whole species of cowboy singers on radio like John I. White broadcast regularly on network radio shows. This was followed by the singing cowboy movie stars like Ken Maynard and Gene Autry. The songs collected by Cowboy Jack Tharp and John Lomax were sung around the campfire or out on the range with the sole intention of pleasing the cowboy and his compadres. One of the goals of this book is to examine how traditional music related to these attempts to market it to a mass audience.

During the 1920s country music and folk music contained many common elements in terms of instrumentation, song structure, and the use of traditional songs. Radio provided an outlet and an audience for cowboy singers, country music string bands, and solo performers. The Grand Ole Opry in Nashville and WLS in Chicago with its Barn Dance Show provided opportunities for musicians to perform for a large radio audience. Smaller local stations offered similar opportunities, although for years the rationale for such performances was to promote performances in the area where the radio station signal could be received. The goal for musicians was to build an audience for live shows rather than to expect any real income from the radio station.

These live country radio shows included comedians and comediennes, references to allegedly authentic country tropes such as moonshine and drunken parties, and a genial sort of hell-raising with performances and recordings capturing such events. WLS in particular required a sort of dress code and ersatz rural identity from its performers. Sociologist Richard Peterson has written at some length about how country music created images of authenticity that often were contradicted by the urban or sophisticated origins of some of its artists. In a local community performing jobs might be available at churches, schools, parties, and dances. When record companies realized that country music and blues were saleable items, talent scouts from New York traveled to southern towns like Bristol, Virginia, placed ads in newspapers, and auditioned talent. These early record producers would then record the best of the musicians that they had listened to. The sales of these recordings enabled some of these musicians to tour on the vaudeville stages in movie theaters all over the United States.

Similarly, blues songs were originally sung on street corners, juke joints, and at social gatherings. They were performed by local musicians or traveling ones who would go from town to town by hitchhiking or riding freight trains. Oddly, the earliest recorded blues (Mamie Smith's recording of Crazy Blues, 1920) were sung by women who were generally versatile vaudeville entertainers. The songs themselves were usually composed by professional jazz musicians like Clarence Williams or W. C. Handy. It wasn't until 1924 that Papa Charlie Jackson recorded anything resembling what we might call folk or traditional blues songs. When such folk blues artists as Blind Lemon Jefferson or Son House recorded, their phonograph records did not alter their status as street corner singers. Blues artists did not have performing opportunities on radio or in movies, but they did perform with traveling medicine shows.

Another controversy that persists to this day is the notion that the performance of "sinful music" would necessarily result in a trip to Hell after death. Some performers like Blind Lemon Jefferson or a young Josh White had it both ways, performing both religious and secular music. The strength of these sentiments was powerful enough that even today some blues musicians turn to religious music in their later years. The peculiar nature of this dichotomy is also present in reverse. Reverend Blind Gary Davis was originally a Piedmont blues singer who became an evangelical minister. After he moved to New York City, he became an influential figure among young white blues enthusiasts who were fascinated by his guitar style. He generally avoided singing blues songs. When his wife Annie was not present, he was more apt to be persuaded to sing them.

## Imitation and alteration

In all of these idioms certain key figures became popular and in turn spawned a group of musical imitators. There were countless mountain string bands, solo blues artists, and cowboy singers. Many of them were influenced by prior artists. In some cases, regional musical styles centered around specific musical gestures, such as banjo or fiddle styles, prevalent in a particular region or even county. Artists like the Carter Family, Jimmie Rodgers, Skip James, and Gene Autry had their share of imitators. In a traditional folk setting someone might be influenced by another artist but would rarely devote studious attention to copying their precise styles or performing mannerisms.

## The subject matter of folksongs in the 1920s and 1930s

Folksongs have never followed one specific subject in their lyrics. There are lullabies, work songs, songs about failed love and separation, songs about tragic events both personal and historical, and songs expressing social–political views. Conditions in the cotton mills of the Carolinas and the coal mines of Kentucky influenced songs protesting wages and working conditions. When the Great Depression of 1929–40 occurred, these songs varied between songs written and performed by the people in these communities to those inspired by outside political agitators. In particular, the Communist Party encouraged the use of traditional folksongs with new words expressing political ideas. They even celebrated and lionized a few of these singers, notably Aunt Molly Jackson who was transported to New York City where she became a sort of spokesperson for the Kentucky miners. Initially, composers who were members of the Communist Party wanted to use more sophisticated music to upgrade the taste of the working class. Avant-garde composer Charles Seeger changed his mind about this issue after he encountered Jackson's music.

This contrasted with the work of America's first union political singers, the members of the Industrial Workers of the World (IWW or Wobblies). IWW singers wrote new lyrics but put them to old hymn tunes, not traditional folk tunes.

Over the years, political folksongs represent another controversial aspect of folk music and the folk music revival. It is one thing for a Piedmont cotton mill worker or ex-cotton mill worker to sing about working in the mill. It is another thing entirely to witness a professional folksinger in Manhattan or Hollywood singing a mournful ballad about working in the coal mines. Later on I will explore the question of why someone like Pete Seeger could sing a song about the murder of a striking coal miner and achieve some level of credibility. After all Pete was the son of a composer-ethnomusicologist and a violinist mother, with a stepmother who was a groundbreaking composer of modern classical music. Why does an audience attribute credibility to one artist, yet deny that label to another seemingly equally sincere artist when neither of them have "authentic," political credentials or a personal working-class background?

As the Depression deepened, political music became an increasingly important aspect of the urban folk music scene. A corps of political, mostly urbanized political folksingers migrated to New York City. By 1940 this included Oklahoma troubadour Woody Guthrie, Pete Seeger, "Arkansas Lee" Hays, Millard Lampell, and a number of other singers who coalesced into the politically oriented *Almanac Singers*. The Almanacs were all young radicals with a burning desire to support unions and to make an impact on the American political–social scene through the medium of music. Although the group was originally opposed to entering into a conflict with Germany, after Russia was attacked they changed their viewpoints overnight.

The impact of political music on the folk music scene in New York went beyond the existence of the Almanacs themselves. Such artists as Burl Ives, Marais and Miranda, Susan Reed, Richard Dyer-Bennett, and others were generally sympathetic to left-wing causes.

## The Weavers, People's Songs, political music, and the blacklist

Several of the Almanacs served in the armed forces during the Second World War. When Pete Seeger returned from the war, he developed a vision of a kind of union of politically oriented left-wing artists that transcended the folk idiom. He spearheaded an organization called People's Songs, which was designed to unite musicians in such efforts. Initially Broadway and classical musicians joined alongside Seeger and other folksingers. What Seeger had not counted on was the transformation of the USSR from faithful ally against the Nazis to our principal antagonist in the Cold War. The Depression was over and America turned away from left-wing causes into a concerted effort to mobilize against the new enemy. Unions lost interest in performances by left-wing singers, and the AFL and CIO kicked out and marginalized some of the unions that had been in effect patrons of the Almanacs. People's Songs could not sustain itself economically and many of the artists dropped out. They feared that they would be identified, correctly or not, as communists or communist sympathizers. People's Songs folded, later emerging in a less ambitious form as People's Artists.

## Politics versus folk music

Although radical politics in effect dominated the ideology of most professional folksingers in the 1930s and 1940s, with the advent of the Cold War some artists and folklorists openly began to question the validity of political, newly made folksongs as opposed to a political traditional folk music. For some this process was a matter of career survival because blacklisted artists were avoided by major record labels, agents, and managers. Some artists' careers were heavily impacted by the blacklist and Burl Ives, for one, openly recanted his ties to left-wing politics, revealed the names of communist musicians, and denounced communism. Other performers preferred to focus on the music as an artifact of a gentler, kinder time rather than involving themselves in the political sphere. A few musicians like Oscar Brand and Tom Glazer had never been supporters of communist ideology and now became more openly critical of Russia and Stalinism.

## The folk-pop revival: Harry Belafonte, the Tarriers, and the emergence of the Kingston Trio

In the early 1950s in addition to the hit recordings of the Weavers folk music emerged in the pop music marketplace through the work of certain songwriters.

Frankie Laine, Jo Stafford, Patti Page, and Kay Starr all enjoyed hits with songs that combined folk imagery in their lyrics with pop music arrangements. Songwriters Terry Gilkyson, Irving Gordon, and co-writers Paul Mason Howard and Paul Weston all had written hit songs with the above pop artists in 1950 and 1951. The Weavers disbanded in 1952 after they were blacklisted and their records ceased to be played on American radio stations. Possibly as a partial response to this climate of "anti-folk" sentiment, pop songwriters appeared to turn away from composing the sort of folk-themed lyrics described in the previous paragraph.

Meanwhile Belafonte, who had experienced only moderate success as a jazz singer, turned to singing calypso and American folk songs. His 1956 album *Calypso* brought folk music back into play in the mass music market. This was followed by the milder successes of *The Easy Riders*, a group that included songwriter Terry Gilkyson, *the Tarriers* and *the Gateway Singers*. All of this set the table for the arrival and mass popularity of *The Kingston Trio*.

## Image versus political concerns and commerciality

All of the artists mentioned in the preceding paragraph had connections to left-wing causes, except for the Kingston Trio. The anti-communist political climate that now prevailed made such connections dangerous for entertainers' careers. Moreover, many of these artists had turned away from asserting their social–political views during their performances. During their brief period of mass popularity, even the Weavers did not actively promote their political ideas, but their prior associations with radical causes were so deep and extensive that this temporary political hiatus did not save them from political persecution or prosecution.

The Kingston Trio presented an entirely different image. Young, fun loving, clean-cut, and enthusiastic, they would leap onto the stage in their candy-colored button-down shirts. No one knew or cared about their political beliefs. The ironic aspect of their success was that the Trio who had little specific background in traditional folk music recorded with virtually no outside accompanying musicians while the Weavers, at least two of whom were extremely well versed in traditional folk music, used choral and instrumental back-ups on their records. Although a few purists had criticized the Weavers for "selling out their music," from the very beginning traditional folk music fans were outraged by the Trio's easy-going no-holds-barred association with mass popularity. This in turn set off arguments that continue to this day about musical integrity, greed, and loyalty to traditional music.

## The end of the revival, and folk music turns genre specific

The Kingston Trio spawned numerous imitators and would-be successors like *The Highwaymen, The Brothers Four,* and *The Limeliters* and most notably, *Peter, Paul & Mary.* In the world of mass market pop, any single musical style of necessity has a limited shelf life. By 1964 *the Beatles* and subsequent other British rock groups and Bob Dylan's self-transformation from protest singer to rock-inflected songwriter led to the demise of pop-folk as a significant presence on the American music scene. Various pop-folk artists employed a number of strategies to ensure their livelihoods. Some turned to folk rock, some to country rock. Others used Dylan as a role model and transformed themselves into singer-songwriters.

Meanwhile the discovery and rediscovery of such artists as Mississippi John Hurt, Son House, Dock Boggs, and Doc Watson led the more dedicated folk music enthusiasts to more traditional music. Some fans of this music, many of whom were themselves far removed from traditional music, became what singer-songwriter-storyteller Utah Phillips referred to as "folk Nazis." These people established their own rulebook that outlined what was praiseworthy or objectionable in the work of various musicians. Musicians and fans had three fundamentally different attitudes toward folk-pop artists. Artists like John Hurt or Doc Watson were venerated, "compromise" artists like Judy Collins or Ian and Sylvia were considered acceptable, and folk-pop groups like the Kingston Trio or The Brothers Four were scorned by these dedicated adherents of traditional music. Their very popularity seemed to induce suspicion and even hatred. Rather than seeing the revival as one big tree with numerous branches, the audience for folk music broke down into tribal factions. Other such controversies developed around the use of electric as opposed to acoustic instruments, and the question of whether it was musically or socially acceptable for white musicians to perform black music.

In the pop-folk world, there were few black musicians. Although there were dozens of (mostly) male white musicians in the various popular groups, I can only think of two members of The Tarriers and one member of The Gateway Singers who were African Americans. Since almost all the groups were singing

African-American folksongs, and group members were almost uniformly social liberals, why was this? In fact, in the entire pop-folk idiom it is difficult to come up with more than twenty or so black artists in a musical style that in its heyday boasted hundreds of performers. Virtually no black booking agents, record company executives, or personal managers were actively involved in the pop-folk world or the folk music revival as a whole.

## Women's music

During the 1970s women's music emerged as a social–political statement. Most of the music issued by Olivia Records (1974–93) was singer-songwriter music, often anchored in folk music but drifting over into folk rock as well. The label made its political statement not only with its music but by placing virtually every aspect of its recordings from audio to distribution in the hands of women. The label was fueled by the feminist movement, which in itself included large-scale festivals limited to female artists. This caused some controversy because men were basically excluded from some of these events.

Holly Near is a singer-songwriter who ran her own label, Redwood Records, from 1973 to 1992. Her orientation was both feminist and generally socially progressive. Because she included some male artists on her label, she was a somewhat controversial figure in the women's music movement.

## The folk music "business"

Once folk music became viable as a business, managers and agents, record companies, music stores, music publishers, venue owners, and concert presenters all entered the picture. Although the fatter corporate cats left the scene after the end of the pop-folk revival in the mid-1960s, a more stable if less lucrative market has continued to this day.

There are music stores throughout North America and a good part of Europe that specialize in folk instruments, and there is an intense trade in vintage instruments as well. There are folk music and folklore societies that present concerts and coffeehouses that feature the music. During the summer months there are numerous folk festivals in the United States and Canada, as well as instructional camps that serve as music schools for folk enthusiasts.

In 1989 the Folk Alliance International (known previously as North American Folk Alliance) began to hold annual meetings where artists and people in the business got together to hear music and develop business networks. I will return to the subject of the alliance later.

## Contemporary developments in folk-style music

Examining all of the musical branches of the American folk music tree is a confusing experience in 2018. The musical niches can be broken down into various musical styles as follows:

- Blues: Includes soloists, bands, acoustic and electric artists.
- Bluegrass: Encompassing traditional bluegrass music styles and the so-called "New Grass" artists.
- Celtic music: Irish or Irish-based music.
- Freak folk: Folk music with a sort of punk orientation.
- Instrumental music: Artists whose emphasis or entire work is based on music without lyrics.
- Old time: Mountain music that pre-dates bluegrass.
- Political-protest music: Advocates social change, and discusses various social issues.
- Pop-folk today: Music by such artists as the Avett Brothers and The Lumineers that has crossed over into the folk-pop marketplace.
- Regional and ethnic styles: American Indian music, Cajun music, Tex-Mex, Cape Breton fiddle tunes, Zydeco, etc.
- Singer-songwriters: Artists with a pop edge, but at least one foot firmly planted in the world of folk music.
- Traditional: Musicians who seek to imitate traditional folk artists.
- World music: Musicians who perform the music of other cultures or whose work shows these influences.

Another category that I will explore at length is the hybrid musicians of the twenty-first century. Musicians like Bela Fleck, Ry Cooder, and Chris Thile draw not only from almost every category listed above, but also write new music that is very loosely derived from these styles. There are also jazz artists like Bill Frisell or the late Charlie Haden who work mostly in the jazz idiom but whose work includes collaborations with folk musicians to create a music that is difficult to define or classify.

# Conclusion

In this overview I have offered a brief history of the music and have discussed various controversies that began with the early studies of folk music. These differences have evolved as the music itself has moved into new styles and fusions of existing ones. This book will also include coverage of significant artists like Erik Darling and Josh White, who for a variety of reasons have seemingly been "written out" of the history of the folk music revival.

The Canadian folk scene currently includes many active artists and the only print publication about folk music in North America. I will also examine the ways that folk scenes developed in a number of areas in the United States and Canada, notably Chicago, Texas, Toronto, and the Pacific Northwest. The Canadian scene is mostly known to people in the United States through such singer-songwriters as Gordon Lightfoot, Joni Mitchell, and Neil Young. It also includes a long-running series of large folk festivals, an active market in music for children, and the French-language music of Quebec as well as such regional music styles as the fiddle tunes of Cape Breton. There also have been, and continue to be, a number of Canadian folk artists like Stan Rogers and String Band who remained in Canada, and had comparatively limited exposure in the United States. Currently a number of younger artists, including *The Be Good Tanyas*, *The Dukhs*, and *the Wailin' Jennies* have developed an audience in both the United States and Canada.

Another neglected area in the history of the folk revival that deserves some attention is the development of instrumental music styles that are rooted in traditional folk music but have expanded into a variety of directions. I will examine the beginnings of these musical experiments by discussing the music of such artists as Sandy Bull, John Fahey, Billy Faier, John Hartford, Bill Keith, and Bobby Thompson, and how their music has informed the work of such contemporary players as Ry Cooder, Bela Fleck, and Chris Thile.

The original protagonists in the pop-folk revival are disappearing from today's scene. A separate chapter will evaluate the importance in today's folk music scene of such artists as Woody Guthrie, Lead Belly, and Pete Seeger.

I will now turn to the history of the folk music of Canada and the United States.

# 1

# From the Beginning: Folksong Collectors and Collections and Regional Music Styles in the United States and Canada

Musicologists divide music into three archetypes: folk, popular, and classical. Classical music is relatively easy to categorize: the music exists through the composition and notation of new music that is performed by musicians who are trained to read and write music in the form of traditional music notation.

Popular music carries the connotation of mass marketed music insofar as that is possible during the particular period that the critic may be writing about. Its goal is tied to commercial factors in the sense that there is a long-standing and intense business of creating this sort of music and marketing it in the widest sphere possible. Moreover, it is tied into for-profit business relationships on the part of composers, artists, record companies, music publishers, and the small army of intermediaries who present this music. That includes concert and night club promoters, performing venues, managers, agents, sound technicians, tour managers, and the various professionals and business people who make a living creating and promoting this music.

Folk music has generally been regarded as music that is created in communities and family environments that does not necessarily require performances outside a home or community. This relative freedom from the intrusion of commerciality has long attracted folklorists and utopian philosophers or historians who admire the notion of creating music in communities or families. They see folk music as pure and untainted, compared to the self-conscious way that popular music is created and marketed.

This romanticized view of the music capitalizes on a kind of arrogant view of the folk as "noble savages," people who are entirely unintellectual, live in isolation, and resist the advances of any sort of modernistic or technological innovations. This viewpoint appeared somewhat viable in the late nineteenth and early twentieth centuries when mass communications as we experience them in the twenty-first century were non-existent or present only on the fringes of American culture.

## The Industrial Revolution and the romantic philosophers

Much of the original fascination of intellectuals with folk music derived from the social changes caused by the Industrial Revolution in the last half of the eighteenth century and the first half of the nineteenth century. The days of the idyllic rural life that such intellectuals idolized were transformed by lengthy industrial work days and the transformation of primarily rural lifestyles to the urban slums that became the new homes for the working class.

The German philosopher Johann Gottfried von Herder (1744–1803) also began to worry about the artificiality of "modern" life and its emphasis on the rational. Free flowing folk culture presented a looser and more pleasant way of looking at life. Herder himself collected the lyrics of folksongs and even coined the word folksong. Even before Herder's time, collections of traditional ballads were published in England, and in 1763 an English clergyman named Thomas Percy published his ballad collection *Reliques of English Poetry*, drawing on an earlier collection of ballads.

## Communal ballad making vs. the notion of individual composition and broadside ballads

Herder and the Brothers Grimm, who collected and published fairy tales, believed that ballads were communally composed. This notion of mystical group composition suited their conception of the folk as a sort of anonymous but wonderfully primitive mass. It also suited their skepticism about the new industrialism where products were mass manufactured without originality or "soul."

Cecil Sharp (1859–1924) was an English composer and folksong collector who argued that folksongs had an original and specific author and that the collective effort was the transmission of the songs from that author to other individuals who in turn spread and sometimes revised or re-arranged the original song as they traveled from one place to another.

A further complication ensued when contemporary ballad makers published and sold songs in broadsides or song sheets. During this period, broadsides were regarded as cheap, inferior, and popularized versions of folksongs or simply as trash made for popular consumption.

Later on, folksong collector Edward (Sandy) Ives (1859–1924) studied three folksong makers: Larry Gorman, Joe Scott, and Lawrence Doyle. These three composers were all originally Canadian but worked in the woods of Maine and New Brunswick. All of them wrote original songs. For many folklorists the true test of a folksong was whether it was passed on and continued to be sung by others, and all three of these composers wrote songs that passed that test.

## Child, Kittredge, and John Lomax

Interest in collecting and publishing collections of folksongs in the United States developed somewhat later, but in 1882 Harvard scholar Francis James Child published a collection of English folksongs sung in the United States that derived from Scottish or English sources, focusing on songs that preceded the invention of the printing press. This allowed him to entirely evade the subject of broadside ballads. Child's research continued for forty years, and he published 305 different titles as well as variants. He did not include music in his researches. Child's student George Lyman Kittredge was one of the fathers of American folksong research.

## John Lomax

It wasn't until the early years of the twentieth century that folklorists, musicologists, and ethnomusicologists started collecting American folksongs. The person who became the most famous collector, although not the first one, was John A. Lomax. Lomax was a student of ballad scholar George Lyman Kittredge and Kittredge encouraged Lomax, who began his folksong endeavors by collecting cowboy songs. Later he recruited his son Alan to assist him in collecting folksongs all over the United States, especially in southern prisons.

The two Lomaxes had very different orientations. John was a conservative southerner and Alan's political beliefs placed him on the far left. They both shared a Herder-like attitude toward the black prisoners whose songs they recorded. They saw these prisoners as noble savages, people whose music was virtually uninfluenced by popular music commerciality.

Both Lomaxes were involved in various controversies in their lengthy career, and I will discuss Alan's career much later in this book. John almost immediately found himself in rough waters when he ran up against fellow cowboy song collector "Cowboy Jack" Tharp. Tharp published a songbook in 1908 that included five songs he had written. When Lomax re-printed one of Tharp's original songs without credit, the feud was on! In the 1916 revised edition of the Lomax book he added the other four Tharp originals. Later Lomax claimed that Tharp had "stolen" songs from him, a claim refuted by folklorist D. K. Wilgus.

It was not unusual for the nineteenth-century British ballad collectors to edit the songs they had collected, because either they included bawdy material or the editor felt the songs could be improved upon. Lomax took this process to the next level, by combining various versions of the same song, and then editing them as a single piece of work, and copywriting them in his own name, as though he were the author of the song. When the folksong revival took off in the 1950s and pop-folk groups recorded these songs, these copyrights began to be lucrative. One of the people that Lomax recorded was songster Blind Willie McTell. While recording him for the Library of Congress, Lomax let the tape recorder run during their conversations. In a bizarre and condescending manner Lomax asks McTell if he knows any protest songs. McTell seems puzzled by the request and tells Lomax that he doesn't know any songs like that because things are going well for him. Lomax is quite insistent on this subject and continues to press McTell for such songs. He seems entirely unaware that if McTell knew such songs he might well resist singing them for a white man with a Texas accent.

There is also quite a bit to say about John Lomax's relationship with Huddie (Ledbetter) Lead Belly, which began when Lead Belly was a prisoner in Texas. Because this story includes the extensive involvement of John's son Alan, I will take up this thread of the story in a later chapter.

## Howard W. Odum

Sociologist Howard Odum collected African-American blues, work songs, and religious songs and began publishing the religious songs in 1906. He followed this up in 1911 by publishing 115 secular songs. Together with fellow sociologist Guy Johnson, Odum compiled two books, one of secular songs and one of religious songs that were published by the University of North Carolina Press in 1925 and 1926, respectively. He also wrote three novels about a rambling blues singer named Left Wing Gordon that were published in 1931. Considering that Odum's primary field was sociology, and that he had acquired a reputation as an important scholar who specialized in southern regional studies, this was a remarkable attempt to relate to the world of a bluesman.

Odum's articles were not the first published studies of African-American music. Charles Pickard Ware, Lucy McKim Garrison, and William Francis Allen's *Slave Songs of the United States* appeared in 1867. This was a collection mostly, but not entirely, of religious songs collected after the Civil War in the South Carolina Sea Islands. The book has been re-printed several times. In a sense, it was before its time because it preceded the interest in American folksongs that was created by the Lomax and Odum and Johnson books. It even preceded the formation of the American Folklore Society in 1888.

## The settlement schools and Cecil Sharp

A number of schools were opened in Appalachia in the early years of the twentieth century. They were called "settlement schools." This movement was influenced by schools founded in London in the late nineteenth century, and by social worker Jane Addams' Hull House in Chicago. The teachers and administrators of these schools came from both Kentucky and New England. Because they were located in relatively isolated geographic areas, the schools also came to function as community centers that included dormitories for the students. The schools grew much of their own food, ran health clinics, included cooperative stores, sold local arts and crafts, and collected local music and stories. The earliest settlement schools included the Hindman Settlement School, founded in 1902, and the Pine Mountain Settlement School and the Stuart Robinson School, both founded in 1913.

One of the women who migrated to Appalachia was Olive Dame Campbell who migrated south when her husband was appointed president of Piedmont College in Demorest, Georgia, in the northern part of the state. In 1908–12 Ms. Campbell began to collect folksongs while she was accompanying her husband during trips through the southern mountains. He was conducting a study of social and economic conditions while she pursued her music collecting. By 1913 the couple had moved to Asheville, North Carolina, where she pursued these interests while he became CEO of the Russell Sage Foundation. Campbell also founded the John C. Campbell Folk School in North Carolina in 1925, years after the Sharp expedition.

In 1916 Campbell heard that Cecil Sharp, an English composer and folksong collector, was visiting the United States and she visited him in Lincoln, Massachusetts, to show him her folksong collection. Sharp believed that he could stimulate a revival of interest in folksongs in England by collecting American versions of the Child ballads. She accompanied Sharp and his assistant Maud Karpeles (1885–1976) on a nine-week collecting trip that proved to be very fruitful. They published this collection of 122 songs and ballads in 1917.

During the next two years, Sharp made two other trips to the United States, this time accompanied only by Maud Karpeles. All told, Sharp spent forty-six weeks in Appalachia, and collected 1,612 songs. He died while compiling all of this music, but Karpeles was able to continue the work and she compiled the book *English Folk Songs from the Southern Appalachians* in 1932.

Because he was a trained musician, he included tunes with the songs. Sharp was a worshiper of the "primitive," and he had no interest in collecting anything resembling the popular music of the day. Sharp also had no interest in the culture of African Americans, and in fact saw their music as part of the vulgarization of American life. This contributed to the romantic view of Appalachia espoused by scholars of the day, in disregard of Benjamin Filene's findings that African Americans in fact constituted 13.4 percent of the population of the region at the time of Sharp's collecting work. It also led to scholars ignoring the fact that there was a strong tradition of black-white musical interaction, and quite a few black banjo players and fiddlers who worked from the same general repertoire that white musicians were playing. Subsequent recordings by such white musicians as Uncle Dave Macon and Dock Boggs, which included such songs and instrumentals along with the researches of such folklorists and collectors as Stuart Jamieson, Kip Lornell, and Mike Seeger amplified the importance of this error.

Although Sharp had little interest in any original American music, he included a few songs that were native to America like *John Hardy* and *The Lonesome Prairie*. Despite these limitations, the work that Sharp, Campbell, and Karpeles did was enormously important and stimulated folklorists and music historians to collect music in many remote corners of the United States. According to folksong scholar D. K. Wilgus, Sharp established rapport with regional folksong collectors by meeting them. Thereby, he eliminated the potential for the sort of territorial feuds that had erupted between John Lomax and Jack Tharp.

## Regional collectors

There were scholars and inspired amateurs collecting songs all over the United States. Some restricted themselves to particular states, like the *Frank C. Brown North Carolina Collection* and Henry M. Belden's work in Missouri. Other collectors focused on regions, particular groups of working people, or specific ethnic groups. Vance Randolph spent his lifetime collecting songs and folklore in the Ozark Mountains, Dorothy Scarborough compiled collections of both southern mountain and African-American songs, Phillips Barry collected songs in Maine, and Charles Lummis compiled four hundred Spanish-American folksongs in California. Occupational songs were represented by Joanna C. Colcord's collections of sailors' songs in 1924 and 1938, Charles J. Finger's *Frontier Ballads*, George Pullen Jackson's collections of white spirituals, George Korson's collections of mining songs beginning in 1927, George Milburn's *The Hobo's Hornbook* from 1930, and Franz Rickaby's 1926 *Ballads and Songs of the Shanty Boy*. In later years, scholars compiled collections that basically were compilations of work done by previous folksong collectors but were unpublished or incomplete at the time of publication.

Some scholars focused on specific ethnic groups, including the already-cited works of Howard Odum and Guy Johnson, two books of black spirituals by James Weldon Johnson and J. Rosamund Johnson (1925 and 1926), R. Nathaniel Dett's collection of spirituals published in 1927 and 1936, and Newman I. White's *American Negro Folk-Songs* (1928).

Laura Boulton and Natalie Curtis collected the music of American Indians, while a remarkable woman named Frances Densmore compiled over a dozen books of Native American songs, traveling all over the United States and into Canada through virtually the entire first half of the twentieth century.

## The strange career of Lawrence Gellert

Recently blues scholar Bruce Conforth has written an illuminating book about one of the more mysterious figures in American folksong. Lawrence Gellert was born in 1898, the son of a Hungarian refugee. For many years, he lived in the shadow of his brother Hugo, who was an art editor for the *New Masses*, a magazine that was a cultural organ associated with the Communist Party.

In 2013, the Scarecrow Press published Bruce Conforth's book *African American Folksong and American Cultural Politics: The Lawrence Gellert Story*. Because Gellert was such a mysterious figure whose very place of death is unknown except possibly to a few close-mouthed members of his family, Conforth researched Gellert's life for years before completing this book. Because he was also the custodian at the Gellert Archives at the University of Indiana, Conforth also is the person most familiar with that collection, which includes some 600 songs and numerous folk tales.

As Conforth tells the story, Lawrence Gellert was an unsuccessful, troubled person whose siblings variously owned a furniture business and in Hugo's case, was a successful and prominent art editor for the magazine the *New Masses*. Around 1922, Lawrence found himself adrift and because of either a nervous breakdown or some attempt to establish his own identity, he left New York City for Tryon, North Carolina. Conforth believes that Gellert started collecting music around 1924 with a very poor-quality wire recorder. Gellert had something of a southern white patron who protected him against suspicious townsfolk or unpleasant situations, and Gellert proceeded to travel and record many African-American singers.

The orthodox left-wing view of Gellert was that he was collecting dozens of protest songs, songs that other collectors either never found or didn't bother to record. Initially, a myth developed that Gellert was living with a black woman in Tryon, which gave him access to the black community. Conforth establishes that in fact this woman simply washed his clothes. Further research has led Conforth to the conclusion that many of the songs that Gellert collected were either already found in the prior collections of such collectors as Odum and Johnson, or suggested or partially written by Gellert himself. In other words, Gellert found a market for protest material and so he asked his informants for such songs. He either edited some of them or actually may have written some of them himself.

The initial recordings that Gellert made were so crude that they were basically unusable, even for the purposes of transcription. By the 1930s he acquired better equipment, and in later years several record companies, including Rounder, actually issued some of the recordings. It also took some years before the material was published, outside of a few magazine articles. In the late 1930s two songbooks containing several dozen songs that he had collected were published and had some impact in left-wing circles.

Many folklorists were very suspicious of Gellert's work. He was not a professional folklorist, and he feared that any details of the identity of his sources could lead to imprisonment or harm inflicted on them by white racists. Furthermore, Gellert was a contentious person who openly critiqued the Lomaxes for their treatment of Lead Belly, which he considered to be tantamount to the behavior of white plantation overseers.

If not for the work of Conforth and some preliminary studies by Lawrence Garabedian, Gellert might well be a forgotten figure today. Conforth is working on a boxed set of the recordings that Gellert made. I suspect they will confirm his notions that, although Gellert collected some fine blues songs, other secular songs, and folk tales, there is actually less focus in his collection on protest songs than Gellert may have wished to imply. In any case, Lawrence Gellert was certainly one of the first scholars to record African-American music.

## The Canadian collectors

Generally folk fans divide American folksongs into two key components: English-Scotch-Irish influenced white music, and African American secular and religious music. This is reasonably accurate if one limits the picture to the music of English speakers; but in addition to the music of various American-Indian tribes, there is a rich heritage of the music of various immigrant groups, especially Spanish-language music of the Southwest, and the French language Cajun and zydeco music of Louisiana.

Although these are the most obvious non-English-speaking musical groups, there are a host of others. Among them are the Scandinavians of the mid-west and northwest, and the music of Africans, Arabs, and Asians found wherever those groups have settled. By contrast, the two sources of Canadian folk music are the French language music of Quebec, and the English speakers in most of the rest of Canada. Canada also has a large population of First Nations people, 1,673,780 in 2017. This represented 5.4 percent of the total Canadian population of 36,151,728 people. This compared with a US total population of 323.4 million, and 6.7 million Indians or 2 percent of the total population. Asians are another ethnic group represented in Canada in large numbers and then there are numerous English-born Canadians.

## Canadian folksong collectors

Scholarly interest in French language music appeared earlier than collections in the English language. According to folklorist Edith Fowke, Ernest Gagnon compiled the first large collection of French-Canadian songs, *Chanson populaires du Canada*, in 1865. However, in 1911, when Marius Barbeau began his lengthy career at the National Museum, he not only published a series of books of Quebecois songs but also recorded thousands of wax cylinders of performances of these songs. From 1925 to 1962 Barbeau compiled six published song collections.

W. Roy Mackenzie was a regional collector, who began his collecting in the province of Nova Scotia in the early twentieth century, writing a book describing his collecting activities in 1919, and following this up with a collection of songs in 1928. During the next thirty years, Helen Creighton compiled five books of songs collected in Nova Scotia and New Brunswick, including a book of Gaelic songs from New Brunswick. The earliest Newfoundland collector was Gerald S. Doyle, an amateur enthusiast who published a paperback collection of songs from Newfoundland in 1927. A collection of 189 songs from Newfoundland was compiled by Elizabeth Greenleaf and Grace Mansfield and published in 1933 and three volumes of Acadian songs were compiled by Pere Anselme and Frere Daniel and published in 1942–8.

Many other collections began to appear in the 1960s, including Edith Fowke's work in Ontario and Kenneth Peacock's massive collection of songs from Newfoundland. Other collectors worked in various Canadian provinces.

Other than Barbeau's groundbreaking work in Quebec, there has not been a single major Canadian collector like John or Alan Lomax who collected throughout the United States.

## Folksong and copyright

The question of copyright in folksongs brings up a number of thorny issues. If a song is traditional, what in fact are we copyrighting? The Copyright Act was designed to protect new and original lyrics and melodies. This might apply to a traditional singer like Larry Gorman, who indeed wrote many original songs. But who owns a song like the ballad *Barbara Allen*, which has been collected dozens of times in numerous versions?

Because the Lomaxes originally published songs that they had basically compiled into a single version, often from many sources, they felt justified in copyrighting the songs in their names. However, they followed the same practice when they printed verbatim songs from, for example, chain gang prisoners. Occasionally, they would credit a specific composer, but basically, they avoided doing this when the singers followed their notion of "traditional singers." As we will discuss later, their situation when using Lead Belly's music was more complex because they gave him partial credit, along with their own contributions.

Lawrence Gellert also listed himself as composer of the songs that he collected. In his case, he did not keep records of his sources, so that untangling the process might have been complex. Gellert, however, aggressively pursued a lawsuit against Josh White who recorded an album of chain gang songs. Gellert felt that the songs were drawn from his published collections. White denied this, but Columbia Records intervened and made a settlement with Gellert that apparently satisfied him. Ironically, *The Journeymen*, the band that I performed in during the 1960s, recorded one of Gellert's songs and he split the rights with me without complaint.

## The economics of song publishing

The bulk of folk music collecting was done during the first half of the twentieth century, and certainly before the copyright laws changed in 1976.

During that time, record companies typically paid two cents for each copy of a record sold to the music publisher. Normally, the company then paid half of that money to the songwriter.

Because the early folklorists knew little or nothing about the business of music publishing, it did not occur to them that the logical way to compensate their informants would have been for the folklorist to "do the paperwork" and become the publisher, while the informant retained his or her rights as a songwriter.

Two German-Jewish immigrants named Jean and Julian Aberbach devised another solution to royalty splits. The Aberbach brothers founded Hill and Range Music in 1945. Instead of splitting income with songwriters 50–50, they devised a new system. The songwriter would be paid half of the publishing money, in addition to their songwriting income. In other words, the publisher gave up half of their income to the writer, who now received 75 percent of the pie. Had the folksong collectors made a deal with Hill and Range, the split would have been:

Hill and Range 25 percent, folklorist 25 percent, and songwriter 50 percent. Given that Hill and Range published music written or controlled by bluegrass icon Bill Monroe and many other country music artists like Hank Snow and Jim Reeves, it is a bit surprising that none of the collectors contacted them. This arrangement would also have saved the folksong collectors from having to deal with copyrighting paperwork or collecting money because Hill and Range was skilled at doing so*.

## How traditional songs got copyrighted

Technically, traditional songs should never have been copyrighted, because the original author was generally unknown. Music publishers adopted one of two tactics. One was to ignore that a song was traditional, and simply to copyright it, assuming that no one would contest the copyright. Certainly, the original author of *Barbara Allen* was long deceased and the copyright, had there ever been one, was in the public domain. Songs that are in the public domain can be recorded without the payment of royalties. The second way to deal with traditional music was to give the author credit in the following way: *On Top of Old Smoky*, traditional, adapted, and arranged by Elmer Jones. In this method of copyrighting a song, the author is only copyrighting their (allegedly) original version of the song. Sometimes publishers would add the phrase "adapted and arranged with new material by Elmer Jones."

During the folksong revival, some of the performers, notably Fred Hellerman of the Weavers, and Peter, Paul, & Mary, would actually write new melodies and/or lyrics and add them to traditional songs. If someone else recorded the new version, then they had to pay the normal royalties. For example, Hellerman wrote an introductory bridge and a new verse to the traditional song *I Never Will Marry*, and copyrighted it under his own name. It was recorded by Harry Belafonte and numerous other artists and Hellerman reaped a harvest of royalties.

During the 1930s and 1940s, folksong recordings did not sell in quantity, so none of this would have resulted in a lucrative payoff for traditional singers. However, during the 1950s, the Weavers began to make hit records, and some

---

* The Aberbachs actually borrowed this concept from their previous employer, Max Dreyfus at Chappell & Co.

ten years later, the Kingston Trio recorded both hit singles and albums that sold in the millions. At that point, it became unfortunate that the Lomaxes or other collectors had not either formed their own music publishing companies, or co-owned such companies with Hill and Range Music or some other established music publisher.

## Songbooks

Almost all of the folksong collections referenced so far are serious works compiled by scholars. Other publications were designed for amateur musicians who had basic piano skills. Josephine McGill was a New Yorker who spent her summers collecting songs in the Kentucky Mountains beginning in 1914. She compiled one music folio on her own, and edited two subsequent collections with two classical musicians, Loraine Wyman and Howard Brockway. Bascom Lamar Lunsford, a North Carolina lawyer and banjo player, co-authored another folio with composer Lamar Stringfield. John Jacob Niles was a performer-composer-collector, and he wrote a series of folksong folios and a book called *Singing Soldiers*, which compiled songs sung by African-American soldiers during the First World War.

The above books were primarily designed for singers to use, rather than for scholars to study. They generally avoided extensive historical information about the songs. Folklorists generally included extensive notes on the songs they published and listed additional versions of a song or variations on it in other publications.

The most popular of all the songbooks was Carl Sandburg's *American Songbag*, published in 1927. Sandburg was a renowned poet and biographer of Abraham Lincoln, who also performed folksongs while playing the lecture circuit. Sandburg was not a folklorist and most of his songs came to him through friends and associates. Each song is introduced in a friendly and literate way, rather than in a scholarly manner. The book remains in print today and has gone through numerous editions. Many later books followed the friendly, non-scholarly tone of this book, including several collections of American folksongs compiled by Margaret Boni and Norman Lloyd. Like Sandburg's books, these books included piano arrangements, but not guitar chords.

# 2

# Mass Distribution: Radio, Records, and Pre-World War Two Artists

As I have already pointed out, much of the early interest in American folksong was based on the notion that the music had developed in isolated areas, in a pure way that was in stark contradiction to the ways in which American popular music was composed and transmitted.

Before the 1920s, although such a viewpoint was nostalgic and romantic, it wasn't entirely unreasonable. During the 1920s, two basic factors entered the equation, which transformed the music and the way it was transmitted. First of all, mass media came into play. Although music was available on cylinders before 1890, its production and distribution were relatively insignificant. Phonograph records became available during the mid-twenties, and by 1925, the speed of phonograph records became standardized at 78 revolutions per minute. By 1922 there were 600 radio stations in the United States, and the NBC network was founded in 1926. This was followed by CBS in 1927. Condenser microphones appeared in 1916 and ribbon microphones in 1923.

## Music, the radio, microphones, the phonograph, and the demise of purity

When Cecil Sharp or the other early folksong collectors were collecting folksongs around the second decade of the twentieth century, they were visiting people's homes. People were making music for their friends and families, and not really considering any monetary aspects of music-making.

The recording equipment that the early collectors utilized was extremely primitive, and although it certainly was a cause of amazement by the performers, it would be difficult to argue that it profoundly influenced their performances.

The minute that the radio and phonograph records entered the picture, the entire experience of music-making was transformed. First of all, for the most part, the audiences were not people who personally knew the performers. Second, although radio didn't pay performers to speak of in the early days, it allowed them to advertise their personal appearances where "customers" had to pay to get in the door. Record companies also paid performers and in some cases, performers also received royalties on the sale of their records. (The reader should note that quite a few artists preferred to take their payments without royalties because they had no notion of what sort of income they might be giving up, or they simply didn't trust that the record companies would pay these royalties.) Other money was available for songwriters when songs found their way into phonograph records.

## Ralph Peer: The music publishers meet American folksongs and field recording

Record companies have always employed some variety of talent scouts who bring new acts to their attention. Ralph Peer was originally employed as a record producer by Okeh Records. When he moved over to RCA Records, he negotiated a deal where the record company did not pay him a salary but allowed him to retain the publishing rights of any songs that he recorded. Because of this agreement, Peer was only interested in recording "new" songs that he could copyright.

He recorded both country-folk music and African-American blues. Recording music that existed far outside the New York recording studios often entailed making trips down south and recording musicians in a location near where they lived. Peer and his competitors would go to places like Atlanta, Georgia, or Bristol, Tennessee, and take ads in the local newspapers, or put up handbills in the town. The ads would say that the company was seeking talent to record, and that such talent should come to the hotel, radio station, or some other place where the record company had rented space that was suitable for recording.

Peer's journey to Bristol produced dozens of recordings. The most memorable ones were made by the Carter family, and yodeler Jimmie Rodgers. The Carter family recorded many traditional songs but Peer was either unaware of that, or assumed that since the songs had never previously been copyrighted, he could copyright them and obtain the publishing rights.

## The death of purity

A number of things were involved in making records. For one thing, the recordings took place not in an artist's home, but in a rented recording studio. The audience consisted of a producer and engineer from the record company, not friends or family members. The performers sang into microphones, which were moved around so that, for example, a fiddle didn't drown out the vocal of a song. The length of the recordings was limited by the medium of the phonograph record to three minutes, so a warning light appeared near the end of a performance, telling the performer that they were running out of time. Another aspect of the process was that the record company needed to choose which songs would actually be released on phonograph records, and which ones would be ignored, or tabbed for a future release. Certainly, in the performer's "natural habitat," there were songs or instrumental tunes that their friends and families preferred to other songs in their repertoire. However, these preferences were more personal than a performance on a phonograph record, or the microphones of a radio station.

## The professional musician

Many of the early white and black artists did perform for money. However, the performances took place on street corners, in tobacco sheds, picnics, election rallies, minstrel shows, and traveling medicine shows. Before the 1920s, theater performances were rare for such artists and in fact neither blues singers nor old time country musicians were making records in 1920. Once phonograph records began to sell in quantity, microphones came into use to amplify the singers' voices traveling vaudeville shows became regular events and radio broadcasts provided new audiences; musicians began to believe that they could make a living performing music as a full-time profession. This meant developing a repertoire of songs or instrumental pieces that could please large audiences. It also required the artist to make phonograph records, and to broadcast regularly on radio stations. Performers had to develop an "act," which necessarily included costuming and comedy.

## How professionalism influenced the music

One of the joys of collecting traditional ballads was the widespread collection of songs that were sung without musical accompaniment. Clearly such performances, many of which were quite lengthy, simply were not going to appeal to a broad audience of music fans. The artists who became professional musicians had to adjust their repertoire to the desires of an audience. While a square dance piece played at a dance show might last for seven or eight minutes, this was not going to satisfy an audience who wished to be entertained while listening and not dancing.

Early artists developed spoken word pieces that interspersed instrumental music with some sort of vaudeville-style skit. Because mountain people were identified with the production of moonshine whiskey, there were numerous recordings that created some story around a moonshine still. Others made fun of city slickers who came into a rural environment under the assumption that country folks were ignorant and unsophisticated.

Black ministers developed hell and brimstone sermons that were recorded with something of a live audience affirming their descriptions of hell that awaited sinners. The works of "Sinkiller" Griffin, for example, were bestsellers.

## Early commercial recordings and American folk music

During the 1920s, record companies discovered that there was money to be made in recording folk, country, and blues music. This discovery did not come from a planning process but was accidental. In 1920, New York African-American musician-songwriter-entrepreneur Perry Bradford succeeded in convincing Okeh Records to record African-American vaudeville and blues artist Mamie Smith.

Prior to Mamie Smith's recording, RCA Records had enjoyed some success with white blues-jazz artist Marian Harris. But when Smith's second recording, *Crazy Blues*, sold in hundreds of thousands, record companies realized that there was a market for blues recordings.

# The "classic" blues singers

Although country blues were being performed at least from the turn of the twentieth century, this was not the music that the record companies chose to record. Rather, they recorded female vaudeville-blues artists, many of whom were not particularly blues singers at all. Ma Rainey and Bessie Smith were two exceptional blues singers, whose recordings were very successful. Rainey's music was closer to country blues than Bessie Smith's, who often used distinguished jazz musicians to accompany her. It wasn't until 1924 that Papa Charlie Jackson cut his first recordings for Paramount Records. Jackson was a sort of combination blues-ragtime artist who played a six-string banjo, an instrument tuned like a guitar and quite often used in recordings of Dixieland jazz. Blind Lemon Jefferson, considered one of the most important of the early blues artists, began recording for Paramount in 1926. When both of these artists made big-selling records, all of the labels began to seek out other folk-blues singers. Gradually, the folk blues eclipsed the classic blues singers and a number of the latter found their recording careers at an end by the early 1930s.

# The country side of things

In 1923, Atlanta record salesman Polk Brockman convinced Ralph Peer to record Georgia musician Fiddlin' John Carson. Peer felt that Carson was a terrible musician and was quite surprised that his recordings sold well.

Although Carson wasn't the first country-folk musician to record, he was the first one who proved to be successful on records. After Carson's records began to sell, a number of country instrumental groups like *Gid Tanner, Riley Puckett,* and *The Skillet Lickers* started to record for the major labels. Many of the bands had colorful names, such as *Al Hopkins and His Buckle Busters* or *The Leake County Revelers.*

Another sort of artist was more of a pseudo-country artist than an actual traditional singer. Vernon Dalhart began his career singing light opera, but turned to traditional music, scoring big hits with songs like *The Wreck of the Old 97.*

# Early commercial recordings and traditional music

As I have already discussed, many folksong collectors focused on traditional ballads, and they especially enjoyed a cappella singing. Record companies saw no market in this sort of music, and initially focused on fiddle and banjo tunes, and old-time (pre-bluegrass) string bands. Most folklorists regarded this music as tainted by commercial considerations, and since there were no texts they had no interest in it.

Since relatively few folklorists were collecting blues music, they felt even more negative about blues recordings. Additionally, the Paramount Records were recorded poorly and pressed on cheap vinyl. It was (and is) very difficult to understand the lyrics of many of Blind Lemon Jefferson's songs even with today's digital remastering technology in use.

This snobbery against the fruits of "commercial" recording continued for some years, but in 1940 folklorist-author-performer Alan Lomax edited three recordings of early country-folk artists that started to break down these attitudes. The albums were titled *Smoky Mountain Ballads*, on RCA Records, and *Listen to Our Story: A Panorama of American Balladry*, and *Mountain Frolic*. The latter two albums were on Brunswick Records, a subsidiary of Decca Records. The artists on these records included Dock Boggs, Reverend Edward W. Clayborn, Uncle Dave Macon, and Blind Joe Taggart. These albums were very significant because in effect these "commercial" recordings carried the endorsement of Alan Lomax, one of the premier folksong collectors in the United States. They also mixed white and African-American music on the same albums, which was a revolutionary move at that time.

## Authenticity of spirit

Although none of these recordings were made in folk communities or family households, for the most part they transmitted an authenticity of spirit to the listener. Another way to put this is that the music wasn't pure folk music, but *it felt like folk music*. Many of the songs recorded were indeed traditional folksongs, while others were tradition-based songs with embellishments by the artist. Uncle Dave Macon, for example, was a skilled entertainer who performed regularly on the *Grand Ole Opry* radio show, and many songs that he performed included his interpolations, oral narratives, and enthusiastic yells. Of course, the notion of an authenticity of spirit is extremely subjective. One listener may find a performance compelling and convincing, while another person may find the same performance insincere and artificial.

# Floating verses

In many blues and some country songs of the period, new songs were rewritten around traditional songs or themes. Many of the verses, especially in blues, might reappear in numerous other songs. For example, a common blues verse is:

> You don't know, you don't know my mind,
> You don't know, you don't know my mind.
> When you see me laughing, I'm laughing just to keep from crying.

Verses that appear in numerous songs are referred to as "floating verses." Many of the blue yodels recorded by Jimmie Rodgers made use of floating blues verses. These blue yodels were blues tunes that featured Rodgers yodeling and the texts were often free-form verses in the same way that many of Blind Lemon Jefferson's songs included groups of verses that did not necessarily tell a single coherent story. Most likely in many cases they represented the notion of a stream of consciousness, where the singer needed to fill out a song and simply inserted whatever verses occur to him or her.

# Talent finders

Talent finders beat the bushes, looking for new talent to present to record companies. In return, they were paid fees and sometimes royalties on the records that the companies actually released to the public. Blues singers in particular were outside the purview of most record company personnel, so they relied on people like Henry C. Spier, a music store owner in Jackson, Mississippi, who "discovered" Charley Patton, Skip James, and Tommy Johnson, all major blues figures. J. B. Long in Durham, North Carolina, was responsible for recording Piedmont blues artists Blind Boy Fuller, Buddy Moss, Sonny Terry, and Brownie McGhee. Spier also was responsible for recordings by white artists Uncle Dave Macon and The Leake County Revelers.

Folklorist D. K. Wilgus regards 1938 as the cutoff date when "race and hillbilly records were further removed from their folk roots." By that time, movie cowboys had infiltrated country music, and early rhythm and blues had begun to replace folk blues in the affections of African Americans.

# The significance of early commercial recordings in the evolution of folk music

Many of the early country and blues artists of the 1920s and 1930s grew up or even remained in rural communities. Banjoist Dock Boggs and white blues artist Frank Hutchison were coal miners; many folk, country, and even bluegrass artists worked in textile mills; and many of the early blues singers worked on large plantations in the south. To put it another way, their backgrounds were similar to the ones that folklorists like John Lomax encountered on their collecting trips. One can argue that when someone becomes a professional musician who charges money for a performance that there is a different level of interaction between the performer and the audience than that exists in a community where a group of friends and family members are sitting in a living room taking turns singing and playing music. However, many of the musicians who turned professional did indeed owe the development of their early musical skills to family members. For example, Bill Monroe sang about the influence of his Uncle Pen, and Earl Scruggs's older brother Junie was a banjo picker.

For early blues singers the professional–amateur distinction was not as clear, because so much of this consisted of solo or duo performances in informal gatherings, like parties, picnics, or street singing. Does the singer relying on tips face the same audience pressures that an old-time music band experienced playing live on the radio? At what point does professional stagecraft become part of the picture? Many of the black artists of the period, like Mississippi John Hurt, made a handful of records but never gave up their "day jobs" to become full-time professionals.

Many of the songs on commercial records were loose, spontaneous, and emotional. They might depict train wrecks, fox chases, train whistles, or concern murdered girls or bandits. In other words, they were often quite similar to traditional folksongs.

## The song versus the singer

In traditional music, and in many of the early commercial recordings, the emotion transmitted came from the song not from the performance. Clarence Ashley sings *The Coo-Coo* almost deadpan and the banjo accompaniment remains the same throughout the verses and "solos." Yet somehow, we are transported through song to a remote mountain community, even though we may never have lived there and can scarcely imagine the images depicted in the song.

In his book *The Old Weird America*, music critic Greil Marcus makes a great deal of many of the artists' concerns with the afterlife, and the contradiction between their actual day-to-day hardships and the lives of their artistic imagination. But, it isn't only exotic and strange elements that attract the modern urban listener but also the energy and lack of self-consciousness in the performances. We know many of today's musicians in the way their media representatives want us to know them. What we know about John Hurt or Dock Boggs is what the songs tell us, not what some PR or advertising people have fabricated. It is these stories and those imagined tales that have so attracted the urban revivalists. When some of these artists reemerged in the 1960s, some revivalists were able to develop more direct knowledge of the artists and their music.

Many of the revivalists, like Joan Baez or Judy Collins, for example, sang traditional music but they performed in a dramatic and theatrical way. The emphasis had shifted from the song itself to the singer and her performance.

## Black and white interactions

For years, folk music scholars drew strong distinctions between the music of African Americans and whites. Various researchers and even record producers periodically have confounded these assumptions. Dance historian Kate van Winkle, cited by folk dance scholar Phil Jamison in his book *Hoedowns, Reels and Frolics: Roots and Branches of Southern Appalachian Dance*, cites four hundred black and mixed-race fiddlers during the period 1709–89. Later references to black banjo and fiddle players appear in the various WPA books of slave narratives. Kevin Donleavy's 2004 book *Strings of Life-Conversations with Old-Time Musicians from Virginia and North Carolina Musicians* is a fine source of demolishing this segregation of the mind. He lists dozens of black old-time musicians, some of whom played with neighboring white musicians, and some of whom had black string bands. At the time of the release of his book, the number of such musicians or bands had severely declined, but ironically in recent years largely through the efforts of the *Carolina Chocolate Drops*, a black revival string band, some interest has developed in reviving black string bands and the banjo and fiddle. Robert Winans edited a book called *Banjo Roots and Branches* in 2018, which includes numerous references to nineteenth-century black banjo players, and even a few citations of eighteenth-century black banjoists. He also cites a number of examples of string bands that had both black and white members*.

## Other outlets for the music

Besides the work of folksong collectors and the early blues and country music recordings, the music was also promoted through various mountain music festivals and tours by early folk performers. Carl Sandburg interspersed his lectures on Abraham Lincoln with his songs, accompanying himself on guitar. In the mid-1930s, the Lomaxes toured Lead Belly, initially bizarrely decking him out in chain gang prison stripes. Presumably, John Lomax felt that this provided a touch of authenticity. Country music, including old-time music, was presented on the *Grand Ole Opry* radio show in Nashville and the *WLS Barn Dance* in Chicago.

Folksong collectors, commercial record companies, radio stations, book publishers, and promoters of live musical events each played a role in creating a market for a music that previously had not been marketed. One of the strangest stories in all of the re-discovery odysseys of blues and folk musicians was the re-emergence of Robert Johnson, sometimes referred to as the "King of the delta guitar." Robert only lived for just over 27 years, and he recorded late in the folk blues game, in 1936 and 1937. During his lifetime his records sold poorly, but when Columbia Records re-issued his work, initially on LP in 1961, and in 1990 in a double CD set, his albums had a strong effect on the direction of Chicago blues, and British rock-blues. The CD package has sold over a million copies, which has secured his legacy as a masterful delta blues artist and guitarist.

---

* Dom Clemons and Rhiannon Giddens have also pursued solo careers that display their knowledge of the black string band tradition.

# 3

# Early Protest Music: The Industrial Workers of the World, the Coal Miners, the Cotton Mills, and the Communist and Socialist Agitators

Generally folk fans regard protest songs as music adopted by radical political singers during the 1960s. Other onlookers may be referencing the music of the Civil Rights movement, or songs protesting the war in Vietnam. There was a close association between the early works of Bob Dylan, the songs of Phil Ochs, and their activities with the New Left movement of the 1960s.

The very notion of protest songs is a bit more complex than it first appears to be. Some songs are complaints against social conditions. Others involve specific recipes for inducing or expanding social change. The composers of these songs have different objectives in mind. Some songs are simply complaints about something specific, like working in the coal mines or textile mills, or being underpaid and overworked. These songs are often written by people who are actually experiencing these conditions because they or members of their families are working in the places described, or once did so.

Paul Garon and Gene Tomko's book, *What's the Use of Walking if There's a Freight Train Going Your Way?*, includes a number of such lyrics and other books that include songs about working in the coal mines or textile mills. Many of these songs are written by working people, but don't necessarily include calls for social change.

Another more active genre of protest songs calls for revolt or the resolution of specific issues. Such songs are much more apt to be written by social activists, union organizers, or people specifically involved in movements advocating social justice.

Historically, songs of social complaint go back to the times of the Revolutionary War and the conflict between the American colonies and their British rulers.

There have also been songs associated with virtually every political cause or campaign. One recent example was Bill Clinton's campaign and its use of Fleetwood Mac song *Don't Stop Thinking about Tomorrow*.

An example of a person protesting a specific social situation can be found in the folksong *The Wagoner's Lad*. This version was collected by Olive Dame Campbell in 1907, and contains verses related to numerous other songs, including *Child Ballads* and *On Top of Old Smoky*. The singer offers the complaint:

> Hard is the fortunes of all woman kind,
> They're always controlled, they're always confined;
> Controlled by their parents, until they are wives,
> Then slaves to their husbands the rest of their lives.

This song is about social class as well as gender. The man in the song complains that the woman's parents don't like him, because he is poor:

> Your parents don't like me, they say I'm too poor,
> They say I'm unworthy, of entering your door;
> I work for my living, my money's my own,
> And them as don't like me can leave me alone.

The mountain song *Single Girl* complains about the lot of married women and has a refrain that laments "Lord, I wish I was a single girl again." Another song, *Across the Blue Mountains*, is a complaint from a young woman who wants to go off with her already-married lover but whose parents caution against such reckless behavior.

Other folksongs discuss working conditions. In the song *The Farmer Is the Man*, the singer complains about his broken-down wagon and says that "the middleman is the one who gets it all."

## Nineteenth-century protests

The Hutchinson family toured widely in the 1840s singing anti-slavery songs, and popularizing the abolitionist cause and the temperance movement. Later in the century, labor song-poems and broadside ballads could be found in many labor publications. Scholar Clark D. Halker in his book *For Democracy, Workers and God: Labor Song-Poems and Labor Protest 1865–1895* points out that labor publications proliferated during the 1870s and 1880s and the labor union. The Knights of Labor published a book of labor songs in the 1880s. A book of socialist songs appeared in 1900, and labor historian Philip S. Foner has compiled a large group of nineteenth-century labor songs in his book *Labor Songs of the Nineteenth Century.*

## The IWW (Industrial Workers of the World)

The IWW (often known as "The Wobblies") was a new kind of union for the United States. The Knights of Labor and various other unions organized craft workers, and had no interest in industrial workers, or such specialized groups as migratory farm workers. The Wobblies wanted to organize all workers into one big union. They were much more radical than previous unions in the United States and were happy to accept African Americans and immigrants into their ranks. One of their tactics was the general strike, where all workers in a town would go out on strike in support of the demands of a particular group of striking workers.

The IWW was a singing union, and the near-legendary story of how the singing started is set in Seattle, where the Salvation Army was out on street corners with its small brass bands playing up a storm. In order to be heard The Wobblies started to sing, and to write songs and sing them in as many places as possible. The union published a songbook, *The Little Red Songbook*, in 1909 and it has subsequently gone through many reprints and edits, and is still available today.

A few of the IWW songs became classics, and are still sung at union meetings today. This is especially true of the song *Solidarity Forever*, and to a lesser extent of Joe (Hillstrom) Hill's *The Preacher and the Slave*. Chaplin's song used the melody of the song *John Brown's Body*, while Joe Hill adopted the tune of the hymn *In the Sweet Bye and Bye*. Another Wobbly named Mac McClintock became a professional musician, and his song *Halleluiah I'm a Bum* achieved great popularity.

Joe Hill was a prominent IWW organizer but was indicted on charges of killing a grocer in 1914 in Salt Lake City. The trial was extremely controversial because the prosecution producing no witnesses who identified Hill, and the defense saying only that Hill was involved in a quarrel. Part of the mythology of Joe Hill is that he refused to specifically explain the situation because he was allegedly involved in a romantic liaison and didn't want to identify the woman. Hill was executed in 1915 and he became something of a folk hero among unionists. This status was solidified when poet Alfred Hayes and composer Earl Robinson wrote a song about Hill in 1936. The song has been recorded by a number of artists including Paul Robeson and Joan Baez, and is well known to musicians and fans of the 1960s folk revival.

The IWW opposed America's entrance into the First World War, and the rise of the Communist movement in 1919 also led to its demise. Although the IWW technically still exists today, its importance and its songs are of historical rather than contemporary significance.

## The American Communist Party

Initially, the Communist Party of the United States consisted largely of foreign-born immigrants, according to R. Serge Denisoff in his book *Great Day Coming: Folk Music and the American Left*. The party initially thought that they could organize choruses of working men and women and teach them to sing newly written art songs composed by contemporary composers that included political lyrics.

The 1930s offered fertile ground for radical organizers in the late 1920s and through the 1930s. The farm depression of the mid-1920s and the Great Depression that began in 1928 created widespread unemployment in industrialized cities, and the loss of many small farms in rural areas. The Marxist version of egalitarianism that the Soviet Union promoted was ultimately supposed to lead to a world of absolute economic equality, "from each according to his ability, to each according to his needs." The political state itself was supposed to wither away leading to a world of political and economic equality, free of exploitation.

This egalitarian fantasy was enormously appealing to intellectuals and artists in a country where unemployed workers were selling apples on the street, formerly wealthy stockbrokers and bankers were jumping from buildings, and banks were going out of business. Consequently, artists of all sorts—painters, writers, musicians, actors, and dancers—were attracted to this utopian vision of the future. Quite a few of them joined the Communist Party, and even more of them didn't join but were essentially sympathizers, or "fellow travelers." It was fashionable to accept radical author and journalist Lincoln Steffens's opinion of the USSR "I have seen the future and it works."

# Communism and American folk music

The Communist Party encouraged contemporary composers of the 1930s to form a Workers Musician Club, which was named after a Belgian socialist named Pierre Degeyter. The two dozen members of the club included such prestigious names in the world of musical composition as Aaron Copland, Henry Cowell, Wallingford Rieger, Charles Seeger (Pete's father), Elie Siegmeister, and Marc Blitzstein.

The original goal of these luminaries had nothing at all to do with folk music. Instead, they championed the creation of choruses and orchestras that would marry politically radical song lyrics with modern avant-garde compositional techniques. Their role model was Hans Eisler, a German communist composer who fled Hitler's Germany and immigrated to the United States in 1933. Eisler scorned traditional folk music, which he thought was trivial and old-fashioned, and he championed the writing of atonal music and works that utilized the twelve-tone scale promoted by Arnold Schoenberg.

The notion of writing new and experimental music was attractive to the composers listed above, but they found that such music was too difficult even for the musicians that they were teaching. They also became aware that there was an active singing tradition in the southern United States. The Communist Party had become involved in organizing coal miners and textile workers, and out of political tradition several authentic "labor minstrels" emerged.

One of these songwriters was Ella Mae Wiggins, who impressed a New York radical named Margaret Larkin. Larkin carried Wiggins's song *Mill Mother's Lament* back to New York, sang it at various rallies, and wrote about it for the communist newspaper *The Daily Worker* and for the non-communist liberal magazine *The Nation*. Wiggins was murdered in Gastonia, North Carolina, in 1929 while organizing textile workers and so her music was also infused with her martyrdom at such rallies.

Two years later, a radical committee that included novelists John Dos Passos, Theodore Dreiser, and Sherwood Anderson were enlisted to investigate conditions in the coal mines of Harlan County, Kentucky, and they "discovered" Aunt Molly Jackson. Jackson was a ballad maker and organizer for the communist-led National Miners Union. Like the Wobbly songwriters, Jackson adopted existing tunes for her songs but unlike them, the melodies that she chose were traditional mountain songs, not popular songs or hymns. Jackson sang her song *Ragged,*

*Hungry Blues* for the committee, and resulting publicity in the communist press brought Jackson and her step-brother Jim Garland to New York.

Jackson then performed for the Degyter group, and the strength of her songs caused Charles Seeger to reassess his original negative opinions about American folk music. He began to envision a new radical music movement built around traditional folk music, rather than classical art songs.

Another step in utilizing folksongs for radical causes was the emergence of two singer-songwriters named Ray and Lida Auville. Like Aunt Molly, the Auvilles were actually from the southern mountains and had a repertoire of traditional songs. They moved to Cleveland and began to write songs in both folk and popular music styles, performing them to their own fiddle and guitar accompaniments. For whatever reasons, Charles Seeger and Elie Siegmeister, writing in communist periodicals in 1935, did not like the melodies or the texts to the Auville's songs although *Daily Worker* columnist Mike Gold defended and tried to promote them. In 1936, a couple of songs that the Auvilles had written about the Spanish Civil War were printed in mimeographed songbooks. After that they seemed to totally disappear from sight. I have not been able to find any references to any recordings by the Auvilles. In effect, they had been "written out" of the history of American political folk music.

Lawrence Gellert achieved some notoriety with his songbooks. A few of his songs were published in left-wing periodicals or songbooks and some others were arranged for choral groups. Nevertheless, he too disappeared from the consciousness of scholars of radical folk music.

Looking back at this history eighty years later, it is difficult to know whether the disappearance of these artists and collectors from history was based on aesthetic or political matters, or because of internal feuds in the radical folksong movement. Bruce Conforth's authoritative biography addresses the story of Lawrence Gellert, and he is currently working on issuing a boxed set of the music that Gellert collected.

## Textile mills and non-communist protest music

In addition to the "made to order" politically inspired songs about the cotton mills, there were other mill workers who aspired to be professional musicians who wrote songs about the mills. Country musician Dave McCarn wrote three songs that described conditions in the mills. His song *Cotton Mill Colic* was recorded in 1930. Each verse ends with the refrain: "I'm a-gonna starve, and everybody will. Cause you can't make a living at a cotton mill." The four verses of the song refer to installment buying, difficulties in paying rent or buying food, poor salaries, and the widening gap between the rich and the poor. McCarn himself started working in a cotton mill at the age of twelve.

*Cotton Mill Colic* sold well enough for RCA Victor to record other songs, but it cost McCarn his job when the mill superintendent in South Gastonia heard the song, fired McCarn, and blacklisted him. His subsequent records, including two other songs about the mills, did not sell well enough to allow him to pursue a career in music.

Although working in the cotton mills was a hard life, the mills actually pursued a number of paternalistic programs designed to keep the workers happy and occupied outside of work. According to Patrick Huber's book *Linthead Stomp*, these programs subsidized brass bands, music lessons, and baseball teams.

## Dorsey Dixon

Dorsey Dixon performed with his brother Howard as the Dixon Brothers. Dorsey was a prolific songwriter whose songs focused of religious subjects and his Christian fundamentalist beliefs, but he also wrote about life in the textile mills, tragedies, and natural disasters. In today's world, Dixon probably could have made a living as a professional songwriter but through his own naivete and crooked dealing by a few of his peers, he lost control of all or most of the rights to his most successful songs, notably a song that became a country music "standard," *The Wreck on the Highway*. The Dixon Brothers' recordings were made in 1936 and 1937. As is the case with McCarn's *Cotton Mill Colic*, Dixon's songs about the cotton mills include complaints about wages, working conditions, and the machinery at the mill. Because both of them were writing from the standpoint of grassroots working-class men with no particular political affiliation, these songs do not call for any specific sort of changes, but explain that the singer can't take it anymore.

Patrick Huber points out that between 1923 and 1942, Piedmont singers or musicians from textile towns appeared on over 1500 of 23,000 recorded "hillbilly" songs, and 88 mill workers made records before the Second World War.

## Cotton and coal songs in the revival

A number of artists who come from coal country, or have or had relatives who worked in the mines, have continued to record socially relevant songs about mining to this day. Merle Travis never worked in the mines himself, but had many family members who did. Travis was a superb guitar player, composer, and singer, and in 1947 he recorded an album called *Folk Songs of the Hills*. This record included the songs *Sixteen Tons* and *Dark as a Dungeon*. *Sixteen Tons* became a huge pop hit for Tennessee Ernie Ford and *Dark as a Dungeon* became a staple of the folk revival, and is still sung today. Travis followed this up with an entire album of coal mining songs in 1962.

Jean Ritchie was born in Perry County in Eastern Kentucky. She moved to New York City in 1945 and was well known in the folk music community as one of the few folksingers in New York who actually grew up in a family of traditional musicians. In the mid-1960s, she wrote a number of songs about coal mining in Kentucky. These included *The L&N Don't Stop Here Anymore*, *The Blue Diamond Mines*, *Black Waters*, and *West Virginia Mining Disaster*. In addition to her own recordings and performances, Johnny Cash, Judy Collins, Emmylou Harris, and Dolly Parton recorded their own versions of the song.

Billy Edd Wheeler's song *Coal Tattoo* was a favorite in the folk music revival of the 1960s. Besides Wheeler's own version, it was recorded by Judy Collins, the Kingston Trio, and more recently by Kathy Mattea and rock-blues artist Warren Haynes. Darrell Scott's *You'll Never Leave Harlan Alive* was written in 1997, and has been recorded by Patti Loveless and Kathy Mattea, and was used in several episodes of the TV show *Justified*, sung variously by Brad Paisley and Dave Alvin. Country-folk artist Kathy Mattea recorded an entire album of coal mining songs written by many of the above songwriters in 2008. John Prine's song *Paradise*, recorded in 1971, is another mining song that has achieved some popularity.

Songs about cotton mills have been considerably less prominent among folk revival singers. Hedy West was the only other prominent folksinger in New York during the 1960s who, like Jean Ritchie, came from a traditional folk music background. She learned many of her songs from her grandmother. Hedy's version of *Cotton Mill Girls* was recorded by her, The Journeymen, and many relatively obscure artists. Dorsey Dixon's *Weave Room Blues* was sung by *The New Lost City Ramblers* and Pete Seeger during the 1960s.

Coal mining is a timely issue for environmentalists, and coal mine disasters often result in fatalities and are extensively publicized. Consequently twenty-first-century artists and songwriters regard coal mining as a more important subject for folk revival singers than the plight of cotton mill workers.

## Further thoughts about protest songs

There are numerous other traditional and composed songs that complain about various social conditions. A more recent song, like Si Kahn's *Aragon Mill*, does deal with the destruction of communities resulting from the closing of cotton mills.

Although many of the above singers support progressive political causes, it is difficult to imagine most of them performing on union picket lines. As was the case with Dorsey Dixon or Merle Travis, these songs are mostly descriptive songs about working conditions. They are stronger on complaints than on solutions or calls for specific social reforms.

In that way they differ from the 1940s and 1950s songs performed and composed by political folksingers, whose songs generally included clarion calls demanding social change. Later in the book, I will turn to the work of such contemporary singer-songwriters as Si Kahn and Anne Feeney who do indeed sing at union rallies and gatherings of environmentalists.

## Charles Seeger and Alan Lomax

Through various governmental cultural programs that were part of Franklin D. Roosevelt's New Deal initiatives, Charles Seeger became friendly with Alan Lomax, and the two of them formulated a vision that utilized folksongs as a tool for radical change. Although Alan's father John was quite politically conservative, Alan's political allegiances lay in the opposite direction.

## The vision and the problem

Given that Charles Seeger and Alan Lomax were formulating their notion of using folksongs as a tool for radical change during the Great Depression, it is understandable why they could have come up with this concept. After all, it seemed to work in coal mining and textile mill country. The problem was (and is) that outside of the southern United States, factory workers and most union members had no background or interest in American folksongs. Like most urban Americans, they were consumers of popular music.

Nevertheless, it is important to understand just how powerful an influence these two men had on the development not only of protest music, but also of the folk music revival that followed some twenty years. The two were an unlikely pair, equally opinionated, and sure of themselves, knowledgeable but judgmental on musical matters. Seeger used his various positions as a government employee during the days of the New Deal to collect songs, and also to bring folk musicians working for the federal theater project to small towns in an effort to revive interest in American folk music. Seeger's community program was a dismal failure, but it was an interesting notion.

Lomax was in a stronger bargaining position because he had the ability to advance the careers of folk musicians who he felt were worthy and talented. He did this by helping them get recording contracts and by hiring them for radio shows that he was directly or indirectly involved in, by assisting musicians to find work in nightclubs, and by writing about them in books, magazines, or album notes. Lomax also acted as a mentor for a number of folksingers, employing Charles Seeger's son Pete as his assistant at the Archive of American Folk Song in the Library of Congress, teaching him many of the songs that he and his father had collected and greatly expanding Pete's notion of the scope and history of American folk music.

4

# The Almanac Singers, People's Song, People's Artists, and the Blacklist

For many years New York City was the center for the production of American music. Anyone who wanted a recording contract would eventually go there and it was also the center for the production of network radio shows. Within a few years of one another, Woody Guthrie, Lead Belly, Josh White, Pete Seeger, Lee Hays, and many other folksingers who aspired to become professionals gravitated to Manhattan.

In early 1941, Pete Seeger, Lee Hays, and Millard Lampell moved into a house that occasionally Almanac Peter Hawes had rented. Hawes soon moved out and Woody Guthrie, Bess Lomax (Alan's sister). Gordon Freisen, and Sis Cunningham moved in. They banded together in a group known as the Almanac Singers. A whole group of other musicians and singers, including Hawes' brother Butch, Arthur Stern, Charlie Polacheck, Cisco Houston, Earl Robinson, Woody Guthrie, and blues singers Josh White, Brownie McGhee, and Sonny Terry from time to time also participated in the group.

The Almanacs were an extremely loosely knit group, and anyone who hired them might find any combination of the above names would actually turn up on the gig. It was simply a question of who happened to be available. Rehearsals were minimal, and some of the group members like Woody Guthrie were not exactly paragons of responsibility.

The group sang for many radical causes. During the 1930s, until shortly after the end of the Second World War, a number of unions in the Congress of Industrial Organizations (CIO) were either influenced or dominated by the Communist Party. In 1937, the Communist Party had been heavily involved in the Spanish Civil War. That war pitted a loose coalition of socialists, anarchists, and communists against the fascist forces led by Francisco Franco. Prior to this time, communist propaganda advocated the formation of a united front against fascism. Before them, the party had denounced socialists and liberals or radicals as class enemies.

Franco's forces triumphed in the struggle, and in August, 1939, communists were shocked to discover that Hitler and Stalin had agreed to a non-aggression pact, guaranteeing that the two countries would not attack one another. The communists turned their focus to a hands-off policy, opposing any involvement in European politics. During this period, Russia and Germany carved up Poland between them and Russia invaded Finland, and acquired some Finnish territory. These actions were rationalized by the party as necessary in order to build buffer zones for the Russians against any future conflict with Germany. Meanwhile, the United States and Britain took no position on these invasions. They hoped that Hitler and Stalin would eventually destroy one another leaving the world, so to speak, safe for capitalism.

This ideology was translated into music by the Almanacs when they wrote and recorded an album called *Songs for John Doe*, released in spring 1941. The album included six anti-war songs that strongly attacked President Roosevelt with lines such as "I hate war/ And so does Eleanor/ But we won't be safe/ Till everybody's dead."

Even though the Second World War was underway by that time, the party decreed that the United States should not support the British or the French. The US government had passed the Selective Service Act in October 1940. It required men between the ages of twenty-one and thirty-five to register for the draft, in anticipation that we would soon join the British and French cause. On June 22, 1941, Germany attacked Russia and the album was withdrawn from circulation. It was followed a year later by *Dear Mr. President*, an album that vigorously supported the war effort. The party line had definitely changed! The Almanacs also recorded an album called *Talking Union*, and two albums of folksongs, *Sodbuster Ballads* and *Deep Sea Chanteys*.

## The Second World War and the influence of the Almanac Singers

All of the existing accounts, whether they are histories of the folksong movement or biographies or autobiographies of the various Almanacs, discuss the internal difficulties and conflicts between the various members and partial members of the group. When I use the phrase "partial members" I am referring to such musicians as Tom Glazer and Burl Ives, who sometimes recorded with the group but never lived in Almanac House or were regular members of the group.

The two most personally difficult Almanacs seem to have been Lee Hays and Woody Guthrie. Hays was actually fired from the group when seven members pressured Pete Seeger, the de facto leader of the group, to dismiss him. His various neuroses, ranging from hypochondria to excessive consumption of alcohol, and his generally ornery nature became too much for the others to handle. Guthrie rarely acknowledged any level of personal responsibility. He had strong opinions and even stronger inconsistencies. It is interesting that his persona seems to have captivated many folk-pop-rock performers to this day.

Later in the book I will undertake an evaluation of four major artists of the folk revival, namely, Woody Guthrie, Lead Belly, Alan Lomax, and Pete Seeger.

## Josh White

Of all the people connected to the Almanac Singers, Josh White was the closest to being a tradition-based singer. As a young boy, Josh was the lead boy for various blind street singers in South Carolina, notably Blind Man Arnold. White started his recording career at the age of sixteen, recording blues under the name Pinewood Tom, and religious songs as *The Singing Christian*. Josh moved to New York City in 1932, and he quickly became a major figure on the New York scene during the 1930s and 1940s. In 1939, a chance meeting with choral conductor Leonard de Paur led to a part in the play *John Henry*, which starred Paul Robeson. Josh played the role of Blind Lemon Jefferson. In real life, Josh had played the role of lead boy for Blind Lemon.

The connection with de Paur continued when Josh formed a trio called The Carolinians and they arranged, rewrote a half dozen songs from the Lawrence Gellert published collections. Fabled Columbia Records producer and political radical John Hammond then persuaded Goddard Lieberson, the president of the label, to sign them. The songs were very strong antiracist statements, especially for 1940. When Josh was featured on Alan Lomax and Nicholas Ray's radio show *Back Where I Come From*, he enjoyed national exposure, which led to engagements at the Café Society nightclub, first with Lead Belly, and then with cabaret singer Libby Holman. White then recorded another album of protest songs. These newly composed works were set to poems by a Harlem poet named Waring Cuney.

Josh White did not appear live with the Almanac Singers, but he played guitar on the songs for *John Doe* album, even doing a bit of singing on it. He also recorded with some of the Almanacs in a spin-off group called *The Union Boys*.

A bit later, I will discuss how Josh White's activities on behalf of left-wing causes would seriously impair his performing career. Josh did not exactly fit the image of the Almanacs. He was handsome and articulate, while the group in general tried to portray a rustic image in terms of dress, speech, and repertoire. For some of them this was an affectation, given their college education and middle-class backgrounds. White had become an increasingly sophisticated and professional entertainer and musician. His guitar style was rooted in the blues, but he had modified it in order to play a broad repertoire that ranged from show tunes to jazz-influenced ballads. His guitar work was original and unusual, featuring string bends, interesting rhythmic right-hand patterns, and some showbiz affectations. He had a routine where he deliberately broke a string while playing in an open chord tuning on the guitar. With a cigarette nestled in the head stock of the instrument, he would change the string and keep playing at the same time. I saw Josh White play live a half dozen times. The sixth time I saw him, he had endured a heart attack, and was also having skin problems with his hands. During the other five performances I never saw him make a mistake. He is virtually the only musician whom I have ever seen that I could make such a statement about.

In 1947, Josh White began to cut his ties to the radical movement as the Cold War between the United States and Russia developed. He appeared in front of the House Un-American Activities Committee in 1950. He did not give the committee the names of musicians who were communists or communist sympathizers, but basically said that he was just a young man and didn't know what he was doing. The committee did not remove him from the blacklist, but did not attempt to prosecute him. He was possibly the only musician who was in effect blacklisted both from the right for his radical activities and from the left for his testimony before Congress. Many of these developments are described in detail in Elijah Wald's excellent biography *Josh White: Society Blues*.

Because of the political controversies surrounding White after his testimony, he is seldom covered in any detail in books about the folk music revival. He is yet another person who has been "written out" of the folk music revival. His son Donny, whose stage name is Josh White Jr. is an excellent singer who has performed in concerts and coffeehouses for years and utilizes some of Josh's guitar techniques.

## Lead Belly and the Almanacs

After some conflicts with John Lomax, who with his son Alan had served as Lead Belly's manager, Lead Belly moved to New York City and appeared in some early folk gatherings sponsored by the Almanacs. However, he never traveled or recorded with them. He was friendly with both Pete Seeger and Woody Guthrie and was an influence on their music. As is the case with Woody, I will discuss Lead Belly in more depth in a later chapter. This discussion will also offer an evaluation of the career of the Almanacs' sparkplug, Pete Seeger.

## The Second World War and the end of the Almanacs

When the Second World War began, the United States joined hands with the USSR, Britain, and France to fight Germany and Japan. The Communist Party decreed that all efforts should be directed toward winning the war and that workers should delay protesting working conditions or wages until the fascist menace disappeared. Josh White, for one, was writing songs that pointed out that African Americans were sacrificing their lives in a segregated country that made no promises of improving their situation after the war ended. The other Almanacs continued to sing union songs, but their emphasis was on supporting the war efforts. Listening to the songs on the twelve-CD reissue project *Songs for Political Action*, painstakingly compiled by Ron Cohen and Dave Samuelson, tells the story. There are occasional complaints about war profiteering and the cost of living, but mostly the songs praise the CIO and look forward to the impending defeat of Hitler.

Pete Seeger was drafted in 1942 and Woody Guthrie served in the Merchant Marine until he too was drafted. Various sub-groups of Almanacs continued to record during the war. Possibly the most impassioned recording that the Almanacs ever made was their 1943 album of Spanish Civil War songs. *Songs of the Lincoln Battalion* was recorded for Asch-Stinson Records. The Abraham Lincoln Brigade was the name given to the unit of three thousand American volunteers who fought in Spain. The artists on the album included Pete Seeger, on a weekend pass from the army, Baldwin (Butch) Hawes, Bess Lomax Hawes, and Tom Glazer.

As is the case with many of the Almanacs's topical songs, one rarely hears any of the songs of the Lincoln Battalion today, although in 2004 folksinger

Tony Saletan and a group of several other artists did a lengthy double album that included songs and narration. Some of the performers were children of battalion member George Watt. None of the Almanac Singers were members of the Abraham Lincoln Brigade.

During the Second World War, Almanac offshoots performed in Washington, DC, and Detroit. Without the dynamic presence of Pete Seeger, there was no longer a core group. Alan Lomax employed various Almanacs in his radio shows, which were built around American legends. Lomax even had the legendary feuding family the Martins and the Coys uniting to fight the Nazis in a script co-authored with his wife Elizabeth.

A number of other performers were active in the folk scene during the Second World War, including part-time Almanac Burl Ives, Richard Dyer Bennet, Earl Robinson, and singer-actor Will Geer. Dyer Bennet was an art singer, classical guitarist, and a left-wing sympathizer, whose highly arranged art-folksongs were essentially apolitical. Robinson was a songwriter and composer who, besides co-authoring the previously mentioned revival standard *Joe Hill*, wrote the music for a patriotic cantata, which was performed at both the Republican and Democratic Party Conventions in 1940. That piece and a 1943 cantata about the death of Abraham Lincoln called *The Lonesome Train* were co-authored with lyricist John La Touche. In 1945, occasional Almanac Tom Glazer wrote a widely performed choral work *The Ballad of Franklin D*. Blues cabaret artist and part-time Almanac Josh White became quite friendly with Eleanor Roosevelt and often performed at the White House.

## Pete Seeger and People's Songs

By the time the war had ended, the Almanacs had received some unwanted publicity in the form of newspaper articles reminding readers that the "patriotic" Almanacs were the same folks who had recorded antiwar songs shortly before America had entered the war. They were also cited in several congressional reports on allegedly communist entertainers and artists.

Meanwhile, Pete Seeger returned home with a brand-new vision. He wanted to start a new organization, a sort of super-Almanacs that would include branches all over the country and lead a new fight for social change and a radical America. The name of the organization was People's Songs.

## People's Songs and People's Artists

People's Songs was an organization designed to encourage the writing and transmission of radical protest songs while People's Artists was essentially a booking agency that sought to find jobs for radical performing musicians. People's Songs published a bulletin and put together a songbook of protest songs from all over the world called *The People's Songbook*.

While the Almanac Singers had been a ragtag bunch of folksingers, People's Songs was a more formal organization, not a communal-living collective. The new organization formed a satellite chapter in Los Angeles and there were members in San Francisco and Chicago. People's Songs was intended to be more musically inclusive and it included Broadway and cabaret composers, folklorists, a sprinkling of classical musicians, and even record producer John Hammond.

There was tremendous enthusiasm during the early stages of People's Songs, and many of the Almanacs and neo-Almanacs such as Woody Guthrie, Lee Hays, Millard Lampell, and Tom Glazer served on the national board of directors. Pete Seeger was elected as the national director and Mario "Boots" Casetta was chosen to run the Los Angeles branch. Later Paul Robeson, the renowned black activist, singer, and actor, joined the board of directors.

## The Cold War and the demise of People's Songs

After the end of the Second World War, the United States and Russia became locked in a struggle for political, economic, and military control of the world. Western Europe was aligned with the United States, the Eastern European countries were controlled by communist regimes, and the rest of the world was eventually, and often reluctantly, compelled to choose sides between one camp or the other. The stage was set for what became known as the *Cold War*, an ideological conflict between the two superpowers. Inevitably, left-wing sentiment in the United States became identified with communism and disloyalty to America. Communist ideology was regarded as the enemy and Russia was regarded as a threat to American life.

In the early days of People's Songs, Alan Lomax presented a series of successful concerts. The organization's songbook had a positive impact, and a mutually beneficial relationship with the CIO seemed to point to a continuing friendship between unions and People's Artists. Several workers' choruses absorbed what remained of the Hanns Eisler ideology, and some successful Broadway composers and songwriters were on board.

Problems with Lee Hays fulfilling his work caused Pete Seeger to be handed the unenviable task of asking Hays to resign as executive secretary of the organization. Leonard Jacobson, the booking agent for People's Artists, brought in performing jobs, and there were regular hootenannies group performances in New York. After this positive beginning, a series of Town Hall concerts in New York in 1947–8 lost money.

## Henry Wallace and the election of 1948

Henry Wallace had been Roosevelt's secretary of agriculture and was vice president during FDR's third term (1940–4). He was replaced as vice president during Roosevelt's fourth term. When Truman ran for president in 1948, Wallace decided to run on an independent ticket under the Progressive Party banner. Wallace did not believe in the anti-Soviet ideology of the Cold War, and he ran with the support of the Communist Party and other pro-Russian radical groups.

People's Songs became heavily involved in the Wallace campaign. Alan Lomax and other members wrote songs supporting Wallace; Earl Robinson and Paul Robeson performed at Wallace rallies, and Pete Seeger toured with him. At the same time, the CIO began to expel left-wing unions from the organization, taking a strong anti-communist stance. The connection between the union movement and People's Songs fell apart, and soon a few unions even began to compile their own songbooks. Only a handful of small radical unions retained a connection with People's Songs. These included the UE (United Electrical Workers) and the Mine, Mill and Smelter Workers. Both of these unions had been expelled by the CIO because of their connections with the Communist Party.

The Wallace campaign was something of a disaster. The goal had been to get five million votes, but the party managed to garner only just over a million. J. Strom Thurmond who ran on the segregationist Dixiecrat ticket actually polled more votes than Wallace. By March 1949, People's Songs was in a desperate financial situation. An unsuccessful concert at Carnegie Hall featuring some major jazz and folk artists failed to raise any money, and the organization disbanded.

## People's Artists and the end of the united front

People's Songs was succeeded by a similar organization, named People's Artists. This was the same name that the booking wing of the earlier organization had used.

As the Cold War heated up, non-communist liberals like Oscar Brand and Tom Glazer reined in their radical affiliations. The more that People's Songs interacted with communist or pro-Russian causes, the less useful the organization became to performers seeking gigs. Essentially, the radical movement had developed a symbiotic relationship with performing artists. The singers used the organization to get work, and the organization used the singers to promote radical causes. If the singers didn't entirely agree with the causes, they could simply see the relationship as a way of getting work. After all, most musicians have seldom hesitated to play for organizations from the Republican Party to the Elks Club. This didn't necessarily mean that they agreed with the politics of their employers.

As the Cold War continued, the US Congress became increasingly interested in rooting out communists in the entertainment business. Meanwhile a communist coup overthrew the Czech government in February 1948. Czechoslovakia was the last democratically elected government in Eastern Europe. Non-communist liberals and radicals who had been involved in political music began to question the connection between People's Artists and the Communist Party. After all, it was possible to be a political radical and to disagree with communist ideology.

Richard Reuss wrote what is the most searching analysis of the relationship between left-wing politics and folk music preceding 1960. In his book, *American Folk Music and Left Wing Politics, 1927–1957*, edited by his wife JoAnne, he writes: "Was People's Songs, Inc. really a subunit of the American Communist Party? At the risk of begging the question, it is fair to say no. But there is no doubt that the goals and even the identity of People's Songs, and later People's Artists, were substantially influenced by the worldview of the Communist Party in the post war era."

Reuss goes on to maintain that the Communist Party exercised little direct control over the organization, although many of its members were communists. He then quotes Irwin Silber, who became the driving organizational force behind People's Artists. Silber said that there was a sub-group of folksingers in the party who met to discuss the overall direction of the role of these organizations. He stated that the club had some twenty members from 1946 to 1949, and ten or twelve during the People's Artists era, 1950–2. Silber did not state who these members were, although almost without question he was one of them. It would certainly be interesting to know whether Alan Lomax or Pete Seeger, for example, was among them. By 1950, Seeger had moved upstate to Beacon New York, and had drifted out of the party.

The general tack that Seeger and Earl Robinson have taken in their writings is that they were naïve in regard to Communist Party practices in Russia. According to Silber, this communist sub-group did not attempt to micromanage the direction of the organizations, but was more interested in general ideological discussions.

## Communism in retrospect

Over a period of time, a number of events occurred that drove many radicals away from the party, and hesitant about supporting any aspects of the Russian Revolution. The Moscow trials of 1936–8, allegedly designed to root out Trotskyites, the Czech coup of 1948, followed by the Hungarian invasion of 1956 and the Czech invasion of 1968 all brought into question the vision of a new communist utopia.

When William Z. Foster replaced Earl Browder as the leader of the American Communist Party, Foster suggested that America should adopt the Soviet model of creating separate national states for minority groups. This led to the notion of creating a separate black state in the American South that would consist entirely of African Americans.

It doesn't appear that many party members took this seriously. Keep in mind that People's Songs and People's Artists were attempting to go out of their way to involve black participation in all of their events. Group members promoted economic and social integration and its members often wrote songs promoting these programs. Wouldn't it be natural to assume that communist folksingers would at the very least question Foster's policies? I have never seen any mention of the so-called national question in any autobiographical or biographical books written by radical folksingers. It would appear that if a communist doctrine didn't work for these people, they simply ignored it, rather than opposing it.

Shortly after I submitted the rough draft of this book, I received an email from a New York folk fan named Fred Siesel. He told me that in 1968 he was a thirty-seven-year-old architectural design consultant in New York City with a great interest in folk music, when he decided to take a banjo lesson from Erik Darling. During the lesson, the phone rang and Erik briefly left to take a telephone call. He soon reappeared and told Fred that the call would take a while.

Twenty minutes later, he apologetically returned, and explained that the caller was Pete Seeger, and that Pete was crying bitterly on the phone because "his whole belief system had been shattered," when he discovered that Russian tanks had entered Prague, Czechoslovakia, on that very day.

There are several interesting things about this call. Erik and Pete were friends, but Erik was essentially a non-political libertarian, while Pete was an ex-communist and maintained close associations with communist-led causes for years.

In fact, it wasn't until the late 1990s that Pete openly acknowledged the inhumanity and excesses of the Stalin era. This call demonstrates how difficult it was for ex-communists or communist sympathizers to renounce the dictatorial nature of the Soviet Union. In effect, Pete kept this information and his feelings to himself for some thirty years!

## Who owns and edits the legacy of radical folk music?

If we read any of the books about the relationship between radical politics and folk music, except for Dave Van Ronk's memoir, we get the feeling that the communists entirely dominated political folk music. In fact, there were a handful of liberals or radicals such as Roy Berkeley, Oscar Brand, Joe Glaser, Dave Van Ronk, and folklorist Archie Green who did not "go along with the program." The various small left-wing Trotskyite splinter groups in New York also wrote and sang songs making fun of communism, and even compiled a satirical songbook called *The Bosses Songbook*.

Although some of the music of textile workers and miners was directed or co-opted by the Communist Party, some of the songs really didn't fit into communist ideology. Sarah Ogun Gunning, Aunt Molly Jackson's half-sister, wrote a song titled *I Hate the Capitalist System*. However, not only was Gunning not a communist, but also upon her rediscovery she asserted that she did not approve of communists or communism. Josh White continued to perform some of the strongest political songs of any of the Almanacs long after he repudiated any semblance of communist ideology.

During the 1920s and 1930s, a number of labor schools were established as training grounds for radical organizers. Brookwood Labor College had a politically mixed bag of students who studied for two years in a small town north of New York City. Brookwood was a socialist school founded by Norman Thomas, the perennial socialist candidate for president, and pacifist leader A. J. Muste. They introduced mining songs to the students as a tool for agitation. Although the school fell apart in 1933, another socialist-supported group called the Southern Tenant Farmers Union was organized in Arkansas in 1934 by black and white tenant farmers and socialists. Among its leaders were A. B. Brookins and John Handcox, both black preachers and song leaders. Handcox was an excellent songwriter, and his songs *Raggedy Are We, Roll the Union On*, and *Mean Things Happening in This Land* became well known in the union movement. Handcox had to flee the South in fear of his life, and he became a somewhat forgotten figure in the history of radical folk music until he was rediscovered years later.

The Highlander Folk School in Monteagle, Tennessee, seems to have included both members of the Communist Party and non-communist radicals. Zilphia Horton, wife of founder Myles Horton, was the music director at the school collecting hundreds of songs. Along with Guy Carawan, Frank Hamilton, and Pete Seeger, she is responsible for arranging *We Shall Overcome*, which later became the anthem of the Civil Rights movement*.

During the summer of 1949, a scheduled performance by Paul Robeson in Peekskill, New York, was stymied by an attack engineered by the Ku Klux Klan and various conservative patriotic groups. The concert was rescheduled and performed, but after it ended a similar group of antagonists forced the attendees to go through a gauntlet of rocks thrown at their cars. The Cold War was at its peak and anyone suspected of being a communist or being sympathetic to communist ideas was fair game for congressional investigations. The press lambasted left-wing artists and they were also blacklisted from television and radio work, and their performances were picketed or even cancelled. Alan Lomax fled to England in 1950, safe from intrusion into his political beliefs.

In the 1960s, the role of the Communist Party in radical folk music had moved from a dominant position to a presence barely on the margins of the radar of the youth-led New Left. A contrasting peculiar development was the writing and recording of pro-segregation songs by members of the radical right, on a mysterious record label that featured the Confederate Army Flag.

---

* In early April 2019, a fire burned down the main building at Highlander. The arsonists left a white power symbol in the wreckage.

# 5

# The Weavers and the Beginning of the Folk Revival

The Weavers were formed at the end of the Wallace campaign in 1948. Once again Pete Seeger was the sparkplug and the other members were Seeger's old friend-nemesis Lee Hays and the younger Ronnie Gilbert and Fred Hellerman. Gilbert and Hellerman had a radical folk singing background from their days as camp counselors at a radical summer camp called *Camp Wo-Chi-Ca.*

Initially the Weavers sang at People's Artists hootenannies and for radical causes. Pete Seeger was offered an engagement at the fabled Village Vanguard club in New York City, and Max Gordon the owner agreed to let the four musicians play the gig together for the same $200 fee that Seeger had been offered. What was supposed to be a short engagement turned into a six-month gig. During this time they recorded two songs for Hootenanny Records, a new label formed by Irwin Silber and composer-performer Ernie Lieberman.

Pete Seeger and Lee Hays began to write songs together after the formation of People's songs. Generally, Hays wrote most of the lyrics and Seeger composed the melodies. Their song *If I Had a Hammer* was one of the songs they recorded for Hootenanny. It eventually became a hit song several times over in versions recorded by Trini Lopez and Peter, Paul & Mary.

During the Weavers' Vanguard engagement arranger Gordon Jenkins often came down to the club and through his efforts the quartet recorded for Decca Records. Jenkins was noted as a skilled jazz arranger-composer, and the Decca recordings retained Seeger's banjo and Hellerman's guitar work, but also utilized large orchestras and background singers. In their first hit song, *On Top of Old Smoky*, West Coast folksinger-songwriter Terry Gilkyson was added to the ensemble. Seeger lined out the words to the song, which were then repeated by the ensemble. With no offence to Gilkyson, who was an excellent songwriter, it remains a mystery why the group, Gordon Jenkins or Decca Records thought his presence was necessary.

The Weavers sold over four million records for Decca, with their biggest hit being *Goodnight Irene*, released in 1950 with composer credits given to John and Alan Lomax and Huddie Ledbetter. Although some folk fans thought that the Weavers had gone commercial, Lee Hays confessed that he enjoyed singing with large orchestras, and even claimed, "I'd been wanting to sing with a big orchestra all my life."

## Political seclusion and rejection from the left

The Weavers' managers were Harold Leventhal and Pete Kameron. According to Richard Reuss, the group agreed to avoid left-wing associations in order to keep their high commercial profile going for as long as possible. They knew that inevitably the media would inevitably figure out their prior left-wing affiliations. Of the four artists, Seeger was the least comfortable with mass popularity and even would quietly attend left-wing meetings in cities where the group was appearing.

With Pete Seeger's departure from the People's Artists scene to join the Weavers and Alan Lomax's move to England, Irwin Silber had become the cultural commissar of People's Artists. For Seeger and for People's Artists as an organization, the success of the Weavers represented a difficult dilemma. On the one hand the organization was happy to see their colleagues gain access to large nationwide audiences. On the other hand, there was some bitterness about the Weavers removing themselves from the political arena. There were also attacks on the group for performing African-American music without any black artists being in the group itself. People's Artists even organized another quartet to perform at hootenannies, since the Weavers were no longer available. The group included two men and two women. One woman and one man were black as though to taunt the Weavers "white-bread" appearance.

Listening to the original Decca recordings almost seventy years after the fact, an uncomfortable resemblance to Muzak emerges. Some of the background vocals on *Goodnight Irene*, for example, bear more resemblance to the Norman Luboff Choir or the Roger Wagner Chorale than to traditional folk music. Nevertheless, there were some respects in which the Weavers broke new musical ground. Their recording of *Wimoweh* was an inspired attempt to bring South African music and the political struggles of that nation to the attention of Americans, and their arrangement of the mostly instrumental medley *A Trip around the World* is possibly the first example of world music being recorded by American folksingers outside of the relatively tame and refined South African recordings of Marais and Miranda.

## The blacklisting of the Weavers

As the Weavers had anticipated, within a couple of years the group ran into trouble with the various groups seeking out to communists in the arts. The magazines *Counterattack* and *Red Channels* listed a number of People's Artists stalwarts as communists. By 1951 Decca had dropped the Weavers from the label, a number of gigs were cancelled and television work disappeared. An ex-employee of People's Songs named Harvey (Matt) Matusow appeared before the House Un-American Activities Committee and named the Weavers and other folksingers as communists. He later recanted his testimony but the damage was done.

In perspective, the oddest thing about the censorship of the group was that they themselves had done a superb job of removing their politics from their music. They were being investigated for the music that they had performed *before* the Weavers began. Seeger and Hayes were called to testify before the Un-American Activities Committee to testify about their relationship to the Communist Party and asked to name "other communists." Like most of the entertainment business figures who testified, Lee Hays took the Fifth Amendment, refusing to testify because he might incriminate himself. Seeger took the First Amendment, which questioned the right of the committee to inquire into his political beliefs. Seeger then endured a ten-year legal odyssey. The government backed down in 1962 on a technicality. Other folk artists who refused to cooperate included singer-actor Tony Kraber, Earl Robinson, and Irwin Silber.

When artists were blacklisted, they became pariahs in the entertainment industry. They couldn't get record deals, TV appearances, movie contracts, or any decent gigs. Not everyone defied the red-baiters. Burl Ives not only testified before the McCarran Committee of the US Senate, but he named people whom he accused of being communists. Irwin Silber attacked Ives, Josh White, and Tom Glazer as traitors to the cause, because of either their denunciations of the communist influence in folk music, or their congressional testimony.

A little-known aspect of the left was blacklisting done by the left itself. Seeger, the other Weavers, and the members of People's Artists were able to get some work through the remnants of the radical movement, especially in New York City. Radical groups would no longer hire Brand, Glazer, Ives, or White. Because Ives had named names he was able to preserve his career, although more in the field of film than music. Later he reemerged as a nonpolitical country singer. Brand has described himself as being excluded from work by both the left and right wings. The same strictures applied to Glazer and White, although Glazer reinvented himself as a children's artist and author, and Josh White managed to make inroads on the burgeoning college concert scene.

The Weavers reunited in 1955 for a sold-out performance at Carnegie Hall, promoted by Harold Leventhal, their original co-manager. They then made some successful recordings for Vanguard Records without the orchestral and choral backing that had been employed at Decca Records. In 1958 Pete Seeger left the group, and he was replaced by Erik Darling who left in 1961. The last two replacements for Pete Seeger were Frank Hamilton, who in turn was replaced by Bernie Krause in 1963. The group permanently disbanded in 1964. A final reunion album was made in 1980, and was the center of a film called *Wasn't That a Time?*

During the mid-1990s I did a series of performances at senior centers and residential facilities in northeastern Colorado and south-central Kansas. None of these facilities were located at or near a large city. I usually closed the show with the song *Goodnight Irene*. I don't think I ever did a performance where the seniors didn't sing along. This indicates how pervasive the Weavers' songs were in middle-America where performances of American folksongs were a relatively rare event. They had all learned the song from the Weavers' recordings of the 1950s.

## Folk-pop

The Weavers weren't the only thing happening in folk music in the 1950s. In 1948 Dick and Beth Best compiled a songbook for the Intercollegiate Outing Club. The book went through fourteen editions through 1963, and included 300 songs sung by the various college clubs that were members of the association. The emphasis was on songs suitable for group singing. In a sense this book anticipated the movement that we now call song circles or sing arounds, when a group of amateur folk musicians get together to sing and play.

I mentioned Terry Gilkyson earlier as the man who sang along on the Weavers recording of *On Top of Old Smoky*. In 1950 he wrote a song called *The*

*Cry of the Wild Goose* that became a pop hit for Frankie Laine. A year later Laine followed up by recording Gilkyson's *The Girl in the Wood*. The Wild Goose song portrayed restlessness while *The Girl in the Wood* was a portrait of a romance that scarred the young protagonist forever. Although Laine's arrangements were pop-orchestral, the melodies of the songs and the subject matter reflected Gilkyson's knowledge of American folk music.

Irving Gordon was a New York songwriter who wrote many pop hits, but in 1951 he composed three folk-tinged songs that became big pop hits. *Allentown Jail* was originally recorded by Jo Stafford, and re-recorded during the folk revival of the 1960s by the British folk-pop group *the Springfields,* and the Australian folk-pop group *The Seekers.* The song is a woman's lament for her lover, who stole a ring to give to her and ended up in the Allentown jail. *Mr. and Mrs. Sippie* was another Patti Page hit, written by Gordon. The song depicts a riverboat gambler who has spent his entire life on the Mississippi River. Gordon's song *Two Brothers* was a big success for Kay Starr, and became a staple of later folk revival folk-pop singers. It is the classic Civil War story of a mother's two children, one fighting for the Union cause and the other for the Confederacy. The focus of the song is on the mother of the two boys, who is waiting "by the railroad track" for the remains of her two dead sons. All of Gordon's songs are very dramatic, sort of Broadway realizations of folksong subjects and characters. It would be interesting to know how much these songs were influenced by the popularity of the Weavers. Of all the "Tin Pan Alley" songwriters, Gordon seems to have been the best at adding a folk flavor to his work.

Another 1951 pop-folk hit was the song *Shrimp Boats*, written by Paul Mason Howard and Paul Weston, and recorded by Jo Stafford. Collaborating with lyricist Harry Farmer, Howard also wrote the Frankie Laine hit *Gandy Dancer's Ball*. Shrimp Boats was a tale of Louisiana fishermen, while the Gandy Dancer song is about a celebration by railroad workers. Jo Stafford recorded an entire album of traditional folksongs in 1948. When it was re-released on LP in 1950, she added two songs. Although Stafford's reputation was made as a pop and jazz singer, her performance of folk songs is low-key, and displays her superb intonation, phrasing, and pitch.

Another other example of folk-tinged pop is several songs performed by Guy Mitchell. *The Roving Kind* was Mitchell's adaptation of an old folksong credited to two writers named Jesse Cavanaugh and Arnold Stanton. This is actually a traditional song. These names appear on songbooks published by this particular publisher, TRO (the Richmond Organization). The names appear to be pseudonyms for staff writers at TRO. *My Truly, Truly Fair* is a folk-tinged ballad about the singer's girlfriend, written by Broadway tunesmith Bob Merrill. Merrill followed this up with another hit for Mitchell, a song written in ¾ (waltz) time called *Pittsburgh, Pennsylvania*. The song is a pitiful story about a suitor who is being overlooked for a richer competitor. Consequently, the singer must go to a pawnshop and try to scrounge up a few dollars.

Two other songs from 1952 are Jo Stafford's version of *A Round the Corner*, and Doris Day's recording of *A Guy Is a Guy*. These songs come from more specific folk music sources. Stafford's song was written by South African folksinger Josef Marais, and Doris Day's song was written by pop-folk artist Oscar Brand. The Doris Day tune is based on an old English drinking song, turned into an innocent love story. The Josef Marais song has a similar subject.

With the exceptions of Terry Gilkyson and Oscar Brand, the other songwriters mentioned above did not pursue their interest in folksongs. It seems fair to conclude that when the musical marketplace turned in other directions so did the interests of these writers. Later Gilkyson songs or co-authored songs were recorded by the Kingston Trio, the Brothers Four, and his own group, the Easy Riders.

## Early Weavers-influenced groups

There were two folk-pop groups on the West Coast that appeared after the blacklisting of the Weavers. The Easy Riders was a trio that included Rich Dehr, Frank Miller, and Terry Gilkyson. Dehr and Miller had been members of the West Coast wing of People's Songs, and Gilkyson had appeared on two songs recorded by the Weavers. The trio started writing pop songs together, and their own first album appeared on Columbia Records in 1957. The group's music included quite a few calypso or calypso-influenced songs, and their version of *Marianne* became a big hit. A number of the trio's songs were folksongs dressed up with new titles, and in some cases new lyrics. Two other albums followed on the Kapp label, but were not notably successful. A fourth album consisted entirely of western songs composed by Hollywood writers Paul Webster and Dmitri Tiomkin. By the time of the fourth album Frank Miller had left the group. Soon the group disbanded and Gilkyson continued his career as a songwriter. His daughter Eliza is currently a prominent singer-songwriter.

The other pop-folk group of the 1950s was *The Gateway Singers*. The group was founded in 1952 in Berkeley, California. The original group included Jim Wood, Lou Gottlieb, Jerry Walter, and Barbara Dane. According to Lou Gottlieb, who later founded the Limeliters, the Communist Party forced the group to get rid of Barbara Dane, and replace her with black singer Elmerlee Thomas. Jim Wood left the group, and was replaced by Travis Edmonson, who later teamed with Bud Dashiell to form the duo Bud & Travis. The Gateways made an album for Decca in 1957, and the song *Puttin' On the Style* became both a successful single and was used in a commercial. The group recorded other albums for Warner Brothers Records and MGM, but after Edmonson and Gottlieb left they disbanded in 1961.

It is easy to hear the influence of the Easy Riders and the Gateway Singers in the early works of the Kingston Trio. All of them performed with energy and enthusiasm, and frequently used a sort of bouncy, happy rhythm in their songs. Gottlieb even did some arranging for the Kingston Trio.

## Odetta

Odetta Holmes (Gordon) was an artist whose music had little in common with the pop-folk groups described above. Although she studied opera as a child, and graduated from college with a music degree, she also sang in theatrical productions. In 1954 she teamed up with banjoist Larry Mohr and recorded a live album at the Tin Angel night club in San Francisco. She moved to New York, and recorded several albums for Tradition Records, starting in 1956.

Odetta had a powerful voice and played a large-bodied guitar. With her emotional performances of blues, spirituals, and contemporary songs, she made a big impact on the folk scene where there were few solo black performers. Unlike the pop-folk artists mentioned above, Odetta was to perform into the twenty-first century, and was an important influence on a variety of singers. She was also active in the Civil Rights movement.

## Harry Belafonte

As far as mass popularity goes, Harry Belafonte was as a bridge between the Weavers and the Kingston Trio. Belafonte began his career as an actor and turned to jazz singing in 1949. Some racist encounters with a Miami audience in 1950 turned him off to jazz singing as a career. In 1951 he debuted as a folksinger at the Village Vanguard. He was hired by Max Gordon, the same person who had hired the Weavers for their first major performance.

Belafonte was attractive and sophisticated, and by 1954 he had a recording contract with RCA Victor Records. His 1956 recording of *Day O-The Banana Boat Song* became a major hit. Belafonte excelled at singing calypso songs and soft ballads, and he developed a huge audience, comparable to the one the Weavers had enjoyed. He also became involved in a personal management company, and he acted as a mentor to South African singer Miriam Makeba. Belafonte was very politically engaged, and although he was initially blacklisted, he was able to persuade Ed Sullivan, the TV host, that although he had appeared at many left-wing rallies, he was not a communist. He added that he would not answer in a public setting whether or not he was a communist. Apparently, Sullivan believed him, and booked him on his influential TV variety show. Belafonte continued to record through 1997. At the present time he no longer performs or records, but has recently written an autobiography.

## The Kingston Trio and the folk music revival explodes

Although the blacklisting of the Weavers was a blow to the popularization of folk music, Belafonte, Odetta, and the Gateway Singers and The Easy Riders provided a transition to the "next big thing."

The Kingston Trio was a group of three college students in the San Francisco Bay area who got together to play and sing music. The group performed in the Bay area and were signed by a personal manager named Frank Werber. They cut a demonstration record which led to a Capitol Records recording contract. Their first single, *Scarlet Ribbons*, didn't have much impact, but when the trio's first album came out in 1958, a disc jockey in San Francisco picked up their version of the traditional folk song *Tom Dooley*. Using a tactic occasionally employed by ambitious disc jockeys of that time, he played the song repeatedly, essentially forcing Capitol to release the song as a single. The song described a fatal romance, and the group added an odd spoken introduction that introduced the song. It became an enormous hit, and it is still obligatory for the current version of the trio to perform it at its concerts some seventy years later.

Dave Guard left the trio after four years and was replaced by singer-songwriter John Stewart. Six years later Stewart exited the group and for years various people have passed through the group. Bob Shane continued to perform with the group for years, and Nick Reynolds periodically returned or exited. In 2017 the name was sold by Bob Shane and his wife Barbara Childress to a group that included Nick Reynolds's son Josh. The three (then) members of the group—Richard Daugherty, George Grove, and Bill Zorn—continued to perform, and the new group, which included Josh Reynolds, his cousin Gerald (Mike) Marvin, and their friend Tom Gorelangton filed suit to prohibit these performances. The court ruled against the new group, but then Bob Shane reportedly reached an agreement with some investors to allow Reynolds and the others to have the exclusive use of the name. The irony of all this is that George Grove was a member of the group from 1976 to 2017, longer than any other member of the trio.

It would be difficult to exaggerate the importance of the Kingston Trio in sparking the folk music revival of the 1960s. In addition to the fact that they sold millions of records and performed before millions of people, it seemed as though every college campus in the United States boasted at least one group that consisted basically of Kingston Trio imitators. George Gruhn, proprietor of Gruhn Guitars in Nashville, once commented to me that in effect the entire acoustic music business was built because of the influence of the Kingston Trio. As he put it, young people would go to see the group and their response was "I could learn how to do that." They would then buy banjos or guitars and start to round up friends to sing with them.

## More folk-pop groups

The Kingston Trio's success led to the formation of a number of pop-folk groups who essentially imitated their style and repertoire. Each of them developed some sort of approach designed to distinguish them from the "originators." The Brothers Four were a group of four fraternity brothers at the University of Washington. They signed with Columbia Records and, like the Trio, were able to come up with some hit singles. *Greenfields* was written by the members of the Easy Riders, and it was released in 1959. A year later the group scored another success with the Paul Francis Webster–Dmitri Tiomkin movie opus *The Green Leaves of Summer*. The Brothers Four had a pleasant barber shop quartet vocal sound, and in various incarnations they have continued to tour.

The Limeliters were a completely different story. Each of them was a professional musician, not a college student. When Lou Gottlieb left the Gateway Singers, he joined forces with tenor-lead vocalist Glenn Yarbrough and Alex Hassilev, a classical guitarist who performed in various languages and quickly took up the banjo. Gottlieb had turned himself into a stand-up comic, and between his musical arrangements and Yarbrough's vocal skills their show was pitched to a more sophisticated audience than any of the other pop-folk groups.

Other hit pop-folk groups emerged within the next couple of years, including the Highwaymen, the New Christy Minstrels, and the Serendipity Singers. The Highwaymen had also met at college, in their case Wesleyan College in Connecticut. They had two major hit records with the songs *Michael Row the Boat Ashore* and Lead Belly's *Cotton Fields*. The Highwaymen occasionally sang in French and Spanish, and were in that regard the most versatile of the pop-folk groups.

Dickie and Tommy Smothers were two comedic musicians who formed a duo and gently satirized pop-folk music. They later had a short-running but successful TV show. The Rooftop Singers were formed by Erik Darling, a founding member of the original Tarriers and Pete Seeger's replacement in the Weavers. The group had a monster hit record with Gus Cannon and Hosea Woods' old jug band song *Walk Right In*. The song introduced the acoustic twelve string guitar into American pop music, and featured the expert guitar work of Darling and his friend Bill Svanoe. This sound was much closer to a sound rooted in the blues and African-American music in general than anything that other folk-pop bands were attempting.

The New Christy Minstrels included a number of musicians who went on to pursue careers in other musical contexts. Barry McGuire became a solo artist, Dolan Ellis has been Arizona's official ballad singer for some years, Larry Ramos joined the Association, and Kenny Rogers became a huge country-pop star. Like the Christy Minstrels, the Serendipity Singers included nine people, seven of whom met while they were students at the University of Colorado. They scored a major hit with the song *Don't Let the Rain Come Down*. Various members of the group performed into the 1990s.

There was a sort of second line of successful pop groups who worked regularly but never had any hit records. Among the best known of these were Bud and Travis, the Chad Mitchell Trio, the Journeymen, the later versions of the Tarriers, and the Modern Folk Quartet. Other slightly lesser-known bands included the Cumberland Three with a young John Stewart, the Halifax Three, and the Travelers Three. John Stewart later replaced Dave Guard in the Kingston Trio, and Dennis Doherty sang with the Halifax group. Doherty later was one of the lead singers in the folk-rock group *The Mamas and Papas*.

Bud and Travis were probably the first Anglo-pop group to perform a repertoire that included a substantial number of Mexican songs sung in Spanish. The Chad Mitchell group featured clever topical–political songs, including some written by Tom Paxton. Right around the end of the folk boom in 1965 future country-folk superstar John Denver replaced Chad Mitchell in the Mitchell Trio. The Journeymen featured lead singer Scott McKenzie. He and Glenn Yarbrough were generally considered to be the best pure vocalists in the pop-folk revival. John Phillips soldiered on with a new cast of Journeymen in autumn, 1964, which included his wife, Michelle, ex-Tarrier Marshall Brickman, and a few months later he added Denny Doherty. This group evolved in the folk-rock stars, the Mamas and the Papas. Scott McKenzie found new life as a soloist with his classic recording of John Phillips' song *San Francisco (Be Sure to Wear Flowers in Your Hair)*.

There were other pop-folk groups that got to record and tour but never achieved a high degree of success. For some reason, a number of them were modeled after the Christies, with seven to ten members. Among this line-up was the Christy Minstrels "farm team" group, the Back Porch Majority. Les Baxter's balladeers with David Crosby, America's Children, and the Café Au-Go-Go Singers. The latter included Stephen Stills and Richie Furay. Stills was a founder of the Buffalo Springfield and later a charter member of Crosby, Stills, Nash (and sometimes, Young). Furay was a founder of the band Poco, and later became a pastor of a church and a Christian artist.

## Buying in and selling out

In addition to the transitory fan base that some of the pop-folk groups developed, there were another set of people who became enamored with traditional music. Quite a few of these people were influenced by Pete Seeger's solo performances. Whenever he did solo concerts, Seeger tried to influence the audience to check out traditional artists. He named banjo players, guitar players, and traditional singers and told his audience that if they really liked folk music they should investigate the roots of the music. Some of these young fans became fanatic about traditional music, even considering Seeger himself as being a sort of pop-folk entertainer rather than a serious practitioner of traditional music. As these young people matured, some of them became professional musicians. In their eyes, almost every traditional music recording was a gem, the real thing.

The best known of these musicians were a group called the New Lost City Ramblers. Attending one of their concerts revealed kind of a wild cross between attending an in-group party and sitting at a graduate school folklore lecture. There was an incessant amount of tuning of instruments, partly because the three artists played a raft of instruments. These musicians saw themselves as musical missionaries rather than pop entertainers. As such they also came at the music with something of a perfectionist attitude. Every time the musicians switched off between their guitars, banjos, fiddles, or mandolins, a new volley of tuning erupted. To the general public, Rambler performances were virtually incoherent and dull, but their fans loved the inside jokes and puns, the continual references to obscure records and artists, and even the way the tuning brought out humorous interplay between the musicians.

The three founding members of the group were John Cohen, Tom Paley, and Mike Seeger. Cohen and Paley met at Yale University and Mike Seeger was the half-brother of Pete Seeger. Seeger and Cohen were intent on reproducing the sounds of traditional musicians, although Paley had a somewhat freer approach and a more original style.

The pop-folk musicians mostly wore button-down shirts with candy-colored stripes, or dressed in matching suits. They often literally ran onto the stage and utilized quite a bit of scripted humor in their shows. Often this humor was written by outside comedy writers on commission. The Ramblers could indeed be funny, but a premium was placed on spontaneous planning of shows and maintaining an "honest" approach to the music. It was never entirely clear exactly what this meant, but it included such things as always mentioning the original sources of any song being performed, not using "modern" chords but sticking to the sort of chord progressions that traditional country or blues musicians played. There was generally a non-dramatic, poker-faced dryness in the performance styles of groups like the Ramblers.

Fans of the Ramblers and aspiring tradition-following musicians did not view themselves as beatniks, but they shared the beatniks' contempt for American mass culture and money-making pursuits. In New York most of the revivalists were living either in cheap apartments in the Village, or in various low-rent sections of Manhattan. The male urban-folk uniform was jeans and a flannel shirt, and women wore baggy sweaters or plaids and jeans. Women grew their hair long and didn't wear makeup.

The New Lost City Ramblers were highly influential with the niche group of urban, college-educated traditionalists. Rambler-influenced bands like the Highwoods String Band, the Fuzzy Mountain String Band, the Hollow Rock String Band, and the Red Clay Ramblers certainly were listening to them.

## The folk Nazis

In 1991, I attended a conference on the folk revival in Bloomington, Indiana. All of the guests had been involved in the 1960s folk revival in one capacity or another. Among the guests and speakers were Oscar Brand, John Cohen, Len Chandler, Mimi Farina, Bob Gibson, Lou Gottlieb, Irwin Silber, and folklorist Neil Rosenberg.

The keynote speaker was John Cohen, and he described the experience of the Ramblers when they played on the 1963 TV show *Hootenanny*. As Cohen told the story, during a rehearsal, in the middle of their third song, Bob Gibson entered the room and Lou Gottlieb got up to hug Bob and to talk to him. Apparently, John regarded this as one of the most insulting experiences he had ever had in the music business. Describing it thirty years later his face flushed beet-red with anger.

When Lou got up to speak, he explained that it was because of *his* recommendation that the Ramblers, and other tradition-based acts like Lester Flatt and Earl Scruggs, and Maybelle Carter of the Carter Family were chosen to appear on the show. Lou also pointed out that he doubted that John Cohen had ever deigned to listen to a Limeliter album. Lou's musical taste was much more eclectic, spanning everything from folk music to jazz and classical music. Since John had no response to Lou's comments, I tend to think they were probably accurate. The interested reader can see these comments printed in Ronald Cohen's book *Wasn't That a Time: First Hand Accounts of the Folk Music Revival*.

For me, this exchange encapsulated the culture clashes that arose between the "purist" revivalists and the pop-folk singers. The purists dressed in jeans or what they thought were the sort of clothes that old-time country musicians might have worn in the 1920s, while the pop-folk people wore "hip" contemporary styles. The pop-folk musicians and the more free-wheeling of the urban revivalists referred to the purists as the "folk Nazis." The latter group seemed to feel that they had a monopoly on truth and authenticity. In Cohen's keynote speech at the Indiana conference, he refers to his promotion of traditional music as a "crusade" and there certainly was an almost religious feeling to the purists' war against the pop stars.

There were certain aspects of the revival that purists did not like to acknowledge. Most of the people in the urban folk revival were "Pete Seeger's children." They bought banjos in pawnshops, learned traditional songs, and tried to follow Pete's directions to find the people and the artists who grew up with the music. But many of the people who later became entranced with traditional music heard their first banjo picking from Dave Guard and their first folk songs from the Kingston Trio. I am thinking here of someone like Michael Cooney, who became one of the most dyed-in-the-wool traditionalists but who as a teenager was inspired by pop-folk artists like Bud and Travis.

Then too there is that nagging little matter of Pete Seeger himself being, in a sense, the first folkie to "sell out." The Weavers' Decca Recordings, as I have already pointed out, were a mixture of pop and folk music. It is true that *Sing Out!* occasionally chided Seeger and the Weavers for watering down their music, but the criticism that Seeger got was mild compared to the rants against pop-folk groups like the Kingston Trio that John Cohen and Ron Radosh (later a conservative Cold-War historian) wrote for that magazine. Radosh railed against their musical arrangements, blasted them for telling corny jokes, and even accused them of pandering to racist stereotypes in some of their spoken commentaries. The truth is that because so many of the people in the revival were inspired by Seeger they were reluctant to criticize his musical compromises.

Then there is the ugly little matter of money. When the folk revivalists were learning about the music, no one dreamed that it was possible to make a good living as a professional musician. They didn't imagine that college concerts would pay thousands of dollars in 1963, and didn't expect to have careers as studio musicians or songwriters. Revivalists didn't know that songwriting royalties for a big hit song could sustain a person's musical career for a lifetime.

Most of the real purists did not attempt to sustain lifetime careers as professional musicians. Some of them taught college enabling them to tour on weekends and during the summer. For the pop-folk musician, music was a career that he or she chose. Some of these careers lasted for a lifetime and others provided a temporary living. Popular music has requirements that are difficult for the part-time purist practitioner to grasp. Full-time musician-entertainers are expected to be funny and energetic. If they perform music that is thoughtful or complex they do so at the risk of not developing an audience or losing what audience they do have. Beyond this, the professional musician tends to accept that unless she is extremely successful, when work comes in you take it. The full-timer might find himself playing in bars, in noisy venues, and in places where the audience resents hearing anything that they haven't heard before.

## Discoveries and re-discoveries

As I have described the situation above, there were two polarized groups that were active during the period 1958–64. On the one hand we have the pop-folk groups, especially the Kingston Trio. In the opposite corner, were the traditionalists, epitomized by the New Lost City Ramblers.

There was more than one way that traditional fans gained access to the music. In 1952 Folkways Records issued Harry Smith's six-volume *Anthology of American Folk Music*. This was a six-LP set that contained music recorded in the 1920s and 1930s. Moe Asch, the owner of Folkways, took kind of a Wild West attitude towards copyright and royalties. He figured, with some justification, that the major labels would never reissue recordings by blues, country-folk, Cajun, and string band artists from the 1920s and 1930s. Meanwhile Harry Smith, an avant-garde film maker, owned a huge collection of such records, and proposed to Asch that Folkways issue them. The package included credits for all the artists and Smith summarized the lyrics to the songs without actually printing them. Possibly Asch figured that it was bold enough to ignore the rights of record companies, but that printing the lyrics to the songs would also be a slap in the face to the music publishers who owned the rights to the songs.

Virtually every 1960s musician who was a fan of traditional music owned the set, or at least several of the albums. It is difficult to overestimate the impact of the Anthology. However, Alan Lomax's 1947 reissue albums included some of the same artists that Smith chose. Nevertheless, the Lomax albums simply didn't have the impact that the Smith Anthology produced. It is difficult to judge whether this was because Lomax was in effect premature with his projects, or that Smith's strange annotations and drawings appealed more to the sort of pre-beatnik sensibility of many folk fans and musicians.

Another phenomenon emerged, partly as a result of the efforts of the Ramblers to resurrect the careers of musicians of the 1930s who were still alive during the revival. Mike Seeger and John Cohen, along with a group of people in New York

City organized the *Friends of Old Time Music*. This group brought a number of these rediscovered musicians to New York and also influenced their inclusion in the Newport Folk Festival. Newport began in 1959 and over the next few years moved from being a for-profit concert venue to a non-profit organization that tried to balance the interests of pop-folk and tradition-oriented musicians. These rediscovered musicians included Clarence Ashley and Dock Boggs, and some previously unknown artists like Roscoe Holcomb and especially, Doc Watson.

At the same time, a dedicated group of blues fans including Dick Spottswood, John Fahey, Ed Denson, and Tom Hoskins scoured the south in a quest to find forgotten blues singers from the 1920s and 1930s. Their rediscoveries included Mississippi John Hurt, Skip James, Son House, and Bukka White. Meanwhile folklorist Harry Oster found the previously unknown Robert Pete Williams in the Angola, Louisiana prison, and Arhoolie Records owner Chris Strachwitz found songster Mance Lipscomb in Texas.

All of these artists resumed or, in Hurt's case, initiated performing careers in coffeehouses and concert venues. Suddenly it was possible to actually see artists that Pete Seeger or the New Lost City Ramblers referred to in their own performances. Witnessing a performance by these musicians made the contrast between traditionalist and folk-pop artists even more obvious. Musicians like John Hurt or Doc Watson communicated absolute sincerity in their singing and playing, and they didn't look anything like the pop-folk artists. Nor did they use prepared patter or run out on stage.

## In the middle: "Acceptable pop-folk artists"

A whole group of artists walked a tightrope between traditional folk music and pop-folk. Among these artists were Joan Baez, Judy Collins, Ian and Sylvia, Peter, Paul & Mary, and Simon and Garfunkel. It's a bit difficult to evaluate exactly how these artists managed to satisfy a reasonably large segment of both of these audiences.

Mary Travers had been a student at a private elementary school called *The Little Red Schoolhouse*. Pete Seeger performed there on a regular basis through the worst of the blacklist period. She was also a member of a chorale group called *The Song Swappers* who recorded with Pete Seeger. Peter Yarrow was an urban folksinger who had hooked up with shrewd personal manager Albert Grossman. Al had come up with the idea of creating a kind of more contemporary "hipper" version of the Kingston Trio. He experimented with various combinations of singers, including Bob Gibson, Carolyn Hester, and Dave Van Ronk. Grossman and Yarrow recruited Mary Travers, and she in turn suggested adding Paul (Noel) Stookey. He had been doing solo performances mixed with stand-up comedy in various village coffeehouses. Noel adopted the stage name Paul because Peter, Paul, and Mary rolled off the tongue more gracefully than Peter, Noel, and Mary would have. The act featured a deliberate contrast in appearance between the two men dressing in ultracool mode and Mary playing the role of the "wild chick," with long blond hair that spilled all over the microphone and around her face.

If the Kingston Trio was designed for the middle-American college student, PP&M had an element of bohemianism in their appearance and presentation designed to appeal to a slightly more sophisticated audience. Peter's role was to play the somewhat intellectual, serious folksinger. Paul was the suave hip humorist with his amusing car imitation sounds and one-liners. Mary's role was to appeal to the lustful inclinations of male college students.

Arranger Milt Okun (1923–2016) was brought on board to help the trio to develop a vocal sound. In his book, *Along the Cherry Lane*, Milt claims that he tried to bow out of the job, because he had to teach vocal parts to the three of them by ear, rather than writing them out in sheet music form. He also stated that no one else was willing to take the job!

The group made their debut in 1961 and their first album, released in 1962, sold over two million copies. Their first single record release was a two-sided hit, *Lemon Tree*, a sophisticated folk tune by folk-art singer Will Holt, and Seeger and Hays' chestnut *If I Had a Hammer*.

There are a number of factors that can be figured in to explain why PP&M essentially transcended the pop versus traditionalists battles. For one thing their shows had a more intellectual ring than the work of the prior folk-pop groups. By featuring *If I Had a Hammer* in their first recording, they were making a subtle over identification with the legacy of Pete Seeger's political music. For those "in the know," Mary was essentially a protégé of Pete, and as such carried his implicit endorsement. They were also the first folk group since the Weavers and the Gateway Singers to feature a woman in the group. The Rooftop Singers, who came along a year later, also featured a woman in the group. Lastly PP&M were the only group that had a string of hit singles.

After their initial double-sided hit, further hits included John Denver's *Leaving on a Jet Plane*, Peter's own *Puff the Magic Dragon*, and then two songs by a (then) obscure songwriter named Bob Dylan. Those songs were *Blowing in the Wind* and *Don't Think Twice. Puff* established the group's hip credentials, when a controversy erupted whether the song actually was about smoking pot. By introducing Dylan's songs, the group identified itself as being at the cutting edge of the burgeoning singer-songwriter movement, and *Blowing in the Wind* also placed the group in support of the Civil Rights movement. Purists might not have liked the slick musical arrangements employed by the group, but they were largely in support of their political sentiments.

Not coincidentally the group's manager, Al Grossman, also managed Bob Dylan. He was simultaneously reinforcing PP&M's fame while introducing his "new kid" to the American public, all the way collecting commissions from both of them.

PP&M managed to survive the onslaught of rock 'n' roll with their good-humored satire *I Dig Rock and Roll Music*. The song was written by ex-disc jockey Dave Dixon, record producer Jim Mason, and Paul Stookey, of PP&M. The recording was released in 1967 some two to three years after most of the pop-folk groups' popularity was in severe decline. Six of the band's singles made the Top Ten mark on the pop charts, and the trio released eight albums that went gold (sales of 500,000 or more) before 1970. The trio continued to play concerts for years and were the only pop-folk group that included all of the original members. Mary died in 2009, but Peter and Paul still do some shows together and remain active as solo artists.

## Simon and Garfunkel

Paul Simon and Art Garfunkel were childhood friends who had a hit pop record in 1957 when they were each sixteen years old under the name "Tom and Jerry." They made several unsuccessful attempts to record again, but a 1963 contract with Columbia Records resulted in the album *Wednesday Morning, 3 A.M.* The record was initially a failure, and Simon went to England to play some solo gigs. Meanwhile a disc jockey in Miami became enamored of *The Sounds of Silence*, one of the songs on the album. He pestered Columbia to release the song as a single, and producer Tom Wilson added electric guitar, bass, and drums to the existing track without consulting the artists. As the story goes, Simon had no idea of what was going on, but he happened to leaf through a copy of *Billboard Magazine* in England, and found the record on the pop charts. *The Sounds of Silence* is a song about angst and loneliness, but unlikely as it may seem, it became the vehicle for the duo to reunite, tour, and pursue a very successful career. Their career was marked by break-ups, patch-ups, further break-ups, and occasional reunions.

Simon wrote all of the group's songs, with the exception of their adaptation of the English folksong *Scarborough Fair*. Despite the demise of folk-pop as an idiom, the duo's 1970 release, *Bridge over Troubled Water* was a massive success. Part of the group's continued popularity may have been that since Simon was the only instrumentalist in the group, they really had no obligation to provide a specific repetitious sound, as say the Kingston Trio did. The duo's records featured a snapshot of New York's best studio musicians, and their engineer and sometimes co-producer Roy Halee did a great job on capturing their sound on records. By 1971 Garfunkel was jointly pursuing acting and singing roles, and Simon became disenchanted with having to wait months while Garfunkel was on location shooting films.

At this writing, Simon is on a farewell performing career. His solo career is generally been successful, notably his 1986 album *Graceland,* which featured a number of South African musicians. Sometimes Simon's artistic ambitions have exceeded his artistic grasp and his movie, *One Trick Pony*, was a minor disaster. Even more unfortunate was his attempt at a Broadway musical. His show, *The Capeman,* went through three directors but closed after sixty-eight performances. Garfunkel pursued his film career in the 1970s, but although he had a hit with the Jim Webb Song *For All We Know* in 1973, his recording career has not been especially successful.

## Paul Simon

Paul Simon was one of the first of the breed that we now refer to as singer-songwriters, performers who write their own songs. Because he was a student of English literature and poetry, Simon's songs abound in literary symbols and references to artistic and popular culture figures, including everyone from Emily Dickinson and Robert Frost to Joe DiMaggio and Elvis. It puzzles me why Simon doesn't seem to be acknowledged by the folk establishment. He plays acoustic guitar quite well, and as a songwriter he is one of the few that is even roughly comparable to Bob Dylan in terms of the quality and length of his overall song production. Part of the problem may be that Simon doesn't seem to have retained many folky associations. He tours with New York studio musicians and for the most part he avoids the sort of interactions that Dylan has maintained with important figures in the folk mafia. It would be difficult to imagine Simon appearing at a Woody Guthrie tribute concert, or headlining a folk festival. I do not feel that it is logical or fair to ignore Simon's role as in important figure in the folk revival.

Ian and Sylvia achieved an equal measure of popularity among both folk-pop fans and traditional music adherents. Since they are Canadian artists, I will return to them in the next chapter which covers the folk revival in Canada.

## My life in the world of pop-folk

In 1960 I met a talented songwriter-arranger named John Phillips through my old friend Izzy Young. Izzy was the proprietor of the Folklore Center in New York's Greenwich Village. John had wandered into the store looking for someone to play banjo and guitar on a recording by his pop group *The Smoothies*. The group had been singing jazz-flavored pop music in the vein of a sort of pop Four Freshmen.

I played on their Decca recording sessions and John and I started to hang out together. At the time I was living with Karen Dalton, a talented singer originally from Enid, Oklahoma. John told me that he and the Smoothies lead singer Scott McKenzie wanted to quit the Smoothies and start a new pop-folk group. He asked if I would be interested in joining them. I was about to leave a truly grim folk-pop-rock group called *The Citizens* who were finishing up an album for Laurie Records, destined upon release for the cut-rate record bins.

I told John that that sounded good, and suggested that we include Karen in group. I had a five-room railroad flat apartment in a low-rent district below Columbia University, and we held rehearsals there. We did two rehearsals, which mostly consisted of Karen and John arguing about vocal parts, which John seemed to be able to invent with the ease of someone brushing their teeth.

At any rate, Karen did not work out, and the three of us rehearsed for six days a week, ten hours a day, until we had an album's worth of material. The songs were a blend of traditional songs that I brought in, two songs that John wrote and one of my songs. In a matter of months, we acquired a manager, a booking agency, and after turning down an offer from MGM Records, we signed a deal with Capitol Records.

The Journeymen did a three and a half year stint as a touring act playing college concerts, a few nightclubs, TV shows, and recording a series of Schlitz

Beer commercials. Sometime during our third year, Scott and I decided that we'd had enough.

## Breaking up isn't that hard to do

People often wonder why seemingly successful groups break up. Anyone who had been a member of a touring musical group knows that constant touring tends to make minor personality disputes into major annoyances. In our band John and Scott were very close friends, almost like brothers. After two and a half years on the road, the two of them got so irritated with one another that that they literally did not speak. They communicated through me (e.g.) "Dick, would you tell Scott to tie his shoes." Fifty years later it seems totally ridiculous, but we often rented two different cars so that they would not have to ride together.

Not all groups dissipate exactly this way, but I remember reading that the Budapest String Quartet, who played together for many years, would never sit together on an airplane or in a restaurant. Maybe that's why they were able to stay together! About the time we broke up, the Tarriers and the Highwaymen had also called it a day, although the Highwaymen re-formed with some different personnel. The Beatles were starting to shake up the world of popular music, the Byrds were pursuing folk-rock and a young man named Bob Dylan was about to make his own revolutionary forays into the American music scene.

## Solo pop-folk artists

Another group of artists seemed to bridge the gap between folk and pop music fans. Joan Baez, Judy Collins, the late Bob Gibson, and Buffy Ste. Marie all began their careers in the period 1955–60. With the exception of Gibson, these careers continue to the present day.

## Bob Gibson

Bob Gibson began performing in 1953. Gibson's reputation spread through his 1955 recordings for Riverside Records, and an eleven-month engagement at the Gate of Horn nightclub in Chicago. In 1959 Gibson brought Joan Baez, unannounced to the Newport Folk festival. When she essentially stole the show from him, it basically provided her with an introduction to a mass audience.

Initially Gibson was something of a Pete Seeger banjo imitator but as he developed his own musical style, he took up twelve-string guitar, and formed a duo with Chicago actor Bob Camp. The duo performed to enthusiastic audiences at New York's Village Gate in 1958. Gibson also became friendly with songwriter-cartoonist Shel Silverstein, and they wrote dozens of songs together over a thirty-five-year period. Gibson was always a good musical self-promoter, and he performed in many venues that did not normally feature folk music. He also formed a booking agency and in general was active in the business end of folk music.

Unfortunately, Gibson's casual drug use escalated to a heroin habit and led to several jail terms in Canada. He was never able to really reestablish his career, although he influenced many revival figures, including Peter Yarrow and Phil Ochs. Part of his influence was his ability to rearrange traditional songs with more modern harmonies. Late in his career he experimented with playwriting and became a children's music artist. In 1994 Gibson was diagnosed with progressive supranuclear palsy which effectively ended his career. He invited his friends to a farewell music hootenanny on September 20, 1996 where he was in the audience as dozens of well-wishers performed for him. He died a week later.

## Joan Baez

Joan Baez is the daughter of an astrophysicist. She briefly attended Boston University, but became entranced with the Boston coffeehouse scene. In her autobiography, *And a Voice to Sing With*, she offers many details about her fundamental sense of loneliness and her involvement with social and political issues. Of all the revivalists she has contributed the most time and money to political causes, particularly the antiwar movement.

There is a disconnect between this ideology and the competitive nature that artists and part-time music historians Eric Von Schmidt and Jim Rooney reveal in their book *Baby Let Me Follow You Down*. They describe Baez learning singer-songwriter Debby Green's repertoire and then performing it when she was opening act for Ms. Green. This was then rationalized by Joan's assertion that Debby was not ambitious and would never really apply herself to career goals anyway. The authors also describe Joan sitting in the back of Cambridge's Club 47 and singing harmony from the rear of the club in such a way that she overpowered the performer despite the fact that the performer was on microphone and Joan was not.

Joan recorded an album *Folksingers Round Harvard Square* for local Boston record label Veritas in 1959. Her career took off after her aforementioned performance at the Newport Folk Festival, which led to a contract with Vanguard Records and her 1960 Vanguard album, titled simply *Joan Baez*.

The contradiction between Baez's politics and her ambitions came to a head when Albert Grossman courted her as a management client, and attempted to push her to record for Columbia Records. Baez felt more rapport with Vanguard, and was also impressed that they had fought the blacklist by signing the Weavers. She also decided to sign with Boston manager Manny Greenhill, an ex-union organizer who certainly was not the business shark that Grossman was generally acknowledged to be.

Baez's early repertoire was a combination of English and American folk songs. Her first songs were minimally produced, simply containing her own performances with voice and guitar with some guitar accompaniment by Weaver Fred Hellerman. It became a gold record, which was an astonishing feat for a small label like Vanguard.

## The singer, the song, and the image

Baez had a powerful soprano voice and, because she was half-Mexican something of a sultry appearance. She embellished this with her long hair, simple outfits, and the avoidance of makeup. All over the United States young women followes her lead and wore their hair straight and used minimal makeup, or abandoned it entirely. In Baez's case it wasn't only her physical appearance that resonated with young women. She was a follower of Gandhi's nonviolent approach to social change, and she demonstrated against the war in Vietnam, spent some time in jail, refused to pay federal income taxes a protest against the war, and founded a school for nonviolence in her new home in Carmel, California.

Baez's concerts were fundamentally quite serious, yet she was fond of throwing in such things as excerpts from rock songs by groups like the Diamonds, recreating the high falsetto parts. Audiences couldn't really tell whether she was satirizing the songs, simply having fun, or both.

Because her repertoire included so many traditional songs, even lengthy ballads, Baez struck a chord with the purists. On the other hand, she completely violated the notion of "the singer, not the song." Her renditions were often sung in a loud voice and included the rather harsh part of her soprano range. This drew attention to her voice, rather than to the songs that she was performing. This, of course, absolutely violated the ethic of such traditionalists as the New Lost City Ramblers and their devoted fans. Nevertheless, Baez was "allowed to skate" by such listeners. Her Vanguard Records were far purer than the original Weavers' recordings. They mostly featured her, with occasional help from an additional guitarist.

In 1966 Baez began working with composer-arranger Peter Schickele on her recordings, and within a few years she was writing songs and recording in Nashville. By 1972 she had left Vanguard Records, and was recording for A&M. Her song *Diamonds and Rust*, released in 1975, details her deteriorating relationship with Bob Dylan, and was her most recent successful recording. Just as Joan Baez had in effect sponsored Bob Dylan, she in turn introduced Bob Dylan to her audience. Because Dylan's vocals were an acquired taste, he badly needed the endorsement of more conventional singers who had captured the folk audience.

David Hadju's gossip column-treatise *Positively 4th Street: The Life and Times of Joan Baez, Bob Dylan, Mimi Baez, and Richard Farina* describes the complex web of personal relationships that developed between Baez, Dylan, Mimi, who was Joan's sister, and Richard Farina. Hadju alleges that Farina actually advised Dylan to "go after" Baez because it would assist his career.

Dylan followed Farina's advice. Baez's autobiography asserts that she accepted a role as second banana in the Dylan bandwagon. She followed him to England, assuming that she would be a guest artist on his shows, in the same way that she had paved the road for him. Seemingly Baez had found someone far more ambitious, calculating, and cold-hearted than she was. Instead of accepting a role as a guest artist, she became a mere member of Dylan's entourage. Because she was largely ignored and occasionally humiliated, she left the tour.

Joan Baez is currently on her final concert tour, and has announced her retirement from the performing arena. I will return to the inimitable Mr. Dylan in a later chapter about folk-rock.

## Judy Collins

Like Odetta, Judy Collins is a classically trained literate musician. Her father was a performer and radio personality in Denver, and she studied classical piano with pianist and conductor Antonia Brico. As a teenager she became interested in folk music and the guitar. In her four autobiographical works, Judy discusses her musical and personal experiences at length. Early in her career, she was influenced by a mystical Denver character named Lingo the Drifter. Lingo was a researcher who studied alleged dormant areas of the brain, but he was also a folksinger and a successful contestant on various game shows. He had a summer TV show, which was an influence on Collins. Judy started as a regional artist performing in Boulder and Denver. Because she married and had a child, she was conflicted about pursuing her musical career. Her husband was a psychology student, and when he got a graduate assistantship at the University of Connecticut Judy got some opportunities to perform at the Gate of Horn in Chicago, and also in New York. The first of her many Elektra albums was released in 1961.

Initially Judy, like Joan Baez, performed mostly traditional folksongs. By 1964 she started to perform songs by contemporary singer-songwriters. These included Bob Gibson, Billy Edd Wheeler, John Phillips, and Tom Paxton. She had several gold-selling albums, but her career reached a new level with her 1967 recording of *Both Sides Now*, written by a (then) little-known Canadian songwriter named Joni Mitchell. The song was arranged by Joshua Rifkin, a Juilliard graduate and later professor as well as the ragtime pianist who reintroduced the work of Scott Joplin to America.

Subsequently Judy began to record with classically oriented arrangements and to try her hand at sophisticated cabaret songs by Kurt Weill, Stephen Sondheim, and others. Her recordings of Ian Tyson's *Someday Soon* in 1969 and Sondheim's *Send in the Clowns* in 1975 made the Billboard charts, with the Sondheim version appearing on the charts in both 1975 and 1977.

Collins began writing and recording her own songs in 1967, and several of her songs have been recorded by such artists as Rufus Wainwright and Dolly Parton. Her most covered songs include *My Father*, recorded by 11 artists, and *Since You Asked*, recorded by eighteen artists.

Collins continues to record, now on her own record label, and tours regularly. She was the subject of Stephen Stills's famous *Suite Judy Blue Eyes*, and has recently recorded and toured with him. She has lived in New York City for over fifty years. In 1974 Judy co-directed a film about her early piano teacher, Antonia Brico. The film was titled *Antonia: Portrait of a Woman*, and it succeeded in reviving Brico's somewhat dormant conducting career. It documented the discrimination faced by female orchestra conductors.

Although Joan Baez and Judy Collins are often thought of interchangeably by folk fans, there are many differences between the two of them. Judy Collins has both an alto and a soprano range, which provides a bit more variety in her vocal performances. She has also positioned herself more as an art-folk singer, performing regularly, for example, at the Café Carlyle, a cabaret in New York City.

## Other figures in the folk revival

I will discuss Buffy Ste. Marie in a later chapter. It was difficult to know where to place her, because her career parallels that of Baez and Collins, but she is also both a Canadian and US artist, and she is an important figure in American Indian music, and protest music as well.

Len Chandler, Tom Paxton, and Dave Van Ronk all began their careers in the late 1950s, but I place Chandler and Paxton in the singer-songwriter vanguard, and Van Ronk as a blues artist, and also a sort of inspirational figure on the New York folk scene.

# 6

# Meanwhile, Back in Canada

The Canadian Pacific Railroad sponsored over a dozen festivals in both Quebec and Western Canada between 1927 and 1930. According to folklorist Neil Rosenberg, writing in his book *Transforming Tradition: Folk Music Revivals Examined*, John Murray Gibbon, the company's head of publicity, had a twofold purpose in sponsoring these events. One goal was to bring tourists to the company's hotels. The other objective was to celebrate the music, song, dance, and craft that made up the "Canadian mosaic of cultures." Even before that time, Folklore scholar Marius Barbeau worked from 1911 to 1948 to document the folk traditions of Quebec in Canada's National Museum.

Alan Mills was a classical music vocalist, touring both Canada and the United States from 1935 to 1937 with the London Singers. After the Second World War he sang with the Opera Guild of Montreal. In 1947 he accepted an engagement with CBC Radio as a folksinger, and began a long and distinguished career. Mills did a radio show called *Folk Songs for Young Folk* from 1947 to 1959, and did his first records for RCA Victor in 1949. From 1952 to 1972 he recorded twenty albums for Folkways Records. These albums covered quite a bit of territory, including children's songs, several albums of songs of French-Canada, songs from Newfoundland, an album of Jewish folk songs, and an album of fiddle tunes with renowned French-Canadian fiddler Jean Carignan. He also did a radio show and made an album with French-Canadian folksinger Helene Baillargeon.

Mills toured Europe and appeared in the United States at the Newport Folk Festival in 1960, with Carignan. He also compiled several collections of Canadian folksongs, and he co-authored the song *I Know an Old Lady Who Swallowed a Fly*, with Rone Bonne. The song has become a standard part of the repertoire of artists who sing for children, and was also recorded by Burl Ives.

Jean Carignan was taught to play the violin by his father. He did not learn to read music, but studied everything from traditional Irish and Scottish fiddle styles to the work of classical virtuoso Jascha Heifetz by listening to records and memorizing a huge amount of music. He made a living at various jobs, including driving a taxi, but played at folk festivals and in local dance halls. As a youth he often played in the streets, even charming policemen with his music after he was arrested for busking. According to guitarist Eugene Chadbourne, writing for the All Music website, Carignan took some flak from Quebecois nationalists for continuing to play Scottish and Irish tunes, but he insisted that the majority of French-Canadian fiddle tunes came from these sources.

Carignan recorded for the Philo folk label in Vermont and for Folkways Records, and occasionally appeared with Pete Seeger. Several films were made about him, and he received an honorary doctorate from McGill University. Classical virtuoso Yehudi Menuhin praised his playing in the notes to one of Carignan's albums. He had come a long way from playing on the streets of Montreal.

## Early revivalists in Canada: The Travellers

If Alan Mills was the Burl Ives of Canada, then The Travellers were the Canadian equivalent of the Weavers. The group began in the summer of 1953 through singalongs at a Jewish socialist vacation community in Ontario. Like the Weavers, the Travellers sang at labor events, strikes, and protests. The original group was musically unusual because it featured Sid Dolgay's mandocello playing.

One of the trademarks of the group was their Canadian adaptation of Woody Guthrie's song *This Land Is Your Land*. Their adaptation included one verse that included various Canadian geographical references. This was followed by the two well-known verses that every school child in the United States has heard, followed up by his two rarely sung protest verses. The latter include references to a no trespassing sign, and a relief office.

In 1957 the group released their first album on the minor Hallmark label, followed by one other album, also on Hallmark. In 1960 they became the first Canadian folk group to sign with a major label, recording two albums for Columbia. In 1961 they performed at the first Mariposa Folk Festival. In 1962 they toured the Soviet Union as part of a Canada–USSR Cultural Exchange, and they later toured Britain, and Europe, but the members also worked day jobs. They also appeared on several CBC television shows.

Over the years there were a number of personnel changes in the group. Thirteen different people eventually performed at different times. Although the Weavers had a relatively amicable break-up, in 1965 founding member Sid Dolgay was forced out of the Travellers in a dispute over their musical and political direction. The dispute was a bitter one, and the bad feelings, lasting for over fifty years, are detailed in a 2003 documentary: *The Travellers: This Land Is Your Land*. Despite the bitterness, Dolgay played occasional concerts with the group over the years. The influence of the Travellers can be judged by the fact that they made sixteen albums, including both recordings for adults and children. The group remained active into the 1980s.

## Wade Hemsworth

Wade Hemsworth was a draftsman who performed and wrote music part-time. He took up banjo and guitar as a child, and graduated from the Ontario School of Art in 1939. During his Second World War service in the air force he was stationed in Newfoundland, where he discovered traditional music. During his lifetime he recorded two albums, but several of his own songs, notably *The Black Fly Song* and *The Wild Goose* became well known among Canadian folksingers. The inspiration for many of his songs came from his work as a typographical draftsman, which brought him to the woods of North Ontario, Quebec, and Labrador. Hemsworth also published a songbook in 1990, which contained sixteen of the songs that he had written.

## Omar Blondahl

Omar Blondahl aka Sagebrush Sam was born east of Saskatoon, and studied piano, violin, and voice. In 1944 he assumed the name Sagebrush Sam and sang on country music radio in 1951. He followed this with a two-year stint in Hollywood, moving to St. Johns, Newfoundland, in 1955. During his ten-year stay in St. Johns, he developed a repertoire of local songs, some of which he had collected. He adopted the local accent and performed locally and on CBC, popularizing songs from Newfoundland. He recorded seven albums in the 1960s and 1970s over the course of his career.

Blondahl was probably suitably surprised when a Newfoundland rock band called Lukey's Boat recorded some of the songs he had recorded, adding a rock beat to the proceedings. Folklorist Neil Rosenberg published a detailed article on Blondahl's career in the 1991 *Canadian Journal of Traditional Music*.

The late Ron Hynes, who died in 2015, was a singer-songwriter from Newfoundland who started his career as a member of the Wonderful Grand Band, but went on to record seven solo albums. He was especially known for his songwriting talents, and his songs have been covered by over a hundred other artists, including Emmylou Harris, Christy Moore, and numerous Canadian artists. He also acted in a number of theatrical productions and films.

## Don Messer

Messer was a Canadian fiddle player who had his own network shows on Canadian radio and then television from 1939 to 1969. Messer positioned the show as a down to earth made in Canada alternative to the more glamorous American variety shows, like the *Ed Sullivan Show*. His two lead singers, Charlie Chamberlain and Marge Osborne sang a medley of old-time favorite folksongs, and Messer mostly confined himself to playing the fiddle. Rather than broadcasting from a major city, Messer's show variously originated from New Brunswick, Prince Edward Island, and Nova Scotia. In addition to recording to a large number of albums, a number of folios of his fiddle tunes were available in printed music folios.

Several later Canadian TV shows, including the *Tommy Hunter Show*, the Irish Rovers' show, and a show featuring maritime musician Rita MacNeil and Friends followed Messer's low-key, down-home approach.

## Canadian pop-folk

The Travellers were the best known of the Canadian folk-pop groups, but there were also a few others. *The Mountain City Four* performed from 1963 to 1967 in Montreal. They helped to popularize a number of songs by Wade Hemsworth, who is discussed above. They also performed his song *The Log Driver's Waltz* in a National Film Board animated film. Anna and Kate McGarricle were two of the four members of the group. They achieved some notoriety as both songwriters and artists in both Canada and the United States in later years.

*The Raftsmen* were active at about the same as the Mountain City Four was performing. They performed on multiple instruments in thirteen languages, and recorded four albums for RCA, starting in 1962. They performed in Montreal and also in Miami, and guested on Oscar Brand's Montreal radio show. They also recorded his song *Something to Sing About.* Personnel changes led to two other successor bands which made additional recordings for other labels. Founding member Louis Leroux later toured with pop singer Nana Mouskouri, and did session work and taught guitar.

*3's a Crowd* began as a folk-comedy trio that turned into a folk-rock group. The original members were singer Donna Warner and singer-songwriters Brent Titcomb and Trevor Veitch. The band was formed in Vancouver, moving to Toronto in 1965, and Ottawa in 1967. The group disbanded in 1968, but there were various short-term revisions of the band that included singer-songwriter Bruce Cockburn, and Neil Young's associate Ken Koblun. Titcomb and Veitch went on to establish long-term careers as singer-songwriters. Veitch moved to Los Angeles and worked with a number of artists as a contractor or songwriter, including Elton John and Donna Summer.

Claude Dubois began his career performing with a country band called *Les Montagnards.* Inspired by Bob Dylan, Donovan, and Gilles Vigneault he turned to folk rock, and in 1972 recorded his third album in Paris. He went on to appear at Expo 67 and hosted several TV shows. In 1976 he made an album called *Mellow Reggae,* and later working through some drug problems he recorded two hit singles, and recorded more albums. Dubois was involved in a controversy with the CBC in 2008, when he accused the network of racism for removing all of the Quebecois artists from the 2008 Canadian Songwriters Hall of Fame gala show in Toronto.

# Ian and Sylvia

Of all the North American folk-pop singers, Ian and Sylvia received the most positive across-the-board acceptance from both pop-folk and traditional enthusiasts. Ian was an art school student in 1958, performing in various Toronto coffeehouses. There he met Sylvia Fricker who had moved to Toronto after graduating from high school.

In 1962 they recorded their first album for Vanguard Records, and started to tour colleges in the United States and Canada. Initially they sang traditional songs, but each of them wrote significant songs fairly early in the game. Ian's *Four Strong Winds,* written in 1962, has been a hit many times over, while Sylvia's *You Were on My Mind,* written and recorded by the duo in 1964, was turned into a major folk-rock hit by the band *We Five.* Ian's song *Someday Soon,* about a romance with a rodeo cowboy, was recorded by the duo in 1964, and was later a hit in Judy Collins's 1969 recording. Other artists have covered the song since then, and it has become something of a folk revival standard.

Ian and Sylvia had a very appealing sound, with Ian generally singing the melody, and Sylvia singing harmony. They were able to convincingly perform both quiet ballads and intense soulful work songs. There was a certain reality that their performances exuded which eluded many of the other folk-pop groups. For example, Ian had been headed toward a possible career as a rodeo cowboy until an injury derailed him. This brought a unique aspect to their performances of *Someday Soon.*

Although their concerts were well attended and their albums sold reasonably well, Ian and Sylvia never achieved the spectacular success that some of the American pop-folk groups enjoyed. After the folk-boom crested they made some attempts to record with their country-rock band, *The Great Speckled Bird.* This was followed by a Canadian television Show called *Nashville North*, later called the *Ian Tyson Show.*

Ian and Sylvia married in 1964, but divorced in 1975. Sylvia went on to host a CBC Radio Show, *Touch the Earth* which ran from 1974 to 1979. She recorded two solo albums for Capitol, and then started her own company, Salt Records. Sylvia also sang in *Quartette,* an acapella gospel and rhythm and blues vocal group, as well as recorded with them. She continues to perform as a solo artist and with Quartette.

Ian bought a ranch in Alberta, and morphed into a cowboy poetry writer who performs at numerous cowboy poetry gatherings. He has recorded several albums of this repertoire, and in 1994 wrote *I Never Sold My Saddle*, an autobiography about his life and performing career.

The duo reunited for occasional shows, and their 1986 concert was televised and received a Gemini award for the best variety show from the Academy of Canadian Cinema and Television.

## American Canadians and Canadian Americans

Several folk artists maintained a kind of dual national identity encompassing both the United States and Canada. This was the case for Oscar Brand, Ed McCurdy, and Buffy Ste. Marie. Each of them played an important role in the folk music revival in both Canada and the United Sates.

## Oscar Brand

Oscar Brand was born in Winnipeg, but moved at the age of seven with his family to Minneapolis. By the time he was in high school, his family moved to New York City. He lived there for the rest of his life. In New York he played alongside members of the *Almanac Singers*, as well as Jean Ritchie. He wrote a. number of books that varied from commentary to compilations of ballads. Oscar had a fifty-year recording career, from 1949 to 1999. During that time, he made over seven dozen albums. Many were subject centered, for example, *Marine Corps Songs*, or *Songs for Doctors Only*. Other albums dealt with historical or subjects like American election songs. He also compiled four volumes of *Bawdy Songs & Backroom Ballads*, and recorded many of them.

As if this wasn't enough, he had a radio show on WNYC that ran for seventy years, and as previously mentioned wrote the hit song *A Guy Is a Guy* for Doris Day. Oscar also wrote a number of commercials, and produced over three hundred documentary films.

Although Brand lived in New York, he never gave up his Canadian connections. His Canadian TV show, *Let's Sing Out*, aired on CTV from 1963 to 1967, and then on CBC TV from 1967 to 1968. The show followed a format that was similar to the American TV show, *Hootenanny*, with Oscar hosting the show and introducing several Canadian or American acts. The theme song for the show was a song called *This Land of Ours (Something to Sing About)*, a song that celebrated Canadian patriotism. Oscar being Oscar, he also wrote a set of lyrics applicable to performances in the United States. Unlike the American show, *Let's Sing Out* did not blacklist artists for their political beliefs.

One of Brand's albums called *On Campus Concert in Canada* featured Canadian folksongs. Brand also did a number of performances at the Mariposa Folk Festival.

## Ed McCurdy

Ed McCurdy moved back and forth between the United States and Canada. He grew up in Willow Hill, Pennsylvania, and worked as a gospel singer on radio. In 1945 he moved to Vancouver, where his 1947 CBC radio show *Ed McCurdy Sings* was the first one in the English language network devoted to folksong. Over the next seven years he did a series of radio and TV shows for CBC. In 1950 he wrote an anti-war song called *Last Night I Had the Strangest Dream*. Over the years the song was recorded over forty times in seventy-seven languages, including recordings by Simon & Garfunkel, Garth Brooks, Pete Seeger, Joan Baez, Johnny Cash, and jazzman Charles Lloyd.

In 1954 McCurdy moved to New York City, but he continued to appear on a number of Canadian TV shows, at coffeehouses, and at the 1962 Mariposa Folk Festival. From 1956 to 1958 McCurdy recorded four albums of bawdy English poems, using the title *When Dalliance Was in Flower and Maidens Lost Their Heads*. The bawdy lyrics were set off by exquisite banjo accompaniments by Erik Darling. In 1976 McCurdy toured Europe, and in 1982 he moved to Halifax, Nova Scotia. He performed at the Mariposa and Winnipeg Folk Festivals until 1994, and he took on some acting roles, mostly on CBC-TV.

Like Oscar Brand, McCurdy recorded many albums. His first album, *Folk Songs of the Canadian Maritimes and Newfoundland*, was recorded in 1955. The remaining albums usually did not include Canadian songs. McCurdy became a naturalized Canadian citizen in 1986.

## Buffy Sainte-Marie

It is difficult to describe Ste. Marie in the context of a particular place. She was born on the Piapot Reserve in Saskatchewan, Canada, but her mother died in an automobile accident when she was an infant. She was adopted by an American couple of Mi'kmaq ancestry and raised in Maine and Massachusetts. She has lived in New York, Los Angeles, and Hawaii, but is more popular in Canada than in the United States, and has won numerous Canadian Juno Awards and is in the Juno Hall of Fame. (Juno awards are the Canadian equivalent of the Grammy Awards in the United States.)

Ste. Marie began her musical career while a student at the University of Massachusetts at Amherst, where she earned a degree in philosophy. After graduation she moved to New York City, where she played in coffeehouses and entered into a long-term recording agreement with Vanguard Records. She also performed at the Purple Onion Coffeehouse in Toronto.

In Andrea Warner's biography *Buffy Sainte-Marie, The Authorized Biography*, Warner points out that Ste. Marie had no understanding of the nature of the contract, and in fact used the attorney suggested by the label, who was also their attorney. A similar naiveté caused Ste. Marie to sell the publishing rights of her song *The Universal Soldier* for a grand total of $1 to a member of the band *The Highwaymen*, who were about to record it. The song was written in 1964, and became a hit for Donovan. Ten years later she paid $25,000 to recover the publishing rights.

Ste. Marie is often regarded as a protest song artist, because a number of her songs like *Bury My Heart at Wounded Knee* or *Now That the Buffalo's Gone* concern the treatment of American Indians in the United States. However, her songs move in a variety of directions. *Until It's Time for You to Go* was a hit record for Bobby Darin 1965, and was later recorded by Elvis Presley. In 1969 she recorded an electronic album making abundant use of the Buchla synthesizer, and in 1992 she made the first album entirely recorded on the internet. She also recorded four albums with bassist-producer Norbert Putnam that reflected rock and country influences. She has described her own vocal work as an attempt to use many different voices, something that she points out that rock artist Annie Lennox did later.

Ste. Marie was an actress on the TV show *The Virginians*, in an episode that thanks to her efforts included an all-Indian cast. From 1975 to 1981 she was a regular cast member of the *Sesame Street* show, and she has devoted much time and money to supporting a computer-based curriculum that brings the contribution of Native Americans into the classroom.

After something of a performing hiatus, Ste. Marie has resumed touring and in 2015 she recorded *Power in the Blood*, an album of new material. A 2017 recording featuring rearranged older material and two new songs followed in 2017.

## Bonnie Dobson

Bonnie Dobson has roots and branches in Canada, the United States, and England as well. Originally a native of Toronto, she lived in New York from 1964 to 1965, but moved to England in 1969.

Like her fellow Canadian Ed McCurdy, Dobson was not a prolific composer. However, her song *Morning Dew*, which describes the aftermath of an atomic explosion, became a widely performed and recorded anthem in the folk revival. The song became a subject of controversy when Tim Rose recorded it and managed to cut himself in on the copyright. According to Dobson, speaking in an interview that is on the Roots of the Grateful Dead website, Rose made no change in the lyrics, except that he adopted the change the Fred Neil had made in his recording of *Morning Dew*. Neil changed the "Take me for a walk" lyric to "Walk me out in the morning dew." (Incidentally Neil did not credit himself with any part of the song.) All of this assumed more importance when British pop artist Lulu made a hit record of the song. Other recordings of the song were made by the Allman Brothers, the Jeff Beck group with Rod Stewart, Devo, and the Grateful Dead.

Dobson did three albums for Prestige Records, and four more albums in England. For years she was relatively inactive on the music front because she was an administrator in the philosophy department at the University of London's Berwood College. Since her retirement from that position, she made an album for Hornbeam Records in 2014 and has resumed her performing career.

## Stompin' Tom Connors and Canadian identity

Strictly speaking, Tom Connors was more of a country artist than a folksinger. Some referred to him as the Canadian Johnny Cash, because of his gravel-voiced baritone stylings. I have included him here because of his emphasis on Canadian customs, place names, and geographic locales.

Charles Thomas Connor was an illegitimate child because his father's Catholic family didn't want him to marry his Protestant mother. Tom was so poor that he actually saw his mother stealing food from a Chinese restaurant in order to feed the family. He lived briefly with his mother in a low-security penitentiary, and then was taken away by the Children's Aid Society and subsequently adopted by a family from Prince Edward Island. He soon went away from home and hitchhiked across Canada. During the next thirteen years he worked odd jobs, sometimes sang for his supper, and worked in the mines. This period came to an end in 1964 by accident, not by design.

In 1964 Connors found himself in the town of Timmins, Ontario, a mining town in the northern part of that province. Connors had not slept in a bed in months, and he wandered into the local Maple Leaf Hotel. He was five cents short of buying a beer, but the bartender contributed the nickel. After a while he asked Connors if he played the guitar that he was carrying. A few songs later, Connors launched into Canadian expatriate Hank Snow's iconic tune *I've Been Everywhere*\*. The song mentions any number of locales in the United States, but

---

\*   I've been Everywhere was originally an Australian song, written by Geoff Mack. He re-wrote the song, replacing the Australian place names with American ones. Subsequently the song has been re-worked to include locales in Finland Israel, Germany, the New Zealand and the United Kingdom.

Connors substituted Canadian towns, earning him another beer, and eventually a room in a cheap hotel. The bartender, Gaet Lepine, convinced the owner to hire Connors. Eventually the hotel built a stage for him, and the engagement lasted for fourteen months, led him landing a weekly spot on CKGB radio in Timmins and a series of 45RPM recordings.

During his lifetime Connors recorded some three dozen albums and numerous singles, and wrote two autobiographies. He did not tour in the United States, and seemed entirely disinterested in doing so. He won six Juno Awards but stewing over the prizes given to expatriate Canadians, Connors returned the awards with an angry letter, and took a ten-year hiatus from his musical career.

Part of the reason that Connors never caught on in the United States was that many of his songs referred to Canadian historical figures or political or social events. His most famous song was *The Hockey Song*, which is played at least once in each National Hockey League Event.

In the 1970s and 1980s Connors founded three record labels that promoted a number of acts whose only common ground was that they were all Canadians. This included classical guitarist Liona Boyd, folksinger Rita MacNeil, the Canadian Brass, a bluegrass band called the *Dixie Flyers*, and First Nations Inuk artist Charlie Panigoniak.

Stompin' Tom was definitely a man who walked his Canadian talk!

## Some thoughts about the Canadian folk scene

The Canadian equivalent to the Greenwich Village folk scene was in the Yorkville neighborhood of Toronto and the St. Catherine St. neighborhood in Montreal. According to Professor Gillian Mitchell by the mid-1960s there were forty-seven coffeehouses in the Yorkville neighborhood. Many featured local musicians, although *The Riverboat*, which lasted the longest, also had performers from the United States. In addition to Ian and Sylvia, and later Joni Mitchell, there were a number of lesser-known performers, including Donna Warner, Vicky Taylor, Susan Jains, Carol Robinson, and Elyse Weinberg.

Compared to the proliferation of pop-folk trios and quartets in the United States, there seem to have been relatively few equivalents. The *Halifax Three*, formed in Halifax, Nova Scotia, had a brief run at fame and fortune with their Epic Records contract and the single *The Man Who Wouldn't Sing along with Mitch*, but by 1964 they had given up the ghost. Denny Doherty went on to join the Mamas and Papas, and Halifax, while lead guitarist Zal Yanofsky became a member of the *Lovin' Spoonful* before leaving to open a French restaurant in Ottawa.

The Canadian music scene had two inherent difficulties compared to the scene in the United States. Until 1971 Canadian radio was not very friendly to Canadian music. Almost all of the major Canadian cities, with the exceptions of Edmonton and Quebec City, easily received radio stations from the United States. American music simply dominated the Canadian airwaves until 1971. The other problem that Canadian artists face is that the geographic distances are great, and there are far fewer major population centers. The larger the performing group, the more difficult it is to finance a tour that customarily includes 500–600 mile hops between performing venues.

Between the domination of radio coming from the United States and the relatively low population of Canada, there was little opportunity for Canadian artists to make bestselling records in Canada. This is one of the main factors why so many Canadian artists, like Joni Mitchell or Neil Young, have ended up moving to the United States, and why other artists, like Gordon Lightfoot has utilized personal managers from the United States. By the same token, this may be why Canada has developed a more eclectic musical scene than the one that dominates the United States, especially in certain genres, like the children's music market or the way that many of the Canadian folk festivals operated. The first of these festivals was the Mariposa Folk Festival, which began in 1961 in Ontario.

The Miramichi Folksong Festival in New Brunswick dates from 1958, but it is a ballad-centered festival that is not as broad in musical scope as Mariposa attempts to be. Mariposa is closer to the model of the Newport Festival, founded in 1959 in Newport, Rhode Island. The difference between Newport and Mariposa is that the United States festival has gone back and forth between being a for-profit event and a nonprofit event. Mariposa has always been a nonprofit festival. Estelle Klein assisted in the first festival, and it was her artistic vision to include both First Nations artists and world music performers, long before Newport entertained such ideas. She also was insistent that all artists be paid the same, which broke down the kind of classist hierarchy that exists at many folk festivals between the pop-folk stars and traditional musicians. Klein inspired entrepreneur Mitch Podolak, who with several other producers started the Winnipeg Folk Festival in 1974, which in turn inspired the Vancouver Festival, whose beginnings date to 1978. Although Mariposa has had its financial struggles, it along with the other festivals, and many others in Canada, still exist today.

Possibly what distinguishes the Canadian scene, at least for the artists who have chosen to stay in Canada, is less reliance on hitting the jackpot with hit records and the subsequent high-paying concert engagements that bring thousands of dollars to artists, their managers, and their agents.

# 7

# Selling the Music: The New York Scene

From 1950 to 1964, New York was definitely the center of the folk music world, especially the pop-folk world. Because at that time the record business was centered in New York, and the Weavers and the earliest folk and folk-pop singers were there, talent tended to gravitate to New York City, and to Greenwich Village in particular. All of the major record labels, except for Capitol, had their headquarters in New York City, and the much smaller folk labels were there as well. Folkways Records was the granddaddy of the scene, which grew to include Elektra, Riverside, Tradition, and Vanguard Records.

It wasn't only the presence of the record companies that made the scene as active as it was. Personal managers, booking agents, and music publishers were mostly located in New York.

## The record companies

The pioneer folk label was Asch-Stinson Records, originally formed as a partnership between Mo Asch and Herbert Harris in 1941. Asch entered into the partnership because Harris had a supply of shellac that he had obtained from the Russian government, and Asch needed the shellac during the Second World War. By 1945 the two partners had had enough of one another, and in 1947 Asch started Disc Records, which quickly went into bankruptcy. By 1948 Asch started the Folkways label, which recorded some 1800 albums before Asch sold it to the Smithsonian Institute in 1987.

Moe Asch was a colorful individual and also a visionary. It was his goal to document the music of the entire world. He was not interested in competing with major record companies, but he wanted to archive music that he personally felt was of historical interest. The label issued recordings of ethnic music from all over the world, and most of them included extensive notes by renowned ethnomusicologists. In order to stay in business, Asch promoted the sales of his recordings to libraries and schools.

In 1952 Asch issued a set of six twelve-inch LPs, *The Anthology of American Folk Music*. These recordings were compiled by the brilliant and eccentric filmmaker Harry Smith, who lived on the Bowery in Manhattan. Smith had amassed a collection of thousands of 78 rpm records, and chose eighty-seven songs for the six albums.

There were a number of peculiar aspects of this project. The recordings were blatantly illegal because they were recordings that had been issued during the 1920s and 1930s by various record labels. Folkways did not ask for permission from these companies, nor did he pay any royalties to the artists. This strategy was not entirely unique, because a record company fittingly called Jolly Roger has followed a similar path in 1950 by reissuing jazz recordings. An amusing sidelight to all this was that RCA's custom pressing division was supposedly pressing records illegally taken from its own vaults.

In effect Asch was taking the position that the original owners of these records had no interest in continuing to market them. He justified this position on the notion that the recordings were of great artistic importance. The records came out with little initial fanfare, and none of record companies, music publishers, or artists initially made any demands for payment. They probably either did not notice the release of these recordings or they felt that pursuing legal remedies would cost more than any income from the sales of the Anthology.

True to Smith's persona, the records came with a booklet that included Smith's plot summaries of the songs and rather odd, surrealistic drawings. The whole package was designed to appear like a crazed surrealistic vision of an old farmer's almanac.

Asch had taken some heavy risks in releasing these recordings. Aside from the possibility of lawsuits, issuing six albums of relatively obscure music was certainly a financial risk for the company. As it turned out, from both an aesthetic and a historical perspective, the risk certainly paid off. No one has ever written about the sales figures of the records, but anyone active in the revival, then or later, was heavily influenced by these albums. They included blues, country, folk, and Cajun music—virtually an encyclopedia of American folk music. The only music that was omitted was the music of immigrant groups or ethnic groups that recorded in foreign languages. The Anthology mixed black and white musical styles and artists without any sort of racial separation. It is interesting that many of the young urban performers who were influenced by the Anthology did not follow this notion, but focused either on African-American or Anglo-American music.

Through these recordings, many young urban performers and folk music fans were introduced to such artists as Mississippi John Hurt, Furry Lewis, and Clarence Ashley. In the subsequent ten or so years the young urban revivalists located these artists and a number of others. Many were still alive, and a few of them resumed their careers, or in Hurt's case started one. Most folklorists were not interested in these artists, feeling that because they had made commercial recordings, they could not be regarded as folksingers.

Moe Asch was a political radical who maintained his independence from the prevailing communist ideology of the old left. When the Weavers were blacklisted, he recorded an extensive series of albums by Pete Seeger. Asch was notorious for not paying royalties to his artists. He even paid Pete a retainer of $15 a week in lieu of "royalties." Dave Van Ronk once told me that he himself never made any attempt to collect royalties from Folkways. In place of what was owed him he would simply go up to the Folkways Records office in mid-town Manhattan and take copies of his own records and whatever other Folkways albums interested him.

## Elektra Records

In 1950 a young college student named Jac Holzman started a record label while he was attending St. Johns College in Maryland. One of his first recordings was of a fellow student named Glenn Yarbrough, later to find fame with the Limeliters and his later solo recordings. Holzman moved up to New York and rented a loft in the western part of Greenwich Village. The loft served as a retail record store as well as the headquarters of the Elektra label. Some of the early Elektra recordings included albums by Tom Paley and Jean Ritchie. Paley was a mathematics professor at Yale who was a renowned guitar and banjo player, and later was one of the founders of the *New Lost City Ramblers*. Earlier in the book I cited Jean Ritchie as one of the few folksingers in New York who actually came from Kentucky and initially learned songs from her family.

Both of these albums were important in the folk revival. Ritchie's 1952 album reminded urban revivalists that there was indeed an actual folk community where songs were learned within families and communities. Paley's 1953 album proved him to be an excellent musician who was steeped in traditional music, but was also not afraid to add some of his own variations to those tunes. He was typical of many young revivalists in the sense that his singing was secondary to his extraordinary instrumental abilities.

Some other early Elektra recordings included international folk music offerings by Cynthia Gooding and Theodore Bikel a blues album by harmonica great Sonny Terry, and a number of recordings by Oscar Brand and Ed McCurdy. Although Moe Asch did record some of the younger revivalists, like The New Lost City Ramblers, Mark Spoelstra, and Dave Van Ronk, he made many more recordings of the older generation of singers, like Woody Guthrie, Lead Belly, and Pete Seeger. It was Elektra that opened up the possibility of recording for the young revivalists.

Elektra was a promotionally aggressive company, and the Ed McCurdy albums of bawdy music grew out of a concept that Holzman developed with McCurdy. They were a big success from the time of their first appearance in 1956. Holzman was less successful in his attempts to release the folk-pop albums of Bob Grossman and the *Travellers Three*. When Elektra struck gold with the *Doors*, first album in 1967, the company turned away from folk music, and moved to the West Coast.

## Kenneth Goldstein: Riverside and Prestige Records

Relatively little attention has been payed to the important role of Kenneth Goldstein in the folk revival. Kenny, as everyone called him, was a journalist who started out in the world of folk music writing liner notes and producing albums for Stinson Records in 1951. He introduced some of the British folksingers to the American scene, notably A. L. Lloyd, Ewan MacColl, and Irish singer Patrick Galvin. In 1955 Kenny persuaded Riverside Records to jump into the production of folk music. Riverside was a strong independent jazz label that had issued albums by such artists as Wes Montgomery and Cannonball Adderley.

Kenny recorded dozens of records for Riverside, including unaccompanied Child ballads sung by Lloyd and MacColl, holy blues albums by Reverend Gary Davis, and songster Pink Anderson, regional collections by some of the young revivalists, and a banjo record featuring Billy Faier, a very young Eric Weissberg, and the author.

In 1960 Kenny moved over to Prestige Records, also previously a jazz label. He produced numerous other recordings for Prestige, including albums by country-folk musicians Harry and Jeanie West, and young revivalists Paul Clayton, Utah Phillips, and Rosalie Sorrels.

Kenny then turned to the world of folklore and for years he was a professor at the University of Pennsylvania. He kept his hand in the revival by co-founding the Philadelphia Folk Festival in 1957 with radio personality Gene Shay. Goldstein was artistic director of the festival for fifteen years.

What Kenneth Goldstein brought to the folk revival was an honest appreciation and enthusiasm for all sorts of folk music ranging from old blues singers to unaccompanied ballad singers and young urban singers and instrumentalists. More than any other single record producer he was open to the entire spectrum of American folk music styles.

## Tradition Records

The Clancy Brothers and Tommy Makem were fixtures of the folk scene in New York in the 1950s and 1960s. In 1956 they formed a label called Tradition Records with the financial assistance of Guggenheim heiress Diane Hamilton. The label issued albums by the Clancys and also by their friends Paul Clayton and Jean Ritchie, as well as some fine field recordings that Clayton had made. The latter included an instrumental album that featured the work of a fine guitarist named Etta Baker. She provided some of the young female revivalists with a female role model who was a fine guitarist.

## The others

Occasionally other labels would issue folk recordings. One such label was Esoteric Records, which was mostly a classical music label. Lyrichord was a label that issued many albums of music from around the world. Various companies jumped into the folk-pop sweepstakes. Monitor released several albums by singer-songwriter Billy Edd Wheeler, and during the 1960s when the revival was at its peak, many of the major labels issued folk-pop albums that failed to find an audience, along with the albums of successful pop-folk groups.

## Infrastructure: Agents, personal managers, music publishers, attorneys, and their relationship to the New York folk scene

For many years the music business has developed an infrastructure designed to promote artists. Booking agents obtain gigs for artists. Personal managers operate in a broader sphere, and essentially function as career guides who advise their clients on all aspects of their entertainment careers. Entertainment business attorneys deal with music business contracts, as well as sometimes promoting artist to record companies in order to obtain recording contracts. Many record company contracts were and are quite complex, dealing with such matters as foreign rights, reissues of existing material, and publishing rights to songs.

The most prominent music publishers exist to promote the songwriting careers of their contract writers. There are two sorts of music publishers. One group exists to obtain recordings of songs, or to place songs in movies, on television, or in commercials. Other music publishers function in the world of print music, printing folios or sheet music of artists' songs. Transforming the songs into printed music makes the songs accessible to other musicians. Print music publishers also publish instructional folios that can be used by amateur musicians to learn songs or instrumental pieces.

During the 1950s and into the 1960s, most of these businesses were based in New York City. Even the more rebellious artists, a la Bob Dylan, utilized personal managers to help them negotiate deals with record companies and music publishers. The huge majority of artists simply did not have access to record labels or music publishers, and those entities generally preferred dealing with business professionals to create such relationships. Furthermore, most musical artists knew relatively little about the music industry, and certainly did not (and do not) have a good working knowledge of how to read contracts.

Before folk was at least partially transformed into folk-pop, major entertainment entities were not courting folk musicians. Contracts with the smaller folk labels were often relatively short. In the biography of Buffy Ste. Marie cited earlier, Ste. Marie states that she used the same lawyers that her record label were using. This is an obvious conflict of interest, but at the time she had no clear idea of what she was signing, or what rights she was giving up.

# Booking agents and managers

One New York booking agency dominated the entire world of folk-pop. ITA (International Talent Associates) was founded in 1960, by two veteran talent agents: Bert Block and Larry Bennett. Starting out with such prominent jazz artists as Gerry Mulligan and Miles Davis they soon leaped into the world of folk-pop. They booked virtually every major pop-folk group, including the Kingston Trio, the Brothers Four, the Limeliters, and Peter, Paul & Mary. They also booked Bob Dylan and Odetta. When a college student rep. called and wanted to book one of the major acts, but couldn't meet their price, the agency would turn to some of their secondary groups like the Journeymen or the Halifax Three.

Although ITA dominated bookings for folk acts, there were a number of personal managers who were on the scene. The major league managers were used to dealing with major record labels, and complex deals. Mort Lewis had managed jazz musician Dave Brubeck in the 1950s and into the 1960s, but then went on to manage the Brothers Four and Simon and Garfunkel. Ken Greengrass handled a group of acts that represented different musical styles. In addition to supervising the careers of The Highwaymen, he managed Bob McGrath of *Sesame Street*, Steve Lawrence, and Diahann Carroll. The crown prince of folk managers was Albert Grossman, who handled Bob Dylan, The Band, Richie Havens, Ian and Sylvia, Janis Joplin, Gordon Lightfoot, and Peter, Paul & Mary. A young Ken Kragen managed the Limeliters.

These were the "big boys." Another set of managers handled acts that were perfectly credible, but did not turn out to be "star material." It is arguable whether this inability to ascend to the heights of the industry was the fault of bad management, limitations of talent, or bad luck. Harold Leventhal managed the Weavers, Pete Seeger, and Judy Collins. These were definitely important acts, but not in pop terms, superstars.

Arthur (Art) Gorson managed Phil Ochs, David (Cohen) Blue, Jim and Jean, and Eric Andersen. Herbert S. (Herb) Gart handled Buffy Ste. Marie, Jose Feliciano, Don McLean, Janis Ian, Mississippi John Hurt, Gary and Randy Scruggs, and early feminist singer Alix Dobkin. Len Rosenfeld managed Josh White. David Wilkes was another of these managers, at various times managing or co-managing Emmylou Harris, Richie Havens, Tom Paxton, Josh White Jr., and Jerry Jeff Walker. He then became an executive at Vanguard Records. The second line of managers certainly represented excellent talent. Whether they were able to do the best possible job for these acts is arguable.

Although the bulk of the action during the early part of the revival was definitely in New York, not all managers were headquartered there. Manny Greenhill, who managed Joan Baez, was based in Boston, until 1976, when he moved to Santa Monica. Manny's company, Folklore Productions, now functions as a booking agency for a number of folk artists, and is operated by his son and grandson. Frank Werber managed the Kingston Trio out of San Francisco.

# Music publishers

From a long-term standpoint, music publishing is often the most lucrative portion of the music business. Publishers benefit from reissue projects, and also from royalties that come from radio airplay; sheet music sales; and the use of songs in commercials, movies, or on television. When a hit song appears, like *Goodnight Irene*, the royalties from radio airplay can mount to thousands and thousands of dollars over a long period of time.

In the 1950s there were many music publishers in New York. Many of them were devoted to traditional pop music, and had little interest in or understanding of the nature of traditional music. Once the Weavers started making hit records, everything changed.

Albert Grossman developed a connection with a music publishing entrepreneur-hustler named Artie Mogull. Artie worked for Warner-Chappell Music, one of the largest music publishers in the world. Mogull arranged for Peter, Paul & Mary to have companies that they basically shared with Warner-Chappell.

Music Sales Corporation was the pioneer in publishing folk instrumental instruction books. Their early notable authors included Jerry Silverman, Happy Traum, and Stefan Grossman. Each of them authored folk guitar methods that covered the various genres of folk guitar styles. Later the company added methods for banjo, fiddle, and mandolin, and many more guitar publications.

In later years Mel Bay, based in suburban St. Louis, Hal Leonard in Milwaukee, and Alfred Music in Los Angeles entered the picture, but none of them seemed to have much interest in folk instrumental styles in the early years of the folksong revival.

# The bottom line

Successful groups or soloists utilized the services of all the people mentioned above. Agents generally charged 10–15 percent of the gross income of performers. Personal managers typically took 15–25 percent. Of the artist's income, although some took as little as 10 percent, a number of managers demanded 25 percent, and a few managers grabbed 50 percent of a performer's income. Artists who really hit it big would often hire a business manager, whose function was to provide accounting services, deal with tax matters, and to invest the artist's money. For these services, typically the act would have to pay an additional 5 percent of their gross income.

For a performer who spent a good deal of time on the road, paying all those commissions, plus travel expenses, and attorney fees, a road trip might end with little money left over for the artist. Solo artists also generally used an accompanist or a band, and they had to pay those expenses as well. During the early days of the revival tech support was not a huge item, but as time went on performers used a road crew that handled sound and lights.

Some managers owned part or all of an act's publishing rights, and also commissioned the writer's share of income. If the manager owned all of the music publishing rights, and then commissioned writer's income as well, the manager might well be earning more from an artist's songs than the artist did. This was ethically questionable, but not illegal. The folk or pop-folk artist at an early portion of their career often had no idea why they seemed to work regularly, experience success as recording and concert artists, but come home with comparatively little money.

# The Folklore Center and Israel G. Young

One of the people who was active in the New York folk scene in the late 1940s and into the 1970s was a young dancer and would-be bookseller named Israel G. (Izzy) Young. Izzy became interested in folk music through his participation in Margot Mayo's American Square Dance groups, and by hanging out in Greenwich Village. In the course of his village excursions, Izzy became friendly with John Cohen and Tom Paley, who later founded the New Lost City Ramblers with Mike Seeger. During the mid-1950s Izzy met Kenny Goldstein, who encouraged him to develop catalog books about folk music. This led to Izzy's renting a space at 110 MacDougal Street, in the heart of Greenwich Village. He called the store the *Folklore Center.*

All of New York's folksingers and aspiring folksingers could be found hanging out at the store. Some used it as a maildrop; some of the pop-folk musicians bought books of folksongs in their quest to find new material for their records and performances. Record company personnel dropped by the shop to see "what was happening," and Izzy himself became a sort of small-time concert promoter and one of the founders of the *Friends of Old Time Music.* Some nights Izzy would tire of the endless parade of tourists thronging the neighborhood. He would lock the doors and the singers stayed and passed around guitars and banjos and play their newest musical arrangements.

Izzy was not involved with the protest music proponents. Although his politics were progressive enough, he had no ties to any existing political viewpoints. Rather he was a music, dance, and book junkie with great energy and enthusiasm for what he thought was honest and musical. As such, he was part of the counterculture that existed in opposition to the pop-folk music of the day. In 1960 he operated a sort of music concession at *Gerde's,* a bar just east of Greenwich Village. He hired artists like Brownie McGhee and Sonny Terry, and folk fans began to gravitate to the club. Never a brilliant businessman because he was never that interested in the *business* aspect of anything, Izzy and his partner Tom Prendergast were soon squeezed out of the club when Mike Porco, the owner, realized that he was onto something that could be a money-maker. Mike had been operating the bar, and after Izzy and Tom left, Mike took over the music booking as well.

Another role that Izzy played was to recommend musicians for jobs and even record deals. Some of the revivalists started to give guitar or banjo lessons, and Izzy would give their phone numbers to prospective students. He was scrupulously fair, and never asked for nor did he receive any commissions from the musicians whose services he recommended.

Izzy's shop was also a center for gossip, personal, musical, or otherwise. He wrote a column for *Sing Out!* That was outspoken about everything from music to politics and literature, and this sometimes irritated both his friends and enemies. He was even known to throw people out of his store either because they were obnoxious or simply because they irritated him. By 1965 rents on MacDougal Street had skyrocketed and Izzy moved from the street to nearby Sixth Avenue (Avenue of the Americas). Marc Silber, a musician and guitar repair specialist, opened a shop in the adjoining building. Izzy had always carried a handful of fretted instruments, but now a visit to the two shops allowed a musician to acquire new strings, old instruments, or new recordings. In 1973 Izzy sold the business and moved to Sweden. He opened a similar store in Stockholm, which closed in November, 2018, after Izzy turned ninety years of age. He passed away in Stockholm in February, 2019.

## Lessons and teachers

During the folk revival there were several key facilities that offered guitar and banjo lessons. The Metropolitan School of Music opened in 1934. During the 1950s and 1960s it featured many lessons in banjo, guitar, and as a host of other musical instruments. Jerry Silverman taught there, and he went on to become the most published author of musical instruction books and collections of folksongs for guitar and voice.

West 48th Street between 6th and 7th Avenues was a block that featured many musical instrument stores located from one end of the street to the other. Noah Wolfe Guitars also had teaching studios where lessons were taught. Both Happy Traum and his brother Artie taught there in the 1950s and 1960s before moving upstate to Woodstock. Today all the music stores are gone, victim to ever-rising rental rates. Happy went on to found Homespun Tapes, the largest company producing audio and video instructional tapes that specializes in folk music.

In the Village Jack Baker started teaching banjo and guitar in 1970. His teaching practice was located at Marc Silber's Fretted Instrument shop, next door to the Folklore Center. One of his fellow teachers was Stefan Grossman, performer, record company owner, and author of many blues instruction folios. He has had a long and distinguished career. Jack still teaches in Greenwich Village, but no longer at that location. Other teachers affiliated with him offer fiddle and mandolin lessons.

Kent Sidon founded the Guitar Workshop in 1963 in Great Neck Long Island. Soon afterward it moved to nearby Roslyn Heights, Long Island. One of the teachers, Jeff Warner, was the son of dedicated folksong collector Frank Warner, who has collected the folksong standard Tom Dooley from banjoist-singer Frank Proffitt in North Carolina. Kent died in 1976, but the school continued into the 1980s.

Lessons were an important way of teaching younger people folk music instrumental styles. They also were a source of much-needed income for the teachers.

# Bob Dylan

A young performer who called himself Bob Dylan started to hang out at Folk City and Mike Porco decided to hire him to sing in the fall of 1961. Porco operated the club under union contracts, and when Dylan told him that he was an orphan(!) Porco vouched for him at the union. At this point in his life Dylan was creating his own legend, steeped in mythological rather than actual adventures. The last thing that he wanted publicized was that he was the son of a middle-class Jewish family from Hibbing, Minnesota. In a matter of months *New York Times* folk columnist Robert Shelton had boosted Dylan's career with stories and reviews in that paper. When Dylan played harmonica on an album by folksinger Caroline Hester, he met legendary record producer and talent finder John Hammond. Dylan then signed a management agreement with notorious management shark-starmaker Albert Grossman.

Dylan's story has been told all too many times in volume after volume of carefully researched, obsessively detailed, or fan-based tributes. The quick summary is that Dylan's first album was a financial bomb but when Bob started writing his own topical material, and Peter, Paul & Mary successfully recorded it Dylan became the toast of the New York radical left. By 1965 Dylan turned to rock 'n' roll, and his 1965 appearance at the Newport Folk Festival with a very loud electric band sounded one of several death knells for the pop-folk revival. The rest of the obituary was delivered by the success of the Beatles.

In Dylan's many subsequent albums he has gone through a number of musical incarnations, ranging from country rock, to gospel music, his recent excursions into pop music standards and to occasional returns to his folk roots. It seems redundant to recapitulate all of these events, and his appearances with The Band, his participation in the *Traveling Wilburys*, or his continued concert appearances. The point that I am making here is that Dylan was in effect the leader of the singer-songwriter movement in New York, and he was in the forefront of the folk-rock movement. In his travels he gained millions of fans around the world, and alienated a small group of purists and radicals who had anointed him as the new Woody Guthrie.

## The New York scene: Venues and training grounds

New York had a number of non-professional venues that in effect constituted a training ground for would-be professional folksingers. Starting around 1950 folksingers would gather on Sunday afternoons in Washington Square Park, near New York University in Greenwich Village. By the mid-1950s such musicians as Roger Sprung, Marshall Brickman, Bob Brill, John Cohen, Jack Elliott, Billy Faier, Dick Greenhaus, Johnny Herald, Barry Kornfeld, Roger Lass, Paul Prestopino, Dick Rosmini, Happy Traum, Dave Van Ronk, Winnie Winston, and Bob Yellin would get together the square and sing all afternoon. All of these musicians went on into pursuing performing and recording careers in the succeeding years. Many of these musicians were better instrumentalists than singers, but they generated enough excitement and enthusiasm to interest and amuse the crowd of onlookers who gathered around the fountain in the square. Colorful characters would appear in the square from time to time, including a self-styled black cowboy named Lightnin' who did tricks with a long lasso rope.

Singing in the Square was somewhat factional in the sense that bluegrass musicians might be found in one area, old-time musicians in another, and singalong enthusiasts in another area around the fountain. After a long afternoon of singing, musicians would grab a light supper and go over to the American Youth Hostel on West 8th Street, a short walk away. Others would head to an apartment at 190 Spring Street where first Paul Clayton and later Roger Abrahams lived. Both of them were folklorists and collectors as well as performers and the Spring Street sessions tended to favor traditional music. Some of the people who gathered at Spring Street included Ellen Adler, Gina Glaser, Susie Shahn (who was the daughter of visual artist Ben Shahn), and an excellent banjo player named Luke Faust. Luke Faust later recorded with an experimental folk-rock band called *The Insect Trust*. Clayton made numerous recordings, and Abrahams did one solo album and *The Kossoy Sisters*, who recorded an album for Tradition Records, could sometimes be found at Spring Street or the AYH jams.

Once a week Tiny Ledbetter, lead Belly's niece, hosted evening jam sessions that were mostly a vehicle for aspiring blues enthusiasts to listen to, and/or play along with Reverend Gary Davis*. Davis was a remarkable guitarist and gospel singer who had moved to New York from South Carolina. He made a living playing on the streets of Harlem but he also taught guitar informally or formally to a host of white urban revivalists, including Barry Kornfeld, Dave Van Ronk, Roy Bookbinder, Ernie Hawkins, and Stefan Grossman. From time to time any of these musicians and many others, including Erik Darling and Woody Guthrie, would drift into the apartment

---

* Although almost all of Gary's students were white, Larry Johnson was a young black student of Gary's who went on to record several albums of his own.

to play with Gary. These sessions often included John Gibbon, an excellent guitarist who went on to become a psychologist, and Fred Gerlach. Fred was one of the few musicians at the time who specialized in twelve-string guitar. Gerlach had an encyclopedic knowledge of Lead Belly's style on the instruments, and he threw in a few variations of his own. He went on to record a couple of relatively obscure albums. Gerlach and Stefan Grossman each recorded Gary Davis singing and playing, and even preaching at a small church in the Bronx. Stefan also transcribed a number of Gary's songs and instrumental pieces, and compiled them in print.

Old-time pickers in New York gathered at Allan Block's leather sandal shop in the West Village to play fiddle and square-dance tunes. Allan's daughter Rory grew up around this beehive of old-time string band music, and she later became a well-known blues artist and singer-songwriter.

After 1958 Alan Lomax's downtown loft became a venue for music sessions, and another scene developed around Theodore Bikel, who sang songs in a number of foreign languages. He held occasional sessions at his apartment, and his Elektra recordings opened the door for Israeli singers Geula Gill and Ron and Nama, who also recorded for Elektra. Martha Schlamme also sang in a number of languages, and her repertoire moved folk music into the cabaret and art song area with songs by Bertold Brecht and Kurt Weill.

In addition to the various gatherings described above, there seemed to be a constant round of parties where would people would jam and sing. Some of these gatherings took place uptown. Three young musicians named Art Rosenbaum, Tam Gibbs, and Robby Robinson were in various stages of their academic careers at Columbia University. Robinson was a painter who had a graduate fellowship, Gibbs was a blues fanatic, and Rosenbaum was a young banjo player who later became an art professor at the University of Georgia. Rosenbaum continued his musical career, both as a live performer and by producing recordings by traditional musicians and compiling books of songs accompanied by his paintings and the photos by his wife, Margo Newmark Rosenbaum.

In the spring of 1960 I was at the opening act for Brownie McGhee and Sonny Terry at the Fifth Peg. This was the club that later became Gerde's Folk City. Brownie McGhee asked me to host a blues party after the show Brownie announced my address to the audience. When I arrived home, there were almost a hundred people camped on my doorstep! Ultimately this led to two more blues parties. Some of the musicians who attended this or two subsequent parties included Brownie and Sonny, John Lee Hooker, Bruce Langhorne (Mr. Tambourine Man), a jazz guitarist named Dave Woods, and Erik Darling. I literally did not know three-quarters of the people who were at the parties. I cite this experience simply to demonstrate how informal these social and musical networks were. If you bought a few six packs of beer and wine, you too could have a music party!

## Other clubs and coffeehouses

There were a number of other coffeehouses and clubs in the Village. The Café Au Go Go on Bleecker Street was open from 1964 to 1969. Judy Collins, John Lee Hooker, and a number of blues bands played there and owner Howard Solomon created the *Cafe Au Go Go Singers*, who recorded one album. The most notable thing about the band was that Richie Furay and Stephen Still were members. They later founded the *Buffalo Springfield* and Furay moved on to Poco, while Stills became a member of *Crosby, Stills and Nash*.

The Gaslight which was practically next door to the Folklore Center went through a series of owners, starting in 1956. John Mitchell, the second owner, hired mostly beat poets and folk singers were initially an afterthought. It was home to Len Chandler, a talented singer-songwriter and one of the few black musicians active in the New York folk scene. Initially musicians had to pass the hat to get paid, but Bob Dylan eventually was paid $75 a week. Dave Van Ronk and Tom Paxton were other musicians who played there. Mitchell sold the club to Clarence Hood and he and his son Sam and daughter-in-law Alix Dobkin ran the club on a less eccentric and more professional basis. Because people lived upstairs from the club, the audience was told not to applaud but to snap their fingers in appreciation. This gesture then was adopted in other venues that simply thought that this was a cool and appropriate way of expressing appreciation to the artist.

The Bitter End, opening its doors in 1961, was a club on Bleecker Street that projected more of a slightly uptown vibe than the other clubs did. It was also friendlier to pop-folk, which was not in vogue at either Gerde's Folk City or the Gaslight. The original owner was Fred Weintraub. When the folk boom calmed down, the club began to book comedians and pop and rock musicians. It continues today under a different ownership.

There were a number of "basket" coffeehouses on the scene. They employed performers paying them something like $3 a night, but allowed them to collect tips by passing the basket. These clubs included the *Four Winds*, the *Commons* (later changing its name to the *Fat Black Pussycat*), and the *Night Owl*, where *the Lovin' Spoonful* woodshedded their sound.

# Hootenanies

"Hootenany" was a word Woody Guthrie and Pete Seeger brought back from a Seattle sojourn in 1941. *The Almanac Singers* transformed the term onto a medium that featured group performances involving multiple artists and audience participation. People's Songs presented these events three or four times a year in New York starting after the end of the Second World War. After the demise of People's Songs People's Artists and then *Sing Out!* magazine assumed sponsorship of the hoots, as they were called. A number of performers including Leon Bibb, Laura Duncan, Betty Sanders, Pete Seeger, Jerry Silverman, and Osborne Smith were regular participants.

Hoots tended to feature politically oriented music, and they continued into the 1960s. Just as *Sing Out!* itself became de-politicized, the word and the events became removed from their original radical connotations. Gerde's Folk City for example, had Monday night hoots that bore no connection to politics. By the time of the Hootenany TV show in 1963, the word had lost its original connotations. The show honored the blacklisting of Pete Seeger by refusing to hire him. Occasionally the word hootenanny is still used today in its older, political context.

# Radio shows and journalists

Besides Oscar Brand's aforementioned radio show, George Lorrie, Skip Weshner, Bob Fasse, Cynthia Gooding, Henriette Yurchenko, and banjo virtuoso Billy Faier all had their own radio shows. Although these shows were consigned to non-commercial stations like WNYC or WBAI, they did provide a forum for folk music and folk musicians.

*The Village Voice* was the earliest alternative weekly paper published in the United States. It was founded in 1955. *The Voice* covered the folk scene sporadically and had one regular writer who despised the folk music scene. When Robert Shelton began to write reviews for the *New York Times* in the late 1950s, it became apparent that the audience for folk music was expanding well beyond Greenwich Village. Shelton was part booster, part fan, and part-time music critic. Shelton was a stringer—paid by the *Times* on a space basis rather than being a regular on-staff music critic. He supplemented his income by writing liner notes, using assumed notes, because he sometimes reviewed the same albums for which he had written the original notes. Lawyers call this a conflict of interest. Later he became the editor of the short-lived *Hootenanny Magazine*. Shelton's lengthy biography of Bob Dylan, *No Direction Home*, was written in 1986 and revised in 2011.

*Caravan* was a folk fan magazine founded by Lee Hoffman in 1957. It was a combination folk gossip column and cheerleader for folk music. She soon became tired of putting out the magazine, which was a time-consuming labor of love. Billy Faier took over the editing tasks, and brought a more serious tone to the magazine. By 1960 the magazine had folded. Shaw found that she missed having a journalistic outlet and she published and edited a few issues of a mimeographed fan magazine called *Gardyloo*. Other folk music publications located outside New York are discussed in the next chapter.

## Diversity and fragmentation

The purist–traditionalist–folk faction would never have acknowledged it, but the pop-folk explosion opened up opportunities for virtually everyone on the New York folk scene. The kings of the traditional music scene were the New Lost City Ramblers. Ironically, they formed in 1958 the same year that the Kingston Trio hit the jackpot with their hit song *Tom Dooley*.

Rambler John Cohen was a photographer as well as a musician. He recorded Roscoe Holcomb and made a movie about him called *The High Lonesome Sound*. He later wrote a combination book and photo essay about Roscoe. Cohen went on to make movies about traditional musicians, as well as publish his photos of a young Bob Dylan. Dylan seemed to fascinate Cohen, who conducted a lengthy interview with Bob published in *Sing Out!* This was rather peculiar given Cohen's negative attitudes toward commercial music.

Mike Seeger recorded Piedmont songster Elizabeth Cotten. Her odyssey is one of the stranger stories in the folk revival. Cotten helped Ruth Crawford Seeger find her daughter Peggy who went missing in a Washington, DC, department store. The Seeger family then hired Cotten as a maid. One day Elizabeth picked up Peggy's guitar, playing it left-handed and upside down. The family was astonished to find that their maid was an original and excellent composer and instrumentalist. Mike recorded an album with Cotten and her tune *Freight Train* became a hit record in England for Nancy Whiskey. It also became a staple among urban revivalists, and has been recorded dozens of times, including versions by Joan Baez; the Grateful Dead; Peter, Paul & Mary; and contemporary singer-songwriter Laura Viers.

Mike Seeger also recorded the influential album *American Banjo Tunes in Scruggs Style* in 1956. It featured Earl Scruggs's older brother Junie, pre-Scruggs bluegrass banjoist Snuffy Jenkins, and a very young Eric Weissberg.

Although the Ramblers did not necessarily recreate the sounds of old records on a note-for-note basis, they tended to fuse various traditional styles in any one song. Creative differences developed by 1960 when Tom Paley wanted to return to playing music on a part-time basis and preferred a more spontaneous and improvisational approach than the other Ramblers did at that time. In 1961 Paley left the group and was replaced by Tracy Schwarz. The group continued to tour and record, and to regroup for reunion shows, but some of their activities were limited by Cohen's day job as a professor in the fine arts department at Purchase College, SUNY.

By the end of the 1960s, bluegrass and old-time musicians had separated into different camps, and there was relatively little interaction between them. Old-time music, sometimes called string band music, generally utilized the fiddle as the lead instrument. The guitar kept the rhythm going and the more proficient players added bass runs. The banjo also mostly supported the fiddle although some of the early virtuoso players, like Charlie Poole, played more modern styles that were influenced by non-folk ragtime players like Vess Ossman or Fred Van Eps. Some bands used two fiddles or included the mandolin. Old-time music was often used as the back-up for square dances.

Bluegrass added the acoustic bass to the mix and it often included the mandolin and sometimes the dobro. In early bluegrass, although the fiddle remained important, all instruments were expected to play solos. Bluegrass also featured more intense vocal harmony and usually the singing included high-voiced baritones and an upper-register tenor above that. The tempos of many of the songs were rapid. The banjo was now played in the fast and percussive three-finger style popularized by Earl Scruggs.

There was a certain amount of mutual antipathy between practitioners of the two styles among urban revivalists. Old-time musicians thought that their music was closer to "the true vine," while bluegrassers felt that old-time music was boring. These differences were also reflected in the practitioners' choice of instruments. Bluegrass instruments were intended to be played at high volumes. Old-time musicians prized older, vintage instruments, although bluegrass players also favored specific models like the F5 Gibson mandolin, or the pre-

Second World War Martin D 28 guitars. There were very few musicians who were as versatile as Mike Seeger, who seemed relatively comfortable playing in both of these styles.

## Bluegrass in New York

The first bluegrass band in New York was a trio called *The Shanty Boys*, formed in 1957. Roger Sprung was the banjo player, probably the first bluegrass banjo picker in the City. John Cohen's brother Mike played guitar and Lionel Kilberg played washtub bass. The group were never full-time professionals but played regularly in Washington Square on Sunday afternoons. Sprung was one of the first New Yorkers to go south to the various festivals that featured bluegrass, such as the one in Union Grove, North Carolina. Roger had recorded for Stinson Records in 1953 with a group called the *Folksay Trio*. The other two members, Bob Carey and Erik Darllng, later formed *the Tarriers*.

The *Greenbriar Boys* formed when multi-instrumentalist Eric Weissberg, banjoist Bob Yellin, and guitarist-vocalist Johnny Herald were students at the University of Wisconsin in 1958. Weissberg left the group in 1959 because Yellin was doing the lion's share of the banjo work and Eric had been consigned to playing the mandolin. Yellin came from a very musical family and he had studied violin, voice, piano, and trumpet as a child. His older brother Peter became a renowned jazz saxophone player. Herald was an excellent guitarist and one of the few early singers in New York who captured the bluegrass vocal sound. Eric was replaced by Ralph Rinzler, and that trio performed from 1959 to 1964, recording three influential albums for Vanguard Records. Yellin was a crisp and fast banjo player who had won several banjo contests at Union Grove and Rinzler was a steady anchor for the group with his mandolin playing, back-up singing, and extensive knowledge of folk music. The group also performed and recorded with Diane Edmondson during the height of the folk-pop boom and also appeared on the ABC *Hootenanny* TV show.

In 1964 Rinzler left the group and went on to briefly manage Doc Watson and Bill Monroe, coordinated talent for the Newport Folk Foundation and directed the music festivals of the Smithsonian Institute in Washington, DC. By introducing Watson and Monroe to urban and college audiences, Rinzler played a seminal role in spreading the influence of traditional music and bluegrass. When Rinzler left, he was replaced by the spectacular and idiosyncratic mandolinist

Frank Wakefield and fiddler Jim Buchanan. Wakefield was a Tennessee native, and Buchanan hailed from North Carolina. This may have been the first band to combine urban revivalists with "authentic" traditional players.

Another New York-based bluegrass band was the *New York Ramblers,* who won the band contest at the Union Grove festival, and appeared at the Newport Folk Festival in 1965. The band included a number of musicians who went on to musical careers in various musical styles. The lineup included David Grisman on mandolin, Sandy Rothman and Jody Stecher on guitar, Fred Weisz on fiddle, and Winnie Winston on banjo. Eventually Grisman played everything from jug band music to Django-ish jazz; Rothman became a record producer and did a number of projects with Jerry Garcia of the Grateful Dead; Jody Stecher studied East Indian music and is a fixture on the old-time music scene in Berkeley; Weisz played in the *Goose Creek Symphony* country-rock band; and Winnie Winston turned to pedal steel guitar and wrote an instructional book for that instrument.

The Shanty Boys and the Greenbriar Boys were highly visible on the New York scene and because of their influence, more urban revivalists developed an interest in bluegrass. Other New York pickers of the 1960s were Steve Arkin, who later played with Bill Monroe, and Roger Lass, who did not pursue a career as a professional musician. An excellent fiddler named Tex Logan lived in New Jersey and had a day job as an engineer. Another fiddler was Gene Lowinger, who sometimes played in the Square and at jam sessions. He later played with Bill Monroe, and pursued a career as a photo-journalist. Mandolinist Andy Statman was a presence on the scene before turning to a career in klezmer music. Banjoist Marc Horowitz has drifted in and out of performing and teaching careers and guitarist (and banjoist) Steve Mandell was the guitar player on the hit album *Dueling Banjos.* Paul Prestopino is a multi-instrumentalist who has also worked in recording studios as a maintenance and mastering engineer. He has recorded with the *Chad Mitchell Trio,* Peter, Paul & Mary, Tom Paxton, and plays in various bands and for contra dances today.

## Blues in the City

There were a handful of authentic blues musicians on the New York scene. Although Josh White became a sophisticated cabaret artist and concert performer, no one could question his musical apprenticeship with a variety of blind singers in the Carolinas. Brownie McGhee and Sonny Terry were born respectively, in Tennessee and North Carolina, and both had been influenced by the legendary Blind Boy Fuller. Gary Davis did not perform blues in public, but did record some blues and ragtime pieces, and his guitar accompaniments were closer to these musical genres than the gospel songs that he was singing. Both Davis and McGhee taught many white urban revivalists. Ralph Willis was a Piedmont blues artist who relocated to New York. Although from time to time he recorded with McGhee and Terry, Willis had little impact with the young white blues enthusiasts that seemed to cluster around Davis, and to a lesser extent, McGhee. Alec Seward recorded with Louis Hayes using the sobriquet Guitar Slim and Jelly Belly, and he moved to New York City in 1924, Josh White in 1932, Brownie McGhee and Sonny Terry in 1942, and Ralph Willis during the 1940s. Seward recorded with Louis Hayes using the sobriquets *Guitar Slim and Jelly Belly, the Blues Servant Boys*, and *the Back Porch Boys*. Seward also recorded with Terry and McGhee. White, McGhee, and Terry all performed and recorded widely not only in the United States, but also in Europe.

## The white blues boys

Dave Van Ronk was one of the first white blues singers in New York. Through his regular performances at the Gaslight, his numerous recordings over the years, his friendships and mentoring relationships with such notables as Bob Dylan, as well as his work as a guitar teacher, he influenced many of the urban wannabe blues artists. Van Ronk was only an occasional although excellent composer but he was a skilled interpreter of other people's songs. He even recorded some probing emotional versions of some Joni Mitchell songs. Possessed of a harsh, rather growly voice, on the surface he would not have seemed suited to such a role but in fact he performed it with subtlety and grace. Dave began recording in 1959 and continued to record for some forty-five years. The 2013 movie, *Inside Llewyn Davis* is very loosely based on Dave Van Ronk. In 2005 Van Ronk's student and mentee Elijah Wald with Dave's help compiled a memoir of Dave's life called *The Mayor of MacDougal Street*. This entertaining and informative book is probably the best single portrait of the New York folk scene.

John Hammond Jr. was the son of the famous record producer John Hammond. His 1962 Vanguard recordings influenced many young aspiring white blues singers. Hammond is not a composer but a musician who interpreted many blues classics, first as a soloist and from time to time with blues bands. He initially played acoustic guitar but turned electric in the band albums.

Happy Traum, who studied with Brownie McGhee, is better known for his blues instructional books than for his performances or recordings. He later founded *Homespun Tapes*, a leading producer of instructional videos. Danny Kalb was an aggressive blues guitarist who did some session work and who formed *the Blues Project*, a blues rock-band. John Sebastian was a young blues harmonica player and guitarist whose father was a classical harmonica virtuoso. During the early 1960s John spent a great deal of time hanging out in Greenwich Village, and informally studying the blues techniques of country blues artists. In 1963 Elektra Records put together the *Even Dozen Jug Band*. Their goal was to compete with Boston-based Jim Kweskin and his *Jug Band*, whose Vanguard recordings appealed to the urban revivalists. Besides Sebastian, the band included Maria D'Amato, who later married Geoff Muldaur from Kweskin's band, David Grisman, Stefan Grossman, Steve Katz, Joshua Rifkin, and Peter Siegel. Although not much came of this project, every one of these musicians pursued careers as musicians, record producers, composers, and band leaders.

Mark Spoelstra was both a blues guitarist and a singer-songwriter. In the early 1960s he was part of the Greenwich Village folk revival, and he recorded several albums for Folkways Records. Mark was a good musician who managed to develop excellent control over the twelve-string beast. Because he was a conscientious objector, he performed alternative service in Fresno, California. He spent the rest of his life in California, eventually becoming a minister and recording two albums of gospel music.

I have already mentioned John Gibbon, who was one of Gary Davis's first students. Gibbon recorded one album in England but pursued a career as a psychologist. Ian Buchanan was an excellent blues guitarist and singer who was an early influence on Jorma Kaukonen of the Jefferson Airplane. Buchanan did some recording, but his career was stymied by a fall that left him as a paraplegic. Buchanan may have been the best vocalist of the lot. Nicky Thatcher was a legendary and soulful blues singer and guitarist cited in Erik Darling's autobiography. Thatcher never did much professional work but performed in London and was a fixture at New York parties and jam sessions, until he was overcome by his heroin habit.

Another group of young revivalists became determined to promote ragtime music on the guitar. The difficulty was that ragtime is a complex style even on the piano and it presents more difficult technical problems for the guitar. Guitarists

Dave Laidman and Eric Schoenberg made finger-busting transcriptions of ragtime guitar pieces for guitar, and recorded an album of them. Dave Van Ronk was less of a purist but his guitar arrangements of such tunes as the *St. Louis Tickle* were more playable for the medium-to-advanced-level guitarist. Stefan Grossman also transcribed and recorded a number of ragtime arrangements for guitar. Subsequently Joshua Rifkin made an important album of Scott Joplin's piano rags, which he played on the piano at the slow tempos that Joplin advocated. In 1971 Grossman established the Kicking Mule record label with Ed Denson, and they recorded a number of European guitarists who played ragtime guitar.

## Other artists in the New York revival

Hedy West came to New York from her native Georgia to study for a master's degree in the theater program at Columbia University. Hedy was the daughter of radical poet and union organizer Don West. Like Jean Ritchie she had learned folk songs from her family and from other traditional musicians. She began to perform at concerts, and recorded two albums for Vanguard. Her song *500 Miles*, which she had originally learned from her grandmother and had rearranged partly because she hadn't remembered the exact original melody, went on to become one of the most popular songs in the folk revival. The Journeymen made the first commercial recording of the song, but most people learned the song from the Peter, Paul & Mary version on an album that sold several million copies. Many other recorded versions of the song also exist including a hit country version by Bobby Bare, who added a recitation and rewrote some of the lyrics. Hedy was one of the few people in the entire folk revival with a legitimate claim to the copyright of a traditional song. Because Hedy was a well-trained musician who had studied flute and voice, she brought some original stylings to her music, especially the syncopation that she sometimes used in her banjo playing. Some of the folk purists in New York really objected to such instrumental flourishes but because Hedy had the traditional background that they lacked, she was allowed to skate for committing such sins.

Robin Roberts sang English and Irish ballads. She recorded for Tradition and Stinson Records and performed in the New York area. The folk revival was not particularly kind to ballad singers, emphasizing performers who presented themselves in a more dramatic instrumental or vocal manner. Consequently, Robert's influence was not commensurate with her vocal talents.

Carolyn Hester was a folksinger who came to New York from Texas. She did an album for Columbia but when Bob Dylan played harmonica on it, her producer became more interested in Dylan than in her work. Her other bad piece of luck career-wise, was her marriage to novelist-songwriter Dick Farina. He was a talented songwriter and vocalist, who, like his friend Bob Dylan tended to invent his identity in accordance with his own fantasies. When he encountered the beautiful Mimi Baez, Joan's sister, he left Hester and formed a duo with Mimi. They subsequently recorded for Vanguard.

Texas-born singer Hally Wood (Faulk) was active in the early days of People's Songs. She recorded two solo ten-inch LPs, one for Elektra and the other for Stinson. Hally had a harsh but very expressive voice and on her Elektra album she recorded unaccompanied songs that were a bit outside what was popular in the revival. The Stinson album featured the superb banjo and guitar playing of Joe Jaffe, one of the early but little-remembered folk instrumentalists in New York. Wood was a skilled musician and she transcribed the music for the New Lost City Ramblers songbook. After a 1970s sojourn in Puerto Rico, she returned to the United States and made one self-produced album before her death in 1989.

Connecticut native Judy Roderick started her performing career during the late 1950s and early 1960s while attending the University of Colorado. She was a small woman with a powerful voice, particularly adept at singing blues but also quite capable of singing folk and country music. She came to New York in 1962, and landed a Columbia Records contract. Her first album was produced by jazz-pop pianist-songwriter Bobby Scott. He attempted to turn Judy into a white Billie Holiday accompanying her with New York jazz musicians. The album didn't sell and a second album was tabled when Judy and Scott were unable to agree on its musical direction.

In 1965 Judy recorded an album called *Woman Blue* for Vanguard. The Music Hound Essential Folk Album Guide describes it as "some very original treatment of original material." Unfortunately, by this time the folk boom had ended and the album was largely overlooked, although it was later reissued on CD. She returned to Colorado and recorded one folk-rock album for Atlantic with the band *60 Million Buffalo*. That album never caught fire and Judy moved to Montana where she died in 1992. There's an old cliché that timing is everything, and had Judy's Vanguard album come out in 1962, she might well have become one of the better-known folk revivalists. In the music business, talent is definitely not everything.

Karen Dalton was one of the more enigmatic artists in the folk revival. She was originally from Oklahoma, and came to New York City in 1960. She sang in coffeehouses, and recorded an album for Capitol Records in 1969. While in the Village Karen completely changed her vocal style. Earlier she sang quite loud, and excelled at singing wild mountain harmony. From her Village days until the end of her life she began to sing very quietly with a hoarse vocal delivery and was essentially promoted as a white Billie Holiday.

After her Village days she moved back and forth from Colorado to Woodstock, New York. She cut a second album with bassist Harvey Brooks in 1971 in Woodstock and did some occasional touring. Since her death she has for whatever reason become something of a feminist icon. Her two albums have been rereleased, and there has been a steady flow of new albums that are extracted from various coffeehouse performances. In 2015 her friend guitarist Peter Walker circulated a number of Karen's poems to various artists, and Tompkins Square Records released an album of these songs performed by various artists, including Patty Griffin and Lucinda Williams. Karen is better known in Europe than in the United States. There is a French graphic novel about her, as well as a biography, and several documentary or impressionistic films about her life. Karen is certainly more popular now than at any time during her lifetime.

Richie Havens was one of the few black artists on the Greenwich Village scene. He was a native New Yorker who became famous because the producers of the 1969 Woodstock Festival begged him to do an extended set to open the festival when several bands were late due to traffic jams. Richie would have been a perfect Americana artist, because his singing utilized elements of folk, rock, and rhythm and blues and had an unusual and dynamic guitar style.

Lisa Kindred was originally from Buffalo but was active in both New York and Boston in the mid-1960s. Her first album was made for Vanguard Records and released in 1965. Through a bizarre set of circumstances her second album was delayed for four years after the master tapes were stolen. They then were released by Warner Brothers-Reprise Records under the aegis of harmonica player Mel Lyman's Family. The album was billed as a Lyman Family record crediting Kindred only as the vocalist for the band! Subsequently Kindred moved to the Bay area. She works with a blues band and continues to perform and record. Besides performing blues, she sings songs by various singer-songwriters.

America has never had a widespread sophisticated cabaret scene like the one in France that has spawned such artists as Jacques Brel and George Brassens. Will Holt, who died in 2015, would have fit comfortably into such a world.

Holt's connection to the folk scene was largely through his songs *Lemon Tree* and *Raspberries, Strawberries*. These songs were recorded by major pop-folk groups, as well as many other artists bands. Holt performed as a soloist, and also performed songs by Kurt Weill and Berthold Brecht with international singer Martha Schlamme, as well as wrote several Broadway and off-Broadway shows.

## The Folksinger's Guild

You might assume that given the radical political ideology of many of the urban revivalists, that they would be actively involved with the musician's union, the American Federation of Musicians (AFM). In fact, many of the folksingers were either not union members or joined only because their recording contracts required them to do so. Major label agreements specify that all artists must join either the AFM or, if they are vocalists who do not play an instrument, AFTRA-SAG (American Federation of Radio and Television Artists-Screen Actors Guild). This is not because the record companies are pro-union, but because their agreements with these unions specify that all recording artists must join the union. All of the folk musicians who did extensive studio work were union members and received union wages for playing on recording sessions. As more of the young revivalists became professionals, they began to feel that they really had no organization that would protect their interests, because the union had little knowledge about the folk scene. Most New York coffeehouses, for example, paid pitiful wages, and it became customary for musicians to pass a basket to implore the audience for tips. Many union officials were scornful of folksingers, because they themselves were swing musicians who played from musical scores and many folksingers did not know how to read music.

As a reaction to the circumstances described above, in 1958 Dave Van Ronk, Roy Berkeley, Dick Greenhaus, and several other New York revivalists organized a sort of Folksinger's Union that they called the Folksinger's Guild. The organization tried to get folksingers to avoid doing free performances, and they attempted to establish a $5 minimum wage at Village coffeehouses. This may seem laughable but it was more than performers were being paid at the time.

The Guild sponsored several concerts by its members but the initiators discovered that folksingers were not an easy group to organize. The Guild disintegrated when its members violated their own rules. Most of the members were more interested in playing and performing music than in holding meetings and actively supporting one another.

## The revivalists turn pro

By the late 1950s a number of urban revivalists realized that they could become full-time professional musicians. I met Dave Van Ronk in Washington Square around 1958. He had been a merchant seaman, and had just come off a ship. He was astounded at the number of musicians and fans gathering in the square, and asked me whether it was possible to make a living "doing this." I responded that it was, possibly, if you combined some guitar instruction, performances, and recording.

Erik Darling was highly respected as a guitarist, banjoist, and singer-songwriter. He was one of the few artists who seemed to move back and forth between the commercial and more tradition-oriented folk worlds. In addition to his recordings with the Tarriers and the Rooftop Singers, he replaced Pete Seeger in the Weavers in 1957. Erik was one of the first revivalists to do studio work, playing on a number of recordings by Ed McCurdy.

Other revivalists who made their way into the world of studio work included Bruce Langhorne, a very creative young black guitarist who recorded with Bob Dylan, Odetta, and Peter, Paul & Mary, Dick Rosmini, Paul Prestopino, Barry Kornfeld, and myself. Eric Weissberg was the premier folkie studio musician of us all. A bass student at Juilliard, Eric replaced Darling in the Tarriers. Weissberg, Kornfeld, and I all played on a number of pop-folk records recorded under the names of other artists including the Brothers Four, New Christy Minstrels, and Peter, Paul & Mary. We were not generally credited in the album notes in order to preserve the illusion that the band themselves had played these instrumental parts.

There were also a number of musicians who moved into other professions. Roger Abrahams became a noted folklorist who wrote a number of well-respected books about folklore and folk music. Lee Haring, who was a talented banjoist, singer, and arranger, published some instrumental method books and rehearsed various vocal groups. He later became an English professor at Brooklyn College. Robin Christianson was a singer with a large musical repertoire who opted to become a book salesman.

## Early singer-songwriters, political and otherwise

Although it's a bit of an oversimplification, the singer-songwriters could be divided into two groups: the politically oriented writers and those who specialized in writing songs that were either more personal or oriented toward commercial success.

On a trip to England, Pete Seeger observed a number of young singer-songwriters who were writing topical songs about political issues. As mentioned earlier, *Sing Out!* had become increasingly a political and turned into a more general journal of the folk music revival. Seeger discussed this problem with Agnes "Sis" Cunningham and her husband Gordon Freisen. Sis had been a member of the Almanac Singers, and Gordon was a published writer who could be counted on for editing and proofreading chores. They agreed to start *Broadside Magazine* in 1962. The concept was to create an outlet for political songwriting. It was put together in their small public housing apartment. The initial major support came from Israel Young, who bought a large number of copies of the first issue to sell at his Folklore Center. Pete Seeger also offered some financial support.

The magazine barely survived financially but it was a labor of love. It lasted for twenty-six years. The importance of *Broadside* was that it provided a forum for a group of young singer-songwriters who often had no outlet for their work. Gil Turner, who wrote the folk standard *Carry It On*, was one of the early strong supporters of *Broadside*. Since he was an MC at Gerde's open microphone night, he brought many of his friends to the uptown "office" of the magazine. Some of the early performers whose songs appeared in *Broadside* include Bob Dylan (during his political phase), Malvina Reynolds, a San Francisco singer-songwriter best known for her songs *Little Boxes* and *What Have They Done to the Rain*, Phil Ochs, Tom Paxton, Len Chandler, Bonnie Dobson, Peter La Farge (author of the song *Ira Hayes*), and Mark Spoelstra. Other songs published in the magazine came from the pens of Eric Andersen, Peggy Seeger, Julius Lester, Janis Ian, Buffy Ste. Marie, Nina Simone, Ernie Marrs, and Lucinda Williams. Oak Publications also issued several songbooks of the songs from the magazine. Folkways released an excellent set of recordings with detailed information about the songs that includes a history of the magazine and eighty-nine songs.

There were a number of outstanding singer-songwriters in Greenwich Village. Fred Neil, who held forth at the Café Wha, wrote *Everybody's Talking*, and co-authored the Roy Orbison hit *The Candyman* with uptown songwriter

Beverly Ross. Several of his other songs, including *The Other Side of This Life*, *Blues on the Ceiling*, and *The Dolphin* were popular with other artists. Tim Hardin, originally from Eugene, Oregon, lived variously in New York and Woodstock and wrote Bobby Darin's hit song *If I Were a Carpenter*, as well as folk standards *The Reason to Believe*, *Don't Make Promises*, *The Lady Came from Baltimore*, and *Misty Roses*. Neil and Hardin also recorded several albums without much success.

Although Eric Andersen had some involvement with Broadside, most of his songs were romantic fantasies, like *Violets of Dawn*. Andersen toured and recorded for Vanguard, and continues to tour today. Other singer-songwriters on the scene were David (Cohen) Blue, advertised as the "most authentic" Dylan imitator, and Paul Seibel whose most popular song was *Louise*. Tim Buckley was a spectacular-voiced singer-songwriter whose career fell victim to his drug habit, which also cut down Tim Hardin.

## The instrumentalists

A number of innovative instrumentalists were part of the urban revival. Some of them have already been mentioned in the context of bands that they formed or studio work, but their ambitions generally extended beyond playing on other people's recordings. Chapter 15 will discuss these instrumentalists, the development of "American primitive" guitar style, and the various creative musicians who have transformed the folk music revival by bringing musical influences from a myriad of styles and genres.

## Folk-rock

Folk-rock will be covered in detail in Chapter 11. Some of the important early folk-rock artists were middle-period Bob Dylan, John Sebastian's group, the Lovin' Spoonful, and the mostly Canadian group, *The Band*, which was based in Woodstock.

# 8

# Beyond the Big Apple: The Coffeehouses, Folk Music Organizations, and Folk Music Instrument Shops in Boston, Chicago, Denver, Los Angeles, Philadelphia, the Pacific Northwest, San Francisco, and Toronto

During the 1960s virtually every city of any size had something of a folk scene. In this chapter I will look into some of the more influential scenes. The reader should take into consideration that although certain artists are often identified with a particular scene, there was a great deal of back and forth traffic between different cities. Odetta, for example, started out in San Francisco, achieved popularity in Chicago, and then moved to New York. She was an important figure on all of those scenes, and she also traveled widely. Placing her as a Chicago or New York artist isn't really logical.

There were certain commonalities between all these scenes. There were always performance venues, whether they were bars, coffeehouses, or major folk festivals. There were generally, although not always, one or two music stores where professionals and aspiring players hung out, often taught lessons, and networked with other musicians to search for other performing gigs. In some cities, especially Chicago, there was a folk music school that taught lessons. Professionals worked at such venues and aspiring professionals and dedicated amateurs learned about the music at such facilities. In a number of these cities there were key radio shows which served to bring folk music to the attention of a wide audience and provide an outlet for performers.

## Boston and Cambridge

Eric Von Schmidt and Jim Rooney have written an entire book, *Baby Let Me Follow You Down,* about the Boston–Cambridge folk scene of the 1950s and

1960s. The book details the various personalities, clubs, and musicians on the scene, centering on the Club 47 in Cambridge.

There are more colleges in the metropolitan area surrounding Boston than anywhere else in the United States. Consequently, it is of no great surprise that there were a large number of participants in the area's version of the folk revival. Von Schmidt himself was a blues singing visual artist who functioned as a source of songs for the young revivalists. Wearing his other hat, he went on to design many of their album covers. Rooney was a singer, guitarist and author who broke into the national limelight when he recorded an album with his friend Bill Keith, one of the fathers of the so-called melodic banjo style. Rooney subsequently has had a long career as a record producer, music publisher, and part-time vocalist.

Jim Kweskin is a guitarist and singer who started a successful jug band in 1963. A number of its members went and pursued other music careers in later years and Kweskin himself still performs and records today. Geoff Muldaur has a unique blues sensibility with his light, airy vibrato. He later made records with his wife Maria (D'Amato), studied arranging at the Berklee College of Music, and writes chamber–folk–jazz musical arrangements today. In 1973 Maria scored a major pop hit with the eccentric song *Midnight at the Oasis*, written by David Nichtern. Kweskin's original banjo player was Bob Siggins, who was replaced by Bill Keith. Keith's musical adventures included playing his new banjo style with Bill Monroe, mastering the pedal steel guitar, and creating tuning pegs for the banjo that allowed a player alter the tuning of the instrument while playing with a simple gesture of the left hand. Fritz Richmond played the jug and the washboard bass. He went on to become a recording engineer in Los Angeles and to play on numerous recordings. Mel Lyman played harmonica with the band, but quit when one of his lengthy harmonica solos was cut off by a vocal, as described in the Von Schmidt and Rooney book. He was replaced by the mysterious Bruno Wolfe, a nom de plume for David Simon. Lyman became something of a prophet, spiritual guide, and avatar in Boston, and operated a construction company that built houses. Kweskin still works with that company today.

The Kweskin band was just the tip of the Boston iceberg. Flamenco guitarist Rolf Kahn moved from Berkeley to Boston. Tony Saletan was a performer in the Pete Seeger mold, expert at getting audiences to sing along with him. Peggy Seeger, Pete's half-sister was a music student at Radcliffe College in the mid-1950s and she often performed at jam sessions at a house known as Old Joe Clarke.

Because she grew up in a house where her mother was transcribing music for some of the Lomax's songbooks, Peggy had an enormous repertoire. Inventive instrumentalist Sandy Bull attended music school in Boston before returning to New York. Tom Rush was a student at Harvard University, and he became famous for recording songs written by other songwriters, notably Joni Mitchell. Both Taj Mahal and Buffy Ste. Marie were students at the University of Massachusetts at Amherst. Mahal has credited his days hanging out at the Club 47 and later at the Ash Grove in Los Angeles as basic building blocks in the development of his music after some years working in Los Angeles he has returned to Boston.

In the blues world Al Wilson, later a member of the blues band *Canned Heat*, was a music student in Boston. Chris Smithers, who became one of the most convincing of the white blues artists and an excellent singer-songwriter began a lengthy performing and recording career which continues today. Another important white blues artist was Paul Geremia. Fanatic blues enthusiast Dick Waterman was beginning his career as a blues entrepreneur, booking many of the rediscovered blues artists of the 1960s. He was also managing a young blues singer named Bonnie Raitt. Raitt was a Radcliffe College student just beginning a long and distinguished career as a blues singer-guitarist and singer-songwriter that continues to this day.

Robert L. Jones gave up his singing career to become a concert promoter working for impresario George Wein. Wein organized the original Newport Folk and Jazz Festivals, and many other festivals and concerts around the world. Bobby Neuwirth is a performer-songwriter and a road pal of Bob Dylan. Neuwirth is a visual artist who studied at the Boston Museum School in the 1950s. He has done his own album covers and exhibited at various galleries. Over the years he has continued to be involved with Dylan, helping to organize the Rolling Thunder tours.

Juan Candido Washington majored in theater arts at Emerson College in the mid-1950s, and he played at coffeehouses under the name Jackie Washington. He recorded four albums for Vanguard. Washington was born in Puerto Rico, and he traveled south to work in voter registration. He was an assistant to Martin Luther King but then pursued an acting career, working with various theater groups in New York under the name Jack Landron.

Debby Green was an excellent guitarist and singer who never pursued a professional career and later married Eric Andersen. Joan and Mimi Baez often held forth at the Club 47. Joan's first album, *Folksingers' Round Harvard Square*, featured Boston performers Bill Wood and Ted Alevizos. Other local musicians included Jerry Corbett, later to join Jesse Colin Young's folk-rock band *The Youngbloods*, and Paul Arnoldi, a student at Harvard who was a native of Wyoming. Arnoldi was a singer-songwriter who had a brief run on the pop music charts with his song *One Note Man*.

## Bluegrass in Boston

In 1952 the Lilly Brothers, two West Virginia bluegrass musicians featuring brothers Bea and Everett, moved to Boston. They formed a group called *the Confederate Mountaineers*. Bea played guitar and Everett the mandolin, and they added Tex Logan on fiddle and Don Stover on banjo. They performed on the WCOP Hayloft Jamboree, and various Boston clubs, including the Hillbilly Ranch. They changed the name of the band to *the Lilly Brothers* and appeared at concerts and folk festivals until Everett's son died in an auto accident and they left the Boston area. Along the way they recorded for Folkways and Prestige Records, and were an important influence on various young bluegrass aspirants. Don Stover gained a national reputation as an important banjoist, while Logan, who had earned a PhD in electrical engineering, continued to played part-time while working at Bell Labs.

*The Charles Valley Boys* were a young bluegrass band influenced by the Lilly brothers. Three band members were students at Harvard, and the fourth at MIT. In 1961 they did an album partly recorded in England and Cambridge, and in 1962 record producer Paul Rothchild produced an album for his own label, which was reissued on Prestige Records in 1962. A second album on the label included fiddler Tex Logan, mentioned above in relation to the Lilly Brothers. Various musicians were in and out of the group including Fritz Richmond on washtub bass, and Joe Val on mandolin and vocals. Rothchild became a producer for Elektra Records, and in that capacity, he produced an album of Beatles songs in bluegrass style in 1966.

Peter Childs was a young instrumentalist who played dobro and guitar with a short-lived bluegrass band called the *Knoblich Upper Ten Thousand*. Peter Rowan was another young musician who went on to play with Bill Monroe, some of Grateful Dead leader Jerry Garcia's side projects, and a folk-rock band called *Earth Opera* that included mandolin player David Grisman. They recorded two albums for Elektra in 1968 and 1969, but broke up because of a lack of success.

## Venues and other matters

There were many clubs in the Boston and Cambridge area. These included Tulla's Coffee Grinder, The Golden Vanity, The Jolly Beaver, The Orleans, The Unicorn, Turk's Head, The Loft, and the Café Yana. The Club 47 eventually turned into the Club Passim. It remains open today, and also has a music school associated with it.

Manny Greenhill was an ex-union organizer who promoted concerts with local and touring artists and became Joan Baez's manager. Greenhill was a dedicated radical with a reputation for honesty, and he also represented Pete Seeger in Boston during some of Seeger's blacklisted years. He and Baez ended their business relationship in the mid-1970s, and Greenhill moved his booking agency to southern California.

Boston boasted a folk magazine called *Boston Broadside*. It was founded in 1962 by David Wilson, and lasted some ten years. The magazine featured articles, record reviews and a calendar section, and several regular columns.

Earth Opera was a folk-psychedelic rock group formed by Peter Rowan and Joan Baez left for northern California in the mid-1960s. During the 1970s the Jug Band split up, and members of the band left Boston. At that point Boston's influence in the folk revival had diminished, although subsequently there have been numerous singer-songwriters from Boston and New England.

## Chicago

There were two major breeding grounds for the Chicago folk scene in the 1950s. The Gate of Horn nightclub, initially owned by Les Brown and Albert Grossman, opened its doors in 1956. Two performers made their mark at the club. Odetta had a four-month run as a soloist at the Gate. Bob Gibson performed as a soloist and then in a duo with singer-actor Hamilton Camp. He later made a live album at the club. Other Chicago folk venues in the 1960s and 1970s included the Earl of Old Town, the 5th Peg, the Old Town Pub, and Somebody Else's Troubles.

One of the two house musicians at the club was guitarist Frank Hamilton. When he decided to get married he started to think more seriously about establishing a more stable and secure life for himself. He began giving guitar lessons at the home of Dawn Greening, who Hamilton has described as "a magnet for the folk community." Greening lived in suburban Oak Park and in addition to letting Frank use her home as a teaching studio, the house was a virtual hotel and jam session headquarters for traveling folksingers.

In 1957 Greening, Hamilton, and a Chicago vocalist named Win Stracke established a teaching facility in Chicago called the Old Town School of Folk Music. Stracke had dreamed of starting a music school that would serve as a bridge for all the ethnic communities in Chicago. Over time the school has fulfilled that vision.

Frank used a teaching method that had been originated by Bess Lomax Hawes at UCLA's Extension Department. Students would take lessons in large groups, with different classes teaching banjos guitar, mandolin, or fiddle. One-hour group lessons would be followed by a break for coffee, snacks, and socializing. After the break all the students would gather in one large room and sing and play together. The teachers had their hands full, because trying to keep all the instruments in tune and supervising players with different levels of skill could get a bit chaotic. The school created its own songbook which the students would use in the second hour of the classes. Dawn Greening's role was to be the school's administrator. Around the school a core of musicians grew who taught classes, and did concerts. This included banjoist Fleming Brown, vocalist Ginny Clemons, singer-storyteller Art Thieme, and dulcimer players-singers George and Gerry Armstrong. George also played the bagpipes.

Over the years Old Town welcomed many visiting performers, including Pete Seeger, Mahalia Jackson, and Josh White. The school has had its ups and downs, and in the late 1980s almost went out of business. One of the school's two buildings was sold, and banjoist Michael Miles was hired to work on the school's programming while Jim Hirsch worked on the business side of the school. This resulted in a more ethnically diversified student and teaching base and an increased emphasis on children's programs. Today the school has revenues in excess of several million dollars a year and is located in two buildings, one of which has a 400-seat concert hall. There are also children's classes in other suburban locations. There are currently some seven thousand students a week. Both locations contain music stores that sell musical instruments, books, and CD's and offer instrument rentals.

Old Town has had a major impact on the audience for folk music in Chicago. Roger McGuinn, who later founded the Byrds, was one of the early students at the school. Fred Holstein, John Prine, Steve Goodman, Bonnie Koloc, and Bob Gibson all had some association with the school. Some twenty years after its founding Old Town became the inspiration for the second largest school of its kind, Denver's Music Association of Swallow Hill.

# Record companies

Bruce Kaplan founded Flying Fish Records in 1974. From that time until his death in 1992, the label recorded such contemporary folk artists as Claudia Schmidt, Bryan Bowers, John Cephas, John Hartford, Linda Waterfall, Sweet Honey in the Rock, and Tom Paxton. The label was one of the primary outlets for folk music during this period. Kaplan died unexpectedly in 1992 and soon afterwards the label was sold to Rounder Records, which in turn has become part of the Concord Music Group.

Chicago is often regarded as the "home of the blues." Alligator, Delmark, and Earwig Records have all helped to solidify that reputation. Alligator was founded in 1971 by Bruce Iglauer and continues today as a strong specialty blues label. Delmark began as a jazz label in St. Louis in 1973 but founder Bob Koester moved it to Chicago in 1978. The company has many releases in both modern jazz and blues, and continues today under new ownership. Earwig was founded by Michael Franks is 1978, and is both a record label and a personal management company. None of these labels restrict themselves to Chicago artists but many local blues artists are found in their rosters.

Another impetus to the blues scene was the magazine *Living Blues*, founded in 1970 by Jim O'Neal and Amy van Singel. The magazine dedicated itself to writing about black blues artists which caused some controversy as white artists like Johnny Winter and Stevie Ray Vaughan developed large audiences. In 1983 the magazine was moved from Chicago to the University of Mississippi where it continues to be published today.

# The artists and Old Town

Fleming Brown learned to play banjo from Doc Hopkins, a traditional musician who hosted a morning radio show on WLS in Chicago. Brown was a mentor for banjoist Stephen Wade, who is discussed later in this chapter. He also recorded an important album in 1963 of traditional banjo player and multi-instrumentalist Hobart Smith.

Greg Cahill is a bluegrass banjo player who has been touring with band *The Special Consensus* since 1975. He has composed numerous instrumentals and recorded a number of albums with his band as well as three solo albums. Cahill teaches at Old Town and has played at hundreds of schools throughout the United States.

Steve Goodman was a student at Old Town, and became something of a musical icon in Chicago through two songs that he wrote about the hapless Chicago Cubs baseball team. He also wrote the hit song *City of New Orleans,* which became an oft-recorded folk standard through Arlo Guthrie's recording. Goodman toured widely and recorded sixteen albums. The last eight were recorded on his own label *Red Pajamas,* starting shortly before his death from leukemia in 1984. Seattle author Clay Eels has written an extremely thorough and detailed biography on Goodman titled *Steve Goodman: Facing the Music.* Goodman was closely associated with the Old Town School, and met fellow songwriter John Prine there. Prine was working as a mailman and was a student at Old Town. Throughout the 1960s he played many clubs in Chicago. He went on to record a number of albums. Several of his songs have been covered by important artists, notably Bonnie Raitt's cover of *Angel from Montgomery.* By 1977 Prine moved to Nashville and has lived there after since.

Both Ed and Fred Holstein taught at the Old Town School. They both performed at numerous venues in Chicago during the 1960s, and they owned and operated a club called Holstein's from 1981 to 1987. Fred did not write songs but had an encyclopedic repertoire. Ed is a songwriter and his best-known song, *Jazzman,* has been recorded by a number of artists, including Bette Midler and Martin Simpson. Ed still teaches at Old Town, but Fred died in 2004.

Jo Mapes performed pop-folk music locally and nationally during the 1960s and also taught at Old Town. During that time, she recorded for Kapp Records. She was a songwriter as well as a performer whose songs were recorded by *the Monkees, the Association,* and *Spanky & Our Gang.* She was a regular on the *Hootenanny* TV show, and after the folk-pop boom ended she returned to Chicago where she was a copywriter for the J. Walter Thompson advertising agency. She sang on a Raisin Bran commercial that she wrote, and according to her daughter Hillary Mapes Levine, the residuals paid from singing on that commercial supported the family for thirteen years.

Michael Miles is a banjo player and guitarist who has created over a dozen stage shows that combine musical performance with literature, politics, and music. He is among a small handful of banjoists who performs a one-man show that is entirely devoted to the banjo.

Stephen Wade was a banjo student of Fleming Brown at Old Town. He also was mentored by Brown's teacher Doc Hopkins. Hopkins had an early morning radio show on WLS. By the mid-1970s Wade had taken over Brown's classes at the school. In May 1979, Wade developed a theater piece called *Banjo*

*Dancing*. The show ran for thirteen months in Chicago and from there Wade and the show moved to Washington, DC, for a ten-year run. Since that time Wade has recorded five albums as a soloist, and has produced and/or written the liner notes for a number of others. Wade's other activities include writing scholarly books and articles, TV shows, and additional theatrical endeavors. His book *The Beautiful Music All around Us* is a required reading for any fans of traditional music.

## Other Chicago artists

Terry Callier was one of the few black artists in the revival in Chicago. His music included jazz and soul influences. Although he achieved some success as a songwriter with a 1972 hit for The Dells, and a single R&B song that made those charts at #78, he pursued a full-time career as a computer programmer at the University of Chicago. He continued to record, but without much success.

Two other black Chicagoans in the revival were LaRoy Inman and Ira Rogers. Both were originally theater students but became interested in folk music through meeting a Chicago student who had a large record collection. The duo made one album for Columbia that included some gospel and folk songs.

Ella Jenkins is nationally known as a children's music artist, song leader, and storyteller. She has made dozens of albums, and at one time was the bestselling artist on Folkways Records. Jenkins has toured internationally, and made many television appearances on both PBS and commercial television. In 2004 she won a Grammy Lifetime Achievement Award and in 2017 she was awarded a National Heritage Fellowship.

Bonnie Koloc was a strong presence on the Chicago folk scene in the late 1960s and into the 1970s. Koloc is a versatile artist who has also enjoyed careers in the theater, in the visual arts, and as an illustrator for her husband Robert Wolf's books. She continues to perform and record, and has recorded fifteen albums.

## More things Chicago

In 1957 Riverside Records released an album called *Chicago Mob Scene*. It featured Moe Hirsch, Bob March, Pete Stein, and "Samuel Hall." The latter was a pseudonym for Bob Gibson. The album mostly consisted of traditional songs, and did not circulate widely outside of Chicago.

Frank Fried was a presenter of folk and popular music in Chicago whose promotions ranged from artists like Pete Seeger and the Chad Mitchell Trio to the *Rolling Stones* and *Led Zeppelin*. Fried was a committed radical who started his career in the entertainment business as an assistant to Albert Grossman. He then managed the racially integrated group The Gateway Singers and also the Chad Mitchell Trio with his Triangle Productions. He also produced a commercial recording for the SNCC Freedom Singers. In the early 1980s he sold his company and moved to Los Angeles.

WFMT was a local radio station that began to broadcast a folk show in 1953 called *The Midnight Special*. The original host was actor-director Mike Nichols. He soon left the show and hosting duties were undertaken by Ray Norstrand and Norm Pellegrini. Rich Warren became a cohost in 1983 and took over the show in 1966. In 1972 the show became nationally syndicated, and it remains an important outlet for both local and nationally known artists.

## Denver

The first Denver folk club was a Calypso club called The Windsor, which appeared in 1958. The Denver folk scene really began to crystallize in 1959 when Hal Neustedter opened a folk club The Exodus in the downtown area. Prior to the opening of the Exodus, Neustedter had a short-lived club called The Little Bohemi, which he sold prior to opening The Exodus. Hal also signed Judy Collins and Walt Conley to perform at the Exodus on a regular basis. He booked a number of touring artists, many of whom were on their way from one coast to another. Neustedter died in an airplane crash in 1962, and although his wife kept the club going for a while it didn't last long.

Walt Conley was one of the pillars of the Denver pop-folk scene. He was an African-American singer-storyteller who booked the talent at the Satire bar and restaurant, a down-to-earth Mexican restaurant east of the downtown area. Walt replaced eccentric local folksinger Lingo the Drifter as the club's manager in 1960 partly because of his ability to book the Smothers Brothers, who were then beginning their comedic folk-pop act. Walt frequently performed at the club, and a traveling performer could almost literally walk in off the street and

Walt would hire them as an opening act at the club. Walt was friendly, funny, and generally even-tempered, and everyone in town seemed to know and like him.

A little-known fact about Walt was unveiled in Rose Victoria Campbell's master's thesis on Walt and Pop-Folk Music in Denver. Walt had worked at the Jenny Wells Vincent's San Cristobal Ranch in New Mexico, and was recruited by the FBI as a paid informant to attend radical meetings in the 1950s.

Over the years Conley vacillated between singing and pursuing an acting career in Los Angeles, eventually returning to Denver in 1983 and opening a club called Walt Conley's Nostalgia. He closed the club in 1991, and for the remainder of his life specialized in singing Irish music.

## Harry Tuft and the Denver Folklore Center

Meanwhile aspiring folksinger Harry Tuft moved to Denver from Philadelphia. Fresh from conferring with Izzy Young in New York on strategies for opening a folklore center, Harry opened his store six blocks east of the downtown in 1962. In the beginning, Harry drove a taxi all night and lived in a loft in the store.

Over the years, the Folklore Center became the key to the folk revival in Denver. There are a number of distinguished alumni who worked at the store in one capacity or another. Early alumni included the late Mike Kropp, a banjoist who later became a studio musician and record producer, the late Kim King the lead guitar in psychedelic-electronic rock group Lothar and the Hand People, Mac Ferris, later a folk-rock musician, and Ray Chatfield, who became a professional banjo player and moved to Galax, Virginia, and the late Paul Hofstadter, a luthier and musician in Northern California. David Ferretta managed the instrument shop for a while, and later became a friendly competitor by opening an instrument shop and later a coffeehouse that featured local music. There was a well-understood but unspoken distinction between the two shops. Ferretta Music catered to the bluegrass audience while the Folklore Center dealt with other folk music styles. Other alumni pursued music as a part-time profession, like George Downing, a fine ballad singer and a professional carpenter who helped to design the store. The entire bluegrass band *Hot Rize* worked for Harry in one capacity or another, and was formed at the store.

Gradually Harry's store took over an entire small city block. Harry added a concert hall at one end of the street, one store sold musical instruments, there was a separate record shop, a space for repairing instruments, and a "funk shop" that sold beads and fashionably hip clothing. The concert hall provided a regular venue for local musicians and for everything from rediscovered blues greats to touring revivalists. Harry also rented a nearby space that served as a teaching facility for aspiring banjo, guitar, fiddle, and mandolin players.

The Folklore Center was a major factor in the Denver folk revival of the 1960s. The store was a place for musicians to hang out and to participate in constant jam sessions. The teaching studios provided musicians with a way to make a living. It was a place where people felt at home, friendships were made, romances were struck up, and people felt a sense of community. A great deal of this "vibe" was established through Harry's personality. Traveling musicians with Denver gigs dropping in and other musicians who were just passing through town got in the habit of checking out the action at the store. Another part of the store's character was its encouragement of a broad musical pallet. The same people who liked blues could be found singing country songs or even traditional ballads. People played together and learned from one another. They experimented and their music and their personalities matured.

Later alumni of the store included the late Jerry Ricks, an excellent and versatile guitarist who moved out in 1970s and became an in-demand teacher before continuing on his expatriate meanderings, going back and forth to Europe. Otis Taylor took lessons in the store when he was a teenager, and has gone on to become a prominent singer-songwriter rooted in the blues. Mary Flower, who is currently an active blues guitarist, singer, songwriter, and teacher in Portland, Oregon, was often found at the store, where her then husband Jeff Withers worked. The members of the bluegrass band Hot Rize all worked at the store.

Another influence in Denver was an organization called the Denver Friends of Folk Music. It sponsored concerts, regular song circles, and jam sessions. By the mid-1960s Denver was a hotbed of folk music and people from both coasts knew about it. Following the example of San Francisco's free-form radio stations, KFML in Denver broadcast with a format that was idiosyncratic and unstructured. Among the DJ's were Harry Tuft and mandolin player Jerry Mills. Both of them featured generous helpings of folk music in their shows. KVOD was the local classical music station, and folk enthusiast John Wolfe had a regular show there and also was active in the Denver Friends of Folk Music.

For a brief period in the mid-1960s there was a coffeehouse near where the Exodus had been located. It was called The Analyst, and was owned by a local entrepreneur named Al Chapman. He became the manager of a local singer-songwriter named Bob Lind. In 1965 Lind had a national hit with his song *The Elusive Butterfly.* Lind left Denver and moved to New Mexico, before settling in Florida in 1988. In recent years he has resumed his performing and recording career.

From 1973 to 1979 Biscuit City Records produced albums with a number of local folk artists. This included Tim O'Brien, who made his first recordings with the label, Dan McCrimmon, Grubstake, and the City Limits bluegrass band. City Limits featured vocalist, banjo, and guitar player Lynn Morris, who has made a number of recordings including some for Rounder Records. She now lives in Winchester, Virginia. Michael Stanwood made a duo album with violinist Bruce Bowers called *Fingers Akimbo.* He has toured internationally, and is a world music specialist who plays autoharp, didgeridoo, and guitar, and teaches at Swallow Hill and elsewhere.

During the 1970s, there were three different clubs that served alcohol and also featured folk music. The back room at the downtown Oxford Hotel operated during the 1960s and into the 1970s, booking agent and manager Chuck Morris managed another downtown club named Ebbets Field from 1973 to 1975, and Nashville booking agent-to-be ran the York Street Café during the 1970s.

From the early 1970s into the 1990s, a unique women's folk group made a definite impact on the Denver scene. The group was called *The Mother Folkers,* as they put it, the most carefully pronounced name in the music business. They originally got together to do some performances for International Women's Week, and they became an annual fixture in the community by doing annual performances during that commemoration. Mary Flower, Celtic music performer Eileen Niehaus, and bassist and raconteur and bass player Mary Stribling were the original sparkplugs, and a number of other musicians including dulcimer builder and player Bonnie Carol, protest singer Elena Klaver, versatile singer Suzanne Nelson, autoharp player Bonnie Carol, country–folk–blues–jazz singer Mollie O'Brien, performer-teacher Julie Davis, and multi-instrumentalist Ellen Thompson Audley performed with the group at various times. The performances were musically varied and often quite funny. Occasional male performers were allowed if they observed a feminine dress code. Over the years the number of performances expanded to about ten a year, but keeping it together became too much of a burden.

# Boulder

The town of Boulder is about thirty miles northwest of Denver, and is the home of the University of Colorado's main campus. Boulder had its own folk scene. A club called Tulagi's featured such artists as a young Judy Collins. The Attic was a coffeehouse that featured blues singer and songwriter Judy Roderick, blues guitarist Ed O'Riley, and legend-to-be Karen Dalton. Other performance outlets for folksingers were Michael's Pub and The Huddle.

Chuck Ogsbury was a student in Boulder when he started building a line of reasonably priced banjos in 1960 under the name *Ode Banjos*. Soon he had half-a-dozen employees, including Kix Stewart, who went on to found his own banjo and guitar supply company in Ohio. There was a lot of music played around the banjo factory, and there were many parties, jam sessions, and social gatherings. In 1966 Chuck sold the business to Baldwin Pianos, but he resumed making banjos using the name *Ome* in the early 1970s. He designs and manufactures banjos to this day.

Max Krimmel was making fine finger-style guitars in Boulder, and his wife Bonnie Carol made and sold dulcimers. They lived in an unincorporated town on a dirt road near Boulder, jokingly named *Wall Street*. Folk Arts Music opened in 1972, and has survived to the present day, as H.B. Woodsongs. Nick the Greek had a music store in the downtown that specialized in folk instruments.

Between Boulder and the surrounding mountain towns there were lots of music parties and any of the people mentioned above were apt to show up, along with a banjo player named Mike Ford who later wrote one of the early bluegrass banjo methods.

In 1991 Nick Forster of *Hot Rize*, started the etown radio show. This is a syndicated radio show that features many folk and folk-pop performers, and has an environmental focus. In 2012 the program moved into a building in downtown Boulder building that houses the show, concerts, and a recording studio.

# Swallow Hill Music Association

When Harry Tuft moved his store to South Broadway in 1980, it became clear that the loss of a teaching facility and a concert hall was going to limit the scope of the Denver folk scene. A group of volunteers including Tuft, formed a nonprofit organization called the Swallow Hill Music Association. The current building has three performance facilities, seating from 80 to 250 people. There are dozens of music instructors and also two rented facilities in different parts of the city that offer lessons. Swallow Hill does outreach to schools, and the organization also promotes concerts in larger facilities when appropriate.

## Los Angeles

Los Angeles had two major clubs in the Hollywood area that specialized in folk music. The Ash Grove opened in 1958. It began as a home for both folk-pop and traditional acts and the Limeliters recorded a live album there in 1960. The club quickly moved more and more in the direction of traditional music. Many of the rediscovered blues artists of the 1960s played there, and it was also a home for everything from ballad singers to flamenco guitarists. Ry Cooder got his start playing back-up guitar at the club when he was sixteen years old and Linda Ronstadt met Kenny Edwards there, which led to the formation of the *Stone Poneys*. Three mysterious fires led to the demise of the club in 1973. In 1996 owner Ed Pearl reopened the club on the Santa Monica Pier, but it closed after a year.

The Troubadour opened in 1957, and it featured more commercial pop-folk acts than the Ash Grove booked. Many of the folk-rock acts played there including the Buffalo Springfield and the Byrds. The club remains open today.

Both clubs had regular open-mic nights, and a large group of future recording artists would attend and hang out. Many of these artists enjoyed important music careers in various bands and musical formats. The Dillards and the Kentucky Colonels were the preeminent bluegrass groups, with the latter featuring the sensational guitarist Clarence White, who later joined the Byrds. The Troubadour was much more "Hollywood" in its style and selection of acts and record company executives could often be found there scouting for new talent.

There were other performing venues in the Los Angeles area. The Ice House in Pasadena opened in 1960. Under the management of Bob Stanes, the club featured both pop-folk musical acts and comedians until in 1978 new management came in and the club changed to an all-comedy format where it remains today. In 1998 Stanes returned to the club scene and opened a music club called the Coffee Gallery in Altadena. It is still operating today.

Personal manager-entrepreneur-hustler Herb Cohen was involved with two 1950s Los Angeles coffeehouses, The Unicorn and Cosmo Alley. The latter was initially bankrolled by actor-singer Theodore Bikel. Both clubs were gone by the 1960s.

Another music scene was happening in suburban Orange County. The Paradox Club and the Mecca were operating there, and Disneyland employed, and continues to employ a variety of musicians. Teenagers and friends comedian-banjo player-magician Steve Martin and John McEuen, a fine multi-instrumentalist and later a member of the Nitty Gritty Dirt Band, were Disneyland employees in 1955. Some of the participants in the Orange County scene included Penny Nichols, Mary McCaslin, Jeff Hanna, Steve Noonan, and Jackson Browne. Former Monkee Mike Nesmith was another participant.

Other Los Angeles-area clubs included the Garret in Pasadena, the Golden Bear, and Ledbetter's in Hermosa Beach, and Santa Barbara venues in the late 1950s included The Noctambulist, the Iopan, and Mephisto's.

McCabe's Guitar Shop, Originally founded in 1958 in Santa Monica was the music store where folk musicians and fans hung out. It was the center of the action and today it has evolved into an outlet for lessons and musical instruments and a weekend concert space where folk-oriented performers play. Westwood Music, near UCLA, was another music store where quite a few musicians hung out or taught lessons. When Frank Hamilton left Chicago, he resumed his teaching career at Westwood. Originally opened in 1947, the store remains an active part of the folk scene.

The city of Claremont is about thirty miles east of downtown Los Angeles in the San Gabriel Mountains. In 1958 Charles and Dorothy Chase opened the Folk Music Center there. The store sold and repaired instruments, and Dorothy taught banjo and guitar lessons in their home. From 1961 to 1966 the Chases and some friends opened a music café that featured such performers as Brownie McGhee and Sonny Terry and the New Lost City Ramblers. In 1976 the Chases opened a nonprofit museum that exhibits old and rare instruments. The museum also presents an annual folk festival. The Chases' daughter, Ellen Chase-Verdries, now manages the shop and her son, well-known performer Ben Harper, has purchased the store from his grandparents. Judging from the photos on the store's website, the Folk Shop may be the folklore center that has remained closest to the original vision that created such stores as the Folklore Center in New York and the original McCabe's.

Bess Lomax Hawes established a curriculum for group guitar lessons while teaching for the Extension Department at UCLA. Another influence was the radio shows that were hosted by Les Claypool, Ed Cray, Jeff Miller, and John Davis. Howard and Roz Larman had a show that had a thirty-year run, and is currently being broadcast on internet radio by their son. After Theo Bikel moved to New York, he had a radio show called *At Home with Theo Bikel* which was taped in New York but played in Los Angeles.

In 1961 the Topanga Banjo and Fiddle Contest began. It was entirely oriented toward traditional music, and continues today. It in turn inspired the Santa Barbara Old Time Fiddlers' Convention, which began in 1972 and is also still active. The Topanga event went through a variety of venue changes but settled in 1990 at its present home on the Paramount Ranch in the Santa Monica Mountains.

By the 1960s Los Angeles had started to become an extremely important recording center, and at the end of the decade it had surpassed New York as a center for record production. New York has remained the center for recording commercials, but Los Angeles has been the movie capital of the United States for decades. It is also the source of most television work as well. Doug Dillard played banjo on many recording sessions and David Cohen was playing guitar on pop, folk, and country records. David Lindley and Ry Cooder were sought after multi-instrumentalists who were used as colorists—people who could add exotic instrumental sounds to a record or a film. Since the 1970s Ry Cooder has composed a number of film scores where he utilized various traditional and urban revivalist musicians. Both of these musicians have also earned reputations by playing with world music musicians, and in Lindley's case, playing such instruments as the oud. Cooder and Lindley will be discussed later in the chapter on instrumentalists. Bill Knopf is an excellent banjo player who has played on many recordings, written a number of instruction books, and toured with Doc Severinsen from 1979 to 1985.

## Other artists

There were a number of pop-folk singers who established niches for themselves during the folk music revival. Don Crawford and Bob Grossman toured constantly and also recorded. Their successful performing careers for one reason or another did not translate into mass sales of their records. By 1968 Grossman had formed a cabaret act with his then wife Mary Hazel. In the 1970s he turned to a career in acting using the name Robert Grossman. Crawford toured into the 1970s, and began writing his own songs.

Don Crawford was one of the rare black pop-folk performers in the revival. Coloradans used to call musicians like Crawford and Grossman "West Coast folksingers." They were noted for slick and aggressive performing styles. There seemed to be certain staples of their repertoire, including *John Henry* and a dramatic ballad called *The South Coast*. The South Coast was a song about a card game where a Mexican of noble birth loses his wife in a card game. The song came from a poem written by Lillian Bos Ross. Folklorist-performer Sam Eskin wrote the melody, and Rich Dehr and Frank Miller, members of the folk-pop band The Easy Riders, adapted it for performance purposes.

Jennifer Warnes has had a long career singing movie title songs and recording songs by Canadian singer-songwriter Leonard Cohen. She was one of the major impetuses for Cohen's rising popularity in the United States. Warnes had one major hit song, *The Right Time of the Night*, which reached number 6 on the Billboard Hot 100 chart in 1977. Warnes has sung solos or occasional duets on over twenty movie soundtracks, and continues to record today.

Many of the Los Angeles artists, like Linda Ronstadt or Karla Bonoff, developed very successful music careers. They clearly crossed over the folk-rock and country-rock genres. Chapter 12 discusses them along with folk-rock and country-folk-rock groups like The Buffalo Springfield, the Byrds, Poco and Crosby, Stills, Nash, and sometimes Young.

## The Pacific Northwest: Portland

In 1959 Ron Brentano and Mike Russo sang and played at the Thirteenth Avenue Gallery and the Way out Café in Portland. Mike was a twelve-string guitarist who made records for Arhoolie and Folkways and made a living painting elaborate house signs in the beach community of Gearhart, Oregon. Ron was a banjo player who continued to play music on a semi-professional level, but became Director of Field Services for the Oregon Historical Society.

By the 1960s a number of coffeehouses opened in Portland. The Agora, the Ninth Street Exit, and the Folksinger were among them, but by the mid-1960s the coffeehouse scene turned more toward folk rock.

## Instrument shops

In 1971 Artichoke Music opened as the Portland version of a folk instrument store. Over the next ten years it passed through four different owners before Steve Einhorn took over the shop in 1981. He moved the store to the Southeast part of town and included a performing space and a teaching facility as part of the store's offerings. The café featured both local and touring artists. Irish fiddler Kevin Burke relocated to Portland in the early 1980s and was one of the artists who performed at Artichoke. After twenty-seven years Steve and his wife Kate Powers decided to spend full-time performing and the store became a nonprofit organization, spearheaded by Richard Colombo and Jim Morris. Continual financial difficulties resulted in them handing off the store to a new board of directors who moved it to a new, lower rent location where it continues to sell instruments, present concerts, and offer lessons.

Pioneer Music was a local friendly competitor to Artichoke that was founded in the late 70s. It was owned by local guitarist and steel guitarist K. C. Wait and was located in the downtown area for almost thirty years. Wait moved the store to a relatively remote southeast location in 2008 but retired in 2012. Like Artichoke, the store was a place for musicians to hang out and offered lessons. Pioneer specialized in vintage instruments.

## Other folk music matters

A number of cities have some sort of folk music society or group that promotes folk music by presenting concerts, establishing song circles where amateur enthusiasts can play and sing together, and by publishing some sort of newsletter that typically includes a calendar of folk music–related events. The Portland Folk Music Society was founded in 1976. It originally was an umbrella organization that spun off the Portland Country Dance Community and the Oregon Bluegrass Organization. The organization does all the things described above, and also sponsors an annual *Singtime Frolic,* where members gather each March in a summer-camp sort of venue to sing and play together, and to receive instruction from a prominent member of the musical community. They also maintain a website which lists events and helps promote the Society's concerts.

KBOO, founded in 1968, is a public radio station that has regular folk music programming. *Rise When the Rooster Crows* is a weekly early morning show that features folk music of all sorts programmed by such knowledgeable local fan musicians Gordy Euler and John Kellermann. The station also has several other shows that program folk music and encourages musicians doing local concerts to come in and perform live on the radio.

Two events that are unique to Portland are the annual *Pickathon* and the *Old Time Music Gathering*. Pickathon is a summer event that is held on a farm near suburban Happy Valley, Oregon. It tends to book the younger set of folk artists, rather than ones that are in the category of "stars." The *Old Time Gathering* is held in January, and is entirely oriented toward traditional folk music and dance. There are workshops and dances with little emphasis on the performance aspect of things. *Bubba Guitar* is a website that has a calendar of folk music–related events. It also sponsors concerts and is heavily involved in the *Old Time Music Gathering*.

There are quite a few Portland venues that sometime feature folk concerts, and many artists make their homes in town. These include Denver expatriate Mary Flower, Steve Einhorn and Kate Power of Artichoke fame, Bill Murlin who has been instrumental in the organization of the folio of Woody Guthrie Columbia River songs, bluesman and author Steve Cheseborough, Irish fiddler Kevin Burke, and a variety of folk performers in many genres. The singer-songwriter Tom May has become a fixture of the Portland music scene, performing in many venues in the Pacific Northwest, and hosting a syndicated radio show called River City Folk.

# Eugene

Eugene, 105 miles south of Portland has its own folk scene. The school and concert facility The Shedd presents concerts and offers lessons on all sorts of instruments. It is located in downtown Eugene. Radio stations KLCC and KRFM provide some folk programming. Corvallis is about eighty-five miles southwest of Portland, and has several stores that feature folk music instruments, especially the well-stocked Fingerboard Extension. Founded in 1978, it features drums as well as folk instruments.

# Seattle

Like the Portland group, Seattle has the Seattle Folk Music Society. It dates from the mid-1960s when folk fan and later promoter John Ullman graduated from

Reed College in Portland and noticed that Seattle lacked venues for traditional music performances. Initially the society presented only touring traditional musicians but during the early 1970s the membership grew and that policy loosened up to include local performers and some of the younger touring professionals. Like the Portland society, the Seattle group sponsors concerts and has a monthly newsletter.

Another group the Pacific Northwest Folklore Society was founded by local folksinger Walt Robinson in 1953. It has an e-zine with articles and a calendar section and the group presents coffeehouse concerts monthly at the Couth Buzzard Bookstore. The concerts feature both local and touring performers. The group also sponsors a monthly jam session at the same bookstore.

In 1972 the annual *Northwest Folklife Festival* was launched. This is an eclectic event that includes a considerable slice of music from different parts of the world. Some of these performers are not professional musicians but are local residents who wish to maintain the traditions of their culture and transmit them to an audience for whom this music is little known. Over 200,000 people attend the four-day event which doesn't charge admission but collects donations. The festival is somewhat controversial to professional folk performers because performers are paid only a small honorarium for transportation costs, although the organization has a full-time paid staff.

The late Phil Williams and his wife Vivian were actively involved in the festival, and they also established Voyager Records in 1967. Voyager is devoted to issuing recordings of fiddle music not only in the Northwest but all over the United States. They have also issued instruction manuals, and their website is a great source for all things about the fiddle. Vivian, herself an accomplished fiddle player, continues to operate the company today.

## The Folkshop, etc.

The Folkshop located near the University of Washington opened in 1972, but closed its doors in 2012. The much larger Dusty Strings opened in 1982. Dusty Strings is a quality maker of hammered dulcimers and levered harps, and they added a folklore center in 1982. They employ a number of music teachers and sponsor workshops. The store carries many musical instruments and music instruction books.

Radio outlets for folk music include KCBS in Bellevue and KSER in Everett. Another outlet is the all-volunteer organization Victory Music, founded by Chris

Lunn in 1969. Victory sponsors many open-mic shows, periodically produces workshops to help performers learn how to promote their music, and instruction in running sound boards, and creates opportunities for fans or performers to become MCs. Their online site offers performers the opportunity to list their gigs. Chris Lunn has gone on to found a magazine called *Ancient Victories*, which reviews CDs and books and also sponsors open mics in the Seattle-Tacoma area.

## Artists

There are many folk artists who reside in the Seattle area. Jim Page is a protest-oriented singer from Chicago who has recorded twenty-two albums and toured internationally. *Magical Strings* is a Celtic music duo that has widely performed and recorded. Bryan Bowers is an outstanding autoharp player and storyteller who has toured and recorded for many years. The Late Linda Waterfall was a singer-songwriter who is a formally trained musician who has recorded, toured, and taught at the Cornish school of Music. Reggie Garrett performs original songs and some covers and is an African-American musician on a mostly white scene who incorporates a variety of musical influences in his work. These are a few of the veteran artists in Seattle. Another set of younger musicians will be discussed later.

## Outside the city

Port Townsend is fifty-six miles northwest of Seattle. In a partnership with Fort Worden State Park, it sponsors a series of workshops in the arts that include fiddle and blues workshops. These one-week classes bring in students and teachers from all over the country and even abroad. Centrum is one of the best established of the many summer folk music instructional camps.

Port Angeles, which is eighty-two miles northwest of Seattle, has an annual folk festival that has been running for twenty-five years. There are other folk music scenes in Richland, Olympia, and Bellingham.

## Philadelphia

Philadelphia is only ninety miles south of New York, but there were a considerable number of artists who developed there, many of whom could best be described as semiprofessionals. This is not to demean their talents, but simply a realization that they were not full-time touring and recording professionals. In the Rittenhouse Square section of downtown Philadelphia there was a coffeehouse called the Gilded Cage where folksingers gathered in the back room on Sunday afternoons and took turns singing or playing. On weekend nights Esther Halpern, the wife of owner Ed Halpern, sang in the back room. Some of the people who gathered on Sundays, beginning in 1956, included Harry Tuft, who later founded the Denver Folklore Center, Donny Leace, later a protégé of pop singer Roberta Flack, performer Mike Miller, and guitarist Linda Cohen. The Cage closed in 1969.

Another group of performers, notably Joe and Penny Aaronson, Tossi and Lee Aaron, and Mike Miller did some teaching and played quite a few gigs in the area. George Britton became known as the most popular folk guitar instructor in the area and his wife Charlotte later became a booking agent. Raun Mackinnon was a local singer-songwriter who moved to New York to pursue her songwriting and performing career.

By the late 1950s an entrepreneur named Manny Rubin opened the Second Fret, a folk club and coffeehouse in the downtown area. A young African-American named Jerry Ricks started out working in the kitchen and later became manager of the club. During his sojourn at the club he learned how to play guitar. Many of the club's visiting performers including Mississippi John Hurt and Doc Watson stayed at Jerry and Sheila Ricks' near-by apartment. The black blues artists who stayed there were thrilled to find a twenty-something black man who wanted to learn how to play the blues. Country-folk picker Doc Watson has credited Jerry with essentially saving his career when he played the Fret during one of his first trips away from home. He has written that Jerry and Sheila's friendship and hospitality enabled him to understand that his work was important and appreciated.

In 1964 a club called the Main Point opened in Bryn Mawr, a suburb of Philadelphia. It lasted until 1981 and any number of touring artists including Bonnie Raitt played there. In 1976 a former donut shop in Bethlehem, Pennsylvania, about seventy miles north of Philadelphia, was turned into Godfrey Daniels, a folk venue which is still operating today.

Although Steve Kenin briefly had a folk instrument shop during the folk revival, it wasn't until 1974 when Fred Oster opened Vintage Instruments in the Chestnut Hill neighborhood that there was really a full-service guitar shop. Oster moved the shop to current downtown location in 1983. However, this is more of an old-line classic store which doesn't offer lessons or do repairs. It simply stocks many fine-fretted instruments, as well as high-quality violins. It is not a place to hang out and jam. However, in suburban Bucks County there is an acoustic music store called the Bucks County Folk Shop, which opened its doors in 1962 and continues to this day under the same ownership and management.

The Philadelphia Folksong Society began in 1957. It sponsors a regular concert series but its main event is the Philadelphia Folk Festival, which began in 1962, and still runs today. It takes place on a farm in suburban Philadelphia, and draws thousands of people and many well-known performers.

Another significant development in Philadelphia is the strong folklore and folklife program at the University of Pennsylvania. A number of revivalists, like harmonica and guitar player Saul Brody, received doctoral degrees in the program. Many of the professors, including McEdward Leach, Kenneth Goldstein, and Roger Abrahams were nationally known figures in the field of folklore. Another college scene built up around the interest in folk music was at suburban Swarthmore College. The school held folk festivals from 1945 to 1967 and one of the young students there in the late 1950s was Ralph Rinzler, whose musical and folkloristic activities were discussed earlier in the book.

Gene Shay is a radio personality who has been broadcasting folk music on various stations since 1962. He often interviewed folk musicians live on his program, and he was also involved for many years in the Philadelphia Folk Festival.

# San Francisco

The North Beach section of San Francisco had two clubs across the street from one another. During the 1960s the Smothers Brothers held forth in an extended engagement at the Purple Onion. Across the street the Hungry I featured a combination of folk, jazz, and pop acts and comedy. The club's fame was reinforced by the hugely successful *Kingston Trio at the Hungry I* album. During the mid-1960s another San Francisco club was the Drinking Gourd where Marty Balin, Paul Kantner, and the original lead singer Signe Anderson met and formed *Jefferson Airplane*. These three outlets represent the pop-folk aspect of the San Francisco scene in the 1960s. A sort of beatnik coffeehouse called The Fox and the Hounds was also located in North beach.

The San Francisco Folk Music Club was dedicated to both traditional and political music. It grew out of several high school friends meeting in each other's homes in 1948. In 1959 the club was organized by Herb Jager with the goal of promoting concerts, benefit performances, and other community activities. He left the area and Faith Petric became the leader of the club in 1962. In 1964 she started the publication of their newsletter, called *the folknik*. Petric died in 2013 at the age of ninety-eight and today the club is a nonprofit organization of musicians, songwriters, dancers, and folk music aficionados. They hold twice monthly jams and song circles at a San Francisco club called Cyprian's ARC. The folknik contains a calendar of Bay area activities and articles of interest to folk music fans. The organization also sponsors music campouts on three holiday weekends and *Camp New Harmony* that lasts from four to five days is held at a more rural location for members and their families. The group also presents an annual two-day free folk festival in San Francisco and a one-day festival in neighboring town El Cerrito.

## Berkeley

Berkeley was a stronghold of traditional folk music. The Blind Lemon was founded in 1958, and The Steppenwolf in the early 1960s. In 1963 Rolf Cahn, opened the Cabale, which lasted until 1965. In the mid-1960s The Jabberwock became the primary folk club in Berkeley, but it disappeared in 1967. The Freight and Salvage opened in 1968, and it is the only one of these clubs that has survived. Other clubs at that time included the New Orleans House, Mandrake's, Tito's, and the Lucky 13.

The Berkeley Folk Festival was held on the campus of the University of California from 1958 to 1970. It featured many of the prominent musicians of the folk song revival and presented a mix of concerts and workshops. The festival was directed by Barry Olivier, a Berkeley-raised guitarist and folk fan. The event actually pre-dated the Newport Folk Festival. The talent included folklorists, traditional performers, and even some folk-rock artists. Another local promoter was Mary Ann Pollar, a rare African-American woman folk promoter.

Lundberg's Fretted Instruments was an integral part of the Berkeley scene. Jon Lundberg opened the store in 1961, and stocked vintage instruments and also was nationally known for doing extensive repairs to guitars. In addition to being a great hang-out spot, many musicians worked for Jon at one time or another. Fiddler-swing guitarist Tony Marcus, innovative guitarist Janet Smith, and folksinger-philosopher Larry Hanks were employees of the shop. By 1980

Jon had moved the shop to a neighboring town called Kensington, and began to specialize in men's haberdashery, eventually to the exclusion of musical instruments. A fire in the shop forced its closure in 2000.

Both San Francisco and Berkeley had free-form and community radio stations, and free-form radio essentially started in San Francisco. These stations offered an outlet for folk music, depending on the taste of specific disc jockeys.

## Artists

Berkeley spawned a bunch of talented artists whose lives eventually moved outside of the music scene. Al Young was a smooth-voiced young African-American performer who had a large and varied repertoire of folk songs and would become a well-known novelist, poet, music critic, and college professor. He often sang at the Blind Lemon. Steve Talbot had a reputation for being a fine blues and ragtime guitarist, but he made a living working on the railroad. Pete Berg was an excellent musician and a creative jazz-influenced guitarist who seemed to be attending the University of California on a ten-year plan. He changed his major repeatedly, ending up with a degree in anthropology and becoming a bamboo farmer in the Philippines. Marc Silber was a creative blues and ragtime guitarist who only performed occasionally, but repaired instruments and designed guitars that were made in Mexico. Perry was another prominent local guitarist. Terry Garthwaite and Toni Brown were active on the scene, and later founded a successful folk-rock group called *The Joy of Cooking*. The band was founded in 1967, and was a rare example at that time of a mixed gender band where the leaders were women.

The San Francisco–Berkeley area was a key incubator of folk-rock music, which is covered in the next chapter of this book.

## Toronto

During the 1960s The Yorkville section of Toronto in effect was the Greenwich Village of Toronto. It had a similar mix of clubs, coffeehouses, art galleries, and boutiques. At the time the drinking age was twenty-one, so coffeehouses provided an alternative to drinking establishments for young bohemians. As was true in Greenwich Village, there were a number of coffeehouses that featured live folk entertainment. They included the 71 Club, the Half Beat, the Village Corner, the Penny Farthing, the Mousehole, the Gate of Cleve, the Cellar, The First Floor Club, The Fifth Peg, and the Riverboat. The Riverboat featured many American folk artists, ranging from Brownie McGhee and Sonny Terry to Tim Hardin, but it also booked many Canadian artists, including Gordon Lightfoot, Joni Mitchell, Bruce Cockburn, and Murray McLauchlan. The clubs also featured poetry readings, and jazz and rock musicians. American blues and jazz singer-guitarist Lonnie Johnson moved to Toronto in 1966 and even briefly had his own club. After it closed he often played at the Penny Farthing. Buffy Ste. Marie and Lucy and Carly Simon played at the Purple Onion, as did Gordon Lightfoot, Joni Mitchell, and Ian and Sylvia. Many less famous local singers also performed in these venues.

Gillian Mitchell, in her book *The North American Folk Music Revival: Nation and Identity in the United States and Canada, 1945–1980*, points out that Yorkville was a residential neighborhood until the 1950s, but shopkeepers driven out of the downtown area by higher rents replaced the original population. She writes that by the mid-1960s there were forty-seven coffeehouses in the neighborhood. During the 1950s the venues had mostly featured jazz but by the 1960s they had turned to folk music. There was also an influx of young Americans who moved to Canada to evade the draft.

Estelle Klein was the president of the Guild of Canadian Folk Artists. This organization put on shows at various venues in Toronto. The organization also published a magazine called *Hoot* from 1966 to 1969. This was a folk fanzine that contained articles, reviews, photos, and songs. Klein later was one of the driving forces behind the Mariposa Folk Festival, held near Toronto.

## Artists

Gillian Mitchell points out that both in New York and Toronto there were quite a few female artists although often they were the lead singers in male bands, such as Susan Jains, who sang in the *Dirty Shames Jug Band*. Amos Garrett was the guitarist in that band, and he went on to tour with Ian and Sylvia, and eventually to relocate to the United States to become a session musician. Al Cromwell was a black Canadian blues musician who was popular in Toronto in the 1960s and 1970s. CBC Radio and TV featured a number of Canadian folk artists. Nancy White, who is both a folk and cabaret singer, had a program on CBC Radio from 1976 to 1994 on the public affairs show *Sunday Morning*. White also performed at everything from children's concerts to folk festivals and symphony pops to concerts and has made a number of recordings. Her own songs ranged from topical–political songs to humorous ones. I have covered a number of other artists in the chapter on Canada. By the end of the 1960s the Yorkville clubs had turned to rock and the folk boom was effectively over.

American expatriate Eric Nagler and his ex-wife Martha Beers operated the Toronto Folklore Center from 1971 to 1976. In 1977 long after the end of the boom, the Twelfth Fret Guitar Shop was founded. It follows the model of many of the folk music shops I have already discussed. It is particularly noted for its stock of vintage instruments. Jean Larrivee is a luthier who started in Toronto in 1970, but moved to Victoria and Vancouver in 1977 and 1983, and to Oxnard, California in 2001. He continued his North Vancouver operation until 2013 when he shut that shop down. Renowned Canadian luthiers Grit Laskin and Linda Manzer started their careers in his shop. Laskin is also a performer and in 1996 he partnered with musicians Bill Garrett, Paul Mills, and Ken Whiteley to start Borealis Records, a distinguished folk label that now has over 125 releases. Whiteley is a producer, arranger, and artist who produced and played on many recordings.

## The rest

In most major cities and in towns that had large colleges there were people who seemed to play a central role in the folk revival. In Salt Lake City Jim Sorrels and his then-wife Rosalie and Utah Phillips were at the center of the action. Intermountain Guitar and Banjo started in 1973 and developed a reputation as a nationally known vintage instrument store. In Phoenix Dolan Ellis, later to be an original member of the New Christy Minstrels, was a key performer, and later was named balladeer for the state of Arizona. Paul Endicott booked and managed acts out of his Detroit office.

In Minneapolis Koerner, Ray, and Glover were white blues singers who gained national popularity, and Glover wrote an important blues harmonica instruction book. A young Bob Dylan was on the scene during his brief tenure at the University of Minnesota in 1959. In 1974 Garrison Keillor started the

*Prairie Home Companion* radio show, and he utilized guitarist Dakota Dave Hull and mandolin player Peter Oustroushko in his house band. The show was hugely successful and nationally syndicated and versatile guitarist Pat Donohue eventually replaced Hull. Keilor had many guests who performed folk music on the program. From 1959 to 1965 Paul Nelson and Jon Pankake edited and published a folk magazine called *The Little Sandy Review*. The editors were dedicated traditionalists who panned any record that had even a smidgeon of pop-folk content.

There were folk scenes all over Texas that nurtured such singer-songwriters as Guy Clark and K. T. Oslin in the 1960s, and later brought forth Steve Fromholz, Townes Van Zandt, Lyle Lovett, and many other talented writers. A number of Texas singer-songwriters, including Guy Clark and Rodney Crowell moved to Nashville, although in Clark's case his songs often referenced his Texas roots*.

Washington, DC, had clubs like *The Cellar Door* and a very strong bluegrass scene that spawned the Country Gentlemen and the Seldom Scene. Mary Cliff, John Dildine, and Dick Cerri were all influential disc jockeys who could be counted on to play folk music on their shows with Cerri especially inclined toward pop-folk recordings. ex-Chicagoan, Stephen Wade, Cathy Fink, Marcy Marxer, Hazel Dickens Alice Foster, Jennifer Cutting and Lisa Moscatello were or are influential singers on the DC-Baltimore scene.

For a folk scene to really emerge in a city there needs to be an infrastructure to support it. This includes

- Music stores: Not just any music stores, but ones that featured old and new acoustic instruments, and offered lessons on the instruments and repair services, with a friendly atmosphere that encouraged jamming and hanging out.
- Entrepreneurs: Business people who promoted concerts, booked and/or managed talent, and who could access record companies for their clients.
- Clubs or venues: Bars or coffeehouses or even churches that featured live acoustic music.
- Teachers: Instrumentalists who could impart their skills to aspiring talent and to devoted amateurs who would become the core audience for the music.

---

* Austin also spawned an important blues scene, centering around the Antone's, which was both a club and a record label. The label recorded a number of blues and blues-rock musicians, notably white blues artists Marcia Ball, Lou Anne Barton, Sue Foley, Angela Strehli, and Jimmy Ray Vaughan.

- Radio stations: DJs and station music directors who had folk shows and also featured interviews with local and touring artists.
- Recording studios and record companies: For anyone seeking to develop a professional career making records was (and in a different way still is) a necessity. Many cities didn't have record companies or well-equipped recording studios in the 1960s. That situation has entirely changed over the years.
- Studio work: For accomplished musicians and vocalists, good paying work was available for singing or playing on commercials, records, and even films.
- Folklore societies: In cities like Portland, Seattle, and San Francisco, the folklore societies sponsored concerts and song circles, and provided a support network for people interested in folk music. They also published newsletters with schedules of concerts and articles on performers.
- Colleges: Many of the pop-folk groups met in college, or were actively involved in folk song clubs at colleges. They were also a source of gigs, either in the form of concerts or folk festivals. The University of Michigan, UCLA, and the University of Chicago sponsored large festivals with numerous performers. Oberlin College in Ohio, for example, was a nurturing environment for Joe Hickerson, who was the archivist at the Library of Congress' Folk Song Division for many years. Bill Svanoe, later in the Rooftop Singers, folk performer Fred Starner who specialized in hobo songs, folklorist-performer-author Neil Rosenberg, author-editor-performer Richard Carlin, and Brad Leftwich, an excellent fiddle and banjo player, recording artist and author of instructional music were all Oberlin students. Leftwich was the rare college student who came from a family of traditional musicians. Oberlin even spawned a group called *The Folksmiths*, who recorded for Folkways Records. Similarly, blues artists John Hammond Jr., Ian Buchanan, and Jefferson Airplane flyer to be Jorma Kaukonen all attended Antioch College, in Yellow Springs, Ohio.
- University folklore departments: Despite the fact that during the 1950s and 1960s many folklorists looked down their noses at the folk music revival, many people who graduated from these programs themselves played a role as performers in the revival. Roger Abrahams, Gene Bluestein, Neil Rosenberg, and Ellen Stekert all fit that description.
- The intangibles: Sometimes it was the presence of a particularly magnetic individual who might be a performer, a teacher, or a club owner or someone

who opened a place to hang out and play music that created an atmosphere that seemed to inspire people to take a deeper interest in the music.

- Folk dancing: The folk revival also included and was fed by an interest in square dancing, contra dancing, or world folk dance styles.

It wasn't necessary for all of these elements to exist in a single city to develop some sort of cachet in the folk revival. In the larger cities more of these ingredients were apt to be present or to develop, but sometimes the very isolation of a smaller city or a college seemed to bring people closer together and helped develop a sense of community.

# 9

# The Riddle of Authenticity

The original line-up of the Weavers generally performed traditional music, together with a few songs written by their friends or the occasional world music songs that Seeger brought to the group. The pop part of the equation was the Gordon Jenkins arrangements that featured orchestral and vocal back-up. Harry Belafonte's basic repertoire was a combination of traditional music and calypso songs, composed, arranged, or brought to the table by his associate Irving (Lord) Burgess.

The odd, but little-noticed notion about the Kingston Trio is that their early records were really closer to traditional folk arrangements than those that the Weavers or Belafonte had recorded. Only extreme purists like *The Little Sandy Review* editors or their writers dared to criticize the Weavers. Because of Seeger's blacklisting most progressive folk fans accepted that the Weavers were simply trying to reach a large audience rather than the relatively small number of already committed folk fans that attended New York hootenannies. After the Weavers were blacklisted and no longer made pop records, the records that they made for Vanguard omitted the choral and orchestral arrangements. Although the bestselling records were the Decca "pop" records, most folk fans identified with the second incarnation of the Weavers.

Because the Kingston Trio was up-beat, seemingly a political, and used scripted comedy material rather than spontaneous humor, dedicated fans of traditional folk music found their music almost insulting. In the John Cohen keynote speech at a 1991 folk revival symposium referred to earlier in this book, he characterizes the Kingston Trio and other roughly similar groups as the enemy, and musicians and bands like his own band The New Lost City Ramblers as the keepers of the holy grail of purity and authenticity.

On the other hand, record producer and annotator Dave Samuelson at the same conference described Dave Guard, the Trio's original leader, as "knowledgeable about traditional music." He goes on to compare Guard to banjo player and singer Charlie Poole in the sense that they both "freely draw ideas and songs from popular, non-traditional sources."

Most of the pop-folk groups drew from the example of the Kingstons and recordings of groups like The Highwaymen, the Limeliters, the Brothers Four, and Peter, Paul & Mary used little or nothing in the way of orchestrations or back-up singers. They did make slight or substantial changes in the lyrics and/or melodies of traditional songs that may have been distasteful to some tradition-oriented listeners. And, like the Weavers before them, they copyrighted songs in their own names that were traditional songs or even songs that they had sourced from a particular traditional singer. Remember, however, that even the vaunted folklorists like the Lomaxes did the same thing. The question then arises, what did John Cohen and the Little Sandy Folks find so distasteful about the pop-folk groups? To explore this question, I think it is necessary to look at the whole notion of authenticity and the folk-pop revival.

## The riddle of authenticity

The early 1960s recordings by the pop-folk groups used mostly traditional songs, with the occasional Woody Guthrie song or material composed by veteran folk and pop-folk writer Terry Gilkyson thrown in. Yet there was something about the rhythms that these groups utilized that seemed to relate more to pop-folk than to traditional folk. These rhythms were frequently kind of an up-beat, bouncy 4/4 time constructs that made the audience do what my friend John Phillips used to call the "folk clap." The folk clap is the notion of clapping on all four beats of a measure, rather than the African-American notion of accenting the second and fourth beats of the measure. I attribute some of this to Pete Seeger's influence when he had audiences sing along with him. The musical experience seemed very "white" and somewhat mindless.

In my opinion this is some of what the "folk Nazis" objected to. Then there was the undeniable issue of money. All the groups listed above had hit records and hit albums, and toured for what passed as big money in the early and middle 1960s, although top stars in the world of rock and pop-rock make many times more money per show and perform in much larger venues than the pop-folk artists ever did. Hand in hand with the issue of money go feelings of jealousy. None of the purist singers were earning a tenth of the money that the Trio or Peter, Paul & Mary were hauling in from touring, record sales, and publishing rights. (The reader will recall that many of the groups were copyrighting traditional songs with minor modifications, and therefore earning additional income from sheet music sales, radio or television airplay, or other uses.)

Most of the pop-folk groups, with the exception of a few people like Mary Travers, Peter Yarrow, or Erik Darling did in fact not have a serious background in traditional folk music. They learned their songs from recordings of people like Pete Seeger and the Weavers, from songbooks, or music directors like Milt Okun. For the most part they were not seeking out the work of traditional musicians like Uncle Dave Macon, Blind Willie McTell, or the old-time string bands, but were relying on groups like the Ramblers to bring this music to light.

I once attended a music party where a friend of the Brothers Four got quite drunk and insulted me, calling me a beatnik and accusing me of having poor hygiene habits. One of the Brothers Four looked at him and told him that he should be nice to me, because the Brothers made quite a bit of money by attending parties and learning songs from folk music enthusiasts like me! This struck me as rather cynical, but largely accurate.

As the folk revival moved on and the groups started on their fifth or sixth albums, they began to run out of traditional songs, at least ones that they knew. In the case of the Kingston Trio, John Stewart replaced Dave Guard in 1962. Stewart was an excellent songwriter, and the trio began to do more and more of his songs, throwing in occasional songs by their friends or associates. By 1965 folk-rock had reared its head, and it seemed as though the number of singer-songwriters had grown exponentially. It became easier and easier to find songs to fill out albums and many of the pop-folk groups dropped out of the marketplace. The demand for their wares was replaced by folk-rockers, British rock groups, and Motown artists.

## The loss of traditional models

In the 1960s a number of important traditional blues and mountain music artists were rediscovered or found for the first time. This was a result of the work of Mike Seeger and John Cohen on the mountain music side and a number of dedicated blues fans in the case of African-American music. There were also dedicated folklorists like Kip Lornell, Harry Oster, and Art Rosenbaum who were still collecting music from traditional musicians at that time. Groups like the New Lost City Ramblers or the young white blues revivalists were literally able to sit at the feet of these traditional music masters like Tommy Jarrell or Reverend Gary Davis and learn from them formally or informally. Today all of these people have passed on. It is of course still possible to hear the music of these musicians on the internet or on CDs, and in some cases videos, but this is a very different matter from getting to know these musicians face to face. In a world where the entire world is a mouse click away we have seen the end of traditional music in the way it was created and expressed from the 1920s to the 1960s.

## What is authentic?

We still haven't come to grips with the question of exactly what constitutes authenticity. Is it the reproduction of already-existing traditional music? Is it possible to write new songs in a style that is so similar to traditional songs that the new songs can be accepted as folk music? To put this another way, are songs like Dylan's *Blowing in the Wind* or *Don't Think Twice* today's folksongs?

In my mind, these are subjective issues. A composed new song will never literally be a folksong. Under a traditional definition, folksongs are supposed to be passed along and changed in oral transmission, not in the form of recordings on the internet. It is possible to make the argument that these are the contemporary ways of transmitting music rather than learning them in isolated areas from family or friends. If someone writes new or additional words to *Blowing in the Wind*, does that meet the "traditional" test? In point of fact *Don't Think Twice* was a folksong, with the same melody but different words. The melody and the lyric idea came from a song that Paul Clayton, then a Dylan friend and associate, had collected in Virginia. Should we therefore say that Dylan met the test, and the song could be seen as a traditional one? Or is that not possible unless someone else changes the words yet again?

Here is another confusing example. Many of Woody Guthrie's songs were in effect quasi-folksongs because he was borrowing melodies from existing traditional songs. *This Land Is Your Land* originated with a melody used by the Carter family in both the songs Little Darling Pal of Mine and *When the World's On Fire*. This melody was based on an earlier gospel song called *My Loving Brother*. The Canadian pop-folk group The Travellers added a verse to Woody's song that refers to Canadian locales. Does that make *This Land* into a folksong? Probably not, unless other people start to add new verses and to make further changes in the lyrics and/or the melody. As I was writing this sentence, I went on YouTube, and sure enough there was a 2017 version of the song by a singer-songwriter named Jerome Rubin which indeed included a couple of new verses that he had written. I also found another revised lyric that refers to American Indians, which brings to bear a whole other notion of what that "your land" means. Do these various versions automatically turn *This Land* into a folksong, or do we need to wait and see whether anyone else picks up these lyrics when they sing the song?

Nancy K. Dillon is an Oklahoma-born Seattle-based singer, who wrote and recorded a song that she calls *O Susanna* a few years ago. (The reader should be aware that it is not possible to copyright a song title.) Nancy's song has an entirely different melody than Stephen Foster's 1848 classic. However, she refers to the banjo and she also uses the phrase "don't you cry for me." Has Foster's song become a folksong, or do we need to wait and see whether another artist covers either Foster's or Dillon's song and adds their own lyrics or music?

Let's turn to one additional complication. Blues songs utilize floating verses. A floating verse is a song that is not necessarily native to a particular song but one that appears in many songs. The well-known blues *Key to the Highway* was first recorded in 1940 by blues pianist Charlie Segar. Soon afterward Chicago bluesman Big Bill Broonzy recorded a slightly different and more popular version of the same song. Since that time there have been dozens of other recorded versions. I remember hearing Brownie McGhee singing additional verses to the song at a performance in 1958. Does that mean that for practical purposes, it has become a folk song? Finally, and I suppose inevitably, here's another variation on this theme. I have a friend named Marc Silber, who sings songs that are traditional, or well-known songs by artists that range from Hank Williams to Mississippi John Hurt. He often doesn't sing the songs as they were literally written or recorded, but adds and subtracts works according to his mood and taste. Does that alone make a song composed by Hank Williams into a folksong?

## Bringing it up to date

Later in the book I will discuss the ways that younger musicians are adopting or transforming traditional music by bringing other musical idioms and musical styles into the mix. I am uncertain as to how this fits into the notion of folk music, but I am certain that this is happening. In an ironic twist, a few of the newer groups that I have heard are replicating that bouncy rhythm that I referred to above as a kind of characteristic Kingston Trio sound. I have no idea whether these groups have heard the Kingstons, or have simply found these rhythms appropriate to their own, newly composed songs.

## Authenticity of spirit

There is another aspect of all this that is intangible. Earlier in the book I called it "authenticity of spirit." There are some musicians and songwriters who manage to be compelling and convincing. Once again this is something of a subjective call. My critical analysis of a particular artist as a sell-out or someone who is tastelessly violating the spirit of folk music may be the reader's choice of the most sincere, heartfelt singer that they have encountered. It is also true that some artists come into the arena as interesting and innovative, and over a period of time appear to become parodies of themselves.

Pete Seeger is one of my favorite artists and in many ways the inspiration for me (and hundreds of others) to become musicians. However, he performed so long and was so over-recorded, that some of his records sound as though they were completed in the space of an hour or two with little thought or editing time. In a rather odd and anonymous letter to *Sing Out!* magazine he essentially said this about his own work. Some other artists seem to be entirely unconscious that they are simply presenting stylized, repetitive, and dull versions of what they did thirty or even forty years ago. It isn't so much a question of instrumentation style, or instrumental or vocal ability as it is the artist's willingness to aspire to improve one's performances, arrangements, or interpretations. Any two people with different tastes may have different opinions about whether a particular artist has become stale or is still inventive and inspiring.

# 10

# The Civil Rights Movement

The end of the First World War was a harbinger of the struggle for civil rights struggle that erupted some four decades later. The Ku Klux Klan was revived in the South in 1915 two years before the United States entered the war. When black soldiers came back from serving in the armed services, there were some instances of southern blacks attempting to assert their rights. The organized system of Jim Crow prevalent in the South that included segregated schools, the poll tax, lynchings, and other oppressive measures kept the status quo operative. According to distinguished historian John Hope Franklin, there were more than seventy lynchings of blacks in 1919. There were also twenty-five race riots all over the United States, including a serious outbreak in Chicago.

Black soldiers in both the First and Second World Wars served in segregated units. The Second World War lasted much longer and many more blacks were drafted for that war. These soldiers were surprised to find that many of the racial barriers and sexual taboos found in America were not as strictly observed in Europe. When these soldiers returned home in 1945, they were determined to change social conditions especially in the South. Having risked their lives for their country they wanted a level playing field in education, employment, politics, and other aspects of daily living.

Franklin Delano Roosevelt had generally stayed away from attempting to create profound changes on the racial front. Under pressure from black leaders though, he did create the FEPC (Federal Employment Practices Committee). This was an attempt to increase the number of black employees in the federal government and the defense industry. Roosevelt died in 1945, and his successor was Harry S. Truman, a moderate Democrat and a former senator from the border state of Missouri. In 1948 Truman issued an executive order that mandated fair employment by the federal government. Truman was still president in 1950 when the North Koreans invaded South Korea. After some initial experiments at integrating some army units in 1951, all American forces were integrated. Truman also appointed some African Americans to various federal court positions and to his cabinet.

Seeking educational equality, in 1946 African Americans sued for admission to white universities, and in 1954 segregation in the public schools was outlawed. These efforts were followed by successful efforts to integrate restaurants, hotels, and transportation systems. To summarize a number of the events that occurred in the early days of the civil rights movement:

- In Montgomery, Alabama, Rosa Parks refused to move to the back of a city bus. This led to a boycott of the bus company, and to the emergence of Martin Luther King Jr. as the most important leader of the Civil Rights movement. There were sit-ins at lunch counters and dozens of blacks, mostly college students, were arrested. Freedom Riders came South to test segregation in transportation. In many instances, the integrated groups of Riders were beaten up by angry white mobs. In 1960 John F. Kennedy was elected president and he was successfully pressured to protect civil rights workers. Despite the intervention of the FBI, civil rights workers were beaten and murdered. Black political organizations became increasingly militant. The NAACP, traditionally the forum for black leadership, was replaced in the fore-front of the struggle for civil rights struggle by SNCC (Student Non-Violent Coordinating Committee) and CORE (Committee for Racial Equality).
- Many African Americans and some of their white supporters went to jail during this period of social and political agitation.
- The civil rights movement was a singing movement. Music sustained and supported the cause, and participants sang in jails and on the picket lines.

A number of folksingers, mostly the younger white urban revivalists, came to the South and sang their support for the cause of civil rights.

## Music and the civil rights movement: Movement music

There were three streams of music that were associated with the civil rights movement. These musical styles represented the various artists and protesters involved in the struggle. The music of the movement itself was an ideological compadre of the music of the 1930s.

Earlier I examined how the political singers of the 1930s and into the early 1950s attempted to initiate social change through the use of folk music. In virtually every case, with the partial exception of the music of the coal miners and textile workers, the impetus for change was initiated by largely urban, educated artists who had little or no connection with the working class. This is why so much of this music had relatively little effect. For a Pete Seeger or a Millard Lampell to sing at a union rally and to expect to change the ideology of the workers was naïve and, to some extent patronizing. What made these middle-class performing artists think that they knew enough about local issues or working conditions to feel that they could offer guidance or solutions to the problems that the average longshoreman was experiencing? The average worker only wore work clothes at work, and the visiting folksingers in their flannel shirts and blue jeans were in effect playing at being workers. Moreover, the visiting folkies were singing songs that represented their own tastes, but not necessarily the musical preferences of, for example, black auto workers in Detroit.

The music of Kentucky coal miners, by contrast, was music that the miners had grown up singing. It wasn't something imposed by New York radical intellectuals but was part of the culture. It was a different story in New York. The Almanac Singers may have been casual, but they were professional musicians, and more to the point they were entertainers. They knew how to work a crowd, and their singing was not nasal or difficult for city folks to understand. Although some of the textile singers were also union organizers tied in with communist-led unions, quite a few of the songs sung by mill workers were more localized and they were sung by people who were or aspired to be professional musicians, not protest singers.

This brings us to the music of the civil rights movement. There is a long and rich tradition of African-American music in the South, ranging from the music of formal and store-front churches to secular work songs, hollers, blues, and protest songs. These musical forms were widely known to African Americans and were used on a daily basis at work, in dances parties, or in rough juke joints. Furthermore, it was a living tradition easily familiar to the people in the community. It isn't really surprising that when the sit-ins resulted in jail time, the prisoners sang. They sang songs that they had grown up with but, because so much of black music is highly improvisational, they changed the words to reflect the times. Religious tunes were often used because the call and response pattern enabled a song leader to improvise new words while the "back-up" singers sang a consistent part. SNCC even formed a group called the *Freedom Singers*, which included Bernice Johnson Reagon. Later she was one of the founders of the group *Sweet Honey in the Rock*. Fifty years later that group carries on with different personnel.

## Highlander Folk School

Another key source for the use of music in the movement was the Highlander Folk School in Monteagle, Tennessee. The school was founded in 1932 by two white radicals: poet Don West and Myles Horton. Highlander held workshops for union organizers and civil rights workers from the very beginning. Horton's wife Zilphia was a musician and a song leader who encouraged and nurtured the music of the "students" who attended the school. After her death in 1956, a young folk music revivalist named Guy Carawan gave up his performing career to work at the school and to participate in the Civil Rights movement. Guy and his wife Candy helped civil rights workers put new words to some of the old gospel-flavored songs, and he landed in several southern jails for his trouble. The Carawans also compiled two books of movement songs that were reissued in one volume under the title *Sing for Freedom: The Story of the Civil Rights Movement through Its Songs*. Guy Carawan, Frank Hamilton, Zilphia Horton, and Pete Seeger all had a hand in reworking an old southern gospel song in the renowned *We Shall Overcome*. This song became the anthem of the movement, and was sung in very many rallies, concerts, and even used as a slogan by President Lyndon Johnson when he signed the civil rights legislation in 1964. The authors donated all of their royalties to the cause of civil rights. Highlander School is outside of Knoxville and it still exists today, although in a different location. The state of Tennessee seized the original property and revoked the charter of the school in 1962, but the school continued anyway.

## Movement songs

Leafing through the Carawan's songbook the reader finds a combination of songs written by individual songwriters like Matt Jones and Len Chandler, and movement songs that were written or half-improvised at rallies or on picket lines. For example, the old spiritual *I'm Gonna Sit at the Welcome Table* was modified to include lyrics about sitting in at the Woolworth's lunch counter.

Mississippi leader Fannie Lou Hamer with Carlton Reese modernized *Go Tell It on the Mountain* by adding negative references to Barry Goldwater and Uncle Toms. Len Chandler jr., who took a sabbatical from his New York folk singing career and was arrested over fifty times in the South, transformed *John Browns Body to Move on Over*, with the catch phrase "Move on over or we'll move all over you."

Another sort of song that appears in the Carawans' collection revised current rhythm and blues songs with some added verses. Curtis Mayfield wrote many songs referring to social conditions for African Americans and movement composer and singer Jimmy Collier even referred to him and his group *The Impressions* as "movement fellows." The movement also adapted and rewrote songs by such popular black artists as Ray Charles and Sam Cooke.

## White revivalists and the civil right movement

A number of the young white urban revivalists traveled to the South to support the Civil Rights movement, especially during the Mississippi summer campaign of 1964. That campaign was designed to assist African Americans to register to vote and to help them to pass the absurd tests that blacks needed to visit to register to vote in Mississippi.

With the exception of the Carawans, who essentially devoted their lives to the Civil Rights movement, most of the visiting singers spent limited amounts of time in the South. The usual commitment was a week or two. It is important to distinguish between white artists like Bob Dylan or Judy Collins who sang at a few rallies and urban black revivalist Len Chandler, who stayed and was frequently jailed. Performers like Joan Baez, Theodore Bikel, Phil Ochs, and Pete Seeger gave their support but the reality of the situation was that these artists took comparatively few risks compared to the black (and white) activists who were in the trenches. In fairness, Baez continued her political work by protesting against the Vietnam War and did log over a month in jail for these protests.

When the white singers performed at rallies organized by black activists, there was a bit of conflict between the music of the folksingers and the music that the audiences wanted to hear. For example, in the famous 1963 March on Washington, Dick Gregory objected to having Joan Baez and Peter, Paul & Mary featured as singers. He appreciated their attending the event but felt that they shouldn't be usurping stage time that belonged to Martin Luther King or other black activists. On the other hand, long-time activist Harry Belafonte felt that it was useful and important to have white artists publicly involved in the event.

In 1965, Malcolm X was assassinated, and in 1968 Martin Luther King was murdered as well. These events radicalized the African-American community and the Black Panther Party and other groups began to renounce King's nonviolent tactics. By that time the Civil Rights movement had fragmented and whites were no longer welcome. After King's death the country became increasingly polarized and there were race riots in a number of cities. The folk boom itself had evaporated, and the major issue in white radical politics had become the war in Vietnam.

At the same time black popular music itself became increasingly political. While most of Curtis Mayfield's songs had been somewhat subtle or metaphorical and his music had sort of a soft-gospel sound, the black-owned record companies like Philadelphia International and even Motown began to release records with strong messages. Even the rather politically conservative James Brown jumped on the bandwagon with his 1969 song *Say It Loud, I'm Black and I'm Proud*. Kenneth Gamble and Leon Huff of Philadelphia International Records ADD recorded songs sung by groups like the Chi-Lites and the O'Jays that even referenced issues like slavery. For years Berry Gordy, owner of Motown, had avoided any open political positions with the company's recordings. By the early 1970s Motown artists Marvin Gaye and Stevie Wonder pushed for and received control of their own recordings and Motown producer Norman Whitfield also wrote and produced songs about social issues. Many of these songs used heavier, angry instrumental textures in addition to their explicit lyrics.

The Civil Rights movement was so intertwined with the music of the movement itself that the two were inseparable. It was not, as so much of the Almanac Singers' music was, an add-on to a social issue. The music and the issues were intertwined. It was probably the most effective use of music as a political tool in American history. Many of the rearranged gospel songs were constructed with lyrics that could be adjusted to a particular march or situation. The lyrics about the Albany, Georgia, jail could easily be revised to fit the conditions in Birmingham. Singers like Jimmy Collier, Matt Jones, Julius Lester, and Mabel Hillary didn't become famous performers, but their songs helped to fuel the movement.

# A personal anecdote

In 1963 my band the Journeymen was involved in a thirty-day Hootenanny '63 bus tour along with Glenn Yarbrough, Texas, comedy-country act the Geezinslaw Brothers, Chicago folk-pop singer Jo Mapes, and Canadian pop-folk group *The Halifax Three*. A few days before we were scheduled to appear in Jackson, Mississippi at the city auditorium, we received a call from the civil rights group SNCC. They asked us not to do the show because the city auditorium, where the show was scheduled, was in effect segregated. The town had an ordinance requiring that the audience be segregated. Because the city fathers knew that this ordinance would never survive a court test, they would simply arrest any black person who got within 100 yards of the building on a loitering charge. The charges would later be dismissed, but the segregation rule in effect remained intact.

The members of the tour held a group meeting. The Journeymen voted not to play, as did *Glenn and Jo. The Geezinslaws* were conservative Texans and they voted to play as did the *Halifax Three*. All the members of the Halifax group were Canadians, and they took the position that American racism wasn't their problem. Their guitarist, Zal Yanofsky, didn't want to play but he had no vote. Yanofsky, who later was a founding member of The Lovin' Spoonful, came from a politically radical family and as a teenager had even attended a socialist youth camp in Canada.

SNCC then pointed out that since we weren't going to do the show, we now had a free night. They asked if we would do a free concert at Tougaloo College, a largely black but integrated college north of Jackson that was one of the centers for civil rights agitation in the South. Jo, Glenn, and my band The Journeymen all agreed, and the Journeymen rented a car to get there. On the way out of town John Phillips pulled up to the Greyhound bus station. He handed me a brown paper bag and asked me to check it in a bus locker. As I walked into the station, I suddenly realized that the bag contained several ounces of marijuana. This incident was rather ironic since John was a "frequent user" and I never had much of an interest in drugs. As I walked into the bus station, I imagined myself getting busted and spending a number of years in a Mississippi prison. Fortunately for me, no one seemed to notice. We then drove to Tougaloo, and ended up doing a full concert for the students. Looking around us, we noticed that some of the students were adorned with a variety of bandages. Clearly they had been beaten up by southern cops or thugs. When we got to the end of the show, we all sang *We Shall Overcome*, locking arms together.

When we left, the students warned us to be sure to drive under the speed limit and to make a full stop at any railroad crossing or stop sign. They informed us that we would most likely be followed by cops, and if we even came close to violating any laws we would have the book thrown at us. We drove back to Jackson without incident. The next day the story of our boycott was carried on newspaper wire services all over the South. We got on the bus the next day and drove to our next concert destination in Louisiana. The first people off the bus were the Geezinslaws. They were met with baseball bats and the crowd shouted that if Jackson wasn't good enough for us then we weren't welcome in Louisiana. Our greeters also tossed the usual epithets at us, like "nigger lovers." We drove away, the tour continued, and a few weeks into the tour John Kennedy was assassinated.

Years later, my friend and bandmate Scott McKenzie sent me a story posted on the internet. It seems that at the time of our performance morale was very low in Tougaloo, and our willingness to honor the boycott and to perform was an important event for the students. It seems embarrassing in retrospect that doing the only humane thing was a significant contribution in the eyes of people who were risking their lives every day for the ideal of racial equality. Granted there were some risks in doing what we did, but they seemed utterly insignificant to me in the over-all scope of courage and risk-taking that was so much a part of the Civil Rights movement.

## The role of black musicians in the folk revival and pop-folk music

When the pop-folk revival exploded, there were several black artists who already had established careers. In the world of hootenannies and People's Songs, Laura Duncan, Osborne Smith, and Leon Bibb performed regularly. Josh White had established a career as a blues singer and guitarist and cabaret performer and Brownie McGhee and Sonny Terry had performed and recorded.

Of all the artists in the pop-folk revival, Harry Belafonte was really the only black (West Indian) artist who managed to achieve superstar status. Odetta was a successful artist but her original manager Al Grossman became too busy with his superstar clients to devote much time to her. Other black artists were Jerry

Moore and Sparky Rucker. Of the People's Songs artists, only Leon Bibb managed to sustain a career over a long period of time. He recorded for Vanguard, RCA, and Columbia, but ran afoul of the blacklist in the late 1950s and 1960s. Paul Robeson, whose talents included acting as well as singing, suffered an even more severe setback for his political leanings.

Of the folk-pop groups, only two featured a black performer. Elmerlee Thomas was in the Gateway Singers in 1960–5, and Bob Carey founded the Tarriers with Erik Darling and Alan Arkin in 1956. Clarence Cooper replaced Alan Arkin in the same group in 1958. When looking at the large number of pop-folk groups that were active in that same period, I was not able to turn up any other black members. When you consider that this number includes, to name a few, the Kingston Trio, The Brothers Four, The Highwaymen, The Limeliters, the New Christy Minstrels, and Peter, Paul & Mary, plus dozens of other "secondary" groups like The Chad Mitchell Trio Three and the Halifax Three, and that virtually every one of them included many African-American songs in their repertoires, this is amazing.

There were indeed various black local and touring acts associated with the revival but for the most part they recorded for minor record labels, or despite having major label contracts, were not heavily promoted. They also were not represented by the sort of big-time personal managers that might have helped them win fame and fortune. This credible but not incredibly successful group included Jackie (Landron) Washington in Boston, Terry Collier and Ira and Inman in Chicago, Walt Conley in Denver, Joe and Eddie in Los Angeles, Reggie Garrett in Seattle, Len Chandler, Jimmy Collier, Julius Lester, Bill McAdoo, the Phoenix Singers, and Hal Waters in New York, Stan Wilson and Don Crawford in San Francisco, Al Cromwell in Toronto, Sweet Honey in the Rock in Washington, DC, and Casey Anderson, who lived variously in New York and Los Angeles. Meanwhile a few black artists, including Taj Mahal, Leon Bibb, Odetta, and Josh White's son, Josh White Jr. were able to build long-term careers. None of them sold as many records as the key pop-folk groups nor were they able to command anything near the live appearance money that these groups earned. Although Odetta was managed by Albert Grossman, her role in his business life was greatly diminished when some of his other white acts like Peter, Paul & Mary and Bob Dylan became superstars.

Looking at the list of black artists above, the question remains why didn't any of these artists taste the fruits of success on the same level as the white artists working in the same genres at the same time. To some extent this is an unanswerable question, because stardom is so tied in to timing, promotion, imaging, and the support of record companies and personal managers. However, it is possible to present some reasonable speculations that might account for this situation.

Personal managers may have decided that taking on black performers in, 1960, a poor risk. Inevitably southern audiences might not want to support artists who might insist upon integrated audiences and hotel accommodations for black artists might prove difficult or impossible to procure. Record companies might have felt some confusion about how to promote black folk artists. For example, Len Chandler did two fine albums on Columbia. One can imagine the promotion department trying to figure out whether they should present him as a protest singer who was active in the Civil Rights movement, or as a singer-songwriter who exhibited considerable vocal and instrumental abilities. In any case, none of the black artists listed above enjoyed mass record sales, even though their recordings were released by both major and minor labels. For many of the same reasons, pop-folk groups might have determined that it would be best not to include black musicians in their line-up. Why add another ingredient to the difficulties of regular touring?

To turn to another personal experience: in 1963 the Journeymen did a co-billed concert with Odetta at Hampton-Sydney College in Virginia. We all knew Odetta from having lived in New York and running into her at various shows or social events. When we got to the venue we got to see that she was upset about something. When we asked her what was wrong, she told us that she had gone to the hotel with the fraternity boys who had booked the show. When they got to the hotel, the proprietor refused to allow Odetta to stay there. After considerable negotiating, during which the frat. boys told the hotel that Odetta was an African princess, the hotel agreed to allow her to stay, but only if she used the freight elevator! That was certainly an appropriate reason to be distressed. The concert went off without incident, and we never had the opportunity to discuss the matter again with Odetta. I have always wondered what accommodations were arranged for Odetta's bass player Bill Lee. Bill was a fine bass player, and film-maker Spike Lee's father, but no one's image of an African prince.

## The audience and the performers

The typical college audience for pop-folk shows *c.* 1960–4 was white college students. Therefore, black pop-folk performers found themselves performing for white audiences. Black musicians of the period were mostly involved with rhythm and blues and soul music. If an aspiring musical group of collegiate pop-folk artists had wanted to include black artists, in all likelihood they would have experienced difficulties in finding black musicians who were interested. On a local level in a Northern or Pacific Coast city, Jim Crow was not openly supported by the government, the media, or the music audience. Many of the touring black professionals avoided or limited doing shows in the South because of any possible difficulties or complications that such gigs might present. It is unpleasant to accuse the folk revival of racism, but in my judgment it is fair to say that although African-American singers and musicians were accepted in the revival, there was something less than a strong effort to involve them in the folk-pop party.

## The Blues Move On

Guy Davis, Keb 'Mo, Otis Taylor, and  Phil Wiggins are black blues-based artists whose music has moved in various directions. In recent years a younger generation of black players includes Corey Harris, Ben Harper, Jerron "Blind Box" Paxton, and Alvin Youngblood Hart, have continued to explore various aspects of the blues tradition. Buddy Guy is the patriarch of Chicago blues, while Robert Cray, like the late B.B. King has had some success bringing blues into the pop music world.

# 11

# Folk-Rock, the British Invasion, and the Rise of the Singer-Songwriters

Pop-folk music was essentially a musical fad. There have been numerous fads in the American pop music business. For example, in 1969 gospel-pop music exploded on the New York musical scene. As a result of the hit record *Oh Happy Day,* night clubs opened that featured pop-gospel music and where audience members were given tambourines. Who can forget the disco fad of the late 1970s with its many artists and dance clubs featuring light shows?

The pop-folk fad lasted from 1958 to 1964. There were a number of elements that came into play that eventually led to its demise. The pop music of the late 1950s was a bit sterile, and artists like Fabian or Bobby Rydell didn't have an indefinite shelf life. Jerry Lee Lewis married his thirteen-year-old cousin in December, 1957, throwing his career into temporary oblivion. An airplane crash killed Buddy Holly, the Big Bopper, and Richie Valens in 1959, and late in the same year Chuck Berry was jailed for transporting a minor across the state line for immoral purposes.

Enter the Kingston Trio. They were three very white, jocular, and seemingly wholesome college boys racing up and down the stages of America. Their repertoire consisted mostly of happy-go-lucky listener-friendly songs that can hardly be accused of any sort of moral or political subversion. Meanwhile the trio's booking agents were pioneering the presentation of college concerts at schools all over the United States and Canada. It was the perfect captive audience for the trio. Fun-loving students meet fun-loving musicians.

## Bob Dylan at Newport, 1965

The ever-increasing number of happy-go-lucky pop-folk performing groups inevitably was going to result in entertainment overload. The 1965 Newport

Folk Festival was the beginning of the end of the road for that portion of the folk revival.

One of the most famous Newport conflagrations featured Bob Dylan's performance in 1965. The dedicated Dylan protest fans were offended, but some members of the audience, as well as some music critics, felt like they were seeing the birth of a new musical world. Bob Dylan had already become known to the pop-folk audience, initially through Peter, Paul & Mary's hit recordings of *Don't Think Twice* and *Blowing in the Wind*. He was also getting considerable attention from *New York Times* reviewer Robert Shelton, and was generally placed at the center of a group of political–topical singer-songwriters that included Phil Ochs, Len Chandler, Tom Paxton, and others. By 1965 Dylan was becoming restless with the image that he had so carefully promoted of being a young Woody Guthrie—a protest singer who railed against injustice, inequality, and the establishment. At Newport that year were electric guitarist Mike Bloomfield, and the entire Paul Butterfield blues band. At an afternoon workshop folk guru Alan Lomax was the master of ceremonies for a workshop where the *Butterfield* band was about to play. Looking at their extensive electronic equipment, he remarked that blues masters like Muddy Waters needed little electronic support, and he wondered whether the Butterfield band could really play. Like Dylan, the Butterfield band was managed by Albert Grossman. Lomax's sarcastic introduction resulted in the overweight Grossman and Lomax rolling on the ground in a wrestling match.

Whether by design or improvisation, Dylan elected to use Butterfield's musicians as his back-up band for an evening performance before thousands of fans. The band was deafening, and more to the point, Dylan's lyrics were impossible to understand over the din.

The story of this performance has been told in many other books, but the bottom line was that Dylan temporarily alienated his protest pro-traditional music audience, and upset the festival fathers, notably Pete Seeger. A prevailing myth that came out of the show is that Seeger took an axe and tried to cut down the sound cables of the electric musicians. No real evidence supports this myth but undoubtedly Seeger was terribly upset about the fact that the electric noise was drowning out the lyrics to Dylan's songs. The audience reaction to Dylan's performance was mixed. Some critics, like Paul Nelson, and some of the audience loved the "new" Dylan, and felt that they were seeing the birth of a new musical world. Others hated the show and booed vociferously. Dylan had already recorded his first major rock hit, *Like a Rolling Stone*, a few weeks before the festival, and it was released simultaneously with that event. The song became a massive pop hit and for the next year or so the folk audience struggled with the identity of the "new Dylan" before accepting the notion that the darling of the protest music had abandoned politics. He had chosen instead to become one of the pioneers of an entirely new musical niche, folk-rock music.

Subsequent Newports were relatively tame, but from 1970 to 1985 the festival took a hiatus. George Wein returned in 1985 with a for-profit organization, which once again turned nonprofit in 2011. The nonprofit aspect of the festival is important, because it has promoted folk music research of various kinds.

## A brief folk-rock history

The Byrds, led by Roger (Jim) McGuinn, released Dylan's *Mr. Tambourine Man* in April, 1965, four months ahead of the Newport Festival. The recording featured McGuinn's jangly twelve-string electric guitar and a group of studio sessions players. They followed that up with their version of Pete Seeger's *Turn, Turn, Turn* in September, 1965. In August 1965, the band *We Five* released a hit version of Sylvia Tyson's song *You Were on My Mind*. This was followed by ex-Christy Minstrels singer Barry McGuire's release of P. F. Sloan's song, *Eve of Destruction*. In March, 1967, the Buffalo Springfield, featuring Richie Furay, Stephen Stills, and Neil Young released their one hit, the song *For What It's Worth*. In July 1967 the Youngbloods released the anthemic *Get Together*, a virtual calling card of hippie idealism. These recordings were all massive hits although neither McGuire, We Five, nor the Youngbloods were able to sustain long-term careers as hit artists. The Los-Angeles based Mamas and Papas included members Cass Elliot, Denny Doherty, and John Phillips. All had paid dues in folk groups. Their song *Creeque Alley*, released in April 1967, actually provides a brief somewhat satirical history of the evolution of pop-folk to folk-rock. In a bow to the folk influence, Phillips' twelve-string guitar began the song on a seventh chord, a device strongly associated with Lead Belly's guitar work. Even Peter, Paul & Mary made a perfunctory bow to folk-rock with the song *I Dig Rock and Roll Music*. Linda Ronstadt got her start in a trio called *The Stone Poneys*. In September 1967, her band had a major hit with the song *Different Drum*. The song was written by former Monkee Michael Nesmith. It is fair to say that folk-rock also influenced some of the pop-rock artists. Dion, for example, had his biggest hit song ever with Dick Holler's song *Abraham, Martin and John* released in August 1968. It concerned three great American leaders who were assassinated. In this recording Dion transformed his prior neo-doo-wop style into a folk-rock anthem.

## San Francisco and folk-rock

If there was anything left of the folk-pop explosion, the San Francisco folk-rock, psychedelic bands delivered the death blow to the idiom. Jerry Garcia, Bob Weir, and Ron "Pigpen" McKernan, Janis Joplin and Peter Albin of Big Brother and the Holding Company, Marty Balin, Jorma Kaukonen, and Paul Kantner of the Jefferson Airplane, Country Joe McDonald and David Cohen of Country Joe and the Fish, and David Frieberg and Dino Valenti of Quicksilver Messenger Service were all steeped in folk music. All of them used electric bass and drums, and they played loud! Every once in a while, the folk-rockers would reveal their folk backgrounds. Sometimes it was through their lyrics, as in Neil Young's *Nowadays Clancy Can't Even Sing*, or perhaps a folk instrumental touch might be added, such as Charlie Chin's clawhammer banjo in Stephen Stills' song *Bluebird*.

## The culture and ideology of folk-rock

There were other differences than instrumentation between pop-folk groups and folk-rock bands. The folk-rock bands were steeped in the use of LSD and other psychedelic drugs. They also openly used drug references in their original songs. For the most part, with the exception of John Stewart, the pop-folk groups did not include members who were prolific songwriters. Compared to the folk-rock artists, most pop-folk bands had relatively few hit singles but relied on the sale of their albums to achieve mass popularity.

Although free-form FM radio existed during the early years of the folk boom, it wasn't until the folk-rock immersion that free-form radio stations were proliferating. The rise of these stations paralleled the popularity of folk-rock.

Partly due to the use of drugs, partly as a sort of philosophical stance, and to save money, some of the folk-rock groups, especially the San Francisco versions, lived in communal houses and shared vaguely anarchistic political ideas. The early folksingers had been connected to radical political ideas, and then to the

Civil Rights movement. The folk-rock artists were loosely intertwined with the so-called New Left Movement. The New Left rejected the traditional Marxist–Leninist ideology and had a more free-wheeling approach to radical politics. The most important group was SDS, Students for a Democratic Society. The SDS members were all college students or recent graduates and, unlike the communists or the People's Song group, they were willing to entertain some criticism of communist ideology. The white left-wingers were essentially kicked out of the Civil Rights movement by the mid-to-late 1960s because that movement was focusing on black power and black leadership and less on racial integration. The SDS turned to the war in Vietnam as their primary issue. Once Bob Dylan turned to the personal and away from the political, many of the folk-rockers followed his example. They could be counted on to play benefits for free medical clinics or occasional anti-war rallies, but for the most part they lacked the sort of direct connection that the Almanac Singers or People's Songs artists had maintained. By the late 1960s a left-wing faction of SDS called *The Weathermen* took a more violent approach to social change. They took their name from a Dylan lyric, even though Dylan himself had long since backed away from taking a role as a political singer and songwriter. The lyric proclaimed that you didn't need a weatherman to know which way the wind was blowing. The Weathermen were involved in bank robberies, shoot-outs, and even kidnapping. This ideology didn't appeal to the peace, love, drugs, and flowers notion of the folk-rock musicians. Many of the San Francisco bands featured long jam sessions, often without too much specific musical form. This format has survived today in the work of a number of jam bands like *Phish, Leftover Salmon,* and others.

## Protest music and Vietnam

Although there were many protests against the war in Vietnam, protest music was not at the center of the action. The song most identified with the protests is the Buffalo Springfield's *For What It's Worth.* This song appears in virtually every movie about the war. In fact, the song concerns teenaged riots on the Sunset Strip in Hollywood which had absolutely nothing to do with Vietnam. John Prine's powerful song *Sam Stone* describes a soldier returning from the war with a heroin habit, but it is not an anthemic type of group-singing song. There was an album called *Soul of Vietnam,* but the songs are in rhythm and blues vein. An album called *In Country: Folk Songs of Americans in the Vietnam War* is a collection of songs written by Vietnam veterans. Although all of these songs were written during the 1960s, the album was not recorded until 1991.

There were some strong anti-war folk-rock songs that were written in the 1960s. Country Joe (McDonald) and the Fish originally recorded his song *I Feel Like I'm Fixin' to Die Rag in* 1965, and it was released on their Vanguard Records album in 1967. The Fish worked up their audiences with a spoken word Fish cheer that preceded the song, which became transformed into another four-letter F word chant. Creedence Clearwater Revival recorded John Fogerty's song *Fortunate Son* in 1969. Fogerty's song contrasted the people who were drafted in Vietnam with those who were able to obtain deferments from the military draft. Neil Young's song *Ohio* was a more specific song about a particular event, the shootings of students at Kent State University by the National Guard. The song was written just nineteen days after the event, and the record was released within weeks.

A number of anti-war songs were written by the protest singer-songwriters of the period, including Phil Ochs and Tom Paxton. None of them were as widely performed as the songs above.

Because the war took place entirely overseas, many Americans especially college students with deferments from the draft were able to ignore it. Seemingly the Civil Rights movement was not so easy to overlook. Civil rights music was deeply rooted in black gospel music traditions and the anti-war songs did not have a single musical style that they could draw upon.

## The British are coming

As if folk-rock hadn't caused enough havoc in the world of pop-folk, American music was invaded by an English rock group called *The Beatles*, starting in 1964. The Beatles recorded for EMI, the company that owned Capitol Records. Because of this ownership chain, Capitol had the right of first refusal to issue records by the group in the United States. Like the many English companies that had rejected the band before George Martin decided to produce the band, Capitol turned them down in the United States, although Capitol of Canada released the first North American Beatles album in 1963. By 1964 Capitol changed its mind, and released the first Beatles album in the United States. Initially the band chalked up numerous teen-oriented hit singles in the United States but the release of *Rubber Soul* in 1965, followed by the even more experimental

*Sergeant Pepper's Lonely Hearts Club Band* in 1967 consolidated the Beatles role as the thinking person's band. Numerous other successful English rock records followed across the Atlantic, but the Beatles totally eclipsed what was left of the pop-folk boom.

## The end of folk-rock

Like pop-folk before it, folk-rock had a limited shelf life. It has never entirely ended as a musical style and some singer-songwriters continue to explore it to this day in the so-called Americana radio format. All of the groups mentioned in the preceding paragraphs either broke up or had so many personnel changes that their original identity evaporated. (Jefferson Airplane had so many personnel changes that the members changed the very name of the group several times.) In many cases group members elected to pursue solo careers. There were often ego conflicts between various group members. In some instances, the members' drug or alcohol habits became so intense that they were unable to continue performing on a regular basis. Some members simply left the music business and others became ill or even died.

The progressive FM radio station formats became clichés in their own right and the stations became boring, predictable, and no longer financially viable. Rhythm and blues music was transformed into soul music and began to make serious inroads into the pop-rock market. By the time the war in Vietnam ended in 1973, followed by Nixon's resignation in 1974, none of the original folk-rock groups existed in their original form. Buffalo Springfield mutated into Crosby, Stills, Nash and (sometimes) Young, but they were reduced to periodic reunion tours. In typical rock 'n' roll fashion, the party was over.

## A note about the party

Around 1967 the Mamas and Papas did one of their concerts at Forest Hills Tennis Stadium in New York. My old friend John Phillips invited me to a post-concert party at the posh St. Regis Hotel. The party was something out of a movie about the last days of Rome. Outside the window of the living room, the road manager of the band was scaling the hotel walls. This gentleman was a skilled mountain climber, but he was also stoned out of his mind. John led me to a table with a well-stocked bar and every drug known to man, and many unknown to me. He smiled and described himself as the perfect host. He then offered me whatever I wanted to drink, smoke, and so forth.

I had never seen anything quite like this, and didn't stay too long. Folk-rock had mutated into Hollywood Dionysian excess, and most of the party guests seemed to fit right in. A few years later John was busted for exchanging pills obtained with a fake prescription pad from a New York pharmacy for prescription-quality heroin. One of the brightest people I have ever known in the music industry had become a heroin addict and taken his life to the brink of destruction. John made a deal with the legal authorities and went into a therapy program, later appearing in schools and on television testifying to the dangers of drugs.

## Country rock

Dylan and the Byrds had led the transition from urban folk music to folk-rock. They also were among the earliest folkies to thrown country music into the mix. Lest the reader become seasick at this point, it is important to remember that musical genres are not as easily subsumed into labels as the average record store display might suggest. What I am referring to as country music here is music played by (mostly) white string bands and modified through what I can only call the Nashville organizational meat grinder.

By the late 1960s, Nashville had a thriving studio scene, and had become the capital of country music. Although it made the occasional obligatory bow to traditional country or western styles, the so-called countrypolitan sound had set in. This included violins played en masse rather than in a solo role, back-up singers and smooth, easy on the ear vocals by the artists. The object seemed to be, to sophisticate the act for urban audiences. The back-up singers always seemed to be members of the Jordanaires or the Anita Kerr Singers.

Folk rockers had begun to view albums as artistic statements and their concept project albums could take weeks or even months to record. Country music sessions were turning out a finished product that took about a single hour for each song recorded. An album of ten songs could be comfortably completed in three days or less, if the singer's voice held out. There was a core group of a couple of dozen people that seemed to play on everybody's records. This included guitarists Chet Atkins, Jerry Bradley, and Hank "Sugarfoot" Garland;

piano players Floyd Cramer or Harold "Pig" Robbins; Henry Strzelecki or Roy Husky on bass; and Pete Drake, Buddy Harmon, or Lloyd Green on pedal steel guitar. Charlie McCoy was the harmonica player of choice.

During the mid-1960s the pop-folk and folk-rock artists turned to Nashville to record their albums. Bob Dylan, Ian and Sylvia, and Joan Baez were among the pop-folk artists who recorded in Nashville. It was fast, efficient, and cheap, and the players were cooperative and less jaded than their New York or Los Angeles compatriots.

In Nashville itself, toward the end of the 1960s a group of younger studio musicians began to tire of playing the same old country licks five days a week. There was even a saying among Nashville studio musicians that if a guitar player came to a recording session and played a new hot lick on Monday, by Friday the same lick would be played by other guitarists on four or five sessions. Among the new players were drummers Kenny Buttrey and Jerry Corrigan, bassist Norbert Putnam, guitarists Mac Gayden and Wayne Moss, pianist David Briggs, steel guitarist Weldon Myrick, banjo picker and rhythm guitarist Bobby Thompson, and harmonica wizard and multi-instrumentalist Charlie McCoy. By the end of the decade, these musicians had played on albums by all the pop-folk icons who chose to record in Nashville. Some accidental free time gave a group of the young Turks an opportunity to record themselves jamming on country and Beatle tunes at Wayne Moss's studio. They had been booked for a Monkees session with Monkee Michael Nesmith when he cut the session short. These initial jams ended up as an album on Polygram called *Area Code 615*. The group even did a few live gigs and a Johnny Cash TV show, but basically none of them wanted to tour because they were doing just fine playing sessions in Nashville. A second album followed and later the group changed its name to *Barefoot Jerry*, with slightly different personnel. *The Area 615* albums were way ahead of their time, and without a touring band, the albums slipped out of sight.

Country-rock wasn't only about Nashville. A group of young musicians emerged in Los Angeles who had deep roots in folk and country music. Among the most important of these musicians were guitarist Clarence White and Florida–Los Angeles émigré singer-songwriter Gram Parsons. The Dillards were a Missouri bluegrass group that settled in Los Angeles, and appeared on the Andy Griffith TV show. Another group of West Coast musicians including lead vocalists Jeff Hanna and Jimmy Ibbotson and multi-instrumentalist John McEuen formed the Nitty Gritty Dirt Band. Chris Hillman, a member of the Byrds, had a solid background as a bluegrass mandolin player, and Herb

Pedersen, who replaced Doug Dillard in the Dillards, was also an experienced bluegrass player.

Gram Parsons transitioned through a pop-folk group called the Shilos, had a brief fling at Harvard, then moved to the International Submarine Band, and then the Byrds. During his short tenure with the Byrds in 1968 he pushed the band in a country direction with their album *Sweetheart of the Rodeo*. Various disputes between the various Byrds, included a South African tour playing for segregated audiences and Parson's fascination with his new friends the Rolling Stones. Parsons quit just before the South African tour and went on to form the more heavily country *Flying Burrito Brothers*. He was eventually kicked out of his own band because of his ever-growing alcohol and drug dependency. He then started to perform with a young singer named Emmylou Harris, who has spread the influence of his music far beyond any success that Gram achieved in his short lifetime. Parsons flamed out in rock-star style, dying from drug abuse. Phil Kaufman, his road manager, stole his casket from an airport loading dock, cremating him in the desert at Joshua Tree, California, where Gram had been living.

Although many of the rock stars who died young, such as Jimi Hendrix, Janis Joplin, and Jim Morrison, they became, if anything, more famous after their deaths, Gram Parsons's reputation has extended primarily to other musicians. A half dozen songs have been written about him. Among the songwriters who have celebrated his life are Richie Furay, Emmylou Harris, Bernie Leadon, and John Phillips.

In the late 1960s and the early 1970s country-rock really caught fire. Poco was formed in 1969 by Richie Furay after the breakup of the Buffalo Springfield. Pure Prairie League was a band in southern Ohio that formed in 1965. It had two hit songs, *Amie*, in 1975 and *Let Me Love You Tonight*, in 1980. The Eagles formed in 1971, and as every reader knows, have had countless hits from that time forward. All three of these bands experienced fairly frequent personnel changes. In several instances the founder of the group himself exited.

The last real roar of folk-rock was the band Crosby, Stills and Nash, founded in 1968. By 1969 they had added Neil Young to the line-up. Young seems to drift in and out of the band, depending on his mood, and his relationships with the other band members. Poco, the Eagles, and Pure Prairie League have generally avoided any sort of social–political statements in their songs, but Crosby, Stills, Nash, and Young have written and performed some songs, notably *Ohio*, by Neil Young that do take positions on current events. Ohio describes the 1970 shootings of unarmed students by the National Guard at Kent State University in Ohio. The students were protesting the bombing of Cambodia.

## Austin

By 1970 many country musicians had become unhappy with the Nashville music establishment. Many of these musicians had backgrounds playing folk, country and rock music, and quite a few of them were songwriters. Leaving Nashville behind, they settled in Austin, Texas. Willie Nelson and Michael Martin Murphy were the best known of the group. J. W. Stevenson had one big hit with a song called *My Maria* that he had co-written with Daniel Moore. Willis Alan Ramsey to this day has only released one album, but his song *Muskrat Love* became a substantial hit by pop group *The Captain and Tennille*. Bobby Bridger was a singer-songwriter-playwright obsessed with western history, and he somehow persuaded RCA Records to issue some of his music based on western themes and legends.

It seemed as though Austin had an endless supply of singer-songwriter-performers. Kinky Friedman had a band called the Texas Jewboys, and he managed to outrage and irritate a sizeable number of people before eventually becoming a successful mystery writer and an unsuccessful candidate for governor of Texas. In 1976 Willie Nelson had a hit with local writer Steve Fromholz's *I'd Have to Be Crazy*, and in 1998 singer-songwriter Lyle Lovett recorded a double album of songs by Texas singer-songwriters that included Steve's brilliant *Texas Trilogy*. Townes Van Zandt's song *Pancho and Lefty* became a folk and country standard as well as a huge hit by Nelson Willie and Merle Haggard, and Van Zandt made a number of interesting albums that were more popular with other musicians than with the general public. Jerry Jeff Walker became an Austin institution, and his song *Mr. Bojangles* struck pay dirt in a recording by the *Nitty Gritty Dirt Band*. R Ray Wylie Hubbard's *Up against the Wall Redneck Mother* is a true Austin classic and Murphy had his share of hits before moving to Colorado, and New Mexico, and turning to western music rather than his own songs.

*Austin City Limits* is a television show that began in 1976 and features country, folk, and country-rock singers. Some are local and others are nationally known artists. The South By Southwest (SXSW) music festival began in 1987, and brought hundreds of bands, record companies, and publishing employees and fans to the town. SXSW began as an alternative venue to existing large music conferences, but has itself become a major music business gathering over the years.

## The Band

I don't know exactly how to categorize the country-folk-rock group *The Band*. They were four Canadians, joined by a funky Arkansas-born drummer. The Band was the backup band for legendary American rocker Ronnie Hawkins who had emigrated to Canada. They later became Bob Dylan's backup band, and after his 1966 motorcycle accident they took up residence in a house near Woodstock. They proceeded to record twenty-four songs, some written by Dylan, some co-authored with him, and others written by members of The Band.

These songs ran the gamut from bluesy rock to country-rock and the instrumentation included keyboards, drums, mandolin, electric bass, electric and acoustic guitars, harmonica, accordion, and tenor sax. The songs written by Dylan were recorded in 1967 and intended as publisher's demos to get other people to record them while Dylan was recuperating from his accident. The recordings were surprisingly well circulated as bootleg recordings and released in 1975 as *The Basement Tapes*.

Prominent music critic Greil Marcus has proclaimed *The Basement Tapes* as the Holy Grail of Americana, a sort of modern realization of the old Folkways *Anthology of American Folk Music*. He appears to be referring to references to the American Civil War, American place names, and biblical allusions. The songs are enjoyable to listen to, and the different singers provide good variety in the ways that they interpret the lyrics. Oddly the songs sound almost more dated than the songs on the Anthology, yet those songs are forty to fifty years older than anything that the Band ever recorded.

Robbie Robertson's song *The Night They Drove Old Dixie Down* was a major hit for Joan Baez in 1971. In a sense the Band shared a common fabricated identity with Bob Dylan. Except for Levon Helm, the other four members were all Canadians; yet, many of their songs related to American history and mythology. A bunch of Canadian rockers transformed themselves into an American roots music-folk-rock band. The band was active from 1968 to 1977. Serious personal and business disagreements erupted between Helm and Robertson, each of whose story is told in separate books. In 1977 Robertson left to pursue a career as a solo artist and record producer. Richard Manuel died in 1986, but the band continued to tour without him. Occasional band reunions continued without Robertson, until Rick Danko died in 1999.

Movie director Martin Scorsese made a film of the original band's last performance in 1976 called *The Last Waltz*, which was released in 1978. The film is still shown on cable TV, and is probably their best-known calling card.

## The singer-songwriters

Before the 1960s, artists were generally singers who recorded songs written by professional songwriters who were not singers. There were some exceptions, like Peggy Lee, who co-authored some of her songs with her then husband guitarist Dave Barbour.

For the most part the urban folk revivalists, at least during the early days of the folk revival, were not songwriters. Although the political songwriters like Woody Guthrie or the Almanacs did write songs, by the 1950s most of their careers were either in decline or had ended. The repertoire of the tradition-oriented singers came from the Harry Smith Folkways Anthology records, or from recordings by earlier singers like Burl Ives or Richard Dyer-Bennett. The folk-pop artists got much of their material from recordings by the Weavers, Woody Guthrie, or Lead Belly. Terry Gilkyson was a singer-songwriter, but once he left The Easy Riders in the early 1960s he concentrated on songwriting, working for the Disney Studios.

John Stewart was first pop-folk group member after Gilkyson who was a committed and prolific songwriter. He started out with a group called *The Cumberland Three*, and then replaced Dave Guard in the Kingston Trio in 1961. John was a competent banjo and guitar player and an adequate singer, but he has never really received adequate recognition for his songwriting skills. Although most of John's material was not political, during the 1960s he became quite involved in the political campaigns of both John and Robert Kennedy. His Kennedy-era songs were idealistic and hopeful, rather than the sort of agit-propaganda songs that the Almanacs had written.

Of all the singer-songwriters of his era, Stewart seemed to be the least swayed or influenced by Dylan's work. John's songs tended to be written along the lines of pop and folk songs. Many of the songs explore various historical and emotional aspects of life and the American historical experience as a whole. His *California Bloodlines* album is generally regarded as one of the best of those works.

It is difficult to categorize the work of Laura Nyro. She had a unique ability to make up or recontextualize words and phrases. Because she played piano rather than guitar, was a bit of a recluse, and her recordings tended to be a bit more commercial than what was considered "folky," Nyro has never clearly fit into one musical category. Moreover, the hit recordings of her songs were usually made by pop-group artists like the Fifth Dimension, Blood Sweat and Tears, and Barbra Streisand. Consequently, her name rarely appears in books about the folk revival although a number of other artists, like Joni Mitchell, have acknowledged her influence and talent.

## The New York scene

There were a number of talented singer-songwriters on the New York scene in the early-to-mid-1960s. Fred Neil held court at the Café Wha in the Village. Fred sang in something of a Johnny Cash vocal register. His biggest successes came through other people's recordings, particularly Harry Nilsson's 1969 recording of Fred's song *Everybody's Talkin'*, the theme from the movie *Midnight Cowboy*. An unusual part of Fred's story is that he was a contract songwriter for music publisher Aaron Schroeder Music. Neil possessed a bluesy, ingratiating voice and several of his other songs, *The Bag I'm In*, *Blues on the Ceiling*, *The Dolphin*, and *Other Side of This Life*, were covered by other artists on records or in performances. Neil recorded for Elektra and Capitol, but his career never took off because of his reluctance to tour. He spent the last thirty years of his life in Florida, concerning himself with the protection and preservation of dolphins.

Like Fred Neil, Tim Hardin had a soulful bluesy voice. His life was embittered by Bobby Darin's hit recording of the Hardin song *If I Were a Carpenter*. Darin's recording closely followed Tim's demo of the song, and although he did receive songwriting royalties, he felt that Darin's record had eliminated his own big chance at success. In addition to Darin's recording, several dozen artists, including the Four Tops and Waylon Jennings also recorded it.

Hardin had another handful of artistic but commercially viable songs that were covered by other artists. *Reason to Believe* was recorded by rocker Rod Stewart, The Nice recorded *Hang on to a Dream*, and *The Lady Came from Baltimore* and *Don't Make Promises* were also covered by other artists. The Baltimore song was the slightly edited version of his courtship and marriage to soap opera star Susan Morss. Hardin's heroin habit led to his death at age thirty-nine.

There were a number of other New York-based singer-songwriters including, Tom Rapp, the leader of the band *Pearls before Swine* and American Indian writer and singer Patrick Sky, who performed traditional songs as well as his own work. In later life Rapp became a lawyer and Sky got a degree in folklore and became a builder of Uillean pipes. David Cohen, who sometimes recorded under the name David Blue, was a singer-songwriter who was strongly influenced by Bob Dylan. He recorded a half-dozen albums in New York and California and also had some success pursuing an acting career in Los Angeles.

Eric Andersen followed the Dylan influence although his songs tend to reflect his individual, literary-poetic style, but nevertheless they have been covered by Mary Chapin Carpenter, Judy Collins, Bob Dylan, and Fairport Convention, among others. Eric has continued to write and perform both in the United States and in Europe, where he has lived since the 1980s. Eric had the bizarre experience of recording an album in 1972–3 that was literally lost in the vaults of Columbia Records, rediscovered and finally issued in 1991. To aggravate matters, this event occurred immediately after an earlier Andersen Columbia disc had actually made the pop charts.

Tom Paxton has written a number of topical, sometimes satirical songs, but his biggest commercial successes have come from his romantic, almost sentimental works. The most popular of these songs are *The Last Thing on My Mind*, *I Can't Help but Wonder Where I'm Bound*, and *Rambling Boy*. He has also tasted success with his children's songs *The Marvelous Toy* and *My Dog's Bigger Than Your Dog*, which was turned into a dog food commercial. Tom even wrote a few hit songs, including *Bottle of Wine*, recorded by Jimmy Gilmer and the Fireballs, and *Wasn't That a Party*, recorded by the Irish Rovers. Paxton has also written and recorded many songs of social commentary. In 2017 he began to tour with the Don Juans, Nashville songwriter-performers Don Henry and Jon Vezner.

Phil Ochs spent a large part of his life and energy trying to compete with Bob Dylan's artistry, hipness, and popularity. The various Dylan biographies claim that Dylan was not kind to Ochs, treating him like a sort of hack pretender to the protest songwriting throne. Ochs, on the other hand, was a staunch defender of Dylan's right to artistic freedom when many of his fellow radicals attacked Dylan for deserting left-wing politics and writing more personal, subjective, and abstract songs. Ochs himself seemed to feel that he was eventually going to best Dylan in some mythical musical competition that took place in his own mind. Later, Ochs started to reference Elvis as his musical hero, and he started to adopt the king's dress code. By 1975 Ochs had become frustrated by his lack of success and the fact that the radical movement in the United States was making so little headway. Ochs suffered from bi-polar disorder and depression, and committed suicide in 1976.

## Here come the Canadians

I have already discussed how Ian and Sylvia transitioned from a successful pop-folk group to a more contemporary format that included their own composed songs. There were four other major Canadian singer-songwriters who had a large impact on music in both Canada and the United States during the 1960s and 1970s and even in later years.

Bruce Cockburn played in various rock bands in the mid-1960s after attending the Berklee College of Music for three semesters. His first solo album appeared in 1970, and since then he has recorded thirty-three albums. Cockburn has had considerable success in Canada but in America his fan base developed out of the 1979 hit *Wonder Where the Lions Are* and his lesser 1984 hit *If I Had a Rocket Launcher.*

Cockburn is one of the better guitarists among the singer-songwriters, and has even recorded some solo instrumental pieces. His songs cover a wide range of subjects, from Christianity to progressive politics to environmental issues. In 2014 his autobiography *Rumors of Glory* was published.

Leonard Cohen was a Canadian poet and novelist who essentially backed into a career as a singer-songwriter-performer. Cohen started out as a poet but his novel *Beautiful Losers,* written in 1966, brought him to the attention of a wider audience, especially in Canada. Cohen's song *Suzanne,* recorded by Judy Collins in 1967 brought his musical talents to the fore. His own records, which featured his own modest vocal talents, brought him success in Canada and England, but less so in the United States. Periodically Cohen would tour and then turn away from touring. He entered a Buddhist monastery in Los Angeles in 1994, was ordained as a monk and then left in 1997. During this period his manager Kelly Lynch stole some five million dollars from him. Cohen was forced back on the road, and despite his initial reluctance, toured successfully. His most successful song was the anthemic *Hallelujah.* Jeff Buckley's record of the song is regarded as kind of the classic version but numerous others recorded it. The list includes Jon Bon Jovi, K. D. Lang, and Rufus Wainwright.

Cohen's singing was definitely an acquired taste. While accepting a Grammy Musicares award Bob Dylan said "Critics say my voice is shot. That I have no voice. Why don't they say those things about Leonard Cohen?" To be fair, Dylan was openly appreciative of Cohen's melodic and lyric songwriting gifts.

Gordon Lightfoot's songs are among the most performed and recorded songs of any North American singer-songwriter. Ian and Sylvia heard Lightfoot performing his songs in a Toronto nightclub in 1963 and added some of his songs to their repertoire. They then introduced him to their manager, Albert Grossman, who signed him. As had been the case with Bob Dylan, this led Peter, Paul & Mary, also Grossman clients, to record Lightfoot's songs *Early Morning Rain* and *For Lovin' Me*. Grossman also engineered a recording contract with United Artist records. Lightfoot recorded five albums for United Artists. In 1967 the Canadian Broadcasting Company commissioned Lightfoot to write a song about the building of the Canadian transcontinental railroad. Lightfoot responded by writing the song *Canadian Railroad Trilogy*, possibly his most Canadian song, in terms of its subject matter and historical references. By 1970 Lightfoot was a major star in Canada but in the United States was best known as a songwriter because of the hit records of his songs by other artists. In 1970 Lightfoot left the Grossman stable and signed a new record deal with Warner Brothers' Reprise Records label. His song *If You Could Read My Mind* became his first hit in the United States, and the album itself became a Top Ten pop offering.

Lightfoot remained a successful touring artist beyond the 1970s although he had to combat an abdominal aortic aneurysm in 2002 and a minor stroke in 2006.

## Joni Mitchell

Many critics consider Joni Mitchell to be the most artistically significant of all singer-songwriters. Mitchell began her career as a coffeehouse singer in her native Canada, moving to Detroit when she married Chuck Mitchell. She performed at many coffeehouses in Detroit and on the East Coast before securing a record deal in 1968. Because Joan Baez and Judy Collins were already well established as important female folk artists, initially record companies were somewhat reluctant to sign her. Her first record was produced by David Crosby, and released in 1968. During that same year Judy Collins had a major hit record with Joni's song, *Clouds (Both Sides Now)*. Mitchell went on to craft an enormously influential group of songs, and had a few hits of her own in the 1970s, which will be discussed in the next chapter.

# K. D. Lang

K. D. Lang is such a spectacular and versatile singer that it is easy to overlook her abilities as a songwriter. As a vocalist, Lang has recorded country music with Nashville guru Owen Bradley, a duet album with Tony Bennett, and has performed in numerous musical genres. Much of her songwriting work was done with Ben Mink, a violinist who produced several of Lang's albums. In 1993, Lang and Mink wrote the songs and did the film soundtrack for the film *Even Cowgirls Get the Blues*. In the context of this book, her two most important albums are her 2004 collection of Canadian singer-songwriters *Hymns of the 49th Parallel*, and her 2016 collaboration with Nekko Case and Laura Vieirs, *case/lang/viers*.

Lang is a social activist, who came out as a lesbian in 1992, and is involved in animal rights, Tibetan human rights, and gay/lesbian causes.

# Neil Young

What are we to make of Neil Young? Is he a rock artist, a folk-rock artist, a punk performer, a folkie, an electronics dude, or a country-rock guy? Or is he all of those things? Neil started out in his native Canada in a rock band called the *Mynah Birds*. The leader singer was Rick James, and they were signed to Motown. Young only lasted for a few months, because the band had managerial problems, and James turned out to be a deserter from the Navy. Although James ended up with a successful Motown career and the band reformed, Neil drove to Los Angeles in a hearse and started the Buffalo Springfield with Stephen Stills and Richie Furay.

Over the years Young has pursued a similar path to the one Bob Dylan chose. Each album seems to be wildly different from the last one. When he plays with his band Crazy Horse it's rock 'n' roll all the time. In between there are singer-songwriter folk or country folk albums with an occasional punk or electronic feature thrown in. To sweeten the pot periodically Crosby, Stills, and Nash become CSN and Young, and folk-rock rules the day.

Like Joni Mitchell Young lives in California not Canada, but both of them are generally identified as Canadians. Each of them has written songs about Canada, including Mitchell's *Oh Canada* and Neil Young's *Helpless*, a tale about a house in Ontario.

## Singer-songwriters: The pluses and the minuses

By the end of the 1960s it became de rigueur for younger folksingers and folk-rock singers to record their own songs. The positive part of this process was that the artists generally had a strong emotional attachment to their own songs. The flip side of the coin was that artists became extremely conscious that writing one's own songs was another opportunity to earn money from records and additional money if someone else recorded the song. It also stoked the artist's ego to have their own songs on a record, and see their own names represented multiple times in the song credits. The situation remains unchanged today. Yet when you think about it, some of the best recordings have been made by artists singing songs that have been written by other people. For example, think of Aretha Franklin's recording of Otis Redding's song *Respect*, Carole King's song *You Make Me Feel Like a Natural Woman*, or Paul Simon's *Bridge over Troubled Water*. Redding and King, in fact, publicly acknowledged Franklin's mastery of their songs.

As more and more artists wrote all or most of their own songs, some singer-songwriters who never imagined themselves as performing artists found themselves having to consider pursuing that avenue because it was the easiest way for them to get their own songs recorded. Other artists like John Denver used the success of a song recorded by another artist as a springboard to their own record deal. In Denver's case it was Peter, Paul & Mary's recording of *Leaving on a Jet Plane* that made his career possible.

## Songs and copyrights: You should never have taken the very best

Under the US Copyright Law there are two elements of a song that produce a copyright. These are the melody of a song and its lyrics. Although clearly rhythms and beats have become increasingly important in twenty-first-century pop music, those elements cannot be copyrighted.

There is a long and unpleasant history of lawsuits that involve copyright infringement. To prove a case of infringement a writer must show similarity in her song and the infringing song and also must show that the violator had access to the original song. Song titles themselves cannot be copyrighted.

To put this in another way, if you have written a song and someone in Kenya two months later writes a song with a very similar melody, unless you can prove that the Kenyan had access to your song, whether through sheet music, a recording, a live performance, or any other existing medium of transmission, you will not win a copyright infringement lawsuit.

In several other portions of this book I have discussed how pop-folk singers copyrighted existing traditional songs either by making changes in them, or by claiming to have "adapted and arranged" them. The current term of copyright is that the rights exist for the life of the last living author, plus an additional seventy years. Because an earlier copyright preceded the current one, anything written before 1923 is currently considered to be in the public domain. This means that anyone can use these songs in any way they wish to without paying royalties.

There have been many well-known copyright suits in the folksong genre involving well-known songs. Some songs that have been the subject of such suits include *Home on the Range* and *Tom Dooley*. In the last two years both songs *Happy Birthday* and *We Shall Overcome* have been declared to be in the public domain, and the copyright owners have even had to provide financial restitution for prior payments.

## "Hey Joe, What You Goin' to Do with Those Royalties?"

One of the strangest songwriting controversies that I know about in the folksong world is the tale of the song *Hey Joe*. The New York folk community was relatively small during the 1950s, and many of the artists and songwriters knew one another through informal picking parties. One of the singer-songwriters was a young woman named Niela Miller. I particularly recall a song that she sang at the time called *Baby, Please Don't Go to Town*. The latter song used an unusual though not unique chord progression, moving in fifths from F to C to G to D to A.

Toward the end of this time, Niela started going out with a bluesy twelve-string guitarist named Billy Roberts. About ten years elapsed, and suddenly I heard a song called *Hey Joe* on the radio. It seemed oddly familiar to me, though the words were different. At some point I realized that this song was derived from Niela's song, and I assumed that she was making tons of money from the many successful recordings of the song by a West Coast band called *the Leaves* and then by Jimi Hendrix's version. It turned out that Billy had learned the song from her, changed *Hey Babe* to *Hey Joe*, and changed the lyric from a song about the perils of a young woman in the city to the story of a man who murdered his lover. Billy never recorded the song but he copyrighted it in 1962 and performed it in his shows. Niela had recorded a demo of her song but had never copyrighted it.

At the present time there are eight hundred documented recordings of the song and it appears in over fifty songbooks. Along the way both Tim Rose and Dino Valenti attempted to copyright *Hey Joe*, possibly believing that it was a traditional song. Robert's publisher Third Palm Music (formerly Third Story Music) fought back and now controls the copyright. Meanwhile Niela Miller pursued her career as a psychiatric social worker and never received any money for her contributions to the song. Billy Roberts received all of the credit and all of the income from the song.

In 1968 I was working as a record producer for a subsidiary of ABC Records and ran into Niela Miller on the street. When she told me that she was not being credited for *Hey Joe*, I took her up to the ABC offices and we talked to a lawyer for the company. Unfortunately, under the old copyright act which expired in 1976, when a song was copyrighted there were no grounds for reasonable error. Therefore, the lawyer told Niela that she had forfeited her claims to the song.

I'm not sure what the moral of this story is, but there must be something in there about warning lovers about the possibility of future larceny when couples break up.

12

# The Increasing Influence of Singer-Songwriters and the Women's Music Movement

As the importance of folk-rock diminished, the mainstream currents of popular music moved further away from any sort of folk sensibility. Elektra Records, once a folk label, became increasingly devoted to rock 'n' roll, and the importance of an artist like Judy Collins receded in the eyes of the label. Rock album sales for artists like The Doors were in the millions. Vanguard did well with County Joe and The Fish. Of the folk record labels, only Folkways remained essentially unchanged with Moe Asch, as always, unmoved by sales or pop music trends. Other folk labels like Folk Legacy continued to release records, but they were definitely aimed at a niche market, not the general public.

In 1971 Paul Simon split from Art Garfunkel and quickly tasted success with his songs *Mother and Child Reunion* and *Me and Julio Down by the Schoolyard*. After several albums achieved only moderate sales, Simon added world music elements to his sound. His 1986 *Graceland* album became his biggest solo success. Graceland caused considerable controversy because Simon ignored the anti-apartheid boycott. Although he treated his African musicians well in terms of payments and royalties for the recording, there was still some resentment against him from the political left.

Bob Dylan continued on his own idiosyncratic path. After something of a creative slump by the end of the 60s, Dylan released *Self Portrait* in 1970. Self Portrait was a strange double album that included everything from old folksongs to covers of songs written by his contemporaries. He also redefined his voice by crooning to replace his usual rasp. Throughout his career critics have written off Dylan's ability to revive his talent, and then changed their minds. His 1970 album *New Morning* and the 1975 *Blood on the Tracks* reinvigorated his career. In 1979 Dylan became, apparently temporarily, a born-again Christian, and his *Slow Train Coming* album testified to that transition.

# Folk-pop and otherwise

Crosby, Stills, and Nash and Jackson Browne were among the singer-songwriters who were extremely popular during the 1970s. Stills' *Suite for Judy Blue Eyes* was a series of songs that documented his relationship with Judy Collins, featuring a heavy dose of acoustic guitar. Graham Nash's *Teach Your Children Well* was a sort of folk-themed appeal to parents to bring up their children in a sane and peaceful world. Browne co-authored *Take It Easy* with Eagle Glenn Frey, and it included a nice dose of bluegrass banjo played by early Eagle Bernie Leadon. The Eagles had one foot in rock and the other in country music, and possibly one sock in folk music. They also recorded an unusual and successful acapella version of country-folk-rock swinger Steve Young's song *Seven Bridges Road.*

Other male singer-songwriters of the 1970s danced back and forth between folk, country, and rock music styles. Chicago singer-songwriter Steve Goodman wrote the hit song *City of New Orleans* which was a huge hit for Arlo Guthrie. Goodman, who was widely regarded as a tremendous performer but who had little success on records, also co-authored the self-described satirical country song *You Never Call Even Me by My Name* with his friend John Prine in 1971.

James Taylor has established a long-term career as a singer-songwriter, beginning with his huge 1970 hit *Fire and Rain.* As is the case with Paul Simon, much of Taylor's connection to folk music lies in his acoustic guitar playing and relatively straightforward delivery. Somehow Taylor recently managed to play in the Telluride Bluegrass Festival. It is reasonable to place him in a variety of musical categories—soft-rock, pop-folk, etc.

Gordon Lightfoot continued his success with his bluesy 1974 Sundown and his 1976 song *Wreck of the Edmund Fitzgerald.* This is a rare A-form song which has no chorus, only verses. It is written in the style of a traditional folk ballad but the repetition is masked by a clever production. Additional instruments enter during the various verses, giving the illusion of change to the music.

The biggest neo-folk artist of the 1970s was John Denver. Denver replaced Chad Mitchell in the Chad Mitchell Trio in 1964. During the 1960s he was best known as the author of Peter, Paul & Mary's hit song *Leaving on a Jet Plane.* In 1969 he began his solo career. After several mildly successful albums he hit pay dirt in 1971 with the song *Take Me Home Country Roads,* co-written with Bill Danoff and Taffy Nivert. Denver moved to Colorado and he wrote a number of songs about the Rocky Mountains, especially *Rocky Mountain High,* which helped to cause a veritable population explosion in the area. Denver's sociopolitical interests were not directed as much toward politics as to environmental change. He set up a foundation to promote environmental causes.

Denver's music was really pop music with mostly acoustic guitars and the occasional fiddle, banjo, or pedal steel guitar. He had a dozen hit songs during the 1970, including the country tune *Thank God I'm a Country Boy*, written by John Sommer, a member of his band. Denver's popularity grew so great that he even won awards from country music associations to the discomfort of the more conservative members. By the end of the 1970s he had drifted into a career as a movie actor and TV personality and his music had diminished in popularity. In 1997 he died while piloting an airplane.

Dan Fogelberg was a folk-pop-country-soft rock songwriter. Like John Denver he was captivated by the Colorado Mountains, and lived in Pagosa Springs, Colorado, during the 1980s. Besides writing many hit pop-folk-country songs, Fogelberg recorded a bluegrass album in 1985, gathering such bluegrass stalwarts as Ricky Skaggs and Doc Watson for the project.

Harry Chapin was another singer-songwriter who experienced a meteoric rise to fame during the 1970s. Son of a well-known New York drummer, Chapin briefly sang with his brothers Tom and Steve during the mid-1960s. Harry specialized in story-songs, pop songs that followed a folk format in the sense that they resembled short films about real or imaginary characters. His lengthy 1972 song *Taxi* concerned an accidental encounter with an ex-girlfriend while he was driving a cab. In 1973 he had another successful single with the song *WOLD*, a sad portrait of a radio disc jockey whose career and life are in decline. The following year he had a #1 record with his song *Cats in the Cradle*, a portrait of a non-communicative father–son relationship that portrays two people who can never find time for one another.

Chapin's academic background was in film, and he wrote a play called *The Night That Made America Famous* that won two Tony Award nominations. He was a very energetic person who became deeply involved in the battle against world hunger, doing many benefits for that cause.

Because Chapin used a cello in his band, and his arrangements tended toward art-rock, he did not receive much recognition in the folk music community. The structure and subject matter of his songs make an argument in favor of such recognition. His songs differed from those of many of his peers in the sense that except for *Taxi*, most of his songs were not about himself. His career was cut short by a fatal 1981 auto accident.

His brother Tom has gone on to establish his own successful but less dramatic career as a singer-songwriter and children's music performer. He hosted an award-winning TV show called *Make a Wish* from 1971 to 1976*.

## *Dueling Banjos*: The deliverance debacle

One of the true wild cards of the 1970s was the hit recording of Dueling Banjos. Poet and novelist James Dickey met Mike Russo and Ron Brentano during a short college teaching engagement in Portland in the late 1960s. Dickey wrote the novel that the movie was based upon. Dickey particularly liked their version of Arthur Smith's tune *Dueling Banjos* and when Warner Brothers began to express interest in transforming the novel into a movie, he promised the duo that they would be doing the music for the film. Dickey later discovered that he didn't control the music for the film. The first call for the score was made to banjoist Bill Keith, but he was booked for some European engagements. He then recommended New York studio banjo whiz Eric Weissberg. Weissberg flew to Atlanta with guitarist Steve Mandell and they recorded many versions of the tune at various tempos. Eric did not know that the song was going to be released as a single, and he had to enlist a New York attorney to receive the proper credit and royalties. Mike Russo in particular was heartbroken that he and Brentano had not gotten to do the song in the film. The record eventually got to #2 on the Billboard charts, and is still a much-requested number at bluegrass festivals, and wherever a banjo is heard.

*Dueling Banjos* very quickly became a hit; so instead of doing an album to follow it up, Warner Brothers Records simply leased an earlier record that Eric had done with his old friend Marshall Brickman on Warner owned Elektra Records. That 1963 album was called *New Dimension in Banjo and Bluegrass*. The new release omitted a really nice original tune of Eric's called *No Title Yet Blues*. The album featured many banjo duets with Marshall and Eric and a strong supporting cast including guitarist Clarence White. The banjo playing on the album was inspired by Bill Keith's melodic banjo playing, which was a more musically complex off-shoot of Earl Scruggs's bluegrass banjo style. Dueling Banjos sold

---

* Jim Croce is a somewhat neglected figure in the folk music revival. After an earlier, commercially unsuccessful recording with his wife Ingrid, he experienced a great degree of popular music success in 1972–3 with his songs, notably Time In A Bottle, and Bad Bad, Leroy Brown. Because he died in an airplane crash in 1973, and possibly because his songs achieved such widespread popularity, he has not received his due as a singer-songwriter.

over two million copies, and Eric toured with a band for several years, going out on weekends and racing home to do studio work from Monday through Thursday.

In addition to Warner Brothers not paying Eric his royalties as an artist, Warner Brothers did not credit Arthur Smith with the songwriting royalties for the tune. Arthur successfully sued to recover these royalties. Smith died in 2014, and in one of the obituaries that I read he was asked about the success of the song. He had a photo of a large yacht in the office of his recording studio. When asked how much money he made from the songwriting royalties, he simply pointed to the yacht!

The *Deliverance* record initiated a tremendous boom in the sale of banjos, records featuring the banjo, bluegrass music in general, and instructional materials for the instrument.

## Female artists and singer-songwriters

Traditionally in American popular music, women have been relegated to the role of "chick singers." Their recordings were produced by male producers, the charts that the studio musicians used were written by male music arrangers and the studio musicians were almost entirely males. The same holds true for live performances, with male bands led by male bandleaders. Swing bands almost invariably had a female vocalist as much for the image as for musical reasons. Even though a number of these performers like Jo Stafford, Billie Holiday, or Rosemary Clooney were excellent musicians, the general public and many of their male accompanists viewed them as a sort of necessary evil.

Women played a more significant role in the folk revival. Susan Reed and Jean Ritchie were soloists during the early part of the revival and Ronnie Gilbert was an important and acknowledged part of the Weavers' sound. Ritchie started out as a traditional singer who learned songs from various members of her Kentucky family. She went on to write a number of interesting songs about the economic hardships that had affected her birthplace and especially the mining areas like Harlan County. Gilbert was an important role model for many of the later urban folksingers because of her powerful voice and her major onstage role in the Weavers. Holly Near has cited Gilbert has an important influence on her own career.

During the 1960s, Joan Baez and Judy Collins quickly established themselves as major figures in the revival. Both Baez and Collins were competent guitar players, and Collins had an extensive background as a pianist. Although both of them used additional musicians on their records, their guitar-centric sound dominated both of their early records.

## More Joni Mitchell

I have discussed the early part of Mitchell's career earlier in this book. Her 1971 album, *Blue,* may be the most outstanding singer-songwriter album ever. In a sense it crystallized the gap that had developed in the revival between the performance of traditional music and the singer-songwriter's emphasis on crafting songs that were about personal, often romantic, situations. In a searching interview with Bill Flanagan in his excellent book *Written in My Soul,* Mitchell mentioned that when she recorded the album she had no defenses. She states that she was so emotionally vulnerable that she and her engineer and co-producer Henry Lewy locked everyone else out of the studio. One of the songs on the album, *Little Green,* describes a mother giving up her child for adoption. Some thirty years later Mitchell revealed that this song was autobiographical and that she was finally able to find her child and meet her.

There are many interesting things about Joni Mitchell's career. She was one of the first women in the revival who assumed an active role in producing her own records. In addition to her superior talents as a lyricist, Joni was also an excellent and original musician. She pioneered the use of numerous alternative guitar tunings which influenced and encouraged other musicians to follow suit. After the Blue album Mitchell started to work with various studio musicians in Hollywood to augment the sound of her records. It is arguable whether their work added another valuable dimension to her music or whether their musical contributions mostly brought her more toward the mainstream of popular music. Although studio musicians are highly skilled and versatile, in the end they are basically skillful hired hands who tend to resist emotional involvement with their work because the various commercial and artistic demands of record producers and artists tend to induce a high degree of cynicism. To put it on a more pragmatic level, how many new ideas or solos can a musician produce when they are doing 15–20 recording sessions a week? In any case, Mitchell was finally able to achieve her own hit record with the song *Help Me* in 1974.

In 1979 Mitchell made a violent left turn and worked on a collaborative album with jazz bassist and composer Charles Mingus. This noble experiment succeeded in losing Mitchell her mainstream audience. She has never quite recovered that audience. In various interviews that she has given Mitchell has expressed some bitterness about the current state of the music business, and especially the narrow policies that govern record companies and the way that radio stations choose which records to play.

Something that she has *not* discussed is the fact that women in the entertainment industry are generally treated like old crones once they get much beyond the age of forty-five. To put it another way, it seems necessary for women to be young and sexually attractive to be famous, while famous male pop idols like Mick Jagger or David Crosby can rock on into their golden, senior citizen years. In the folk music world, women like Joan Baez and Judy Collins were able to maintain a reasonable-sized audience as they aged. I don't know whether Joni Mitchell wanted and need more than that, or whether the Mingus album simply diverted that audience from maintaining their allegiance to her.

Aside from her musical influence on such singer-songwriters as Shawn Colvin and Mary Chapin Carpenter Mitchell's lyrics asserted her right to choose and abandon lovers, while at the same time expressing her personal vulnerability. Some of her songs describe affairs with musical luminaries as Graham Nash and James Taylor. Although Baez and Collins in their own autobiographies reveal that their romantic lives in some respects were parallel to Mitchell's, their own songs for the most part were not as explicit about these experiences. Mitchell was also one of the first female songwriters who also wrote about social–political issues, like suburbanization, conformity, and environmental issues.

For the last several years Mitchell has experienced a variety of medical problems. These include an aneurysm, post-polio difficulties, and a rare disease called Morgellon's Syndrome. She is not currently musically active.

## Other female singer-songwriters

Several of the singer-songwriters who emerged in the late 1960s or in the 1970s have had long-lasting musical careers. Janis Ian, like Bela Fleck, Happy Traum, and Eric Weissberg, attended the High School of Music and Art in New York City.

Janis was a fifteen-year-old when her record of *Society's Child* was released. The song was about an interracial romance and it terrified radio programmers. Conductor-composer Leonard Bernstein talked about the song on a television show, and it then catapulted to become a hit in 1967.

Ian's career included unsuccessful major label follow-ups, until she wrote and recorded the hit song *At Seventeen* in 1975. She moved to Nashville in 1988, and became much more active as a songwriter than as a performer. She had a number of successful co-writes with Kye Fleming for a variety of artists, including Amy Grant, Bette Midler, and Kathy Mattea. Ian has survived some poor business decisions that led to problems with the IRS. In 1993, she came out as a lesbian and since then has become active in promoting gay and lesbian rights. In 2008 Tarcher published her autobiography *Child: My Autobiography*.

Carly Simon is another New York singer-songwriter whose musical career started in the 1960s when she and her sister Lucy had a folk duo. Carly continued to make occasional children's records in a somewhat folkish vein with her sister, but she is best known for her co-authored folk-rock hit song *That's the Way I've always Heard It Would Be* (1971) and her own *You're So Vain* (1972). Simon does not enjoy live performing, and her career has been negatively impacted by that problem, as well as her years raising a family with her (then) husband James Taylor. Simon recorded two albums of pop standards in the late 1980s and early 1990s, moving further away from anything resembling folk music. Her autobiography, *Boys in the Trees,* was published in 2015.

## The women's movement

The modern women's movement in the United States dates from around 1963, when Betty Freidan's book *The Feminine Mystique* was published. This book revolutionized the attitudes and behaviors of middle-class white women. They began to question their family roles and to demand the opportunity to pursue their own career goals in addition to raising children. Technology in the form of various electric household devices reduced the need for women to spend all of their waking hours as homemakers. All over the country women formed groups for "consciousness raising." In 1970, more radical women's manifestos were published, such as Kate Millett's *Sexual Politics,* Shulamith Firestone's *The Dialectics of Sex*, and Robin Morgan's *Sisterhood Is Powerful.* *Ms.* magazine began publication in 1971, and such organizations as the Women's International League for Peace and Freedom and WITCH (Women's International Conspiracy from Hell) moved the women's music in a more radical direction.

A significant stimulant to the women's movement centered on a woman's right to assert her sexual identity. In some cases, this meant coming out as a lesbian or a bisexual. It was inevitable that these notions were more aggressively translated into music.

## Olivia Records

A group of women singer-songwriters formed a co-op that founded Olivia Records. They included Meg Christian, Cris Williamson, and business coordinator Judy Dlugacz. In 1974 Olivia released their first recording, Christian's *I Know You Know*. A year later Williamson's album *The Changer and the Changed* came out. Over the years it has sold over 500,000 copies, an outstanding achievement given that the records were primarily sold at performances, women's music festivals, and women's bookshops, not in record stores. The musical content of Williamson's album fit into the folk-rock genre, and sometimes she added strings to the arrangements as well.

Olivia's ideology was not limited to recording songs by and about women. The goal was to have women assume all aspects of the recording process, including engineering, art work, background singing or playing, and the distribution of the records. The content of the songs celebrated love between women and discussed women's issues, sometimes in a very direct way. During the 1970s, Olivia also recorded other women artists, such as Tret Fure and African-American artist Linda Tillery. Today Olivia has abandoned the record business and exists as a travel agency that sponsors cruises for lesbians. I think it would be fair to say that Olivia was one of the primary factors behind the women's music movement. Tret Fure worked in a duo with Cris Williamson in the 1980s and 1990s, and subsequently has pursued as solo career. She also recently completed a term as president of Local 1000, the so-called Travelling Folksingers Local of the American Federation of Musicians.

## Holly Near and women's music festivals

Holly Near was another feminist music artist and she was also an actress. She established her own label, *Redwood Records*. The label recorded her own music, but also the music of both male and female artists who expressed radical social–

political sentiments. As Near states it in her memoir, *Fire in the Rain ... Singer in the Storm*, Olivia recorded women's music and supported world peace and Redwood recorded political music and supported women's music. Near's role in women's music was a complex one because she was openly bisexual, and she often used men as her piano accompanists. For Olivia and some of the lesbian artists this was not acceptable. Some lesbian artists were opposed to Near appearing at women's music events because they didn't want to have anything to do with women who maintained relationships with men.

Women's music festivals began to appear all over the country in the 1970s. The first one was held at Sacramento State University in 1973 and the first national gathering appeared a year later in Champaign-Urbana, Illinois, the home of the University of Illinois. Festivals in San Diego, Missouri, Illinois, Michigan, and Boston followed. At one of these festivals Near found herself in a bitter dispute with her songwriting friend Malvina Reynolds, composer of *What Have They Done to the Rain?* and *Little Boxes*. The festival would not allow Reynolds' husband, a confirmed political radical, into the event. In Ellen Schwartz's book *Born a Woman*, Canadian singer-songwriter Sylvia Tyson reports that she was invited to perform at one festival, but she refused when she was told that she could not bring any of the members of her male back-up band and she would not be able to perform any songs about men. Although none of the folk festivals in the United States featured women's music artists, the Canadian folk festivals began including them in 1961. The Winnipeg, Vancouver, and Edmonton festivals soon followed suit.

Other women artists issued music on their own labels, including Alix Dobkin and instrumental composer Kay Gardner.

## The folk revival and the omission of women's music

None of the general histories of the folk revival consider women's music as part of the revival, even though it is possible to argue that women's music was one of the most active segments of the folk revival during the 1970s. By the end of the decade, the impetus for women's music became greatly diminished. To some extent the issues in the women's movement had become part of the consciousness and lifestyle of nearly every young woman, even those who did not consider themselves feminists. Gradually, lesbians who had music careers started to publicly come out, as blues-rock artist Melissa Ethridge did in 1993.

# Other female singer-songwriters in the 1970s and 1980s

There were other female singer-songwriters during the 1970s. Melanie achieved some success during the early 1970s with her *Nickel Song* and the somewhat goofy and child-like *Brand New Key*. Kate Wolf was a highly respected folk artist during the 1970s and 1980s, and despite her premature death in 1986, she has retained something of a following, and a festival named after her. There are two printed songbooks of her repertoire, including many of her own songs. She was also honored posthumously by a tribute album recorded by other artists.

During the 1980s, there was something of an explosion of female singer-songwriters. Suzanne Vega was a dance student at the New York High School of Music and Arts. Her first album was released in 1985, but it was the second one that established her career. It included the hit song *Luka* about an abused child. *Tom's Diner*, another song that she wrote was a hit in her 1987 recording and again in 1990 in a dance mix by the British group DNA. Vega was one of a number of songwriters, including Christine Lavin, who were involved in the song magazine *Fast Folk*, established by the late Jack Hardy in 1982. This was a song magazine that included a recording with each issue of the magazine. The group also sponsored shows in New York City clubs.

Michelle Shocked became an unlikely celebrity through a bootleg recording of her singing around a campfire at the Kerrville music festival in 1986. Shocked had been living in Europe and a British record producer recorded the tapes without her permission and without compensating her. The album became a hit in England resulting in a seven-year court battle before she was able to gain control of the tapes. This peculiar incident resulted in Shocked receiving a healthy contract from Polygram Records. Because hers ideology leans toward the radical side, she was never entirely comfortable with the Polygram deal. Eventually she was able to get out of the deal and she has subsequently recorded for several other labels. Some of her recordings, notably the 1992 *Arkansas Traveler*, are heavily based on traditional American folk music, but others highlight her interest in New Orleans jazz and rhythm and blues. In later years Michelle was able to regain control of her entire catalog of recordings and she started her own record label. She also became a born-again Christian, and was involved with some controversial alleged homophobic remarks.

Tracy Chapman made her recording debut in 1988. Two of her songs, *Fast Car* and *Talking 'Bout a Revolution*, became massive pop hits. The album that contained the two songs sold over ten million copies. It was in a folk-rock vein with little instrumentation beyond her guitar and a rhythm section. Chapman is black, and her husky voice as well as the fact that she played acoustic guitar has created many critical comparisons to Joan Armatrading, the excellent British singer-songwriter.

Chapman's socially aware songs and her acoustic guitar playing made her a logical choice for folk venues, but her huge record sales thrust her into arena-rock venues where she was not entirely comfortable. Chapman has many fans but has neither received much recognition for her role in the later reincarnation of the folk revival, nor has she ever received airplay from the urban contemporary radio stations that dominate the market for African-American popular music.

Peggy Seeger was an important influence on the folk revival in the mid- and late 1950s. She grew up in a household where her mother was transcribing music for some of the Lomax's books as well as her own collections of children's songs. Peggy was also Pete's half-sister. The result of these circumstances was that she developed an enormous repertoire, and she taught a number of songs to various revivalists. In 1958 she moved to England and married Ewan MacColl, a British playwright and folksinger. In 1958 she co-wrote *The Ballad of Springhill* with MacColl, and in 1971 she wrote the feminist anthem *I'm Gonna Be an Engineer.* Many of her songs, like the two mentioned, concern social and political issues. After MacColl's death in 1989 she moved back to the United States for sixteen years, returning to England in 2010. She continues to tour, write, and record.

## Female folk artists markets as country artists

By the 1980s the word folk was not one that led to recording contracts with major labels. Several artists drifted into this world by coming in the back door marked "country." Mary Chapin Carpenter, Nanci Griffith, and Kathy Mattea are three women whose records were classified as country but whose folk influences were clearly evident.

Griffith's first recordings were released on the homegrown Austin record label B.F. Deal. In 1986 she moved to the folk label Philo/Rounder and in 1987 shifted to MCA. The label could never quite figure out how to market her and her continual frustration with the label caused them to move her from their Nashville country music division to the pop-rock roster in Los Angeles.

Many of Griffith's songs, like Harry Chapin's, are short stories. Her biggest songwriting success came from Kathy Mattea's recording of Nanci's song, *Love at the Five and Dime.* Although Griffith was widely respected in the revivalist movement as an excellent songwriter, her own most successful American record was from her 1993 album *Other Voices, Other Rooms*. On that album she recorded seventeen songs by songwriters that had influenced her. For some years her recording career has been more successful in England and Ireland than in the United States.

Mary Chapin Carpenter has pursued a clever and extremely successful strategy on her Epic albums. Carpenter has sprinkled country-rock hits like Down *At the Twist and Shout, Passionate Kisses,* and *I Feel Lucky* amid albums that contain sensitive and literate offerings like *John Doe No. 26,* a song based on the death of an anonymous homeless man. Many of her successful albums were produced by the late John Jennings and recorded not in Nashville, but in a studio in Virginia. They include elements of folk music, country, and rock.

Carpenter writes songs that vary from social–political concern, to literate and intelligent songs about romance. She has acknowledged the influence of Joni Mitchell, not exactly a member of the Nashville songwriting mafia. I have always wondered what the fans who liked her dance and upbeat songs made of the more introspective and complex songs that comprise a large amount of her recorded material. As the 1990s disappeared Carpenter stopped writing the country hits and has continued to write about the complex nature of human beings and their feelings. She no longer has a major label contract, but continues to perform and record for the audience that she has developed over the years.

Kathy Mattea is not a songwriter but she started out as a country star whose work has leaned more and more toward folk, bluegrass, and Celtic influences. In addition to her first hit, she has recorded a number of Top Ten country songs, including two by bluegrass-country-folk-singer-songwriter Tim O'Brien. In 2008 Mattea released an album of coal mining songs by such songwriters as Merle Travis and Hazel Dickens. The album was packaged with a handsome book that discussed the songs and the troubled world of coal mining. Mattea grew up in West Virginia, and her father, grandfathers, and uncle worked in the coal mines. Dickens and Alice Foster used country and folk influences in their work.

## Women in music

During the 1990s and 2000s there was a proliferation of female artists in the rock field, many of whom were also singer-songwriters. Some of them, like Fiona Apple, Patty Griffin, The Indigo Girls, Jewel, and Sarah McLachlan showed strong folk influences. Others such as Tori Amos, Sheryl Crow, Melissa Ethridge, Alanis Morrissette, and Ann and Nancy Wilson with their women-led band *Heart* were more pop-rock derived. McLachlan is also important in the world of women's music, because she started a three-year series of performances of women's artists called Lilith Fair. It ran from 1997 to 1999 with a brief attempt to revive it in 2010*.

The thread that ties these artists together is their songwriting. Although there had obviously been female artists well before the 2000s who wrote songs, like Grace Slick of Jefferson Airplane, or Carole King, or Karla Bonoff's successes of the late 1970s, it was not a common occurrence.

Although Holly Near and Cris Williamson continue to perform, there is no important women's music label as such. As Williamson and others have pointed out, perhaps there isn't a need for these labels today. Melissa Ethridge, K. D. Lang, Janis Ian, and the Indigo Girls have all outed themselves as lesbians. In traditional music and the early years of the folk revival, women were rarely featured as instrumentalists. Exceptions include blues artists Memphis Minnie and Geechie Wiley, Piedmont guitarists Etta Baker and Lena Hughes, and autoharp and guitarist, Maybelle Carter the Coon Creek Girls string band, and early Roy Acuff band banjoist Rachel Veach.

An increasing number of women have also established careers as instrumentalists, including guitarists Nina Gerber, Molly Tuttle, banjo players and Patty Larkin, bluegrass music superstar Alison Krauss, guitarists Patty Larkin and Molly Tuttle, fiddler Laurie Lewis, multi-instrumentalist Sarah Jarosz, K.C. Groves, banjoist and Compass Records owner Allison Brown, mandolinist Sierra Hull and banjoist and guitarist Lynn Morris. Prominent women dobro players include Cindy Cashdollar and Sally Van Meter.

Although the music business is still clearly dominated by white males, there are important female music business executives, including Sylvia Rhone, the black executive who heads Epic, Julie Greenwald, co-CEO at Atlantic Records, and Jody Gerson, CEO of Universal Music Publishing. Ani difranco does not fit comfortably into a specific category. Her music reflects folk, punk and rock influences. She has also recorded socially political albums with the late Utah Phllips, and was one of the first artists to successfully release music on her own label, Righteous Babe. She also owns a performing venue in her hometown of Buffalo, New York.

There is little question that the women's music movement opened the doors for many of the artists and executives above, and the #MeToo movement will undoubtedly expand these gains.

---

* The Dixie Chicks were an enormously popular trio during the 1990's and into 2003. Their music showed country, folk and rock\influences, and their records sold in the millions, until their lead singer, Natalie Maines, made some critical remarks about president George W. Bush. This effectively ended their career as country music superstars, although it gained them a sort of alternative music audience. Since 2003, the three women have occasionally toured and recorded.

13

# North American Folk Festivals and Summer Teaching Camps

The experience of attending a folk festival is quite different from participating in a teaching program designed to increase one's knowledge of folk music instrumental styles. What the experiences have in common is that each, in its own way, creates a sense of community for its participants.

These days, there are quite a variety of folk music festivals. Some of them are genre-oriented like bluegrass or blues festivals. Others are musically varied folk festivals which include a variety of performers in different sub-genres of folk. Many of the festivals are run by nonprofit organizations whose primary goals are to present music and to make enough money so that the event can continue to occur.

The large festivals, like the Newport or Philadelphia Folk Festivals, share a general format. During the afternoon, there are workshops; and in the evening, there are concerts. The workshops are informal instructional sessions where musicians or singers not only perform music but also explain what they are doing and how they've learned to do it. There are usually several performers and sometimes they informally jam with one another or one performer will take a concept cited by another artist and explain how they would do something similar or different. Workshops generally draw a limited number of festival attendees and are not really intended to be shows or highly organized events. The evening concerts draw thousands of people. They generally feature well-known artists who can attract a large audience and bring revenue into the festival. Artists sell CDs, DVDs, or instructional books at these events. Sometimes, as was the case with Bob Gibson introducing Joan Baez at Newport, a performance by a little-known act at a major festival actually is a huge lift-off point for that artist's career. The major festivals draw thousands of people from a wide geographic area, so word of mouth about such an event can be a huge boost to an artist's career.

Another sort of festival is one that is devoted to traditional music played, sung, or danced by traditional musicians or dancers. In many instances, these artists are not professional musicians, and so the impetus is more about promoting the music than the careers of the artists. Examples of such festivals include the National Folk Festival and the White Top Festival. Even before these events began, banjo picker-folksong-collector lawyer Bascom Lamar Lunsford ran a festival called the Rhododendron Festival in Asheville, North Carolina, in 1928.

White Top ran from 1931 to 1939, and after flooding cancelled the 1940 festival, it did not resume operations. The National Folk Festival began in 1934, and continues today. It was founded by Sarah Gertrude Knott and is operated by the National Council for the Traditional Arts. Initially, it was held in a different location every year, but since 1971 it has gone into residence in different locations, usually for two- to three-year periods, except for an eleven-year stint at Wolf Trap, Virginia, from 1971 to 1982.

The National Folk Festival is not an event oriented toward popular taste. Ethnomusicologists and folklorists choose the acts, along with a professional staff. The group also sponsors national tours of traditional musicians, and the festival has spawned a number of local festivals. This is not an event that welcomes pop-folk groups, but rather it seeks to expand the reach of traditional musicians, whether or not they are professionals.

## The Newport Folk Festival

The most imitated models of festivals take place at Newport, Rhode Island, and Mariposa, in Orillia, Ontario. Newport began in 1959 promoted by impresario George Wein. Wein was a jazz pianist himself and began his role in the festival business by promoting the Newport Jazz in 1954. As the pop revival exploded in the late 1950s, starting a folk festival was a logical step. The initial festival featured both Pete Seeger and the Kingston Trio.

Over the years, Newport has had its ups and downs. Initially, Wein booked the festival with the help of some professional talent managers including Albert Grossman. By 1963, the folk festival was taken over by a nonprofit board of directors. At various times, the directors included performers like Pete Seeger and Peter Yarrow of Peter, Paul & Mary. They encouraged the notion of afternoon workshops, which often featured lesser known artists or traditional singers who might not be effective performers in night-time shows that were attended by thousands of fans, tourists, and drop-ins.

## Mariposa

In an earlier section of this book, I discussed the Canadian-Pacific folk festivals of the 1930s. The Miramichi Folk Festival in New Brunswick was established in 1950, and it still operates today. This makes it the longest running folk festival in North America next to the National Folk Festival.

Mariposa is the Canadian equivalent of Newport but it has been a nonprofit organization from the start. Over the years, it has struggled with where the festival is held, returning to its original Orillia, Ontario site in 1999. In general, Mariposa has had the same sort of trials and tribulations that afflicted Newport. These include problems with the town itself, acquiring commercial sponsorship for several years and then losing it, and problems with rain. Since most festivals are held outdoors, weather can be an unpredictable variable. Weather can not only result in the cancellation of performances, but also drastically affects those who have chosen to camp out, rather than stay in motels.

There are some differences between how Mariposa and Newport have been run. Early in the history of Mariposa, a woman named Estelle Klein provided an artistic vision for the festival. This included a separate stage for children's music and early inclusion of music by First Nations performers. (First Nations is the name that Canadians use for tribal groups.) Klein also utilized workshops in a particularly thoughtful way with many lengthy discussions between board members and artistic staff about what performers should be put together and what subjects would be appealing in a workshop. In addition to Klein's work, the late folklorist Edith Fowke also assisted the festival by being a great resource for traditional musicians. Part of Klein's original vision was that all performers would be paid union scale, and no more than that. Although that notion also prevailed during the 1960s Newport festivals, it has long gone by the wayside.

Newport certainly influenced the creation of other folk festivals, but Mariposa literally gave birth to the Canadian festival scene. Klein was a mentor to Mitch Podolak, who was one of the founders of the Winnipeg Festival as well as being involved in the Vancouver and Edmonton Festivals.

Michael Hill's book, *Mariposa Folk Festival: A History*, contains a detailed description of how Mariposa started, and where it has been. My favorite story in the book concerns the 2012 festival. A young volunteer noticed an "older gentleman" pull up in the parking lot and walk toward the gate. The volunteer initially denied the man admission, but a board member noticed that the "gentleman" was Canadian icon Gordon Lightfoot. Of course he admitted Gordon, who asked if he could do a few songs. Gordon explained that he had come to the festival because his daughter wanted to see Jane Arden perform, but that he had also brought his guitar along. The board member then asked Arden whether that was acceptable to her. She replied: "Hey, it's Gordon (expletive deleted) Lightfoot, he can play all night if he wants to."

Perhaps, this story delineates the difference between the Canadian and American folk and folk festival scene. I cannot imagine ANY American folksinger, except possibly Pete Seeger, who would so cheerfully relinquish the stage at a major performance to a folk icon, performing for no fee. Hill goes on to say that Arden afterward delivered a "fantastic and memorable concert."

## Folk festivals today

There are dozens of folk festivals today throughout North America. Manitoba alone has eleven festivals, including the well-established Winnipeg Folk festival. In the United States, in addition to large and well-established festivals like the Smithsonian Folklife Festival, the Kerrville Festival in Texas, and the Philadelphia Folk Festival there are blues festivals, bluegrass festivals, winter weekend festivals, and festivals that feature traditional and/or revival artists only.

As these gatherings have grown in size, there is increasing pressure to attract funding sources from corporate sponsors or government agencies.

There is less desire to take musical risks, because the boards of directors always have to keep an eye on the bottom line. Nonetheless, festivals are an opportunity for performers to develop larger audiences and to meet and interact with other performers. They also give folk music fans the chance to hear dozens of artists in a single setting, rather than have to attend eighteen different concerts.

## Summer folk workshops

There are hundreds of thousands of guitars that are bought every year in the United States and Canada. There is also a good market for five string banjos, mandolins, and fiddles. In every city of any size and in any smaller cities, there are capable instructors for these instruments. Many students develop an interest in a specific folk genre, like Delta blues, but their local instructor may only have a general idea of all of the elements of that style. Other students simply don't have enough time to practice during the year, but they still have the desire to learn more.

For such people, whether they are adults or younger people, there are summer instructional programs in many parts of the United States and Canada. The goals and direction of these programs differ. The Augusta Heritage Festival has a five-week program that offers classes in Cajun music, bluegrass, old-time music, voice, and dance. It was established in 1973, and moved to the campus of Davis & Elkins College in Elkins, West Virginia, in 1981.

These summer programs offer intensive training in segments ranging from long weekends to an entire week. Students stay in college dorms, cabins, or camp out at the facilities. There is very intense contact between students and teachers, and usually a high ratio of teachers to students. Some of the people who attend these camps come back year after year because they are amateurs who have many commitments that keep them from progressing as quickly on their chosen instruments as they would like. Others use the camps to study a particular style one summer and then move on to another style, or even another instrument.

The larger camps offer a choice of teachers and styles within a particular genre of folk music. Some camps are run by well-known musicians, like Jorma Kaukonen's Fur Peace Ranch in Ohio. Jorma was a member of the original Jefferson Airplane, and plays acoustic guitar with the Airplane's bassist, Jack Cassady in the band *Hot Tuna*. Other camps are run by British folk and rock guitarist Richard Thompson, flat-pick guitar specialist Steve Kaufman, flashy guitarist Tommy Emmanuel, and fiddler Alasdair Fraser. Generally, other musicians teach at these camps as well as the person the camp is named after. Clawhammer banjoist Ken Perlman teaches at four or five camps each year in different locations. Many of the camps feature a faculty concert, and at night, there are often opportunities to jam with the instructors and the other students. Often the camps are located in scenic parts of the country so that there are also opportunities for recreation and sightseeing.

The reader should understand that many famous players are not necessarily good teachers. I remember watching an instructional video by a world-famous guitar player where he counted off tempos at breakneck speed. It was clear to me that this musician had done very little, if any, teaching. Some of the camps also have classes in traditional crafts and folk dance. Although some do include some vocal instruction, it has always surprised me that so little emphasis is placed on vocals and harmony singing. Many of the urban revivalists became excellent players, but could clearly use help in their singing.

Sometimes instructional camps are part of the offerings at folk festivals. The Lyons Folk Festival in Colorado, for example, has a song school with classes in instrumental styles and songwriting. This program takes place a few days before the actual festival.

For folk fans who are hungry to learn specific musical styles in a friendly, rural environment, folk music summer camps provide a great opportunity to meet others with the same interests and to learn more about the music. Not all camps are limited to American folk music. Summer Camp Canada, in Ontario, for example, specializes in the music, dance, and crafts of Eastern Europe.

For teachers, these camps provide a good opportunity to work in a friendly environment that includes room and board as part of the paycheck. There are a number of instructors like Ken Perlman and Mary Flower, who teach at four or five workshops every summer. The income that a teacher can earn varies according to the particular camp and how well it is funded. Camps also present an enjoyable way to interact with other teachers, who often come from other parts of the world.

# 14

# Instrumental Music: The Development and Expansion of Musical Possibilities

## Contests

There is a long tradition of fiddle contests in the United States, dating back to 1736. That first contest, like the ones that followed, offered a prize to the winner, in this case a Cremona fiddle. Fiddle contests continue today, and similarly some large music festivals feature contests for banjo, guitar, mandolin, or bands. The contests themselves are frequently categorized by specific music styles, for example, clawhammer banjo or guitar played with a pick or with the fingers of the right hand. As with the first fiddle contest, high quality instruments are often awarded to the winner.

Some fiddlers developed trick instrumental techniques such as playing the instrument behind the back, and certain tunes became closely associated with contests. Over the years, rules have been developed that codify exactly what is supposed to be judged and the judges themselves are often professional musicians who presumably have elevated the standards for winners beyond sheer display. A few tunes are even banned from contests, because the very nature of a tune like Orange Blossom Special encourages trick crowd-pleasing techniques that are frowned upon by high-level professionals.

## Instrumental music: String bands and soloists

As previously mentioned, the 1920s brought technological advances to the performance and recording of music. These included the introduction of 78 RPM records, microphones, and radio broadcasts. Some of the earliest country music records were instrumental solos by string bands. These might or might not include spoken interjections, especially if the song was about moonshine and stills. As the Grand Ole Opry radio show became a fixture of country music, vocals gradually replaced instrumental solos, although for years the show continued to feature old-time music performers like black harmonica player De Ford Bailey, the Crook Brothers, and Uncle Dave Macon's brilliant instrumental accompanists Sam and Kirk Magee.

Instrumental soloists appeared on virtually every instrument in string bands. On the guitar, there were soloists who played so-called parlor guitar.

Parlor style was played with the fingers of the right hand and was sort of a marriage of classical guitar technique with tunes associated with popular or folk music. The guitars used were small-bodied guitars, often played by women, like the late Lena Hughes, dating from the late nineteenth century. Harsher and more dynamic right-hand techniques were used by such musicians as Sam Magee or Hobart Smith. Blues players like Sylvester Weaver and Lonnie Johnson also played instrumental solos, the latter being variously oriented toward blues and jazz. Some amazing five string banjo soloists developed in the early part of the twentieth century who played classical music concertos or excerpts, as well as ragtime-flavored tunes. Foremost among these were Vess Osman and Fred Van Eps. These gentlemen were not folk or country musicians, but they influenced such players as Charlie Poole who did fit into that category. As for the fiddle, early players included Fiddlin' John Carson, Eck Robertson, and Gid Tanner. Tanner's band, the Skillet Lickers, even featured as many as three fiddlers.

## A few thoughts about musical structure

Instrumental music is inherently more abstract than songs are. Traditional songs in peculiar often tell specific stories, with a beginning, a middle, and some sort of resolution, whether the song described a love affair, a train wreck, or a flood. Although country blues could combine verses that didn't necessarily tell a specific story, still the song's title and some of the verses were something that the listener could readily grasp.

Vernacular, or non-classical songs, utilized various structures. A form songs, most commonly found in children's music, simply have verses that use the same melody over and over. AB form songs utilize verses and a chorus. The chorus has the same, or at least similar, lyrics each time it is sung, and listeners often remember choruses to songs when they have forgotten the verses. AB songs may utilize the same melody for the verse and the chorus, or the chorus may have a different melody than the verse employs. Woody Guthrie's famous song *This Land Is Your Land* uses the same melody for the verse and the chorus, while Lead Belly's famous song *Goodnight Irene* has different melodies in the verse and the chorus.

## More matters of song form

Popular music often utilizes yet another melody called the bridge, or to put it another way, ABC form. A bridge is not utilized in traditional American folk music but can be found in country-folksongs like Jimmy Driftwood's classic *The Battle of New Orleans*. Usually a bridge only appears once during a song, and it provides a sort of left turn in a song that is fairly lengthy. In the case of Driftwood's song, which is quite lengthy, he used the bridge more than once and to my ears it is in some ways the most attractive part of the song.

There are two other aspects of form that are sometimes utilized. Popular music standards of the 1920s and 1930s often used an introductory bridge that was present at the beginning of the song and was never used again. Many musicians who play these sorts of songs, like Hoagy Carmichael's classic *Stardust*, simply ignore this portion of the song.

Finally, some songs use a refrain, which is kind of a fragment that can substitute for using a chorus. For example, the traditional folksong The Devil and the Farmer's Wife contains a nonsense refrain after each verse that goes: Come a fi-di, fiddle-i-di, diddle-i-diddle-di day. This fragment is not long enough to be a chorus, but in its way it is "catchy" and relatively easy to remember.

## Fiddle tune form

Fiddle tunes generally use a form that is AABB. There are two parts of the tune and they are each repeated. I recently attended an old-time music festival where I witnessed a fiddler happily sawing away repeating the exact same tune for many minutes, with a banjo player playing in support of him using the same repeated rhythmic technique as well. The neo-traditionalists who constitute a strong segment of the current audience for old-time music are, in effect, musical conservatives. They not only prefer to hear fiddlers play using these repeats but also they tend to be unhappy if they don't observe this custom.

## Pete Seeger

Of all the folksingers who also had a bit of a pop-folk audience, Pete was a powerful influence on other musicians. Even Bruce Springsteen, hardly regarded as a "folksinger," recorded an entire album called The Seeger Sessions and did a tour performing that music with an entirely different group of musicians than his E Street band. In 1954, Seeger recorded an album called The *Goofing Off Suite*. That recording featured an original short piece that was essentially the centerpiece of the suite, and it was followed by Bach and Beethoven excerpts played on the banjo, an Irving Berlin song, several traditional American folksongs, an original and somewhat eccentric guitar piece called The *Mexican Blues*, and Woody Guthrie's solo mandolin piece *Woody's Rag*. Possibly because this album was so different from anything Pete had ever done, the album attracted little attention. In 1959, he partnered with multi-instrumentalist Frank Hamilton to record *Nonesuch and Other Folk Tunes*. This album was quite a bit looser than the Goofing Off project, kind of a jam session by two excellent players enjoying each other's work. It included the Russian army song *Meadowlands*, and a colorful pygmy tune for two banjos. Pete's last instrumental effort was *Indian Summer*. This was music for a film made in 1960. For this album, Pete partnered with his half-brother Mike.

None of these albums received much notice, but they are important because they foreshadowed an outpouring of instrumental music by various artists whose experiments moved in a variety of directions, played on many different instruments. Other than abstract guitar pieces, practically every direction that these albums attempted was present to some extent on one or more of Seeger's three albums.

## Following in Seeger's footsteps (or not)

The pop-folk revival, starting with the Weavers in 1950 and continuing and expanding through the Kingston Trio era, some ten years later, stirred a widespread interest in folk music. In all of his solo concerts, which started around 1955, Seeger acted as an advocate for traditional musicians urging his largely college audiences to go and seek out fine traditional musicians like banjoist Pete Steele in Hamilton, Ohio, or multi-instrumentalist Hobart Smith in Saltville, Virginia. Many of the younger folk enthusiasts did exactly that, but they went a step further. Artist Art Rosenbaum started recording traditional white and black musicians in his hometown of Indianapolis. Art is a painter, and when he went on to teach at the University of Iowa, he recorded musicians, often painted them, and his wife Margot Newmark Rosenbaum photographed these musicians. When he moved on to teach at the University of Georgia, he continued to pursue his musical interests. Rosenbaum also wrote several banjo instruction books that documented the music of traditional musicians. Mike Seeger and John Cohen of the New Lost City Ramblers pursued similar goals, with both of them recording musicians, and John photographing them.

Billy Faier was a banjo player who grew up in Brooklyn and Woodstock, New York. In 1957, his recording *The Art of the Five String Banjo*, with simpatico guitarist Frank Hamilton, caused a minor earthquake in the New York folk world. Billy's playing is hard to define, because he integrated techniques used by classical nylon string banjoists with traditional mountain playing and various techniques that he himself had invented. He really did not specialize in either mountain banjo or bluegrass banjo, and he also didn't play much in Seeger style. The album included an Israeli tune, a Yugoslav dance, Irish and English songs, a Lead Belly tune, and one original tune in lute music style. The effect was breathtaking, inspiring, and confusing to banjoists.

Over the years, Faier recorded several other albums but none had the impact of his first offering. Billy is rarely mentioned in folk music histories and is essentially unknown to younger folk musicians. Nonetheless, he was truly an original and a pioneer in opening up the instrument to other banjo players.

By the end of the 1960s, a variety of old-time music string bands emerged, many of whom learned their music from traditional musicians. The Red Clay Ramblers started recording in 1969, and they were among the more experimental of the string bands. They did everything from square dance tunes to ragtime to a Fats Waller tune, and their personnel included a piano player and a member who played trumpet and trombone. They also wrote some original music, and one of their members, Bland Simpson, was the co-author of a successful 1974 off-off Broadway show called Diamond Studs. The show concerned the James Gang, and the Red Clay Ramblers constituted the orchestra.

John Hartford was another pioneer in writing and recording original instrumental music. Hartford played fiddle, banjo, mandolin, and guitar, and he was able to pursue various musical experiments because of the enormous success of his song *Gentle on My Mind*. He originally recorded the song in 1967, and a cover version by Glen Campbell was recorded during the same year. When it was rereleased in 1969, it became an enormous hit, and over the years has been one of the most played songs on the radio.

What Hartford brought to the party was multi-dimensional. His songs were often abstract and colorful, and he experimented with integrating the banjo with orchestral instruments in his 1969 composition: *Dusty Miller: Hornpipe and Fugue for a Major for Strings, Brass, and Five String Banjo.*

## Bluegrass banjo

Earl Scruggs was an extremely important influential bluegrass banjo player. He synthesized various elements of three-finger banjo style with a system that players refer to as rolls. This technique uses finger picks worn on the thumb, index, and middle fingers of the right hand. Scruggs and the players who followed shortly after him played near the bridge of the banjo, producing a loud and percussive sound that was electrifying compared to what earlier mountain players did. Scruggs joined mandolin player Bill Monroe's Bluegrass Boys in 1945, and he essentially defined the role of the banjo in bluegrass for the next two years. His contemporary Don Reno utilized some techniques of his own, and other early bluegrass banjo players like Sonny Osborne, Eddie Adcock, and Don Stover all had stylistic mannerisms that were particular to them, but Scruggs was the best known and most successful of the bunch. This was partly due to his composition Foggy Mountain Breakdown, recorded after Scruggs left Monroe and teamed up with Monroe guitarist Lester Flatt in the band The Foggy Mountain Boys.

## Beyond Scruggs style

Bill Keith and Bobby Thompson were the two banjo players who carried Scruggs style to the next dimension. In an interview that I did with Bobby for Frets Magazine, he told me that when he was playing with Jim and Jesse in the late 1950s, the fiddle player constantly tormented him by asking why bluegrass banjo players could never play a straight melody, but had to fit the melody into their right hand patterns. In revenge, Bobby worked out how to play fiddle tunes in a style that is now referred to as melodic banjo. A simplified explanation of this technique is that it entailed fretting the short (fifth) string of the banjo and trying to avoid playing consecutive notes on the same string.

At about the same time, a New England banjoist named Bill Keith was experimenting with the same ideas. In 1962, he recorded an album called *Livin' on the Mountain* with singer-guitarist Jim Rooney. The album included some impressive melodic banjo playing. A year later, Keith was hired by Bill Monroe to play in his band, and so the technique became exposed to large numbers of bluegrass fans. Meanwhile, Thompson found that when he played a solo piece with Jim and Jesse's band, the public had little interest in what he was doing.

Because of Monroe's "endorsement" of Keith and also because of Thompson's disinclination to perform live as a soloist with his career evolving entirely into studio work, Thompson's contributions have been largely minimized or even ignored. This is peculiar because Thompson was in the studio band and periodically on camera in the popular television show Hee Haw, and also because he made two albums in 1969 and 1970 with a group of younger studio musicians banding together in a band called Area Code 615. These revolutionary albums go beyond the subject matter of this book, since they included elements of rock, pop, country music, and bluegrass and even performances of Beatles' songs and Mason Williams's guitar piece, *Classical Gas*, beautifully played on the banjo by Thompson.

Beside the work of Thompson and Keith, there was also banjo player Carroll Best, who after two months of playing with the Morris Brothers decided to return to his family's farm. According to an article by Ted Olson, in the Old Time Music Herald, Vol.13, Number 20, Best may have evolved his version of melodic banjo playing as early as the mid-1940s. He also apparently had some contact with both Thompson and Keith at various times, in Thompson's case at a TV studio where they were both working with different bands. To further complicate the situation, Best played an open-back banjo, not a Gibson banjo with a resonator, and he played without picks.

In today's banjo world, players like Bela Fleck, Danny Barnes and Noam Pikelny have carried melodic banjo into newer musical territory. Steve Martin and Tony Ellis play in a variety of styles, rather than adjusting their music to fit a particular picking pattern.

# Fiddle

The fiddle is an instrument that like the banjo crossed racial lines. Originally, there was the European influence, which stemmed from Scots-Irish or English roots. As slavery developed, plantation owners encouraged slaves to pick up the fiddle and to provide entertainment for their masters and their guests. There are numerous descriptions in nineteenth-century handbills or publications that demand the return of runaway slaves and describe them as being proficient on the fiddle or banjo.

Fiddles along with banjos were also featured in minstrel shows that offered mostly stereotypical descriptions of slaves and their lifestyles. Minstrels initially were white entertainers who blacked up their faces in imitation of slaves. Later, there were also black minstrels, who were freed men or escaped slaves who found a way to make a living performing music for white audiences.

The first fiddler to become well known through his recordings was Fiddlin' John Carson. Later Gid, Tanner's band The Skillet Lickers had three fiddlers, and their first recording sold over 200,000 copies. Almost all of the old-time string bands had fiddlers, and fiddle was the most prominent lead instrument in these bands. Some other early old-time fiddlers were Eck Robertson, Fiddlin' Arthur Smith, and Clayton McMichen. Ed Haley was well known as a mountain fiddler but did not record professionally because he was warned that record companies might take advantage of him because he was blind. Some other important old-time fiddlers were Tommy Jarrell and Clark Kessinger. Jarrell influenced many of the younger revivalists, who made pilgrimages to his home to play with him.

Many of the old-time fiddlers played in different tunings, as did old-time banjo players. These were known as "cross tunings." These tunings enabled the fiddler to achieve the same sort of drone effect that the fifth string on the five-string banjo offers. Partly due to the prevalence of fiddle contests, fancy Texas fiddling made a major impact on fiddle playing. Benny Thomasson was one of these fiddlers. He moved to Washington state and was a strong influence on a young Mark O'Connor, a superb multi-instrumentalist who has gone on to do extensive recording work, write string quartets and classical concertos, and a series of instruction books for violin, viola, and cello.

Notable bluegrass fiddlers include Kenny Baker, Bobby Hicks, Howdy Forrester, Byron Berline, and Chubby Wise. As is true with all of the instrumentalists we have discussed here, there are a younger group of newgrass or experimental players that include Darol Anger, Casey Dreissen, Stuart Duncan, and Sarah Watkins of the band Nickel Creek. There was an older generation of Cajun fiddlers that included Harry Choates, Doc Guidry, and Dewey Balfa, and contemporary Cajun fiddlers like Michael Doucet, and Appalachian-fiddler-turned Cajun fiddler Dirk Powell. Flashy fiddler Doug Kershaw was situated between these two groups.

Another group of fiddlers were blues players. Lonnie Johnson, who is best known as a guitarist also played fiddle while Big Bill Broonzy played fiddle before moving to Chicago in 1920 and becoming a renowned blues guitarist. Another early fiddler was Eddie Anthony, who played on Peg Leg Howell. Papa John Creach played with both the Jefferson Airplane and its acoustic spin-off, Hot Tuna, and Clarence "Gatemouth" Brown played fiddle as well as blues guitar.

Rhiannon Giddens, who plays with the Carolina Chocolate Drops and also performs as a soloist in a wide variety of musical styles, represents the younger generation of fiddlers. Bruce Molsky is another fine fiddler and multi-instrumentalist. Laurie Lewis and Rayna Gellert are also fine fiddlers.

## Guitar and guitarists

Many of the pop-folk groups, like Peter, Paul & Mary, utilized a form of picking, which became to be known as "Travis picking." Numerous country pickers played in this style, including Chet Atkins who modified the technique for his own uses.

The style is named for the late Merle Travis and features the right thumb keeping the beat going while the index finger picks out melodies. Travis himself learned this technique from two musicians in his Kentucky childhood days. They were Ike Everly, father of the Everly Brothers, and Mose Rager. In terms of folk music, Travis's technique is best heard on his oft-reissued album Folk Songs of the Hills, originally released in 1947. His 1956 album, *The Merle Travis Guitar* includes standards, blues, and rags, and electric guitar. Travis-style guitar was ubiquitous during the folk revival, and up to this day.

Another group of guitarists established a role for guitar as a solo instrument, or at least an instrument capable of taking solos in a bluegrass band. One of the pioneers in this style was George Shuffler. Shuffler joined the Stanley brothers band The Clinch Mountain Boys in 1951. He played bass for ten years, but when Curly Lambert left the group in 1961, Shuffler played lead guitar. He developed a cross-picking style that was patterned after Scruggs banjo playing. Before cross-picking began to appear, bluegrass guitarists either alternated picking up and down with a pick or simply picked down. Cross-picking is a bit tricky and can be done in several different patterns. One way is to play two downstrokes followed by an upstroke. This pattern is then repeated, and then the final two notes use alternate down and up strokes. This 3+3+2 pattern is similar to the "roll" patterns that Earl Scruggs used. As is true in Scruggs picking, the roll can be executed in reverse, starting with two up picks followed by a down pick.

Doc Watson was another cross-picker. Although he did not usually play in bluegrass bands, he used the technique to play fiddle tunes at rapid tempos. Clarence White and Tony Rice also utilized this technique, in White's case playing in a variety of contexts including bluegrass bands and folk-rock group the Byrds. Rice played with banjo player J. D. Crowe's band New South in 1970, and went on to become a member of the Dave Grisman Quintet, which ventured into gypsy jazz and other jazz variations of bluegrass. Dan Crary was yet another guitarist who played the guitar as a lead instrument in bluegrass and other contexts.

Another reason that the guitar was able to assume a role as a lead instrument was the development of acoustic–electric guitars, where an acoustic guitar can be played with a pickup or amplified internally. This enabled the guitar to play at a much higher volume.

Many other guitarists, including Charles Sawtelle, with the Colorado-based bluegrass band *Hot Rize*, David Grier, Russ Barenberg and Norman Blake all played dynamic guitar solos in or out of a bluegrass band. Grier even does instrumental-based solo gigs without a band. In recent years, guitarist and songwriter Molly Tuttle was honored as songwriter of the year by the International Bluegrass Music Association. Ross Martin is an excellent and versatile flat-picker.

## American Primitive Guitar

The late John Fahey was the initiator of what has become known, somewhat misleadingly, as American Primitive Guitar. The reason I say "misleadingly" is that Fahey himself earned a master's degree in ethnomusicology, and his various disciples and followers had varying amounts of musical training that contradict the notion of the style being primitive.

Fahey started recording in 1959 on a home-grown album called *Blind Joe Death*. He founded the Takoma label with San Francisco record store owner Norman Pierce and entrepreneur Ed Denson. The second release was Fahey's 1962 album Death Chants, Breakdowns, and Military Waltzes. Takoma then signed other guitarists who, to a greater or lesser degree, had been influenced by Fahey. These included Robbie Basho, who was particularly interested in East

Indian music, Harry Taussig, and Leo Kottke. Kottke's album sold very well, and he has established a long-standing career as a six- and twelve-string guitarist.

Each of these artists, and later guitar soloists, has something of their own style. What characterizes American Primitive Guitar as a whole is that it is played with the right-hand fingers, not a flat pick, and the sound is kind of a marriage between classical guitar playing and the fingerpicking styles of musicians like Sam Magee. The music itself includes blues and jazz influences, depending upon the skill and background of the player. In general, the music is much more abstract than what traditional musicians would play and the titles of the pieces, especially Fahey's, tend to be obscure literary or historical references or even humorous in-jokes.

There are also quite a few excellent guitarists whose style does not comfortably fit into the American primitive category. In the Portland, Oregon area guitarists Mark Hansen and Doug Smith are versatile fingerstyle composers, players, and teachers who walk the line between jazz and folk guitar. Kelly Jo Phelps is an excellent slide guitarist who is also a capable singer, and Thad Beckman is a versatile songwriter, guitarist, composer, and singer. Hansen has also written many useful instruction books for guitar, many of which are published by his own company, Accent on Music. Washington state resident Tracy Moore specializes in twelve-string guitar. He is an interesting composer whose work crosses over into many musical genres. Another fine guitarist is Pat Donohue, from Minneapolis.

## Kicking Mule Records

In the mid-1960s, Ed Denson sold his interest in Takoma Records to John Fahey. In 1971, Denson teamed up with blues guitarist and author Stefan Grossman to found Kicking Mule Records. During the 1970s and into the 1980s, the label recorded many artists who specialized in folk, blues, ragtime, and occasionally jazz guitar, including Stefan himself. A number of the artists were European players, partly because Stefan lived variously in England and Italy. The label recorded blues players more than anything else, and some of its artists like Duck Baker, Roy Bookbinder, and Dale Miller remain active today. Very few of these albums were related to the abstract sort of music that John Fahey had specialized; although in 1979, Woody Harris did record a tribute album to Fahey. Grossman left the label in the 1980s and Denson added some albums of banjo and dulcimer music before the label became defunct in 2002.

# Windham Hill Records

Windham Hill Records was started in 1976 by Will Ackerman and Anne Robinson. At the urging of his friends, Ackerman, who was a carpenter by trade, recorded an album of his guitar pieces. Somehow a Seattle DJ named Jeff Heiman got a copy of the album and started playing it. He received many phone calls about the album, and people became frustrated because it was not being sold in record stores. Heiman called Ackerman and told him that unless people could purchase the album, he would have to stop playing it. Consequently, Ackerman pressed a small number of albums. The album did well, and Ackerman added his cousin Alex De Grassi, an excellent guitarist to the roster. Eventually, the label also recorded a number of other guitarists, including Michael Hedges, harp guitarist John Doan, and classical guitarist Andrew York. In 1979, Ackerman recorded George Winston. What began as a possible guitar project for Winston turned into a best-selling piano album.

Most of Windham Hill's guitar albums bore some resemblance to what Fahey had done with Takoma Records, but the label became identified with "New Age" music. New age music involved lyrical motifs that were repeated at some length in a sort of trance-like effect. Not all of the label's work fit the category. But the stark black and white album covers and very clear direct-to-disc engineering techniques gave people the impression that the music fits this mold. The great exception was Michael Hedges who utilized all sorts of dynamic rhythmic techniques that involved the technique of tapping. In tapping, the left hand actually plays notes in addition to fretting the strings. From 1991 to 1996 BMG Records gradually took over the label and merged it with Private Music, which had more pop-oriented artists like Yanni and Vangelis. In 2007, the label closed down and was merged with RCA and later acquired by Sony.

# Tompkins Square Records

As of this writing, Tompkins Square Records is the most prominent label that specializes in guitar music. It was founded in 2005 by Josh Rosenthal, who was a veteran executive at Sony Music. The label has issued a series of guitar albums that it calls Imaginational Anthems. This includes music by both contemporaries of Fahey like Max Ochs and Harry Taussig and many artists who are essentially unknowns. There are also reissue albums by blues and gospel artists, and a few by singer-songwriters.

In today's internet world where record sales are modest, the label seems to have found a workable formula. Some albums are released on CD and some on LP to take advantage of the increasing interest in vinyl and some in both mediums. The number of records pressed seems to be limited and a large percentage of sales come through the artists selling their own albums or through the company's own website. In most cases, it appears that when the initial pressing of the record is sold out, the company moves on to the next project.

## Mandolin

More than any other player, Bill Monroe brought the mandolin to attention as a lead instrument in bluegrass. Monroe began his career playing with his two brothers in a trio. His brother Birch was a fiddler, but when Birch left the trio became a duo with brother Charlie playing guitar and Bill mandolin. They began their recording career in 1936 but by 1938 their personal feuds led to Bill starting his own band, the Blue Grass Boys.

The original band included old-time banjo player Stringbean, who really didn't fit into the hard driving sound that Monroe had in mind. In 1945, Earl Scruggs joined the band and basically with Monroe created the sound that became known as "bluegrass music." Monroe wrote many instrumental pieces, which featured the mandolin, and continued to perform after Scruggs and guitarist Lester Flatt left the band in 1948 to form their own band. In 1953, folklorist and mandolin player Ralph Rinzler took on the job of managing Monroe and introduced him to both the audiences outside the south and college audiences.

Just as George Shuffler adapted Scruggs style banjo to the guitar, Jesse McReynolds pioneered the use of cross-picking technique on the mandolin. McReynolds performed with his brother Jim and their first album was made for Capitol Records in 1952.

Mandolin is often used in a rhythmic role in bluegrass bands but a number of players have developed a more intricate solo style on the instrument. David Grisman moved the instrument in an experimental direction, playing everything from jazz, his own compositions, and jug band music. Mike Marshall played in the David Grisman Quartet and then organized his own quartet in 1985. Mike has played in various groups, including the Anger Marshall Band with fiddler

Darol Anger. Marshall has also played with classical violinist Joshua Bell and experimental bluegrass pickers Bela Fleck and Sam Bush in a style which has become known as new acoustic music.

Sam Bush is an adventurous mandolin player who was a pioneer in what has become known as newgrass music. In 1972, Bush along with banjo player Courtney Johnson, guitarist Curtis Burch, and bass player-vocalist John Cowan formed the band the Newgrass Revival. Newgrass used an innovative approach to bluegrass incorporating elements of rock and roll, jazz, and blues into their music. Cowan, their lead singer, had one foot in bluegrass and another in rhythm and blues music. The initial reaction of bluegrass festival attendees to Newgrass was a combination of enthusiasm, skepticism, and even hostility. Gradually, the band won bluegrass fans over because of their excellent musicianship. An example of their innovative spirit was Bush playing mandolin with a slide on their tune *Fly through the Country* while Cowan sang the lyric in a style that was heavily influenced by soul music.

There are several current bluegrass mandolin soloists including Sierra Hull, John Reischman and Ron McCoury, as well as multi-instrumentalists like Tim O'Brien who features mandolin as one of the several solo instruments he plays. Jethro Burns was another influential mandolin player who was best known to the general public as part of the country comedy group Homer and Jethro but was an excellent and versatile player who ran the gamut from country music to jazz. Yank Rachell was a noted blues mandolin player who often played with guitarist Sleepy John Estes. Chicago blues player Johnny Young also was known for his mandolin work.

In the world of folk music, Ry Cooder is a musician who defies category. Although he is probably best known for his slide guitar work and his film scores, he is also an excellent mandolin player. Peter Ostroushko is a versatile mandolin player who was featured during the 1970s on the radio show The Prairie Home Companion. He has also played with a variety of classical chamber groups and symphonies and in theatrical productions. Although he was not credited in the album notes, he also played on Bob Dylan's big-selling *Blood on the Tracks* album.

## Other Instrumentalists

There are other instruments and instrumentalists that I have omitted from this brief survey. The dobro is less frequently used in bluegrass bands than the instruments discussed above, and it is even more unusual to find it on folk music recordings. Uncle Josh (Buck) Graves was an important early player who played with Earl Scruggs and Lester Flatt, and Mike Auldridge was in the Seldom Scene band and played on many recordings. Jerry Douglas is ubiquitous on today's bluegrass and newgrass records, and Sally Van Meter has also played on many recordings. Ivan Rosenberg and Orville Johnson are other well-known dobro players.

Accordions were and are an important component of Cajun and zydeco records. Nathan Abshire and Amede Ardoin were important earlier players. Marc Savoy is important as both an accordion player and a builder, and some of the younger players include Gene Delafose and Jo-El Sonnier. Clifton Chenier was the king of the zydeco accordion players and his contemporaries include Boozoo Chavis and Buckwheat Zydeco. Clifton Chenier Jr. carries on the tradition.

Other instruments found in traditional folk music include the autoharp, played by Maybelle Carter, and the mountain, and hammered dulcimer. Among important dulcimer players are the late Jean Ritchie for mountain dulcimer, and Howie Mitchell for hammered dulcimer. The late Richard Farina played a sort of folk-rock dulcimer on his albums with Mimi Farina. Other contemporary dulcimer players include Bonnie Carol, who also builds dulcimers, Steve Eulberg, and Neil Hellman. The late David Schnaufer, who played, taught, and recorded, was also an important player as well as the late Bill Spence. Some musicians are known for their instrumental abilities, but are also singer-songwriters and record producers. David Bromberg is a well-known guitarist who is also a singer-songwriter, and has recorded some influential albums. Larry Campbell is a guitarist and multi-instrumentalist who has toured with the Levon Helms band and with Bob Dylan, and also performs with his wife Virginia.

There is a long and distinguished history of both country and blues harmonica players. De Ford Bailey was an African-American harmonica player who played for years on the Grand Ole Opry. Little Walter and Sonny Terry were influential blues harmonica players, and a number of singer-songwriters, including Bob Dylan and Neil Young regularly play harmonica. Howard Levy is a virtuoso harmonica player, who has played with Bela Fleck, and he has also toured and recorded with many other artists. Phil Wiggins and Charlie Musselwhite are renowned contemporary blues harmonica players.

Cindy Mangsen is a fine concertina player who performs with her husband guitarist and songwriter Gillette Steve.

## 15

# The Folk Music Business

As bizarre as it might seem, there is indeed a folk music business. The real beginnings of a folk music business infrastructure began with the Weavers in 1950. The Weavers recorded for Decca Records, a major label and they had two managers, Harold Leventhal and Pete Kameron. Musical publishing companies were set up to publish their original compositions and their arrangements of folk songs. Clearly there was money to be made.

When Harry Belafonte followed by the Kingston Trio and its various progeny emerged, the folk business was off to the races. Although the popularity of folk-based music is not as great today, the infrastructure of the business has expanded in a variety of ways.

## Organizations

Organizations devoted to the spread of folk music include both local and national groups. Folklore societies or organizations with names such as "friends of folk music" exist in many major cities. These groups have meetings, organize song circles for amateur musicians, publish newsletters, and promote jam sessions and open microphones at local clubs. They also organize concerts of local and traveling musicians and have a board of directors that follow some sort of mission statement. Some folklore societies release CDs of local musician-members.

I have already mentioned that Chicago and Denver boast two large nonprofit organizations who give music lessons and sponsor concerts and master classes. The Old Town School in Chicago also includes a music store and Swallow Hill Music operates a recording studio. Both groups operate with financing from their member, and through grants and contributions. Each organization has a full-time staff, a board of directors, and many teachers who make a full-time or part-time living by giving lessons.

St. Louis and Atlanta have mini-version of these organizations, and some cities have groups that fulfill some of these functions, like sponsoring concerts, but rent facilities for these activities.

## The International Folk Alliance

The Folk Alliance was founded in 1989. Since then, the organization has run annual conferences that include workshops in the business aspects of folk music, panels of various subjects of interest, juried showcases where performers hope to solicit future employment, and an exhibition area that has booths staffed by artists, record companies, managers, and agents. Attendees at the conference include all of these groups plus amateur musicians, would-be professionals, fans, and scholars. The annual conference in recent years has been held in Kansas City* four out of five years, but in the fifth year is held in a major Canadian city. This is because there are many members of the organization in Canada.

In addition to the formal showcases, there are "guerrilla" showcases held in hotel rooms rented by performers. Some of these are sponsored by record companies or booking agents or by performers who enlist their performer colleagues to share the expenses of renting the room. Because the logistics of running a five-day conference are complex, attendance at the conference has become expensive. For those who do not live in Kansas City, by the time the conference fees, lodging, exhibition fees, hotel rooms, airfare, promotional giveaways, and related expenses are factored in the cost of attending this conference can easily be $1500 or more. There are also far more conference attendees than record companies, agents, managers, or presenters. The guerrilla showcases are of questionable value because so many of them occur simultaneously that the audiences are relatively small.

In addition to the main conference, there are also regional conferences that are held in various parts of the United States. Each one of these sets its own fees, and determines what city the conference will be held in. These conferences are similar to the Kansas City event and are more affordable if you happen to live near or in the city where the conference is being held.

Despite the expense involved, the conferences are enjoyable to many of the attendees. This is partly because many of the musicians rarely see one another and can get together, and play music and exchange tips about possible gigs. Each

---

* The 2019 conference is scheduled to take place in New Orleans, which reflects a change in Folk Alliance policy.

conference also provides some opportunities for fans or musicians to volunteer in order to offset the costs of registering for the conference.

## International Bluegrass Music Association

The bluegrass community has its own organization, the International Bluegrass Music Association. It holds two separate conferences. One is a two-day business conference and the other is a three-day festival where many bands perform. It gives awards and has exhibits and educational events. Many states also have bluegrass associations which publish newsletters and sponsor jams or events.

## Local 1000, American Federation of Musicians

For many years the American Federation of Musicians was built entirely around the notion of members being from a specific geographic area in the United States or Canada. Consequently, many traveling folksingers didn't bother to join the musician's union. This was ironic, since many of these same musicians were singing songs about unions and strikes. Folksingers led by Charlie King, John McCutcheon, and John O'Connor lobbied to establish a new kind of local, the traveling folksingers' union.

The union sets wage minimums and offers a number of benefits including a pension plan and contract guarantees if an employer defaults on payment and instrument insurance. The larger record companies sign national agreements with the union which provide pension benefits, wage minimums, and bonus funds based on the sales and streaming of all records. Because the folk labels are relatively small companies, most of them are not signatories to union agreements. Additionally, many artists produce their own records, usually at minimal cost and using friends as back-up players.

## Record companies, music publishers, and performance rights

There are a handful of relatively small record companies that issue the bulk of folk-based recordings. Rounder was the largest of these companies, but in 2010 it was acquired by the Concord group of labels, and it is not nearly as active in issuing new projects as it used to be. Rounder had acquired Sugar Hill, an important bluegrass label, so it too is housed at the Concord group. Recently Minneapolis-based Red House Records was acquired by Compass Records, which is headquartered in Nashville, and was previously known as a bluegrass and newgrass-oriented label. Smithsonian-Folkways is the successor to Moe Asch's Folkways label. When Asch died he left an enormous catalog of mostly folk and world music recordings. The terms of Asch's agreement with them were that they promised to keep all of the existing records in print. Folkways also has acquired Arhoolie Records. In addition to folk and blues albums, they have released many recordings of Mexican and Mexican-American music.

Consequently, the label issues relatively few new recordings, and much of what they do is to repackage existing material in the form of new compilation records. Appleseed, June Apple, Folk Legacy, and Folk Era/Wind River are all labels that produce few new recordings. Shanachie is still active but involved with other musical styles in addition to folk music. Many recordings from the 1960s revival have been reissued on the Fantasy label, which is part of the Concord group. This means that recordings originally issued on the Prestige and Vanguard have been reissued by the Concord group. Budget label Everest has picked up The Tradition Records catalog, along with their other label acquisitions and Field Recorders Collective specializes in old-time music.

Although County Records is defunct, many of its recordings, along with a large number of other bluegrass and old-time music albums are available through County Record Sales, now operated by different management. Patuxent Record is a small label that produces bluegrass and old-time recordings.

Dust to Digital Records and Archeophone Records are reissue labels and Light in the Attic has mostly reissued albums along with some new recordings. Only a small portion of what Light in the Attic does is folk music. Signature Sounds is a label that releases albums by such singer-songwriters as Tracy Grammer and Chris Smither. Pine Castle Records releases many bluegrass albums.

Current blues labels include Alligator, Blind Pig, and Delmark. Telarc Records is a blues label that has been acquired by the Concord group. In the last chapter I also mentioned Tompkins Square Records which specializes in various forms of roots music*.

Very few folk musicians receive significant royalties. Record sales have greatly diminished, streaming royalties are insignificant unless an artist get hundreds of

---

* Music Maker Records specializes in recordings by older traditional blues singers, but also includes some gospel artists. The label also manages some of these artists and arranges tours for them.

thousands of streams, and royalties are not paid for records that the artist buys from the record company and sells at their own performances.

Music publishing royalties are partly based on the sales of records, but they also include money paid for domestic and foreign airplay and television uses.

These royalties are paid through performing rights organizations that monitor airplay. These organizations include ASCAP, BMI, SESAC, and Global Rights. Unfortunately, the fees paid by NPR stations or community radio stations are small, so folk music is rarely picked up by performing rights groups. Bands like *The Lumineers*, who have enjoyed several pop hits, can receive considerable income from these sources. The performing rights organizations do pay money to singer-songwriters who are performing their own work live. In order to collect this money, the songwriter must fill out a list of these performances on a regular basis. If the performance takes place in a small venue that does not have the necessary licenses with the performing rights organization, the songwriter will not be paid and the organization may very well file a lawsuit against the venue. This in turn may cause the venue to discontinue presenting any live music.

When folk songs receive airplay in foreign countries, the writer usually does get paid. This is because in many countries the government owns and controls radio stations and pays money based on all airplay, rather than through the sophisticated logging systems that the American performing rights groups use. These logging systems are akin to polling in the sense that they are representative rather than specifically accurate.

Other publishing income that comes to singer-songwriters is from songbooks or instructional books. The leading music print publishers, as opposed to publishers who concern themselves with royalties from record sales, radio, TV and movie uses, are Alfred Music and Hal Leonard. Their instruction books often include CDs or have codes available to the consumer that allow her to hear the content of the books via the internet. These are great sources of instruction for aspiring players, and provide income to the person who has written the instruction book. Mel Bay Publications and Centerstream Music are also important players in the music instruction business. A few well-known performers/instructors like Stefan Grossman, Steve Kaufman, Jerry Silverman, and Happy Traum have written dozens of such books.

One of the great success stories of the folk business has been the odyssey of Homespun Tapes. The company was started by Happy Traum in his hometown of Woodstock, New York, when some of his students expressed frustration at his abandoning their lessons when he went on tour. He literally started to duplicate reel-to-reel tapes in his living room. Today the company boasts dozens of videos, as well as some audio and printed music titles. Stefan Grossman has a similar company that is more specifically dedicated toward blues through his *Stefan Grossman's Guitar Workshop* in Sparta, New Jersey.

Songs that are placed in movies can be lucrative to artists and songwriters. Each are paid separately when a song is used in a movie. If the song goes on television, the songwriter will be paid additional money based on the number of markets the movie is shown in and the way the music is used in the movie. For example, uses that involve music used in the foreground pay better than those that are simply backgrounds to the action of the movie. Artists in the United States do not receive further payment for television showings of a movie.

There are a number of reasons why royalties can be difficult to collect from record companies and music publishers. Any money that it costs to make a record, including any cash advances, is deducted from artists' royalties. Often musicians or songwriters move and do not send their new address or banking information to the company. It is questionable how great an effort record companies or music publishers make to locate the artist or songwriter. The same thing applies to union bonus funds and to Sound Exchange. If the reader goes online, they will find a list of hundreds of musicians who are owed money from these funds. If a musician ceases to be a member of the union then the union has no current address for them. Reuses from recorded performances may result in generating new payments, but the money cannot be distributed if the funds can't locate the musicians. The solution would seem to be to create an industry database that could be shared by music publishers, record companies, performing rights organizations, and the bonus funds of talent unions.

To summarize the royalty situation for artists: at a music business conference that I attended a few years ago the business manager of a major rock band stated that collecting royalties from record companies was the most difficult part of his job.

## Magazines

For many years *Sing Out!* magazine was the best-known periodical about American folk music. Currently the magazine publishes only in digital format. From 1987 to 2010 *Dirty Linen* was an attractive bi-monthly magazine that covered various aspects of the folk music scene. *No Depression* is devoted to music that falls in the cracks between country, blues, and folk music, in an idiom that used to be called alt. country, but is now essentially known as Americana. It started out as a print journal, switched to digital only, and now publishes in both formats. *Elmore* is in a somewhat similar vein to *No Depression*, but with more emphasis on independent rock. It also started as a printed magazine but is now exclusively digital.

The last existing printed North American Journal is the Canadian *Penguin Eggs*, which is devoted to Canadian folk music and folksingers, but also includes artists from the United States. *Ancient Victories* is a regionally oriented publication published near Seattle, and *Victory Review* is another northwest magazine that used to be printed, but is now available only online.

## Musical instruments

Along with the folk revival came a tremendous interest in folk instruments. The guitar is the most popular folk instrument, with annual sales in the hundreds of thousands. Martin and Gibson were the most popular instruments through the 1970s. Taylor Guitars appeared in 1976, and has become a strong contender in the acoustic world. Companies like Breedlove, Collings, Goodall, Huss & Dalton, Larrivee, and Santa Cruz are smaller companies with less of a mass production feel. There are also individual luthiers like Linda Manzer and Grit Laskin in Canada and Bill Tippin, James A. Olson, and Jeffrey Elliot in the United States who produce a small number of expensive hand-crafted guitars. Other moderately priced acoustic guitars that are frequently seen in North America are made by Alvarez, Aria, Cort, Fender, Guild, and Takamine.

Deering, Gibson, and Ome are the major players in the banjo market, but there are also smaller, boutique makers who generally sell out of their own shops, as well as smaller manufacturers like Stelling and Ramsey. Gibson, Weber, Collings, and Rigel are well-known mandolin makers, and again some musicians swear by smaller, boutique makers.

Ukuleles are extremely portable and generally cheaper than any of the above instruments. Thousands and thousands of ukes sell each year and some music stores are actually virtually sustained through the sale of ukes. Martin has been making them for years, but there are numerous Hawaiian-based makers, and other companies like Deering have jumped into the market as well.

## Imports

A large portion of the market for guitars and other instruments comes from moderate-priced instruments that are imported from China under various brand names. Saga and Johnson are two of the companies that sell these instruments in the United States. Yamaha and Takamine are two Asian-owned companies that sell thousands of guitars in the United States and Canada. There are also American distributors of musical instruments whose guitars are made by Chinese factories but marketed under various American-sounding names.

## Vintage instruments

There is a strong market for older instruments among musicians and instrument collectors. Certain instruments like Lloyd Loar (Gibson) mandolins and pre-war Martin and Gibson Guitars can sell for stratospheric prices. Because this market has become so significant, there are specific stores like Carter, Vintage Guitars, and Gruhn Guitars in Nashville and Intermountain Guitar and Banjo in Salt Lake City that specialize in these instruments. An online site called reverb.com sells many of these instruments on consignment for various music stores. There is even a monthly magazine called *Vintage Guitar* that analyzes prices of vintage instruments and has articles about rare instruments.

## Endorsements

Some of the more famous musicians, particularly guitarists, endorse or even help design instruments or models of instruments that are named after them. Similarly, there are a half-dozen string makers that provide strings for musicians and give endorsers strings, or provide them at high discounts. String makers, instrument makers, and new manufacturers exhibit at the various musical conferences and at the two musical instrument shows sponsored by NAMM, the National Association of Music Merchandisers.

## Music stores

Earlier in this book I discussed the importance of the early folklore centers to musicians during the folk revival. These days there are numerous stores that specialize in fretted instruments. In addition to the ones already named, a few important stores are the Candyman in Santa Fe, New Mexico, Dusty

Strings in Seattle, Westwood Music in Los Angeles, Gryphon Music in Palo Alto, California, Uptown Music in Rochester, New York, the Pickin' Parlor in Arvada, Colorado, Rufus Guitar Shop in Vancouver, British Columbia, and The Twelfth Fret in Toronto. Norm's Rare Guitars in Reseda, California, and Vintage Instruments in Philadelphia specialize in the vintage instruments that so many musicians covet. Elderly Instruments in Lansing, Michigan, is probably the largest and most successful of all these stores. It is situated in a large building and does a huge mail order business in books, recordings, instructional materials, and new and used instruments.

All music stores are experiencing problems due to the proliferation of large big-box chain stores, especially Guitar Center. There are also heavy internet discounters and dozens of entrepreneurs who sell instruments on eBay. Unlike the traditional folk music shops none of these operations do anything to promote a sense of community.

## Folk radio

Folk radio shows are generally broadcast on NPR, community radio stations, or satellite radio. Some of the folk disc jockeys, such as Mary Cliff in Washington, DC, Rich Warren in Chicago, Matt Watroba in Detroit, and Arthur and Andrea Berman in Vancouver have been on the air for years. Many local stations have folk shows at specific times of day.

Two other radio outlets exist for folk-based music. One is the so-called Americana format. I will return to that format in a later chapter. The other radio outlet is live music performances on syndicated radio. Nick Forster hosts *e Town* in Boulder, Colorado, which features quite a bit of live, folk-based music. Songwriter-performer Tom May has a show called *River City Folk* out of Portland, Oregon, that features folk artists and is also sometimes recorded in other cities. *Mountain Stage* in Charleston, West Virginia, hosted by Larry Groce is another such program. Mandolin virtuoso Chris Thile hosts *Live from Here*, which regularly broadcasts from St. Paul, Minnesota, but also does shows in other locations. This program is the successor to Garrison Keilor's *A Prairie Home Companion*. Because Thile is a musician, his show features even more music than Keilor presented.

There is an email list of folk radio stations that can be accessed by artists, music business professionals, disc jockeys, or fans. It includes over 150 radio stations, mostly located in the United States and Canada. It also lists a smaller number of folk music programmers in various countries including Australia, New Zealand, Germany, and Israel. These disc jockeys submit frequent lists of the recordings that they are currently playing on their shows. This is an invaluable source of information for anyone trying to follow which artists are currently receiving airplay.

# The gig business

A few years ago, the late Mike Seeger made a casual comment to me when I asked him how he was doing. He remarked that the folk music pie was about the same size, but that the number of people sitting at the table had grown much larger. Folk is a niche market compared in terms of the overall market for nonclassical music. The sort of coffeehouses and clubs where performers work do not tend to draw large audiences or pay serious money. There are a dozen booking agents who specialize in folk music gigs like Folklore Productions in Santa Monica or Val Denn, who has offices in Austin and in Upper Blandford, Nova Scotia. They book performers at art centers, colleges, and folk festivals. It is possible for performers to do this on their own, but it is a difficult and time-consuming process that requires patience and persistent follow-up. Folk festivals are particularly good gigs not necessarily because they pay that well, but because the audiences are very large and come from different cities, states, or provinces. Most festivals are outdoor events and not all artists are suited to outdoor venues where volume may be more important than subtle artistry. Folklore societies and local music organizations and churches sponsor concerts as well.

House concerts are a relatively recent addition to the world of traveling artists. Typically, these are shows held in the living rooms of houses that may hold anything from 15 to 50 people, with some exceptions for people who have larger houses or outdoor spaces in their backyards. These are intimate shows that generally do not require much if any amplification. The hosts are dedicated music fans who take no fee for providing the venue. Many offer light snacks and coffee, and a few even provide full dinners for additional admission. To avoid insurance and tax problems for the host, admission is almost always by "suggested donation." The host may or may not provide the performer with a free overnight stay. Because of the nature of the venue these shows work best for single or duo performers. Part of the vibe is for performers to be somewhat sociable and willing to talk pleasantly with both the host and the attendees. These shows are an excellent venue for selling CDs because in such an intimate setting the CD provides a remembrance of a pleasant or even memorable musical evening for the fans. A company called *Concerts in the Home* specializes in booking house concerts. It is also possible for an artist to book these events without an agent. The internet can provide listings of house concerts in most major cities.

Artists who prize privacy and are somewhat introverted may best avoid house concerts. The artist should enquire how the host is going to promote the show and how some of their other shows have gone. A concert with four or five people in attendance is depressing for the host and the artist too.

## Grants

Grants are another possibility for musicians. The NEA (National Endowment for the Arts) has various programs for musicians in the Folk Arts. They typically go to traditional musicians rather than to revivalist performers. Recent grant recipients include children's performer Ella Jenkins, harmonica player Phil Wiggins, the late Hawaiian guitarist Cyrus Pahinui, and Cajun accordion player Eve Ybarra. Many of the grants go to preserve traditional folk-art forms which are not limited to music, but also include other folk arts and crafts. Some grants are awarded to distinguished artists in recognition of lengthy careers but others go to fund mentor–apprentice relationships between a folk artist and someone who wants to study with them. The purpose of teacher–apprentice crafts is to enable traditions to continue after the practitioner ceases working or passes on.

A rare example of a revivalist receiving an NEA grant occurred when dobro player Jerry Douglas received a grant in 2004. Since Douglas is a successful studio musician and performer in Nashville, judging from the endowment's own rules this was a peculiar choice.

Several younger folk artists including Rhiannon Giddens, Chris Thile, and blues artist Corey Harris have been recipients of MacArthur Fellowships. These magical grants are five-year awards of $125,000 a year. These are not grants that someone can apply for, but they are awarded by a committee who selects the winners through their work and reputation in the arts, sciences, and humanities. Another grant that uses a similar rationale is a $50,000 grant given to a different banjo player each year funded by Steve Martin. A committee of distinguished banjo players decides on the winner and recipients have varied from young players like Giddens to older players like Eddie Adcock.

## How Canada created a record industry

If you look at a map that includes Canada and the United States, you can discern that Canada is a slightly larger country than the United States. However, the Canadian population is about 11 percent of the population of the United States. Most of the large Canadian cities are close to the US border and receive American radio. As a result, Canadian record companies found themselves unable to compete with companies in the United States. There were always some regional Canadian artists, especially Quebecois artists, but by and large if a Canadian artist didn't have a record contract in the United States they generally received little Canadian airplay.

In 1971 public hearings developed the notion of creating the concept called Canadian content. The idea was designed to force radio stations in Canada to play a substantial amount of music "made in Canada." Initially, stations were compelled to devote 25 percent of their programming to recordings with Canadian content. Gradually this percentage has been raised to 35 percent, and for newer stations 40 percent. Content is defined according to a formula called MAPL. These four elements of a recording are: the Music of a selection, the Artist, the P means recorded in Canada or performed wholly in Canada and broadcast live in Canada, and L refers to lyrics. Stations that program jazz or classical music where there are a limited number of Canadian recordings may be allowed by the Canadian Radio-Television and Telecommunications Commission (CRTC) to broadcast 20 percent Canadian content recordings.

When these rules were adopted, radio stations complained that this was a noble concept but that they simply were not enough Canadian recordings available for them to meet these quotas. Consequently, the government created a program called FACTOR (Foundation Assisting Canadian Talent on Recordings).

FACTOR contributes 75 percent of the total eligible budget of a recording to a maximum of $47,500 spent by an artist. Funding is paid out 50 percent on approval of a project and the remainder upon completion of the project. More money is available if a recording meets a qualifying sales threshold. Both artists and record labels can apply for this funding and a similar fund Musicaction, exists for French language recordings. There are also requirements for Canadian Content for television.

Essentially the CANCON rules and the establishment of FACTOR created the possibility of a Canadian music business that entailed more than the major labels from the United States establishing offices in Toronto, Montreal, or Vancouver.

## Canadian folk labels

Borealis Records based in Toronto has a large catalog of Canadian artists including composer-arranger-instrumentalist Ken Whitely, banjoist-composer Jayme Stone, singer-songwriter Linda McRae, guitar maker and singer-songwriter Grit Laskin, Pharis and Jason Romero and singer-songwriter James Gordon.

True North Records was founded by entrepreneur-talent manager Bernie Finkelstein and has produced over 600 albums. Its most popular artist is Bruce Cockburn, but there are many other albums available from such artists as Buffy Ste. Marie, Old Man Luedecke, Nova Scotia artist Jimmy Rankin, and Blackie & the Rodeo Kings. True North also distributes products from other Canadian labels and Finkelstein has leased these records to various labels in the United States.

Stony Plains Records, based in Calgary, Alberta, has recorded artists from both Canada and the United States. Among the Canadian artists are guitarist Amos Garrett, Ian Tyson, and Sylvia Tyson, and bluesman King Biscuit Boy.

Northern Blues Records specializes in blues recordings, mostly by Canadian artists. Other Canadian labels like Nettwork sometimes release folk-related projects along with work in numerous other musical genres. Nettwork was founded by manager-record producer-entrepreneur Terry McBride. Their most famous folk-related artist is Sarah McLachlan.

Many Canadian artists release their own self-produced albums on their own record labels. The advantage that they have over US artists is that these albums almost invariably qualify under the Canadian Content rules. Although the Canadian Content rules were designed to create a market for Canadian artists on radio, there have been some other effects. Some Canadian pop artists, like Celine Dion, Anne Murray, April Lavigne, and Shania Twain have used recording studios in Canada in order to be certain that their recordings qualify for Canadian Content. In this way the rules have helped to create more business for Canadian recording studios. The reader should be aware that quite a few other countries such as Mexico, Israel, and South Africa have quotas that require domestic product to receive a certain amount of airplay.

As we enter a period where music is increasingly available on the internet through streaming and sites like YouTube, there is some concern that the Canadian Content rules will become less effective.

## The Canadian children's market

The Cancon rules stimulated many segments of the Canadian music business. Because of a combination of CBC Television shows, live performances, and recordings during the 1970s, a strong market for children's music by Canadian performers developed. Although there have been a number of successful performers, the inspiration for the Canadian children's market was Raffi Cavoukian. Originally Raffi performed music for adults, but in the mid-1970s he was asked to participate in the Mariposa Folk Festival's *Music in the Schools* program. Shortly thereafter his mother-in-law invited him to sing at her nursery school and suggested that he make a recording for children. With the help of musicians-producers Ken Whiteley and Daniel Lanois he recorded his first album, *Songs for the Very Young*. Since then he has become a children's music superstar, touring in Canada and the United States, and selling millions of records. Raffi is also known for his environmental activism.

Sharon, Lois, and Bram were a Canadian trio who starred in two Canadian television shows, and made seventeen albums. Their *Elephant* TV Show was broadcast on CBC, and in reruns in the United States on the Nickelodeon channel. They also featured many fellow-Canadian artists as guests on the show. Their second series *Skinnamarink TV* ran for fifty-two episodes on CBC and was broadcast in the USA on The Learning Channel. They were Goodwill Ambassadors for UNICEF and played extensively all over Canada and even at the White House in the United States. In 2002 Lois decided she did not wish to tour any more, but Sharon and Bram carried on until their 1918 farewell tour.

Fred Penner began to perform in schools in the late 1970s and began to record in 1979. In 1984 Penner initiated the popular CBC show *Fred Penner's Place*. Five years later the show was picked up in the United States on the Nickelodeon Channel in the United States. Penner has also created storybooks based on several of his own songs.

The above artists paved the way for a number of Canadian artists who dedicated their career s partially or entirely to children's music. The list includes Heather Bishop, the late Carmen Compagne, Bob King, Charlotte Diamond, Norman Foote, Jennifer Gasoi, and Al Simmons.

Of course, there are children's music artists in the United States but CBC has been particularly influential in promoting children's music. Certainly, no artist in the United States has developed the notoriety that Raffi enjoys.

## The folk business

The very idea that folk music can be regarded as a business is probably enough to give folk musicians and fans a mild or serious case of ulcers. The fact remains that making a living as a musician, whether playing folk music or any other sort of music, is a serious pursuit with an ample set of problems for its participants. For many folk music artists and fans, music represents a sense of community, and they have some difficulty factoring money into the equation.

16

# What's Going On: Expansion, Contraction, and Evolution

As I write this, we are almost a fifth of the way through the twenty-first century. In 1940 there were the political singers, especially the Almanacs, who believed in using music as a tool for social change; there were a handful of concert singers like John Jacob Niles and Richard Dyer Bennett and there were traditional musicians championed mostly by Alan Lomax and his recordings. A few blues artists, notably Lead Belly and Josh White, promoted interest in the blues and African-American secular music. It is also worth noting that virtually all of this activity was centered in New York City.

All of the major twentieth-century figures that played some role in bringing about the folk revival in the days of the 1950s Weavers' hit recordings are gone. At that time it was easy to analyze the various streams of the revival. There were the traditional singers, the people who wanted to use music as a tool for social change, there were the first glimmers of folk-pop, and a few young folk song revivalists who suddenly grasped that it might be possible to make a living from performing American folk music.

Although the Weavers had relatively few imitators, the success of the Kingston Trio brought folk into general acceptance as one of various forms of popular music. By the time the trio's various successors appeared, we had seen the beginning of folk music stores and the increased production and sales of guitars and banjos. The business infrastructure that included managers, agents, record companies specializing in folk music, and even some music publishers helped to turn the music into an industry. A sort of counterreaction to the Trio developed from those who got deeper into the music. They scorned or at least said that they scorned the trappings of commercial success. This was part of what led to the creation of the New Lost City Ramblers and the various groups that were devoted to traditional music that either paralleled their beginnings, or followed in their wake. Another group of folk fans turned to the blues, spurred by the rediscovery of so-many fabled blues artists of the 1920s and 1930s. By the mid-1960s the success of Bob Dylan, the Byrds, and the Buffalo Springfield led to the short-lived success of the folk-rock genre. Dylan soon became the king of the introspective singer-songwriters, and his rise was paralleled and followed by a variety of others who, like Dylan, privileged the exploration of the personal over any explorations of the political.

## The seventies, eighties and nineties

American popular music went through various stylistic changes during the 1970s and 1980s. Some of them involved or influenced the music of folksingers and some did not do so. Rock music moved from folk-rock to art-rock and punk music developed as a sort of revulsion to the pretentious art-rock bands. The basic punk ethic was to keep the music as simple and loud as possible. The art-rockers were proud of their training and technical skills, but the basic punk ethic maintained that "anyone could do this." In a sense this was pretty much the same mentality that had inspired all of the imitators of the Kingston Trio. Certainly, from a technical point of view, it isn't too difficult to learn three or four chords on a guitar or a banjo. Meanwhile, the acoustic singer-songwriter movement experienced a temporary slump, punk was refined into new wave music, glam rock had its day, and heavy metal music and then rap came into vogue. Interest in folk music became more and more specialized by genre, and there were niche markets within niche markets. Although quite a few of the young folk revivalists of the 1960s were interested in a broad variety of musical styles, white, black, and otherwise, the new generation of folk enthusiasts tended to separate into various musical camps who tended to pay little attention to one another. Celtic music fans weren't interested in blues, and blues fans didn't care about mountain music. Certainly, the musical climate was changing. Most of the pop-folk groups were defunct or reduced to playing gigs of secondary importance. Many of the bands like 1950s rock bands began to tour with replacement members and in some instances there were no more replacements than founding members or even no original members at all.

During the early 1990s, there was a brief vogue for reviving traditional country music in the country music industry. Ricky Skaggs was the leader of the pack, and he moved from country-folk labels like Rounder and Sugar Hill to Columbia Records subsidiary Epic Records. Ricky had played in Emmylou Harris's band and had authentic bluegrass chops. It was odd to hear hit country records with his high, lonesome singing style and hot bluegrass licks infiltrating commercial country radio.

If the younger folk artists were becoming more specialized, the younger artists who began to infiltrate rock and country music were increasingly open to musical experiments combining different genres. By the mid-1980s bands like *the Jayhawks* and *Uncle Tupelo* were developing a genre that became known as "alternative country." In 1995, *No Depression* magazine was born. The magazine was named after a Carter Family song that had been recorded by Uncle Tupelo. The alt. country movement was informed by Harry Smith's old Anthology series on Folkways Records which included multiple genres of folk music. The movement even made fun of itself, something the ultra-sincere early revivalists were loath to do. A collection of articles from the magazine was titled: *No Depression: An Introduction to Alternative Country Music: Whatever That Is.*

Another revolution was going on in the bluegrass movement. Bela Fleck carried the innovations of Bill Keith and Bobby Thompson to a whole new level. After studying with Tony Trischka, himself an innovative and creative banjoist, Fleck made his first recording for Rounder in 1978. In 1981 Fleck joined the leading newgrass band, *The New Grass Revival*. During the 1980s, bluegrass musicians and fans were divided between the older, more traditionally oriented musicians, and the younger, more experimental longhaired performers. It paralleled what happened in jazz when bebop came along. The older swing and Dixieland musicians didn't care for the music and felt threatened by its complexity.

Younger musicians turned to the newer styles, and the newgrass players moved further and further toward the musical left wing. In 1988 Fleck started his own group *The Flecktones*. This band featured the Wooten Brothers playing electric bass and an electronically triggered drum set. The brothers were both black. I can't think of another bluegrass musician who was playing with black musicians as regular band members not only then, but even now. Bela also began to integrate jazz influences into his music, adding oboe and English horn player Paul McCandless to the band. More recently Bela has written and performed music for symphony orchestras, recorded with jazz pianists Marcus Roberts and Chick Corea, and traveled to Africa in order to make a video of himself sitting in with various African musicians.

Meanwhile brilliant multi-instrumentalist Mark O'Connor gave up a lucrative career as a Nashville session player. He started a trio with virtuoso cellist Yo Yo Ma and eclectic bass player Edgar Meyer. They played folk-based classical music together culminating in a bestselling crossover album in 1996. Since that time O'Connor has moved to New York, written various classical works including string quartets and symphonic works.

David Grisman cut his musical teeth on jug band music and traditional bluegrass, and he joined up with guitarist-singer Peter Rowan in the psychedelic group *Earth Opera*. During the 1970s he was in the bluegrass band Old and in the Way with Grateful Dead guitarist Jerry Garcia. From there Grisman invented a folk-jazz style that he called *"dawg music."* In the original quartet were innovative bluegrass guitarist Tony Rice and the afore mentioned Mark O'Connor on fiddle. Later versions of the band featured fiddler Darol Anger and mandolin player Mike Marshall. The band was a sort of chamber-folk-jazz group reflecting the influence of Django Reinhardt, Stephan Grappelli, and the Hot Quintet of France. Grisman also started the Acoustic Disc label, largely to release mandolin music of his own and the work of other, often neglected artists.

Among group of forward-thinking West Coast musicians, banjoists-guitarists Herb Pederson and Bernie Leadon and mandolinist Chris Hillman were in and out of various folk-country-rock groups, including the massively successful *Eagles*, the *Flying Burrito Brothers*, the *Byrds,* and the *Desert Rose Band*. If it was difficult to define folk music by the time of the 1960s revival, it became next to impossible by the end of the 1970s.

## The return of the singer-songwriter

During the mid- to late 1980s, another group of singer-songwriters emerged. Many of the most popular of these artists were women. *10,000 Maniacs* featured Natalie Merchant. They began recording for Elektra in 1985, and they sang about a variety of political and social issues, including child abuse, the criminal justice system, and the environment. Merchant left the band in 1992, and has pursued a solo career ever since.

There are a couple of dozen singer-songwriters who never broke through to the major labels, but whose work was issued on various smaller, independent labels. There is a whole contingent of writers from the New England area, including Bob Francke, Patty Larkin, David Mallett, Bill Morrisey, Ellis Paul, and

Bill Staines. Jack Hardy's *Fast Folk* magazine offered support to the New York songwriting community. Smithsonian Folkways issued a double CD reissue of the magazine's work that included songs composed and sung by thirty-three artists, including Shawn Colvin, Steve Forbert, John Gorka, Jack Hardy, Lucy Kaplansky, Christine Lavin, Rod McDonald, Richard Shindell, and Suzanne Vega. The magazine also sponsored live shows in New York City, and in effect the organization was a loose co-op. Many of the above artists had their songs recorded by other artists in addition to their own recordings.

Other singer-songwriters, such as Bob Bossin, The late Spencer Bohren, Chris Smither, John Gorka Maria Dunn, Chuck Brodsky, Greg Brown, Dan Frechette, Eliza Gilkyson, Arlo Guthrie, Marie-Lynn Hammond, the late Jimmy LaFave, Kate and Anna McGarrigle, Iris DeMent, Carrie Newcomer, David Rawlings, Gillian Welch Tom Russell, Ron Sexsmith, David Wilcox, Dar Williams, Victoria Williams, the late Steve Young, Steve Earle, Mary Gauthier, Tom Russell, Susan Warner, Cheryl Wheeler, and Roy Zimmerman came from, or live, in different parts of the United States or Canada. Almost all of these artists remain active today. Texas has its own singer-songwriter scene that has spawned many artists who did not necessarily stay in Texas but were certainly strongly influenced by that environment. This includes Austin patriarch Willie Nelson, the late Guy Clark, Steve Earle, the late Mickey Newbury, Joe Ely, Nanci Griffith, the late Steve Fromholz, Jimmie Dale Gilmore, Butch Hancock, Ray Wylie Hubbard, Robert Earl Keen, Lyle Lovett, James McMurtry, Michael Martin Murphy, the late Chuck Pyle, Willis Alan Ramsey, Townes Van Zandt, and Jerry Jeff Walker.

Another group of singer-songwriters including Mike Dowling in Wyoming, Mary Flower and Tony Furtado in Portland, Kelly Jo Phelps across the river in Washington, travelling man Jack Williams, and the late Artie Traum in Woodstock established themselves as superb instrumentalists whose recordings mix original songs and instrumentals.

There are also singer-songwriters whose work tends to center around specific subjects. Gordon Bok and the late Canadian artist Stan Rogers wrote songs that celebrated the sea, fishermen, and shipwrecks. Some other artists work in the tradition of the Almanac Singers, recording songs about social and political issues. Charlie Brown, Anne Feeney, John McCutcheon, Jim Page, and David Rovics can be found singing on picket lines and at anti-war rallies. McCutcheon and Feeney have also been activists in the Musician's Union, an organization that many radical folksingers have largely ignored. McCutcheon is also an excellent multi-instrumentalist who plays banjo, fiddle, guitar, and hammered dulcimer.

## Crossover and Americana

The word "crossover" is popular in the music industry. It is used to describe artists whose work can fit into more than one radio format or record bin. Artists like Jackson Browne, James Taylor, and Lucinda Williams are among many who fit into this category.

By the 1980s, many artists whose music touched on various genres began to realize that they were at a disadvantage in receiving radio play. During the 1960s FM radio included many free-form radio stations that played a mixture of musical styles rather than limiting themselves to a single genre. At that time artists who played folk, country, bluegrass, blues, or other musical styles were programmed on these stations back to back without undue concern about the limitations of the radio audience. By the end of the 1960s, many of these stations had turned to a more conservative playlist format, and some of the originally adventurous stations were sold to various radio chains. As a reaction to this phenomenon, writer and disc jockey named Marc Humphrey hosted a weekly radio show in Northridge, California, called *Honky Tonk Amnesia*. Humphrey played a mixture of all of the above styles and KCSN, which broadcast his show, advertised it as "Americana."

By the late 1980s Americana had begun to be a term used to describe this mixed music radio format. In 1999 the Americana Music Association was established as an organization devoted to this new musical format. This has evolved into an annual music fest and awards show with numerous musical performances in the same way that the Folk Alliance and the Bluegrass Association have developed their organizations.

There is no question that the creation of the Americana format has been a boon for artists who don't fit conveniently into specific musical niches. The down side of the format can be ascertained by *No Depression* magazine's comment about alternative country music: "Whatever that is." It is fair to question whether Americana really has a musical identity, as opposed to be a hodge-podge of varying, and not always compatible music genres.

## More crossovers

Another kind of crossover has been attempted by Bruce Springsteen and John Mellancamp, among others. Springsteen's albums *Nebraska, the Ghost of Tom Joad* and *The Seeger Sessions* essentially have attempted to transform "the Boss" into a sort of contemporary Woody Guthrie. Mellancamp used a country-folk band to back him up in such albums as *The Lonesome Jubilee.*

It is a matter of opinion as to how successful these transformations have been. In my opinion the ominous *Nebraska* album was more convincing than the other projects. Part of the problem with the *Seeger Sessions* is that the album contains none of Seeger's own songs or anything that reflects Pete's political ideas. The Nebraska album is produced very simply and other than the Dylan-inflected harmonica, seems straightforward and unselfconscious. The energy his regular band generally seems to blend better with Springsteen's vocal talents and songs. Canadian Bruce Cockburn seems to move comfortably between folk-rock and topical songs, anchored by his own excellent guitar work.

## These days

If we look at the performers and the market for folk music today, the easiest way to comprehend the changes that have occurred is to somewhat arbitrarily divide artists into three groups. First, there is the "youth movement," people who are under the age of forty. This includes newly minted professionals, and artists who have come to terms with their particular talents and how they fit into the world of twenty-first-century folk music. Secondly is the artists whose audience is somewhat established and who are forty to fifty-nine years old. These people are close to the peak of their abilities and careers. The last group is sixty years old or older. They are beginning to wind down their careers or at least to think about doing so. In the various sub-genres of folk music, youth may be a necessary component of a particular music style.

## Pop-folk today

The demand for pop-folk is similar to the reasons that some people are still interested in seeing 1950s or 1960s rock groups. The core audience is older people for whom pop-folk made some sort of difference in their lives. It may have been a romantic event in their earlier years, or possibly it was a particular concert that inspired them to play guitar or banjo. Often the current groups have few or any original members. The three groups that are still, to a greater or lesser extent road warriors, are The Brothers Four, the Kingston Trio, and Peter and Paul of Peter, Paul & Mary.

The Brothers Four began their career in 1957, and bassist Bob Flick is the sole original member that remains active in this group. The current version of the Kingston Trio contains no original members of the band, and only one of the founders is still alive. One member of the group, Josh Reynolds, is the son of founding member Nick Reynolds. Mary Travers of Peter, Paul & Mary died in 2009 and both Peter and Paul are active in individual tours and periodically play together.

There is definitely still a market for this music, but it is mostly restricted to audiences that saw these groups during their 1960s glory years. Pop-folk as a genre is pretty much extinct in terms of new music and new artists. The closest music I can think of in terms of current artists playing music that resembles pop-folk are *The Lumineers*, the British band *Mumford and Sons*, *The Milk Carton Kids*, and *the Avett Brothers*. All of these acts write their own songs but they resemble pop-folk in terms of the accessibility of their songs and the relatively musically simple nature of their music. The subject matter, as one would expect from today's artists, is almost entirely personal and suited for the emotions and pre-occupations of a younger audience.

This book is being written in the winter months of 2019. Joan Baez and Paul Simon are each seventy-seven years old and are doing their "farewell" tours. Each of them has reserved the possibility of continuing to record or doing the occasional concert but by and large, they have concluded that they wish to retire from the concert stage. Although Judy Collins is two years older, she continues to tour, to record, and to write songs. Most recently, she has toured with folk-rocker Stephen Stills, the seventy-three-year-old folk-rocker.

Of the older generation of Canadian artists, both Ian and Sylvia continue to tour in the United States and Canada. At the age of eight-five, Ian is the senior citizen of folk-pop, while Sylvia is a mere seventy-eighty-year-old. Ian has repositioned himself as a cowboy-western artist and is often found at cowboy poetry gatherings. Eighty-year-old Gordon Lightfoot has overcome some serious medical problems and also continues to tour and record. I mention the age of these performers to highlight the idea that the appeal of these artists inevitably does not reach the younger portions of the audience for folk.

# Singer-songwriters today

Many of the singer-songwriters who rose to popularity during the 1960s and 1970s are now themselves in their seventies. This includes Jackson Browne, Bruce Cockburn, Emmylou Harris, Joni Mitchell, John Prine, Bonnie Raitt, Robbie Robinson, and Neil Young. Clearly during the next five years there is going to be a changing of the guard due to illness, retirement, or death.

With all of the major figures gone, say by 2025, will the singer-songwriter genre still be a factor in the audience for folk music? Certainly, there are enough touring artists who are currently in their forties or fifties, like Katie Curtis, K. D. Lang, Gregory Alan Isakov, and Dar Williams who presumably will continue to be active at that time.

# The younger set

It may well be that many of the singer-songwriters of the future will not be solo artists but will be members of a band. Certainly, many of the chronologically younger bands, like *the Accidentals, The Dukhs, the Mammals, the Wailin' Jennies, Tracy Grammer* and *the Be Good Tanyas* all include songwriters in their roster. It is also common for people in such bands to have side projects where they write or co-write songs with collaborators who have their own bands or individual careers.

The late Dave Van Ronk once commented that the music scene would be better off if there were ten artists who interpreted songs for every singer-songwriter. Although Van Ronk was perfectly capable of writing interesting songs, his shows were a blend of traditional songs and songs composed by other songwriters with only an occasional original thrown into the mix. The prevailing cliché is that a songwriter is the best interpreter of her own songs because she is so invested in expressing the emotional aspects of that song. To hear the big, gruff Van Ronk sing a Joni Mitchell song was to grasp a whole dimension of the song that Mitchell herself would not attempt, and might not even imagine. Presumably she appreciated and enjoyed his efforts, just as Paul Simon must have loved Aretha Franklin's stirring version of his song *Bridge over Troubled Waters*. Who is going to play this role today? Some of the younger artists seem to be aware of this dilemma. The Wailin' Jennies 2017 album *Fifteen* consists entirely of cover records of songs written by other songwriters. Possibly this will inspire other artists to pursue this musical direction.

## Jam bands

Jam bands are bands that play extended solos based on the structure of their tunes. The initiator of the jam band mystique was *The Grateful Dead*, founded in 1965 in Palo Alto, California. Jerry Garcia, the lead guitarist, had a rich background in folk music and from time to time did recording projects or gigs where he played bluegrass banjo. The band was famous for its lengthy concerts, and for its fans, who became known as "Deadheads." The Dead had an anarchist business attitude and invited their fans to freely record any of their concerts, even providing space in the venue for this to happen. Their repertoire often included songs with lyrics by Robert Hunter which were loosely based on folksongs or folk themes. Examples include their original songs *Friend of the Devil* and *Ripple.* Garcia died in 1995, but the band has continued on with various guests, including guitarist John Mayer and pianist Bruce Hornsby.

*Phish* was formed in 1991. Although the aesthetic of the band was influenced by the Dead Phish, it was much more rock 'n' roll oriented, and do lengthy jams on particular songs. Like the Dead, they have attracted a large audience.

The Boulder, Colorado, area spawned a trio of jam bands. *Leftover Salmon* began in 1989. It is much closer to folk than Phish, including banjo and mandolin but also featuring a rock 'n' roll rhythm section. *String Cheese Incident* began in the ski town of Crested Butte, Colorado, and like the Leftover Salmon band, has an acoustic music sound, buttressed by bass and drums. *The Yonder Mountain String Band* formed in 1998, and has more of a bluegrass sound than the other jam bands.

The most prominent of the jam bands is the *Dave Matthews Band*, which features Dave's acoustic guitar, but also includes electric violin, and bass and drums that are closer to a rock model. The band is racially integrated, which is unique among jam bands. Dave Matthews is the only exceptional singer in all of these bands. His impassioned vocals, together with a really tight rhythm section, are probably what has made his band the most popular of the jam bands.

The audience for jam band music, except for the Dead, tends to be younger people who find the lengthy songs enjoyable. The emphasis in these bands is not necessarily on any one song, but on creating a lengthy evening of entertainment with its own ambiance. Bands like Donna The Buffalo, Old Crow Medicine Show, and Rising Appalachia incorporate a variety of musical genres in their work.

# World music

As I discussed earlier, world music in the American popular marketplace started with the Weavers recording music from Hungary, Israel, the West Indies, and Africa. They retitled and recorded Solomon Linda's song *Mbube* as *Wimoweh*.

It became a big hit for the Weavers, and was then transformed into song *The Lion Sleeps Tonight* in 1961. Using somewhat reworked lyrics, it was a hit all over again by *The Tokens*. In 1994 the song was used in the Disney hit movie *The Lion King*, which also was turned into a Broadway show.

The Calypso boom of the 1950s was initiated by the Tarriers' recording of *Day-O* but it took wing with the recording of the same song by Harry Belafonte. Belafonte followed up with recordings of both new and traditional, rearranged calypsos. During the urban folk revival of the 1960s, Theodore Bikel, Geula Gill, Cynthia Gooding, and Martha Schlamme all sang in multiple languages, and some California folk-pop artists, especially Bud and Travis, recorded and performed Mexican songs. In his solo performances, Pete Seeger performed music from everywhere—Korea, India, Israel, French, Canada, and Spain. In 1955 he did an album of Bantu choral songs with a very young Mary Travers and two of her students at the Little Red Schoolhouse. In 1962 Old Town School teacher Frank Hamilton did a world music album with Brazilian singer Valucha deCastro.

Despite the above scenario, world music played a relatively small role in the folk revival. British rockers George Harrison and Peter Gabriel played an important role in introducing world music to the British audience and in Harrison's case, to the United States as well. Harrison took some sitar lessons from the famous Ravi Shankar, and even played sitar on a few of the Beatles' recordings. Gabriel started a world music organization called WOMAD (World Music and Dance Organization), and a record label called Real World. Meanwhile Brian Jones, ill-fated original member of The Rolling Stones, recorded Moroccan musicians in 1969, and David Byrne started his Luaka Bop label in 1969 to record Brazilian musicians.

In 1986 Paul Simon brought world music to the attention of the American music fans with his *Graceland* album. He used South African musicians on the record, and also toured with some of them. The album won several Grammy Awards, sold well, and revived Simon's temporarily flagging career. It also served to introduce the notion that world music could find a mass audience in the

United States. According to Chris Nickson writing in the *NPR Curious Listener's Guide to World Music*, Simon's album caused several London entrepreneurs involved in merchandising music to coin the term "world music" as a key to selling this music to consumers.

## American revivalists discover world music

A half-dozen musicians from the United States have explored world music in some depth. These include guitarists Bob Brozman and Henry Kaiser, multi-instrumentalist David Lindley, and guitarist-vocalist Taj Mahal.

The one musician who stands out above others in this area of exploration is Ry Cooder. Ry has had a long and successful career as a singer-guitarist, written over twenty film scores, produced a number of albums, and has also played on the recording sessions of everyone from the Rolling Stones to Neil Young and Randy Newman. Cooder has very broad musical tastes and has always enjoyed throwing together musicians who are generally identified with a particular style of music with musicians who work in an entirely different genre. For example, he might use Tex-Mex accordion player Flaco Jiminez on a song that also featured Delta-style slide guitar.

In 1993 Cooder made an album called *A Meeting at the River* playing slide guitar together with an east Indian musician named Vishwa Mohan Bhatt playing an instrument that Bhatt invented called the mohan veena. A year later he did an album called *Talking Timbuktu* with African guitarist Ali Farka Toure. In 1999 Cooder went to Cuba and produced the Buena Vista Social Club recording with a group of aging Cuban musicians that also became a film, directed by Ry's friend Wim Wenders. The recording was released in 1997, and the film in 1999. The album was an astounding success selling over eight million copies throughout the world. Cooder produced the album and sat in with the band playing slide guitar. More than any other single recording project or film, this project brought world music an international audience.

In 2005 Cooder put together a remarkable album called *Chavez Ravine*. The Ravine is currently the home of the Los Angeles Dodgers baseball team. To make the baseball field possible, a Mexican-American neighborhood was eviscerated and the area became gentrified. The album includes some spoken word reminiscences that highlight the destruction of the neighborhood, together with songs variously in English and Spanish by Mexican-American recording artists who were well known in that community but not among the Anglo population.

Since that time, Ry has done a series of albums that follow in the footsteps of the Almanac Singers, discussing social and political problems and agendas in the contemporary world.

## Bob Brozman

The late Bob Brozman was a slide guitarist who had an encyclopedic knowledge of Hawaiian guitar styles. He recorded over thirty albums in his lifetime. Starting in 2002, he recorded albums with musicians from New Guinea, Hawaii, India, and Okinawa and he toured internationally.

## Henry Kaiser

Henry Kaiser is a versatile avant-garde guitarist with a heavy focus on improvisational music. He also has a career as a diver, and has made a number of trips and dives in Antarctica. Kaiser has recorded with many artists in many idioms including jazz projects with Wadada Leo Smith. Kaiser is also an ethnomusicologist, and he recorded three albums of music from Madagascar with David Lindley who is discussed below. All the royalties from these albums were donated to the Madagascar musicians because Kaiser did not want the musicians to be seen as sidemen and the musicians needed the money far more than he did. He also arranged for the musicians to own 90 percent of all the publishing rights to the songs.

## David Lindley

Multi-instrumentalist David Lindley is an anomaly on the world music scene because he not only records with international musicians but also plays a number of instruments from other cultures. Early in his career Lindley won numerous contests at the Topanga Banjo and Fiddle Contest. He was one of the founding members of the band *Kaleidoscope* who recorded four albums for Epic beginning in 1967. The band was doing wild mixes of flamenco, rock, and Middle Eastern music at a time when no one else was swimming in these waters. Fellow band member Solomon Feldthouse was playing Middle Eastern instruments. Lindley became a session man in Los Angeles and played on hundreds of recordings, including sessions for Jesse Colin Young, Leo Sayer, Linda Ronstadt, Eric Clapton, Dan Fogelberg, and Bruce Springsteen. In 1971 he started accompanying Jackson Browne, playing with him for ten years and later doing occasional tours with him. Lindley has also had his own band *El Rayo-X*, and sometimes tours with Jordanian-born percussionist Hani Naser.

A couple of years ago I attended a Lindley solo concert. He had a battery of Weissenborn slide guitars, acoustic guitars, and an oud. He picked up the oud and started to play something that struck me as a familiar Appalachian murder ballad called *Little Sadie*. About thirty seconds later he started to sing that song. Of all the world musicians profiled here, Lindley is the only one I can imagine attempting such a thing.

## Taj Mahal

In the late 1960s Taj moved to Los Angeles to form *The Rising Sons*, a rock-blues band with Ry Cooder and Jessie Lee Kincaid. The band was quickly beset with creative differences, and each of the founders went their own way.

Mahal's original reputation was as a blues musician and during the 1980s he moved to Hawaii. In 1995 he recorded a project with Indian musicians. During the next few years he recorded Hawaiian music and African music.

## Harry Manx

Manx is a Canadian musician whose music reflects blues influences as well as a serious interest in Hindustani classical music. He studied in India for five years with Vishwa Mohan Bhatt, the inventor of the twenty-string mohan veena, which has become Manx's primary instrument. He has lived and worked in Japan and Europe before returning to Canada, and he has recorded over a dozen albums that include his excellent singing as well as his unusual instrumental work.

There are other musicians who have incorporated world music into specific recording projects. Banjoists Jayme Stone and Bob Carlin, for example, have occasionally worked and recorded with African musicians on albums.

# Irish-American music

Between 1815 and 1844, over one million Irish people immigrated to the United States and Canada. The attraction of Canada was that it was cheaper to embark for Toronto than for Boston or New York. There are currently 34.5 million people who consider themselves to be of Irish descent in the United States and an additional 4,627,000 people of Irish descent in Canada. The population of Ireland itself is 4.68 million people.

Given these numbers, it isn't surprising to know that Irish and Irish-North American music are closely intertwined. According to Dorothea E. Hast and Stanley Scott's book *Music in Ireland*, the most important collection of tunes for Irish musicians was compiled by Francis O'Neill, who came to Chicago from Ireland in 1871. O'Neill's books were published in 1903 and 1907 when he was the Chief of Police in Chicago. He was also a flute and fiddle player. O'Neill, like most collectors or compilers of Irish music, presented the melody of the tunes, and it became the task of the player reading the books to provide the ornamentation that added the meat to the bones of the tune.

Similarly, Michael Coleman, an Irish fiddle player who immigrated to America in 1914, was the most influential fiddle player in Irish music. Coleman recorded and performed widely, and he tended to homogenize fiddle style obscuring regional differences that existed in Ireland.

# The Clancy Brothers, Tommy Makem and the folk revival

Tommy Makem and the Clancy Brothers were Irishmen who immigrated to New York in 1951. All of them were actors but they began singing professionally in the late 1950s. The group sang and played with considerable energy, and sang the melody of the songs in unison. They accompanied themselves with guitar and added banjo on some tunes. The Clancys did not use the sort of vocal ornamentation that had become traditional in Ireland and, like Pete Seeger, their concerts often featured the audience singing along with them. They made numerous recordings, and even started a record label. The Clancys set the tone for the sort of music that worked in pubs and social halls. They appeared on the *Ed Sullivan* TV show, and for years performed an annual concert at Carnegie Hall. Today the *Drop Kick Murphys* are sort of an updated punk version of what the Clancy Brothers offered in terms of energy and enthusiasm.

The Canadian-Irish group *The Irish Rovers* formed in 1963, and for seven years they had an international television series and a major hit record called *The Unicorn*. Four of the five members were born in Ireland but had immigrated to Canada. Over the years the personnel of the band has changed. They have recorded for a dozen record labels and had two additional television series. The various band members play fiddle, tenor banjo, bouzouki, drums, fiddle, percussion, and drums. (The bouzouki is a longer-scale octave mandolin.)

## River Dance and Irish music and dance

If the Kingston Trio was pop-folk, the River Dance shows are pop-folk culture on steroids. It all began as an interval act at the Eurovision Song Contest in 1994. This seven-minute presentation was developed into a full show which has toured internationally for over twenty years. The original lead dancers were Irish-Americans Michael Flatley and Joan Butler and the show features a large chorus and music back-up group. The show is basically super-charged Irish music and dance, with a bit of flamenco, Russian music and dance, tap dancing, and Broadway style energy thrown in. The success of the show's performances, videos, and recordings inevitably has influenced Irish music and dance in both North America and Ireland.

There is another sort of Irish balladry, dance, and music that includes some of the energetic elements in River Dance, but is also more focused on traditional music and ballads. For example, the previously mentioned book *Music in Ireland* prints two ballads that describe the difficulties of Irish immigrants coming to Canada. There are also numerous Irish ballads, including *The Rising of the Moon*, sung by the Clancys, that depict Irish resistance to the British. There also have been many Irish traditional singers, like the late Margaret Barry, whose heartfelt ballads require a listening audience rather than one that has come to see a spectacle.

There are a number of Irish-American musicians who have competed in Ireland and won music contests. Joanie Madden, of the all-female band *Cherish the Ladies* won the All-Ireland Flute and Whistle contests, and violinist Liz Carroll has been junior and senior All-Ireland Fiddle Champion and has also won the Cumadoir TG4, as an American-born composer who writes traditional-based Irish music. Both Carroll and Dr. Mick Moloney have been National Heritage Fellows in the United States. Moloney has a PhD in Folklore and has served as an advisor for many festivals and concerts in the United States. He teaches in the Irish Studies program at New York University. Other prominent Irish-American musicians include punk bands *Flogging Molly* and *the Dropkick Murphys*, and multi-genre fiddler Eileen Ivers.

## Celtic music

The word "Celtic" refers to folk music traditions of the Celtic people of Western Europe. This includes people of Irish and Scottish descent as well as the music of Wales, the Isle of Man, Brittany, and parts of Spain and Portugal. In Canada it includes the Atlantic provinces, especially Newfoundland, Cape Breton, and Prince Edward Island. French-born Cape Breton harper Alan Stivell and Cape Breton fiddler Ashley Macisaac are among the influential Celtic musicians in Canada.

## The music of and about American Indians and First Nations peoples

In looking at American Indian music, there are two separate viewpoints that are worthy of consideration. There is the music that is sung by Anglos and there is the music of Indians. In the popular and folk music of the United States there are two contradictory but equally unrealistic views of Indians. The Indian is represented either as a heartless, bloodthirsty savage or as a dedicated primitive environmentalist, a "noble savage."

The folksong *Sioux Indians* is about a wagon train trip across the plains that ends in Oregon. Along the way, it states that the settlers "while taking refreshment, we heard a loud yell, the whoop of Sioux Indians, coming out of the dell." The song lauds the tribe's "brave leader," but after he is shot the Indians run away and the wagon train safely moves on to Oregon. A similar attitude is presented in Nancy Chase's song *Ballad of Little Big Horn*, recorded by the late country singers Eddy Arnold and Porter Wagoner. The song details the bravery of General Custer's outnumbered forces decimated by the Sioux Indians. The romantic image of the Indian appears in everything from the classic cowboy song *Home on the Range*, to the rock group *Kansas*'s 1975 song Kerry Livgren's *Song for America*.

In addition to the romantic and nasty images that these two categories of songs project, a third type of song protests the treatment of Indians by Anglos. Johnny Cash did an entire album of such songs in 1964. The album was called *Bitter Tears*, and included some of his own songs, and a number of songs by Indian protest artist Peter La Farge. One of La Farge's songs, *The Ballad of Ira Hayes* became a major hit song. Initially Columbia Records, Cash's record label, did not promote the song and Cash took a full-page ad in the music trade paper *Billboard*, denouncing radio people for their cowardice in ignoring it. He then hired his own promotion people to do the job that Columbia chose not to do. The song concerned a Pima Indian who helped to raise the American flag at Iwo Jima, but came home to experience racism and ended up dying in a drunken stupor in a small ditch. In 2005 Cash's friend country artist Marty Stuart recorded an album of songs about racial injustices done to American Indians.

Insulting, racist stereotypes of Indians reflect yet another attitude in songs about Indians. Hank Thompson's 1958 *Squaws along the Yukon*, and Tim McGraw's 1994 *Indian Outlaw* are two of a number of such songs. Thompson's song is generally demeaning in his description of the habits of "squaws." McGraw's song is a more complicated story. The main body of the song was written by Tommy Barnes and Jumpin' Gene Simmons. It contains a group of racist descriptions of Indian life. It depicts Indians in wigwams, playing tom-toms, etc. McGraw's recording then plastered onto the song a chorus from the song *Indian Reservation*, written by John D. Loudermilk and recorded as a hit single by Paul Revere & The Raiders in 1968. Loudermilk's song is actually a progressive piece of work, addressing that whites perpetrated on the Cherokees. The other irony is that McGraw is actually one of the few "out" Democrats in the Nashville music business. *Indian Outlaw* was a career-making record for McGraw, but some radio stations refused to play it when complaints from Indian activist groups surfaced.

## American-Indian music

Although most music consumers think that Indian music is either something that is shouted incoherently to minor chords and insistent drums or a series of plaintive laments played on a wooden flute. In fact, there are a wide variety of music styles found on and near Indian reservations in the United States.

Many tribes sing either acapella or accompanied by drums. The peyote ritual is accompanied by voices and drums and may be sung by men or by women. The music has vocables, which are sung syllables rather than words. The first commercial recordings of peyote music were made in 1940. Jazz musician Jim Pepper adapted a peyote song for his often-recorded song *Wichi Tai Toa* in 1973.

The Indian flute is not a universal instrument among Indian tribes but in recent years a number of Indian musicians, especially Kevin Locke, R. Carlos Nakai, and Mary Youngblood have popularized the instrument. It has found a place with fans of New Age music because it is meditational, somewhat repetitious music that is associated with mediation practices. Nakai has expanded the role of the instrument, playing on a number of classical music compositions by James DeMars.

Besides the songwriters mentioned earlier in the book, there are a number of artists who perform political music that protests the poor treatment of Indians. John Trudell was active in AIM, the American Indian Movement. That paralleled the rise of the Black Power movement in the United States. Trudell made a number of recordings of his poems, initially set to music by Indian guitarist Jesse Ed Davis and later by Mark Shark. Trudell's band was a mixture of Indians and whites and toured as well as performed. Other Indian protest artists include the late Floyd Westerman and the Indian rock band *XIT*. A number of Indian artists like Joanne Shenandoah and A. Paul Ortega perform and write a variety of songs, including political ones. Montana Indian artist Jack Gladstone has written a number of songs that discuss historical events like Custer's defeat from the viewpoint of an Indian. Some Anglo musicians, like Seattle folksinger Jim Page and Larry Long, have written political songs that are pro-Indian.

Another category of Indian music is pow-wow songs, sometimes referred to as "49'ers." These songs are associated with inter-tribal gatherings called pow-wows. Pow-wows take place all over the United States and Canada and include contests with cash prizes, some of which are considerable. Part of the event is ceremonial with honor paid to those who served in the armed forces. The contests include competitions for drummers and dancers and take place in all states and the Canadian provinces. Some pow-wows last as long as a week and include arts and craft fairs.

There are sixty Indian radio stations in the United States. Many of them are in effect successors to the FM radio of the 1960s. During a half hour time period the listener is apt to hear weather reports on the reservation, a Willie Nelson tune followed by an Indian acapella piece, a rock song, and so forth. Pima Indian

Keith Secola's song *Indian Kars* was a big hit on Indian radio. An "Indian Car" is an old vehicle full of dents and scratches and held together with duct tape. Secola's song mentions that he has a sticker that says Indian Power on the back of the car. He adds that is what holds his car together.

## Adaptations and inclusions

Certain musical styles are particularly popular among specific tribes. Kristina M. Jacobsen, in her book *The Sound of Navajo Country*, mentions that there are over fifty country bands on the Navajo reservation. There are several Indian bands including *Red Thunder, Burning Sky*, and *Walela* who work in rock and blues styles. Bill Miller plays guitar and Indian flute and has recorded a dozen albums, with one foot in country and the other in folk music. On the huge Tohono O'odham reservation in Southern Arizona and Mexico, chicken scratch music is the order of the day. This music is a hybrid of German, Mexican, rock, and tribal music and features accordion and saxophone.

There are also quite a few American Indian rappers, including Julian B, Litefoot, City Natives, and Frank Wain, whose raps concern issues relevant to American-Indian life.

## First Nations music

The music of First Nations people in Canada includes almost all of the styles mentioned in the discussion of Indian music in the United States. Manitoba is a hotbed of pow-wow music and various First Nations artists perform blues, protest songs, pow-wow music, etc. A uniquely Canadian musical example is Inuit throat singing, and Tanya Tagaq is an activist singer who has mastered that vocal style. Susan Aglukark is another Inuit singer who combines folk, country, and rock elements and has had a very successful career on records. Aglukark is a feminist activist whose songs reflect her concerns with women's issues.

The Metis are a unique First Nations and American Indian group. They trace their origin to mixed European and First Nations parentage, and they have developed a unique fiddle style. The dances feature a repertoire of European dance styles mixed with First Nations dances. The Metis are spread across Canada, Montana, North Dakota, and northwest Minnesota.

There are quite a few First Nation rappers including *A Tribe Called Red, Shannon Feathers, Litefoot, Willy Mitchell, Art Napoleon,* and *Frank Wain*. During the mid-1980s through the 1990s, the Inuit duo *Kashtin* had hit records, singing in French and English. First Nations singer-songwriters include Tom Jackson, Don Francks, Wab Kinew, Derek Miller, Fara Palmer, and Kinnie Starr.

There are thirty-seven First Nations radio stations in Canada, some of which also stream on the internet.

## American-Indian and First Nations record companies

A number of record companies specialize in American Indian music. Canyon Records was founded in 1961 and features a variety of Indian music styles, including quite a few albums by R. Carlos Nakai. Indian House, founded in 1961, issues more traditionally oriented music. SOAR (Sound of America Recordings) is the only Indian-owned record company and opened its doors in 1989. It tends to feature more contemporary Indian music. Folkways has a number of traditional albums in its catalog, and various labels like Etherean (now defunct) and Silver Wave have periodically issued New Age-oriented recordings of Indian flute music.

There are a number of Canadian record labels that feature First Nations Music. Makoche Records has released many recordings by Indian flutist Kevin Locke. Arbor Records has issued almost 900 titles, and other labels include Sunshine Records, Sweet Grass, and Turtle Island music. Sunshine has a large catalog, including many pow-wow records.

Quite a few artists have their own labels, and sell their recordings at pow-wows, or wherever they perform.

## Mexican-American music

In 1960 there were 4,522,849 people in the United States of Mexican-American origin. At the same time, there were 872,843 Puerto Ricans. Other Hispanic groups were negligible. During the 1960s revival, several Spanish songs made it to the repertoire of pop-folk artists, especially the Mexican *La Llorena* and *La Bamba*, and the Cuban song Guantanamara. The first two of these songs were usually sung by West Coast artists while Guantanamara was performed by artists who sympathized with Fidel Castro. Of the pop-folk artists only Bud and Travis regularly performed songs in Spanish, and utilized Mexican strumming and lead guitar techniques.

Mexican-American artists were simply absent from the revival. One reason for this is that people in the United States were (and still are) backward about speaking any other language than English. This contrasts with the way that Canadians related to French-language French-Canadian songs. Alan Mills, the Canadian Burl Ives, made albums of songs in French. It is difficult to imagine Burl Ives doing an album in Spanish or Mexican songs. Marie Lynn Hammond, co-founder of String Band, had a French-Canadian mother and an Anglo-Quebecois father and sang in both languages. All of this took place before the Canadian government started to legislate bi-lingualism, beginning in 1968. It expanded these programs in 1985 and 2010. The government of the United States has made no such effort even in states where the Hispanic population is a major factor like New Mexico, Texas, California, and Florida.

The southwestern states of New Mexico, California, and Texas were initially settled by Spaniards. Santa Fe, New Mexico, was settled by Spaniards in 1607 and descendants of these settlers, who represent a considerable part of the New Mexico population, consider themselves Spanish and not Mexican. In a sense their musical heritage parallels that of the Southern Appalachian Mountains. Just as Cecil Sharp and other folklorists collected music in the mountains that dated back to sixteenth-century English and Scottish ballads, folklorist-composer J. Donald Robb documented the music of the early settlers in his encyclopedic volume, *Hispanic Music of Old New Mexico and the Southwest: A Self-Portrait of a People.* Jenny Wells Vincent was an active member of People's Songs and is the only fairly well-known Anglo singer in the revival who regularly performed these songs.

While the revival was blooming, there were a number of Mexican-American musicians in Texas who were well known among Spanish-speaking people but were virtually unknown to Anglos. Lydia Mendoza lived in San Antonio for many years and was renowned as a singer and performer. She was extremely popular not only in Texas, but in Mexico and made many recordings. She initially recorded with her family but became a renowned soloist, accompanying herself on bajo sexto, the Mexican version of a twelve-string guitar. Virtuoso accordionist Flaco Jiminez became known to Ry Cooder fans, because he played on Cooder's 1976 album *Chicken Skin Music*. Subsequently Flaco toured with Cooder, and also played on some of his later recordings. Jiminez has played and sung on hundreds of minor label Mexican-American recordings in San Antonio. His father Don Santiago Jiminez Sr. and his brother Santiago Jr. are also well known in the San Antonio music community. In addition to Tex-Mex accordion-based music there are also corridos, essentially ballads that tell a story. The older corridos often discuss injustices done to Mexican-Americans. Other corridos rail against the Texas Rangers, who often beat or jailed Mexican-Americans for the sheer enjoyment of it. In more recent times, the United Farm Workers Union integrated music and theater in its attempts to organize agricultural workers. The union used songs that highlighted wage and social inequities. More current corridos discuss either the narcotics industry or immigration, legal or illegal. The group *Los Tigres Del Norte* is enormously popular both in the United States and Mexico. Their repertoire includes narcocorridos and mojados. Narcocorridos discuss the drug trade, while mojados are songs that detail the living situation of Mexican immigrants who come to the United States. The popularity of the Los Tigres can be ascertained through a story in the music trade paper *Billboard*. That magazine describes how Los Tigres broke an attendance record at the Houston Rodeo in March 2019. The attendance at this show was 75,586, setting a new record.

Although American-Indians' causes seemed to capture the interest of folk revivalists, other than Woody Guthrie's songs *Deportees* and *Pastures of Plenty*, folk revivalists largely ignored these matters. David Rodriguez was a political activist and songwriter who was well known in Austin during the 1980s. He is the father of Carrie Rodriguez, a singer-songwriter and fiddle player. David lived in the Netherlands for over two decades, and died there in 2015. He collaborated with various artists including Lyle Lovett and Tish Hinojosa. Tish Hinojosa is one of thirteen children. She grew up in San Antonio and is a singer-songwriter who sings in both English and Spanish. She plays guitar, and is closest to a folk music performer of the Tex-Mex musicians. She has been recording and performing since the late 1980s.

Doug Sahm was an Anglo Texas musician who fell in love with Tex-Mex music. He formed the band *the Texas Tornadoes* in 1989 with Mexican-American country artist Freddy Fender, Flaco Jiminez, and record producer and organ player Augie Meyers. Sahm died in 1999 and Fender in 2006 but the band continued with Sahm's son and other musicians.

Linda Ronstadt had a Mexican father and an Anglo mother. She became a superstar singing country-folk-rock music but turned away from that music in the 1980s and started to record for many other genres. In 1987 she recorded an album that was a tribute to her father Gilbert, who was a well-known performer in Tucson, Arizona. The album was called *Songs of My Father* and it was sung entirely in Spanish, with a booklet containing the lyrics to the songs in both Spanish and English. Like virtually everything Ronstadt has ever done, the album was a major success, selling over two million copies.

There are a number of other Mexican music styles that have varying popularity in the United States. Mariachi music, which includes a rhythm section and trumpets, is particularly popular throughout the southwest. Banda music is a band style using large orchestral ensembles and is well known on the West Coast.

## Mexicans in Anglo music

Canadians Ian Tyson and Neil Young have written a number of songs about Mexican Americans and their Indian heritage. Young has even written a trilogy of songs about the murder of Indians by the Spaniards.

There are also American folksongs that present a sort of stereotypical view of Mexicans, especially women. *A Border Affair*, also known as *Spanish Is the Loving Tongue*, is a sort of gentle version of the stereotypical hot-blooded Latina lover. The 1959 country song *El Paso*, written and recorded by country artist Marty Robbins, depicts a love affair between an Anglo and a young Mexican girl that results in the death of another suitor and eventually also of the protagonist. Numerous pop songs offer similar romantic views of Mexican women.

Shawn Kiehne is an Anglo artist who calls himself El Gringo. Despite his Anglo origins, he has found an audience among fans of Mexican-American music. He learned Spanish while working on his family's ranch in El Pas, and in 2003 started writing songs in Spanish. This is not unlike someone being a white rapper, or a black country artist, and El Gringo doesn't appear to have many peers at present.

## Other Hispanic groups

New York has always had a large Puerto Rican population and due to the recent disastrous hurricane, many more Puerto Ricans are now living in Florida. It is also home to many Cubans, including those who came to work in the cigar factories of Tampa before Castro and refugees from the Castro regime.

All of these groups have strong music communities, but they have not been part of the folk music revival. Salsa music has developed out of a fusion of Cuban and Puerto Rican music. This music has more of a jazz tinge than anything related to American folk music. There are also smaller Spanish-language communities of immigrants who have come here from Central and South America as well as Haitians, who speak French, and Brazilians who speak Portuguese. Slowly the United States is becoming more bilingual, and in future years it would not be surprising if some of these influences filter into the American folk music community.

Similarly, there are a considerable number of refugees in the United States from Laos, Cambodia, Vietnam, and various countries in the Arab world. Each of them has its own music, and eventually that music will find its way into all forms of American music.

## Cajun and Zydeco music

The word Cajun is a substitution for the Acadian homeland of the French settlers. These two musical styles are found in southeast Texas and Louisiana. In 1755 the British expelled the French from Acadia in Nova Scotia because they refused to pledge allegiance to the British Crown. Hundreds of these displaced people made their way to the French territory of Louisiana. They formed an isolated pocket centering to around Lafayette, Louisiana. A hundred years later German settlers brought accordions into the mix, and the accordion replaced the fiddle as the primary solo instrument in the music of the French immigrants. The nineteenth century brought black slaves and free citizens into the area.

Segregation prevailed in Louisiana, and zydeco absorbed strong blues influences. Cajun music leaned more toward country music styles. Kip Lornell writing in his excellent survey *Introducing Folk Music: Third Edition*, points out that Cajun music tends to emphasize the first and third beats of a 4/4 measure while zydeco accents the second and fourth beats. Zydeco bands usually do not include a fiddle.

In 1964 Cajun music was presented at the Newport Folk festival through the efforts of musicians-folklorists Mike Seeger and Ralph Rinzler. A return trip three years later spotlighted the *Balfa Family* band and helped to revive the music. This resulted in worldwide tours, recordings, and videos about the music.

Zydeco was popularized through the work of sensational accordion player Clifton Chenier. He played a modern piano-accordion with a full keyboard, and added a metal washboard, saxophone, and drums to his band. Beginning in 1955, he recorded a series of successful albums for Arhoolie Records. Since his death in 1987, his son Clifton Jr. has carried on the tradition.

The biggest impediment to the spread of Cajun and zydeco music is that the songs are sung in French. Nevertheless, the music is rhythmic and has attracted an audience of its own. Michael Doucet and his band Beausoleil have toured and recorded widely, and from time to time Cajun-flavored recordings have made their way into movies and flirted with the pop music charts. There are a number of Cajun and zydeco revivalist bands in relatively unlikely places. Examples include the *Bayou-Seco* band in Silver City, New Mexico. Americana band *Donna the Buffalo* includes zydeco music in its Americana offerings.

## Klezmer music

Klezmer music is an Eastern European Jewish version of Dixieland jazz. It became popular on the Lower East Side of Manhattan and in Brooklyn because of the large number of Jewish immigrants who came to New York between 1880 and1920. Clarinetist Dave Tarras was the most famous musician in klezmer.

Henry Sapoznik is an excellent banjo player and urban revivalist. On one of his trips to visit Appalachian banjo player Tommy Jarrell in 1977, Jarrell wondered why Jewish banjo and fiddle enthusiasts didn't explore their own musical traditions. When Sapoznik got back to New York he researched klezmer musicians, started a band called *Kapelye*, and a summer camp called KlezKamp in 1985. Sapoznik also carefully researched and wrote the book *Klezmer! Jewish Music from Old World to Our World.*

About the same time New York bluegrass mandolin player Andy Statman pursuing similar interest located Dave Tarras. Tarras became his mentor and even gave him a clarinet.

Even before these accidental discoveries a Berkeley band called *Klezmorim* recorded an album for Arhoolie in 1977. In subsequent years klezmer music has become a niche in the revival and has spread to Europe and Canada. Canadian banjoist Daniel Koulack plays in several klezmer bands and has even written a klezmer suite. Eclectic composer John Zorn has also been active on the klezmer scene and Knitting Factory Records has released some klezmer music as part of its world music offerings*.

## Freak and punk folk

In general, I have avoided discussing the English folk scene. However, the British group *The Incredible String Band* and the New York-based *Holy Modal Rounders* are probably the best groups to single out when discussing freak folk. The Incredibles were more involved with the fairy tale-mystical-astrological aspects of life that are reflected in contemporary American artists like Sam Beam, who performs as Iron and Wine.

The best way to describe freak folk as a form is that it does not conform to pop-folk or traditional folk but tends to be child like, meditational, and for the most part, soft spoken. The songs tend to be long and to contain more abstract and somewhat literary subject matter than typical singer-songwriter offerings. In the more energetic artists there is a sort of punk influence, an emphasis on energy rather than complexity.

*The Holy Modal Rounders*, who go back to the 1960s, tend to do their own take-offs on traditional music, playing like traditional musicians who are under the influence of psychedelic drugs. The band *Vetiver* has some of the same energy, with a lineup of four acoustic guitars, and occasional plinky folk banjo. Other folk freak artists tend more toward the meditational side of music. Joanna Newsome is a classically trained concert harpist and singer-songwriter. Her vocal sound is child like, a sound that some will find appealing while others find it irritating. She plays a concert full-sized harp, not the Irish version. Devandra Banhart is a Venezuelan-American singer-songwriter whose music is hypnotic and meditational. Sam Beam (Iron and Wine) began his career with a parallel emphasis, but has drifted more toward a pop and jazz direction in recent years.

Sufjian Stevens is a singer-songwriter and a composer-arranger whose albums vary from relatively simple to orchestrated works. He has written two albums of songs that center around the states of Illinois and Michigan and various locales and places associated with these states. Originally, he announced that he would

---

* As is the case with bluegrass, klezmer musicians sub-divide into traditional and more modern artists who compose new music. The New York-based Klezmatics have recorded eleven albums that reflect a more modern sensibility, which includes a variety of musical influences.

do an album for every state in the United States, but he seems to have abandoned that notion.

Many of the above artists have other artistic interests besides music. Newsome has done some professional acting, Banhart is involved with visual arts, and Stevens' literate songs reflect his graduate degree in writing. He is perhaps the most musically versatile of the artists listed with albums of electronic music, Christmas albums, and songwriting that is based on sacred and biblical themes.

Two other singer-songwriters who roughly fit in the freak folk area are Michael Hurley and Brian Cutean. Hurley has worked with the Holy Modal Rounders, and his songs are abstract, somewhat playful, and difficult to categorize. Cutean has recorded both singer-songwriter albums, and solo acoustic guitar works. His songs share some of Hurley's sensibilities, but are unique in their own right. The freak folk practitioners live in various parts of the United States, although Hurley lives in northwest Oregon, while Cutean lives in Eugene.

A few of the younger puck folk bands include *AJJ* (formerly the Andrew Jackson Jihad), *Blackberry Raum* from Santa Cruz, California, and *Mischief Brew* from Philadelphia. AJJ has recorded six albums, and in addition to its current line-up of four members ad an additional touring percussionist, a number of other musicians have been band members at one time or another. Raum is a sort of anarchist combine that developed out of several band members squatting in wilderness areas around Santa Cruz. Mischief Brew shares the anarchist ideology of Blackberry, and has a current line-up of four, with eight members who have been in the band at one time or another.

Two artists that have been influential in the world of freak and punk rock are ani difranco and The Decembrists. Ani's music varies from very personal songs to radical feminist statements. The music itself includes ingredients of folk, rock and punk music, and she has also establish credibility in this area by owning her own recored company and performance venue.

The Decembrists' music is roughly in the vein of the British folk-rock groups Steeleye Span and Fairport Convention. The instrumentation varies fro, acoustic folk-oriented tracks to folk-rock music featuring electric guitar, bass and drums. Much of this music is somewhat like medieval fairy tales in subject matter and imagery, and the band has been enjoyed a #1 album. Considering the nature of the subject matter of the songs and the music arrangements, this is amazing.

# Looking Back: An Evaluation of Four Major Figures in the Folk Revival

Many people contributed to the folk revival in the United States and Canada. There were folklorists, ethnomusicologists, traditional singers, and musicians, and the record producers and record companies that recorded the music. It would be fair to single out four people as the seminal influences in creating the revival.

These four people are Woody Guthrie (1912–67), Huddie (Lead Belly) Ledbetter (1888–1949), Alan Lomax (1915–2002), and Pete Seeger (1919–2014). Every one of these people has become somewhat a mythological figure folkloric in scope. In this chapter I will attempt to evaluate their various contributions to the spread of the music, and to evaluate them as human beings rather than mythological figures. I will start with Alan Lomax because he knew each of the other three very well, and at least in the case of Woody and Pete was a big influence on the direction of their work.

## Alan Lomax

Alan's father John was one of the first people to collect folk music in the United States. Alan joined him when he was a young man, assisting his father by traveling all over the country and recording mostly amateur and semi-professional musicians with relatively primitive recording equipment. He also co-authored two major collections with his father. They were *American Ballads and Folk Songs*, published in 1934, and *Our Singing Country*, published in 1941.

Alan joined his father at the Library of Congress in 1937 and was appointed as Assistant in Charge of the Archive of American Folk Music. During the

Second World War he worked for the Office of War Information (OWI) and produced radio broadcasts for Armed Forces Radio. After the war, he produced recordings, had network radio shows, and was active in People's Songs and the presidential campaign of Henry Wallace. In 1950 he wrote a book about jazz pianist Jelly Roll Morton, partly based on the extensive interviews he had done with Morton for the Library of Congress.

Fearing that he would be investigated by congressional committees for radical activities, Lomax fled to England. For the next ten years he compiled a series of albums of music from all over the world. He collected some of the music himself, and worked with other folklorists and ethnomusicologists on other albums. Lomax returned to the United States in 1959, quickly presenting a concert at Carnegie Hall called Folksong '59. He then resumed his record-producing and song-collecting activities. In 1960 he published his first solo songbook, *The Folksongs of North America*, as well as a novel, *The Rainbow Sign*. The novel was based on the life of Vera Hall, a wonderful black singer from Alabama. The Lomaxes had collected numerous songs from her. He also created a sort of sub-social science theory, which he called Cantometrics. This was a way of looking at the music of the entire world by classifying songs and dance styles as those using either open or closed throat vocal styles. To give a simple example, Hank Williams Sr. would fit comfortably into the category of a closed-throat singer, while Lomax characterized many African singers as open-throat singers. Lomax received foundation funding that enabled him to hire assistants who helped him organize the music and dance of various parts of the world in more complicated versions of this notion. The theory was extremely far reaching and included analyses of hundreds of songs from all over the world. It has proved to be controversial but in a sense was typical of Lomax's visionary thinking.

Some other late-career Lomax achievements include a large collection of CDs of American Music for Rounder Records, a number of videos called *American Patchwork*, and a book about the blues in Mississippi called *The Land Where the Blues Began*.

Lomax was no stranger to controversy. Initially he and his father had combined texts of various versions of songs and copyrighted songs under their own names. In effect, this removed his sources from any ability to collect royalties on their songs. This problem reached its most extreme form when father and son wrote their book about Lead Belly, a biography and large collection of Lead Belly's songs. Both Alan's and John's names appear on the songwriter's credits, which means that they would receive two-thirds of the writer's income from any uses of the songs. Alan Lomax had also battled with Lawrence Gellert, who accused the Lomaxes of treating Lead Belly like a plantation hand because they initially presented him wearing his chain gang clothes. When Lomax went to the Mississippi Delta on a collecting trip with several black professors from Fisk University, he constantly complained about musicologist John Work III's laziness. In fact, it was the Fisk group that had developed the idea for the grant. Lomax was added to it because the Fisk professors felt that they needed the support of a nationally known folklorist. A cynical onlooker might alter that description from the words nationally known to the word white. In Roger Kappers's film about Alan Lomax, Peggy Seeger describes going to a meeting of the American Folklore Society where Alan presented his work on Cantometrics. Various folklorists and other scholars tore him apart because of alleged deficiencies in his research methodology. I feel certain that for some of these scholars, this provided them with a great opportunity to, as the saying goes, "bring him down a peg."

In terms of Lomax's influence on the other three people in this chapter, Lomax used Pete Seeger as his assistant at the Library of Congress and he also helped popularize him by producing a film that featured him, called *To Hear My Banjo Play*. Alan also supervised recordings by Woody Guthrie and Lead Belly for RCA Victor Records, and presented them on his radio shows and in concert.

## Conclusion

It would be difficult to overestimate Alan Lomax's influence on the folk revival. As a collector of folk music he compiled numerous books and records that almost everyone involved in the revival read or listened to. As an entrepreneur he helped all three of these artists get work. Through his recordings for the Library of Congress and later for Atlantic and Prestige Records, he continued to champion traditional music before, during, and after the revival. It is too early to say how influential his researches on Cantometrics will prove to be but through them he has made available recordings from the entire world online. Lomax's choices of what to include or to omit on his records were invariably musically valid. All of these factors make one want to forgive his opinionated and not-always generous nature.

# Lead Belly

Lead Belly was primarily an arranger rather than a songwriter or composer. However, it was his versions of folksong, more than any other artist, that have become part of the folksong canon. *Black Girl, Cotton Fields, Goodnight Irene, The Rock Island Line*, and *The Midnight Special* were all songs that he brought into the folk music revival, and his song *If It Wasn't for Dicky* was adapted by the Weavers for their hit record *Kisses Sweeter Than Wine*.

Lead Belly was born in Mooringsport, Louisiana, in 1888 to a comparatively middle-class black farming family. From an early age he had a restless streak as he details in his song *Mr. Tom Hughes Town*. The song is about him visiting Shreveport, the local version of a big town, and getting his first taste of big city ways. It wasn't long before Lead Belly was in trouble first receiving a prison term and running away from the chain gang and then serving a murder sentence in the Texas State Penitentiary. Texas Governor Pat Neff took a liking to him and witnessed several of his performances at the prison. Lead Belly then wrote a song to the governor, saying that "if I had you like you have me, on Monday morning I'd set you free." Neff had promised never to pardon a prisoner convicted of murder, but he made an exception with Lead Belly. Neff pardoned him during the lame duck period when he was technically still the governor but was about to leave office.

Unfortunately, Lead Belly got in more trouble in Louisiana and was sentenced on a murder charge to the Angola, Louisiana prison. The Lomaxes had met him in Texas, and encountered him again in Louisiana, where Lead Belly rewrote his Governor Neff song for the governor of Louisiana. Alan Lomax spread the legendary but inaccurate story that it was the Lomaxes recording of the song that once again got Lead Belly pardoned from prison. In fact, he was released because of a combination of good behavior as a prisoner and state budgetary problems.

In 1934, John Lomax hired Lead Belly as a valet and chauffeur and also took him on combination lecture-singing tours to various Ivy League colleges. John Lomax was a conservative Texan and inevitably he and Lead Belly clashed when Lomax wanted to keep him on a tight leash, and Lead Belly wanted to pursue his own agendas. John brought Alan into the partnership, because he got along better with Lead Belly, but inevitably it was doomed.

Lead Belly felt that John Lomax had cheated him and sued to get money out of the biography-songbook that the Lomaxes had written. Lead Belly temporarily left the East Coast and returned briefly to Louisiana before moving back to

Manhattan. There he became something of a beloved figure among New York radicals, performed for radical groups, and played at the Village Vanguard club with Josh White.

Lead Belly's attempts to record for the blues market were unsuccessful. Basically, he was not a blues singer but a songster with a large repertoire of all sorts of secular black songs. He never really made much of a living from music and an ill-fated trip to Los Angeles resulted in a bizarre though interesting recording accompanied by a zither. Unfortunately, he died in 1949, not living long enough to see *Goodnight Irene* become a major hit record or to hear his songs covered by everyone from The Highwaymen to Eric Clapton to Kurt Cobain.

## Conclusion

Lead Belly made a number of unique contributions to the folksong revival. He popularized the twelve-string guitar as a musical instrument and certainly influenced the way Pete Seeger and others played it. He also created little vignettes as spoken word introductions to many of his songs. This was partly done at the suggestion of the Lomaxes, who feared that his diction would be difficult for white audiences to understand. His spoken introduction *The Rock Island Line* is virtually a complete short story on its own. Another unusual Lead Belly musical mannerism was to begin a song on the seventh of the tonic chord. If the song was in the key of A, his first chord would be an A7. Years later, John Phillips used that device in the hit song *Creeque Alley,* written by John and his then wife Michelle.

If you combine all of these contributions with the number of songs that he added to the folksong repertoire, you can see how important a figure Lead Belly was in every aspect of the folk and folk-pop revivals. In the discussion of Woody Guthrie I will take up the question on why Lead Belly has not received the sort of credit that he deserved for these contributions.

## Woody Guthrie

Woody Guthrie was the Jack Kerouac of folk music. Kerouac was the beat novelist who was notorious for his free-flowing and unedited prose. Guthrie's songs also seemed to stem from long uninterrupted and unedited sessions at the typewriter.

Guthrie had a long series of careers that did not necessarily relate to one another. He married Mary Jennings in his native Oklahoma in 1931. In 1934 he briefly visited California, returning in 1937, he landed a radio job singing on KFVD in Los Angeles. Initially his radio partner was Maxine "Lefty Lou" Crissman. When she left, he continued to do the show without her. With slight edits from his cousin Jack, Woody wrote a hit song which Jack recorded, *Oklahoma Hills*. Woody also became radicalized during this period, and he wrote a regular column for the *People's World*. This paper was a West Coast version of the East Coast communist paper *The Daily Worker*. In 1940 Woody moved to New York where he became a part-time member of The Almanac Singers. In 1941 he was commissioned to write songs celebrating the building of the Grand Coulee Dam. He had hoped this would provide him with a one-year job but the budget only allowed him a month to complete the project. He wrote twenty-seven songs in thirty days. One of them, *Roll on Columbia*, is well known in the Pacific Northwest though less so elsewhere. He wrote songs with Millard Lampell and Pete Seeger and recorded with the Almanacs. He joined the Merchant Marines during the war and struck up a friendship with actor-singer Cisco Houston. Later they made many recordings for Moe Asch, the owner of Disc and later Folkways Records. In addition to dozens of songs recorded by Asch, Woody also recorded extensively for the Library of Congress. Woody wrote three novelistic memoirs,. two of which were published after his death. Woody also wrote and recorded two charming albums of children's songs.

In another universe, Pete Seeger and Woody Guthrie would have been great song-writing partners. Woody wrote almost no original melodies, and cribbed his tunes from traditional folk songs or from recordings of the Carter Family. His most famous song, *This Land Is Your Land*, was derived from a Carter family tune *Little Darling, Pal of Mine*. The Carter family themselves had borrowed their tune from the gospel song *Oh My Loving Brother*. Seeger wrote many songs, but by far the most popular ones are songs where he wrote the melody, but the lyrics came from another writer. Seeger and Guthrie were friends, but they were total opposites personality-wise. Seeger didn't smoke, drink, or womanize. All of those habits were among Woody's favorite things.

Other than *This Land*, few of Woody's songs were commercially successful, although the Weavers rewrote and somewhat bowdlerized one of his Dust Bowl songs, *So Long It's Been Good to Know You*, and revival musicians can often be heard singing *Pastures of Plenty*, or *Deportees*. *Deportees* is quite distinctive, because it has a simple but attractive melody written by a Colorado schoolteacher named Marty Hoffman. For whatever reasons, *So Long* doesn't seem to have found much of a place in the folk revival, fifty years later.

The tragedy of Woody Guthrie's life was that he was a victim of Huntington's disease. This is a disease of the nervous system which results in uncontrolled body motions. Woody began to become ill in 1947 but was not diagnosed with the disease until 1952. Woody had three children with his first wife Mary, and the two daughters also had Huntington's, dying in 1976 and 1978. Prior to that, his son Bill died in a railroad accident in 1962. Woody's second wife was a modern dancer named Marjorie Greenblatt and their daughter Cathy died in 1947 in an accidental fire. Their other children, Arlo, Nora, and Joady are still alive.

## Woody's legacy

Even a cursory search on the internet reveals two carefully researched full-length biographies of Woody, plus his own posthumously published novels and travel diaries. There are also children's books based on his songs, numerous songbooks, picture books, critical studies of his work and albums of Woody poems set to music by Billy Bragg and the country-rock group *Wilco*. Although there are plenty of Lead Belly recordings available, one biography of him, and a large book of photos of him, there is really no Lead Belly industry compared to what constitutes Woody's current legacy. There are several reasons that this has happened. Woody's son Arlo is a reasonably well-known performer in his own right and influenced by folksinger (Ramblin') Jack Elliott has modeled much of his career and stage persona after Woody's. So did Bob Dylan, in his early Greenwich Village days. The irony is that Arlo and a young Bob Dylan learned how to be Woody Guthrie from Jack, because in Arlo's case his father was seldom around and by the time Dylan got to New York, Woody was in the hospital. Dylan did visit Woody in the hospital and on occasional weekends when Robert and Sidsel Gleason hosted Woody at their home in East Orange, New Jersey. By that time Woody really wasn't Woody anymore.

For years Woody's daughter Nora ran the Woody Guthrie Foundation, which collected photos, songs and biographical materials about Woody. She is responsible for unearthing old poems and encouraging a number of younger artists to write tunes for them. Nora Guthrie has dedicated herself to perpetuating and promoting Woody's work. Currently the archive that she painstakingly collected resides in a museum dedicated to Woody in Tulsa, Oklahoma.

Woody was a major influence on the folk revival. His persona was very relatable to rebellious young people in the 1950s and 1960s as a social rebel. In effect the first beatnik Lead Belly might have been a romantic figure in terms of escaping from the southern plantation and prison systems, but he was not really someone that white middle-class folk fans could relate to. Although his late niece Tiny and her son created a website and did the best they can to keep his memory alive and Lead Belly has long had his adherents and fans, he never had a significant promotional apparatus to promote his career after his death … Given that so many of his songs are still being performed and recorded, it seems unfair and ironic that to the young folk fan Woody is a legend, and Lead Belly is a name that many of them do not recognize.

# Pete Seeger

Pete Seeger has a well-deserved worldwide reputation as a folksinger and as a warrior for social justice causes. Pete grew up in a music-filled environment. His mother Constance was a concert violinist and his father Charles was a composer, ethnomusicologist, and social activist in his own right. After Charles met Aunt Mollie Jackson, he became very interested in the possibilities of using folk music as a tool for social change. Pete played tenor banjo in a jazz band during his year and a half at Harvard, but he fell in love with the five-string banjo when his father took him to a folk festival run by Bascom Lamar Lunsford in North Carolina.

For the next twenty years Pete explored the banjo, writing one of the first modern instruction books, playing music from Spain, Israel, Africa, Hungary, Korea, and the West Indies on the banjo. He even played classical music excerpts and a Tin Pan Alley standard on his *Goofing Off Suite*. Pete also co-founded the Almanac Singers, People's Songs and the Weavers, while often singing free for radical causes that he supported. The Weavers had hidden their earlier political ideology from the media, but it was uncovered by various anti-communist periodicals.

When the House Un-American Activities Committee summoned him to appear before it, rather than take the 5th Amendment to avoid naming names of his radical associates, he took the 1st Amendment. The 5th asserts the right to avoid testifying if that testimony incriminates the person testifying, while the 1st means questioning the legality of the questioning itself.

Seeger's principled stand put him into legal jeopardy and brought him heavy legal expenses. His testimony took place in 1955 and he was indicted by the committee in 1957 and he was convicted on ten counts and sentenced to a one-year jail term in 1961. In 1962 the Appeals Court reversed the indictment on technical grounds.

The Weavers had split up in 1952, but they reunited at a triumphant and sold-out Carnegie Hall concert in 1955. Seeger left the group in 1958 to pursue a solo career. All during this period, and into the late 1960s Seeger and the Weavers were blacklisted. They could not appear on network television and most promoters would not book them. Seeger survived by teaching at schools and summer camps, doing occasional college concerts and by making many albums for Folkways Records. Columbia Records signed Seeger as a solo artist in 1961, which was peculiar in the sense that CBS, the company that owned Columbia, continued to blacklist him from doing any television shows.

## A personal note

In 1955 I was a student at Goddard College in Plainfield, Vermont. I booked Seeger for a concert for $35 and a ride to Montreal, where he had a gig that actually paid him a reasonable amount of money. Like many of his solo shows at the time, his performance was inspirational, including many community singalongs. It seemed as though Seeger could get any audience to sing along with him. On the ride to Montreal, Seeger talked at length about Canadian politics, and how they differed from the way things were done in the United States.

A few years later I saw Seeger perform at a summer camp, and at two concerts at Columbia University. Again, the emphasis was on audience participation, rather than his own talents or performances.

## Other activities and a political mid-life crisis

Seeger had a WNYC TV show, *The Rainbow Qwest*, from 1965 to 1966. He had many guests from virtually every conceivable niche of American folk music. He finally beat the blacklist in the late 1960s, thanks to the Smothers Brothers agitating with CBS to make that happen.

David King Dunaway has written an excellent biography of Pete called *How Can I Keep from Singing?: The Ballad of Pete Seeger*. Dunaway details how Seeger gradually became disillusioned about the notion of using music as a tool for social change. By the late 1960s he had mentally re-grouped, and decided that the primary cause that he wanted to be involved with was cleaning up the Hudson River. With "a little help from his friends" he arranged for the building of a sloop that sailed the Hudson, called the Clearwater. It appears that Seeger had concluded that on a local and regional level he could make real environmental changes that would have a positive effect on the world.

## What happened to the music

During the 1950s and 1960s Pete Seeger established himself as, of all things, a hit songwriter. With the other Weavers he put together the song *Kisses Sweeter Than Wine*. In 1949 he and Lee Hays wrote *If I Had a Hammer* which became a hit several times over, in versions by Trini Lopez and Peter, Paul & Mary.

In 1955 he wrote the song *Where Have All the Flowers Gone* with a lyric influenced by the Mikhail Sholokhov novel, *And Quiet Flows the Don*. In 1960 folklorist Joe Hickerson added a few verses to the song, and it was a hit single for the Kingston Trio in 1961. It was recorded by Peter, Paul & Mary a year later.

Another song that achieved some success was *The Bells of Rhymney*, with Seeger writing the melody to a poem by Welsh poet Idris Davies. It appeared on a hit album by the Byrd, and was recorded by a half dozen artists, including Cher and John Denver. Two of the songs that Seeger wrote both words and music for have been covered by other artists. Judy Collins and Eve Cassady recorded *Oh Had I a Golden Thread* and several artists covered Pete's anti-Vietnam War song *Waist Deep in the Big Muddy*.

Looking at the songs that Seeger composed, I can't think of any that he wrote during the last half of his life that have had the staying power of the songs mentioned in the above paragraph. Clearly, Seeger's strongest abilities were as a composer, not a lyricist. During the days of the Almanac Singers, Pete had a houseful of lyricists to work with, namely Lee Hays, Millard Lampell, and Woody Guthrie, when he was around. After his collaborations with Hays during the early years of the Weavers, Seeger apparently never found another collaborator that suited him. Possibly part of what happened was that as Seeger found himself the father of three children living up the Hudson River in Beacon, New York, he simply did not have regular access to possible co-writers.

Like his friend Alan Lomax, Seeger had many interests and skills. Over the years he wrote instruction books for the banjo, steel drum, and twelve-string guitar, as well as an instruction book on sight singing. He also co-authored a collection of civil rights songs and several children's books based on story-songs that he had put together. For many years he contributed articles to *Sing Out!* magazine, and also partially supported the radical songwriting magazine *Broadside.* He continued to tour and perform, sometimes with Woody's son Arlo.

## Conclusion

Pete Seeger, more than any single other musician, was responsible for the success and continuation of the folk revival. Many of the pop-folk artists didn't necessarily support his political views but they learned songs, singalong skills, and instrumental techniques from either his recordings or live performances. Seeger's sometime-associate Frank Hamilton used to say half-jokingly that Pete had no idea how many kids lives he had ruined by inspiring them to hitchhike, ride freight trains, and even drop out of school.

In my judgment, there is a sad element to his career. His performances became so involved with singalongs that in a sense he crushed his own creative spirit. The experimental instrumental music and the wonderful song collaborations all ended by the mid-1960s. On a certain level he became something of a caricature of himself, strumming the banjo and exhorting audiences to sing along. We will probably never know why he shelved many of his creative impulses in mid-life. It is also not beyond the realm of possibility that indeed Seeger continued to write instrumental tunes but simply chose not to play them in public.

Seeger never quite came to terms with the abuses of Stalinism despite pressure from former radical-turned-conservative, historian Ron Radosh. The anecdote about his phone call to Erik Darling indicates that privately Pete was aware of the excesses of Stalinism. Possibly it was too painful for him to acknowledge that all of those years of radical agitation were something of an illusion. Another possibility is that he simply had to ignore that part of the equation to maintain his friendships with aging radicals and to continue his anti-war demonstrations on the streets of Peekskill as he moved into his 90's. Seeger was an extremely introverted person, and it is difficult to know what he made of Bruce Springsteen touring and recording his songs, and the adulation from other musicians and awards from music organizations that greeted him in the last part of his life.

## Hard hit songs

In 1967, the year that Woody Guthrie died, a final connection emerged between Guthrie, Lomax, and Seeger. In 1940, Lomax had put together a collection of songs about working people. He wanted Woody Guthrie to write most of the notes about the songs, and he was counting on Pete Seeger to transcribe the music of the songs. It took twenty-seven years before Oak Publications actually published the book in 1967. It is a valuable collection of union songs, blues songs, and songs about work and working people. Woody's introductions often read like Jack Kerouac prose. In many instances, it is clear that he has little to say about the specific songs that he is writing about. The songs themselves constitute a valuable picture of songs about social conditions in America during the 1930s. They also remind the reader of the importance of the three authors, together with Lead Belly to the American folk revival.

# Today and Tomorrow

This brings us down to the present day and some speculations about what the future holds for American and Canadian folk music. It seems as though there are an ever-increasing number of sub-genres of the music, each with their dedicated fans. Some of these genres are simply carried over from the years of the folk revival. Groups that use the names of The Kingston Trio and the Brothers Four still tour, although how long they will be able to continue to draw an audience is questionable. Most of the people who cared about this music are definitely in the category of silver-haired. It is possible to see younger groups like The Lumineers, the Milk Carton Kids, and the Avett Brothers fitting into the pop-folk category. Some of them may draw an audience forty years from now who has the same nostalgic feelings that today's audience for The Kingstons exhibit.

The Folk Alliance conferences and many of the billings at the various clubs that feature folk music are largely dominated by singer-songwriters. The idea of performing other people's songs or traditional music as the basic part of a repertoire is virtually non-existent. Outside the singer-songwriter genre are the specialty areas. Bluegrass is divided between adherents of traditional bluegrass and practitioners of newgrass. Old school bluegrass musicians perform the tunes that are identified with the so-called Golden Era of the music, 1950–60, when Bill Monroe, Flatt and Scruggs, and the other pioneers of the music were holding forth. Musicians who favor this style almost always use acoustic bass. The newgrassers write more new songs and more abstract instrumentals, use electric bass, and tend to be generally more musically experimental in outlook. Old-time music, as its name suggests, tends to lean closely to traditional music. The repertoire rarely features new material but centers on the string bands of the 1920s and 1930s. When old-time musicians bring world music into the mix, as with Bob Carlin's album with a kora player, they don't use other old-time musicians.

Singer-songwriter Eric Bibb's 2018 album *Global Griot* is an example of how world music has impacted folk music. Bibb is a black American musician whose father Leon was a well-known solo folksinger in the United States. Eric lives in Sweden, and the album was recorded in Sweden, Canada, Jamaica, and the United States, and includes some African musicians playing with Bibb. Ry Cooder, Henry Kaiser, and Taj Mahal have been exploring various facets of world music for years and continue to do so.

There is a new kind of bluegrass musician that has emerged in the last ten to fifteen years. I will refer to these musicians as post-bluegrass musicians. Bela Fleck and Chris Thile are the most visible of these musicians. Bela has played with jazz pianists and electronic-oriented bass and drums in his band *The Flecktones*, played with African musicians in his video *Throw Down Your Heart*, and has recorded and toured playing banjo duets with his wife, clawhammer banjo player Abigail Washburn. Washburn contributes Chinese music to the mix from her work in the Peace Corps. In recent years, Fleck has also written, recorded, and toured playing symphonic music with various symphony orchestras and chamber groups. Multi-instrumentalist Mark O'Connor's career began with victories in various instrumental contests, extensive studio work in Nashville, and a move to New York City. O'Connor has written several string quartets, toured with Yo Yo Ma and Edgar Meyer, and tours with his violin-playing wife Maggie. O'Connor has also authored a string method for violin, viola, and cello that teaches the instruments by integrating jazz, folk, and country styles, while teaching classical music technique.

Mandolinist Matt Flinner plays with a trio that includes guitarist Ross Martin and acoustic bass player Eric Thorin. They have devised a genre called "music du jour." They all live in different areas of the country. When they meet to do a show, they each write a piece for the trio that morning, rehearse it that afternoon, and perform it at the gig that night. Flinner definitely fits into the post-bluegrass category with this daring experimentalism.

Jayme Stone moves back and forth between his own banjo chamber music compositions and his work reviving songs collected by Alan Lomax in a more modern context with younger musicians. Banjoist Jake Schepps has broad musical interests and has transcribed Brazilian pieces and did an entire album of Bartok transcriptions for bluegrass instruments. He has also commissioned a variety of pieces for banjo and other bluegrass instruments written by other, non-bluegrass composers.

Musician and composer Bill Frisell is generally regarded as a jazz guitarist but he has also made recordings with bluegrass and country musicians. The late Charlie Haden was a jazz bassist, composer, and teacher who grew up in a family that performed country music. In 1970, he formed the *Liberation Music Orchestra*. They recorded two albums, and performed several songs from the Spanish Civil War. In 2008, he did an album called *Charlie Haden and Friends: Rambling Boy*. This recording featured his three daughters and a crew of Nashville studio musicians reliving some of Charlie's childhood musical influences. Marc Ribot, a contemporary jazz-rock guitarist, recently released an album called *Songs of Resistance, 1942–2018*. It includes his own songs, and contributions and performances by such singer-songwriters as Steve Earle and Tom Waits. Ribot's song *The Big Fool* is a sort of rewrite and updating of Pete Seeger's 1967 song *Waist Deep in the Big Muddy*. The original song concerned the war in Vietnam.

Starting with Antonin Dvorak in his 1893 New World Symphony, classical composers from time-to-time have used American folk music in their work. During the 1930s, several classical music composers like Aaron Copland and Roy Harris used American folk music in their work and Wayne Barlow's 1940 composition *Winter's Passed* for oboe and string orchestra is based on the folksong *Black Is the Color*. Three contemporary classical composers who have used various aspects of folk music in their work are Julia Wolfe, Missy Mazzoli and Dave Amram. Amram has written numerous pieces that reference American folk music. Wolfe wrote an opera called *Anthracite Fields* that is about anthracite miners in Pennsylvania. Her most recent work is *Fire in My Mouth*, a cantata about the tragic Triangle Shirt Waist Fire of 1911. The fire killed 146 garment workers. Missy Mazzoli has recently composed *Proving Up*, an opera that includes seven acoustic guitars tuned to open chords. All but one of the guitars are played by a percussionist who uses sticks and mallets. It would have been interesting to see what the late American primitive guitar godfather would have made of that use of open tunings.

How should we look at these various innovations and revisions of the American and Canadian folk song traditions? For me the central question is whether or not the music is relevant to these traditions or is something that musicians are doing out of a sense of boredom or the need to create "the next big thing."

It is undeniable that the bulk of experimentation and innovation is coming out of the bluegrass genre. Bill Monroe and Earl Scruggs, the departed patriarchs of bluegrass, were writing original music from their early recordings. Possibly, there is something about that particular genre that encourages musicians to explore new territory. When old-time music was in its heyday, from 1920–35, even the best musicians in this genre did not tend to write many original tunes. However, it certainly remains true that best musicians like Hobart Smith were synthesizing elements from the musicians that influenced them into their own performances and recordings. I am indebted to Stephen Wade for this insight. When I asked him whether Smith improvised, he said that the answer to this question was that during a specific performance Smith might play repeated versions of the same solo but on another night, although this might still be true, that solo would differ from the one played at a previous time. To put this in another way, there was a certain aspect of maturity about a Smith performance that provided the listener with a feeling that he was playing the right notes at the right time, even when this may not have been literally true.

This still leaves me puzzled at why twenty-first-century younger old-time players seem to lack any interest in expanding the possibilities of the music. This is not posited here as a universal phenomenon, because Canadian Daniel Koulack, for example, does write original tunes and tries to move his music in new directions. I regard him as an exception to the rule. Most of the younger old-time musicians seem content to reproduce sounds rather than to create them.

Without casting stones at particular musicians, I have noticed that some of the post-bluegrass players seem entirely impervious to the influence of African-American music. There is a certain rhythmic tightness without the ineffable and difficult musical factor that jazz musicians refer to as "swing." There is often an emphasis on speed and technique that may be impressive to some audiences, but over time does not wear well.

A similar, though not identical, problem pervades the singer-songwriter community. If you look at the significant singer-songwriters, the fact is that most of their most creative and innovative songs are written before they are thirty- or thirty-five-years old. Why is this? Is it the limitations of the 3–4 minute form, is it the structure of folk and/or popular music with its pre-ordained forms, or is it some sort of burn-out? Bob Dylan, who is certainly one of the high priests of singer-songwriting, has acknowledged that there is no way that he could write a song like *A Hard Rain's Gonna Fall* as he enters the realm of old age. One possible way about this creative impasse is for singer-songwriters to find creative ways to rearrange songs written by other people. Emmylou Harris is one musician who has followed this path.

It seems to me that if folk music has a future in North America it will require that musicians be open-minded about listening to and assimilating both traditional and innovative music styles. The good news is that such an attitude may allow musicians to grow over a long and fruitful career. The bad news is that for musicians to pursue these ends in an honorable way they will have to develop the ability to honestly critique their own work. This means editing, revising, and discarding of materials that do not meet the artist's own standards.

Admittedly, these are aesthetic and creative notions. The other problem for the twenty-first-century folk musician is how to create an audience for new music. Many audiences only want to hear music that they have already heard before as opposed to new music. Without the development of such audiences, folk music is reduced to the role of an art museum, a displayer of archaic work as opposed to something that is living and breathing.

The ultimate answer is that they all need each other. Experimental musicians need to listen to and respect the work of traditional or tradition-bearing musicians. Traditional musicians may not want to walk on these paths, but they need to recognize the possibilities that such work presents. All musicians need to encourage the creation of broad-minded audiences, whose immediate preferences can be modified by new approaches.

The fact that so much musical experimentation is being pursued is encouraging to anyone who cares about North American folk music. Where these experiments will go and how many of them are actually going to prove fruitful are something no one can accurately predict.

Meanwhile, I have a fantasy that includes Guthrie, Lead Belly, Lomax, and Seeger returning to earth. I take them to a series of performances by young singer-songwriters and experimental instrumentalists. I then ask them what they think about it all. Guthrie says "those are some pretty good songs, but they need to get more down to earth. Half the time I didn't know what they were talking about." Lead Belly responds "that's some interesting stuff. I think I'll try a few of those songs." Lomax is not happy. He says "these kids need to listen to traditional singers. I don't think they know what they're singing about." Seeger smiles and says "it's great to see young people interested in this music. Some of the things those kids played, I don't know why I never thought of doing that." Exit, all.

# Appendix

## A note on sources

The bibliography later in this appendix includes many books that will take the reader deeper into specific aspect of American and Canadian folk music. In the chapters on folk music history, I made liberal use of Ron Cohen's various books, especially *The Rainbow Qwest*, and Kip Lornell's survey book on American folk music, as well as Benjamin Filene's work. A good deal of the material on the New York scene comes from my own experience and participation in the folk music revival. The material on Denver also includes my own experiences, tempered by discussions with Harry Tuft, and Rose Victoria Campbell's master's thesis for the University of Colorado: *Walt Conley & Colorado's Popular Folk Revival*, written in 2017. The material on Chicago benefited from conversations with Peggy Fleming, Chris Reitz, and Stephen Wade.

Gillian Mitchell's book was important in my exploration of Canadian folk music, as were the biographies of various important Canadian artists, and the Michael Hill's book on the Mariposa Folk Festival.

The material on the New York scene was greatly enriched by Dave Van Ronk's memoir, and Richie Haven's memoir, together with many long-ago conversation with Israel (Izzy) Young. The sections on folk music and politics benefited greatly from Richard and Joann Reuss's work. I read many of the memoirs written by pop-folk artists. The material on instrumental styles represents endless hours of listening to and playing music. The examination of Woody Guthrie, Alan Lomax, Lead Belly, and Seeger benefited from Joe Klein biography of Woody, the John Szwed biography of Alan Lomax, the Wolfe and Lornell biography of Lead Belly, and the excellent David Dunaway biography of Pete Seeger. I am indebted to Fred Seisel for his story about the Erik Darling-Pete Seeger phone call. I knew Alan Lomax slightly, and Pete Seeger a bit better. Pete was generous with his time in reviewing my earlier book on American folk music.

Stephen Wade has been a great sounding board for my ideas and opinions, and his book *The Beautiful Music All around Us: Field Recordings & the American Experience* is a wonderful reminder of the human connection to scholarship.

# What's been did and what's been hid

A number of books have been written about American and Canadian folk music. These include memoirs, biographies, histories, and books that analyze the music. Certain figures in the revival tend to be put on a very high pedestal, and others have been entirely ignored. I'd like to mention a few people whose contributions have, in my judgment, been neglected.

## Erik Darling

Erik Darling was an important part of the pop-folk revival, and although I wouldn't describe him as a disciple of American Primitive Guitar, he was an influential instrumentalist. Erik had hit records with his first group, the Tarriers. He replaced Pete Seeger in the Weavers at Seeger's own suggestion and he had a huge hit record with his group The Rooftop Singers. He also created lyrical, lute-like banjo accompaniments for Ed McCurdy's popular albums of bawdy songs. Erik also recorded excellent solo albums for Elektra and Vanguard Records and did several other duo and solo albums that had little circulation or traction. His story song, *Train Time*, is a beautifully spun tale that in a sense takes off where Lead Belly left off in his version of *The Rock Island Line*.

If you go to a performance by contemporary folksingers under the age of forty, I would venture to guess that few if any of the audience members have ever heard of Erik Darling. Nor does he get much attention in the work of folk music historians. There are a number of reasons for this. One is that Erik's popular records were by groups, and with most groups only devoted fans know the names of individual group members. Another reason is that Erik was a libertarian in a nest of leftist radicals. He was never a part of the hootenanny crowd in New York, and his political views were much more independent than those of the other members of the Weavers.

Here are some reasons why I urge the reader to check out his music:

1) His instrumental work was always interesting. He played a variety of banjo styles and was possibly the only banjo player who actually expanded on Pete Seeger's instrumental work.
2) Erik's guitar work was exceptionally clean and interesting on both six- and twelve-string guitars. In fact, the two twelve strings played by Erik and his

friend Bill Svanoe essentially introduced the twelve-string guitar to folk and folk-rock music.

3) Erik had a rather high-pitched voice that is distinctively his. He was also an excellent vocal arranger.

4) His autobiography *I'd Give My Life .... A Journey by Folk Music* is essential reading for any young person who is seeking to develop a musical style of their own, and has misgivings about her ability to do so.

5) Probably more than any other folk musician in the revival, Erik had the intangible quality that jazz musicians call "swing." I remember Erik appearing on a television show, and multi-instrumentalist Eric Weissberg looked at me with a big grin and said "He's swinging his ass off."

## Other neglected musicians

Tracy Nelson is an excellent blues and country singer who has recorded solo albums, as well as band albums with the group *Mother Earth*. In her blues albums, Tracy has operated in the same turf inhabited by Janis Joplin. However, Tracy is a more subtle and sophisticated singer than Janis was. I attribute her lack of notoriety to her versatility. The music business tends to categorize people in specific ways, and Tracy is not someone who fits well into that classificatory scheme.

In different ways, Artie Traum and Tracy Moore were and are, respectively, both excellent guitarists. Artie was a songwriter, guitarist, and composer who played on many albums, including solo albums of his own. Like Tracy Nelson, Artie's music does not fit conveniently into a specific category or genre. Tracy Moore has made only two albums, but his twelve-string work is musical and clean. I really do not know why he hasn't been embraced by the fans of American Primitive Guitar.

Steve Young was a superb songwriter and guitarist who was one of those performers who could absolutely mesmerize an audience. I remember attending a show at the Bluebird Café in Nashville where a number of well-known Nashville writers sang for a couple of not all that interesting hours. Steve finally came on and did a handful of his exquisite songs that were clearly in a class by themselves.

Laura Nyro was another songwriter whose work has worn well, but whose popularity seems to have disappeared. Possibly because she wrote a number of hit songs recorded by such pop musicians as the Fifth Dimension, Barbra Streisand and Blood, Sweat and Tears that her own recordings and piano playing has been somewhat neglected. Her song *Save the Country* is as timely in 2019 as it was in 1969, the year that it was written.

## Regional artists

Wherever you live there are probably artists who tour only occasionally or not at all. I am thinking of people like guitarist Rick Ruskin in Seattle, Chico Schwall in Eugene, singer Mollie O'Brien and her husband guitarist Rich Moore in Denver, songwriter-performer-guitarist Thad Beckman in Portland, singer-songwriter Larry Murante in Seattle, multi-instrumentalist-composer Joel Mabus in Michigan, Steve Hansen in Lincopln, Nebraska, and Berkeley musicians Eric and Suzy Thompson and Kate Brislin and Jody Stecher. For your own enjoyment, make it a point to seek out traditional-oriented or innovative folk musicians who tend to be taken for granted in their home towns.

## Chronology

For the convenience and context of the reader below are some birth dates, and where appropriate death dates for some of the people discussed in this book. Note that the dates for Woody Guthrie, Lead Belly, Alan Lomax, and Pete Seeger appear in the chapter about them.

Moe Asch 1905–86
Joan Baez 1941–
Harry Belafonte 1927–
Oscar Brand 1920–2010
Sam Bush 1952–
Fiddlin' John Carson 1868–1949
Len Chandler 1935–
John Cohen 1932–
Bruce Cockburn 1945–
Judy Collins 1939–
Ry Cooder 1947–
Stompin' Tom Connors 1933–2008

Karen Dalton 1937–93

Erik Darling 1933–2008

Bob Dylan 1941–

John Fahey 1939–2001

Bel Fleck 1958–

Sylvia Fricker 1940–

Lawrence Gellert 1898–1971

Rhiannon Giddens 1977–

Terry Gilkyson 1927–95

Lou Gottlieb 1923–96

Archie Green 1917–2009

Frank Hamilton 1934–

Odetta Holmes (Gordon) 1930–2008

Mississippi John Hurt 1892–1966

Flaco Jiminez 1939–

Aunt Molly Jackson 1880–1960

Bill Keith 1939–2015

Jim Kweskin 1940–

Gordon Lightfoot 1938–

John Lomax 1867–1948

Taj Mahal 1942–

Ed McCurdy 1919–86

Alan Mills. 1913–77

Joni Mitchell 1943–

Bill Monroe 1911–96

R. Carlos Nakai 1946–

Holly Near 1949–

Laura Nyro 1947–97

Mark O'Connor 1961–

Howard Odum 1884–1954

Tom Paley 1928–2017

Gram Parsons 1946–73

Ralph Peer 1892–1960

John Phillips 1935–2001

Ralph Rinzler 1934–94

Jean Ritchie 1922–2015

Earle Scruggs 1924–2012

Charles Seeger 1886–1979
Mike Seeger 1933–2009
Cecil Sharp 1859–1924
Buffy Ste. Marie 1941–
Bobby Thompson 1937–2005
Mary Travers 1936–2009
Merle Travis 1917–83
John Trudell 1946–2015
Ian Tyson 1933–
Dave Van Ronk 1936–2002
Doc Watson 1923–2012
Eric Weissberg 1939–
Hedy West 1938–2005
Clarence White 1944–73
Josh White 1914–69
Cris Williamson 1947–
Peter Yarrow 1938–
Israel (Izzy) Young 1928–2019

# Folk music and film

Films or DVDs can be divided into several categories. Instructional DVDs are intended to teach specific musical styles, and will be dealt with later in the appendix. Documentary films capture life stories or sometimes encompass particular concerts. Instructional DVDs teach particular styles of music, and will be dealt with later in the appendix. There are also films that feature music in a prominent role, but one that accompanies a dramatic work. There are also films that focus on the music, or on biographies of particular musicians.

# Documentaries

There are many documentaries that are not feature length films. The two that I want to discuss here in some detail are *The Last Waltz*, the final performance by The Band, and *Wasn't That a Time*, which is the final performance by the Weavers filmed not long before the death of founding member Lee Hays.

The 1978 Band film has received extremely positive reviews, with only a few dissenting voices. I would have to count myself as one of those voices. There are endless shots of Robbie Robertson jumping up and down and mugging for the camera. Director Martin Scorcese talks to the group, but his questions to the individual members of the group reveal next to nothing about them, or the tensions and decisions that have led to this being the final performance of the group. Some of the visiting artists, like Neil Young and Paul Butterfield, seem right in the Band's musical wheelhouse but others, notably Joni Mitchell, seem like musical aliens speaking a language that the band is not conversant with or comfortable speaking. There are endless Robertson guitar solos, and virtually nothing of Richard Manuel's piano playing or vocals. It seems as though Levon Helm were fighting a rearguard action to be heard and filmed. It turns out that he disliked the film and according to him, no one except Robertson and Scorcese profited from it.

On the other hand, *Wasn't That a Time*, released in 1981, is a history lesson about the blacklist and the Weavers. All of the various guests, including Holly Near, Don McLean, writer Studs Terkel, manager Harold Leventhal, and Mary Travers are well aware of the Weavers' history, their place in the folk music revival, and the obvious fact that this will be Lee Hays' final performance. As both a musical and historical document this is an important film.

There are quite a number of other documentary films that are of interest to folk fans and historians. *This Ain't No Mouse Music* is a history of Christ Strachwitz and Arhoolie Records, John Cohen's *The End of an Old Song* depicts the life of mountain musician Roscoe Holcomb, and George West did a film on famed Arkansas ballad singer Almeida Riddle. Most of these films can be streamed for home viewing on FolkStreams.net. The works of the late Les Blanc includes films on Cajun music, Tejano music, Lightning Hopkins, and Mance Lipscomb, through his company Flower Films.

## Dramatic films that feature music

A number of films have prominently featured some form of folk music as part of their soundtrack. The 1967 *Ballad of Bonnie and Clyde* included the Earl Scruggs instrumental, *Foggy Mountain Banjo*. The version used in the movie was the original 1949 recording. Besides being a successful record, it was a large boost to the career of Earl Scruggs and Lester Flatt. The 1972 movie *Deliverance* featured the tune *Dueling Banjos*, recorded by Eric Weissberg on banjo and Steve Mandell on guitar. Instrumentals are rarely pop hits, and this one reintroduced the banjo to the American pop market. It resulted in vastly increased sales of five-string banjos and instructional materials. The 1977 movie *Smoky and the Bandit* starred Burt Reynolds. Spectacular guitarist Jerry Reed was in the cast and co-authored the song *East Bound and Down*, which became a country hit that was also recorded by numerous other artists.

The decade of 2000–10 saw a number of movies that used folk music as a significant part of their musical scores. *Oh Brother, Where Art Thou* was released in 2000. The soundtrack album has sold over eight million copies, although it received very little airplay on country music radio. The artists include such roots music stalwarts as the Stanley Brothers, Alison Krauss, John Hartford, Dan Tyminski, and the Fairfield Four. The music plays a prominent role throughout the film. The only bizarre moment occurs when George Clooney lip syncs *Man of Constant Sorrow* and his two cohorts sing lip-sync the back-up in a style that resembles Homer and Jethro or the *Hee Haw* show.

*Cold Mountain*, released in 2003, featured a number of excellent Nashville musicians including Alison Krauss, Tim O'Brien, and Dirk Powell and the music was supervised by T Bone Burnett. The movie describes the awful carnage that took place during the Civil War, and the music appears both on screen and as background music in a very appropriate role. The 2010 movie *Winter's Bone* uses music to highlight the story of a courageous and abused young woman who grows up in the Ozark Mountains. Instead of using studio players, director Debra Granik chose mostly regional Ozark musicians. The movie is set in the Ozarks and the music is beautifully integrated into the film.

## Full-length bios and music films

In 1976 two feature films were released about Woody Guthrie and Lead Belly. The *This Train Is Bound for Glory* is about Woody's early career, and his radio program in California. Quite a few of Woody's songs are included, as well as the conflict between his desire to make a living from his music versus his political ideology and his desire to avoid staying in one place. The Lead Belly film also is about Lead Belly's life as a young adult, his time in prison, and like *This Train* ends before he moves to New York City. The Lead Belly film is very difficult to find, and is rarely written about.

*A Mighty Wind* is a film released in 2003 that satirizes pop-folk music. Three sets of performers are involved: a Christy-Minstrels type group, a trio very loosely based on the Limeliters, and a duo that references Jim and Jean Glover, Richard and Mimi Farina, and/or Ian and Sylvia. All of the music was written for the film, but it does a great job of gently spoofing the way pop-folk groups sang and related to their audiences. Since the whole plot of the film involves a memorial concert, there is an air of barely controlled nostalgia in these portrayals.

*Inside Llewyn Davis* is a 2013 film that is loosely, very loosely, based on the life of New York folksinger Dave Van Ronk, known as "The Mayor of MacDougal Street." Produced and directed by the Coen Brothers, the film has a number of nasty references to various performers. Jim and Jean were a real married couple who performed and recorded. In the film, the main character impregnates Jean and pays for her to abort the child. Why the Brothers chose to use the name of real people in this instance is a mystery to me. No other characters are literally portrayed, although "Bud" Grossman is clearly Al Grossman. Folksingers in the film are portrayed as money-grubbing, unpleasant, and competitive creatures who barely tolerate one another. As someone who was directly involved in the Greenwich Village, coffeehouse scene portrayed in the film, I can say that this is absurd. Somehow the Coen Brothers have also exiled all African Americans from the film, both in terms of performers and the audience. The ubiquitous T Bone Burnett supervised the music in this film, but I suspect that if Dave Van Ronk had been alive to view the film he would have found the music ranging from mediocre to annoying.

Over the end titles, the viewer hears Van Ronk himself singing *Green, Green Rocky Road*. Suddenly the music is truly relevant and moving. Oscar Isaac, in the Van Ronk role, does a decent job of singing, but he truly is no Dave Van Ronk.

## Magazines

There are very few magazines covering American and/or Canadian that print on a regular basis at this time. *No Depression* prints quarterly editions, and is also available online. *Penguin Eggs* is Canadian-based but it also includes reviews and articles on the folk music. *Old Time Music Herald* is a quarterly magazine that has many interesting articles on old-time music. *Bluegrass Unlimited* fulfills a similar role for bluegrass. *Living Blues* covers music by African-American blues artists, while *Big City Blues* focuses more on younger artists and includes white blues artists. There are also magazines that deal with specific instruments, like the eclectic *Banjo Newsletter, Acoustic Guitar, Fretboard Journal,* and *Fiddler Magazine.* For many years, *Sing Out!* covered American folk music, but it is currently an online publication. The *Oxford American* and *Southern Cultures* publish annual issues that are devoted to regional music. They include articles as well as CDs and/or downloads of the musicians discussed. The *Oxford American* is sold in bookstores, while *Southern Cultures* is available from the University of North Carolina Press.

# Recordings

Almost every artist covered in this book can be heard, and/or seen on YouTube. I have therefore elected not to include an extensive discography. Many artists also have websites, which include some of their music as well as their touring schedules.

For anyone who wants to purchase CDs to enhance their enjoyment of folk music, a good place to start is the Folkways boxed set *An Anthology of American Folk Music,* on Smithsonian-Folkways records. An extensive (and expensive) boxed set of songs of social protest is called *Songs for Political Action,* issued with an elaborate and well-researched book by Bear Family Records. There are also numerous boxed sets of blues recordings.

JSP Records has issued many four-CD sets that are reasonably priced of various blues and old-time music artists. Dust to Digital tends to concentrate on reissued projects that also include books. Smithsonian-Folkways has hundreds of titles available, covering music from all over the world. Tompkins Square concentrates on instrumental music, both new and reissued projects. *Folk Legacy* is very traditionally oriented and has an extensive catalog of ballad singers and as well as younger neo-traditional artists. Other smaller labels fill various niches. Document Records, based in Austria, has released dozens of blues reissue CDs. Patuxent Records covers mostly bluegrass and old-time music, and Jack White's Third Man Records issues music in a variety of genres, including quite a few blues reissues. Most Third Man Records are available only on vinyl, not on CD. Compass Records has issued quite a few bluegrass albums, and also owns Red House Records, primarily a singer-songwriter label. Canadian label Borealis has a large catalog of Canadian folk artists.

Many of the 1960s folk LP have been reissued on CD by one or another branches of Concord Music. They own Prestige, Riverside, Rounder, Sugar Hill, and Vanguard among many other labels.

Finally, an ever-increasing number of artists issue their own recordings. These recordings are available on the artists' websites or at their performances. Many are also available through independent distributor CD Baby. As i was reading the final proofs of this book i encountered a wonderful new recording: songs of our native daughters on Smithsonian Folkways Records. On this album Rhiannon Giddens, Amythst Kiah, Leyla McCalla and Allison Russell sing and play new songs that reflect on the history of Afircan-American women ion the United States. This inspiring work may provide an important direction for future composers and singer-songwriters looking for new ways to expand on traditional music.

# Books

Alarik, Scott. 2003. *Deep Community: Adventures in the Modern Folk Underground.* Cambridge, MA: Black Wolf Press.

Alger, Dean. 2014. *The Original Guitar Hero and the Power of Music: The Legendary Lonnie Johnson, Music and Civil Rights.* Denton, TX: University of North Texas Press.

Allen, Ray. 2010. *Gone to the Country: The New Lost City Ramblers & the Folk Music Revival.* Urbana: The University of Illinois Press.

Allen, William Francis, Charles Pickard Ware, and Lucy McKim Garrison. 1951. *Slave Songs of the United States.* New York: Peter Smith (reprint of 1867 Edition).

Ammen, Sharon. 2017. *May Irwin: Singing, Shouting and the Shadow of Minstrelsy.* Urbana: University of Illinois Press.

Amundson, Michael A. 2017. *Talking Machine West: A History and Catalogue of Tin Pan Aller's Western Recordings 1902–1918.* Norman: University of Oklahoma Press.

Arem, Jocelyn, ed. 2013. *Caffe Lena: Inside America's Legendary Coffeehouse.* Brooklyn, NY: Powerhouse Books.

Author unlisted. 2012. *Authentic American Slave Songs: Thank God A'mighty I'm Free at Last.* No address listed: Mountain Waters Pty Ltd.

Baez, Joan. 1987. *And a Voice to Sing With.* New York: Summit Books.

Barker, Hugh, and Yuval Taylor. 2002. *Faking It: The Quest for Authenticity in Popular Music.* New York: W. W. Norton & Company.

Bastin, Bruce. 1986. *Red River Blues: The Blues Tradition in the Southeast.* Urbana: University of Illinois Press.

Beaumont, Daniel E. 2011. Preachin' the Blues: The Life and Times of Son House. New York, Oxford University Press.

Brand, Oscar. 1962. *The Ballad Mongers: Rise of the Modern Folk Sound*. New York: Funk and Wagnalls.

Brend, Michael. 2001. *American Troubadours: Groundbreaking Singer-Songwriters of the 60s*. San Francisco: Backbeat Books.

Brasseaux, Ryan Andre. 2009. *Cajun Breakdown: The Emergence of an American-Made Music*. New York: Oxford University Press.

Brooks, Joann. 2013. *Why We Left: Untold Stories & Songs of America's First Immigrants*. Minneapolis: University of Minnesota Press.

Browner, Tara, ed. 2009. *Music of the First Nations: Tradition and innovation in Native North America*. Urbana: University of Illinois Press.

Bufwack, Mary A., and Robert J. Oermann. 1993. *Finding her Voice: The Saga of Women in Country Music*. New York: Crown Books.

Burns, Sean. 2011. *Archie Green: The Making of a Working-Class Hero*. Urbana: University of Illinois Press.

Cantwell, Robert. 1996. *When We Were Good: The Folk Revival*. Cambridge, MA: Harvard University Press.

Caffey, Joshua Clegg. 2013. *Traditional Music in Coastal Louisiana*. Baton Rouge: Louisiana State Press.

Cain, Michael Scott. 2017. *The Americana Revolution: From Country and Blues Roots to Avett Brothers, Mumford & Sons, and Beyond*. Lanham, MD: Rowman & Littlefield.

Carawan, Guy, and Candie Carawan. 1975. *Voices from the Mountains*. New York: Alfred A. Knopf.

Carawan, Guy, and Candie Carawan, eds. 1992. *Sing for Freedom: The Story of the Civil Rights Movement through Its Songs*. Bethlehem, PA: Sing Out Corporation.

Carlin, Bob. 2004. *String Bands in the North Carolina Piedmont*. Jefferson, NC: McFarland & Vo.

Carlin, Bob. 2007. *The Birth of the Banjo: Joel Walker Sweeney and Early Minstrelsy*. Jefferson, NC: McFarland & Co.

Carlin, Bob. 2016. *Banjo: An Illustrated History*. New York: Backbeat Books.

Carlin, Richard. 2008. *Worlds of Sound: The Story of Smithsonian Folkways*. New York: Collins.

Castelnero, Gordon, and David Russell. 2017. *Earl Scruggs: Banjo Icon*. Lanham, MD: Rowman & Littlefield.

Charters, Samuel. 2009. *A Language of Song: Journeys in the Musical World of the African Diaspora*. Durham, NC: Duke University Press.

Clifford, Craig, and Craig D. Hillis, eds. 2016. *Pickers & Poets: The Ruthlessly Poetic Singer-Songwriters of Texas*. College Station, TX: Texas A&M University Press.

Cockburn, Bruce, with Bruce King. 2014. *Rumours of Glory: A Memoir*. New York: Harper One.

Cohen, John. 2012. *The High & Lonesome Sound: The Legacy of Roscoe Holcomb*. Gottingen, Germany: Streidl.

Cohen, Norm, ed. 2007. *Ethnic & Border Music: A Regional Exploration*. Greenwood, CT: Greenwood Press.

Cohen, Ronald D., ed. 1990. *Wasn't That a Time: First Hand Accounts of the Folk Music Revival*. Metuchen, NJ: Scarecrow Press.

Cohen, Ronald D. 2002. *Rainbow Quest: The Folk Music Revival & American Society*. Amherst: University of Massachusetts Press.

Cohn, Lawrence. 1993. *Nothing but the Blues: The Music and the Musicians*. New York: Abbeville Press.

Collins, Judy. 2011. *Sweet Judy. Bluer Eyes: My Life in Music*. New York: Random House.

Conforth, Bruce M. 2013. *African American Folksong and American Cultural Politics: The Lawrence Gellert Story*. Lanham, MD: The Scarecrow Press.

Conway, Cecilia. 1995. *African Banjo Echoes in Appalachia: A Study of Folk Traditions*. Knoxville: The University of Tennessee Press.

Cray, Ed. 2004. *Ramblin' Man: The Life and Times of Woody Guthrie*. New York: W.W. Norton Co.

Cox, Bob L. 2007. *Fiddlin' Charlie Bowman: An East Tennessee Old-Time Music Pioneer and His Musical Family*. Knoxville: The University of Tennessee Press.

Cunningham, Agnes ("Sis" and Gordon Freisen). 1999. *Red Dust and Broadsides: A Joint Autobiography*. Amherst: University of Massachusetts Press.

Dahill, Tom. 2017. *Danny Who? Four Decades in Irish Music*. St. Paul, MN: Celtic Collaborative Press.

David, Angela Y. 1998. *Blues Legacies and Black Feminism: Gertrude "Ma" Rainey, Bessie Smith and Billie Holiday*. New York: Pantheon Books.

Darden, Robert. 2004. *People Get Ready: A New History of Black Gospel Music*. New York: Continuum.

Denisoff, R. Serge. 1973. *Great Day Coming: Music and the American Left*. Baltimore: Penguin Books.

Dickens, Hazel, and Bill Malone. 2008. *Working Girl Blues: The Life and Music of Hazel Dickens*. Urbana: University of Illinois Press.

Dickinson, Jim. 2017. *I'm Just Dead I'm Not Gone*. Edited by Ernest Suarez. Jackson: University of Mississippi Press.

Donleavy, Kevin. 2004. *Songs of Life: Conversations with Old-Time Musicians from Virginia & North Carolina*. Blacksburg, VA: Pocahontas Press.

Doubler, Michael D. 2018. *Dixie Dewdrop: The Uncle Dave Macon Story*. Urbana: University of Illinois Press.

Doyle, Alan. 2017. *A Newfoundlander in Canada: Always Going Somewhere, Always Coming Home*. Toronto, ON: Doubleday Canada.

Dubois, Lawrence. 2016. *The Banjo: America's African Instrument*. Cambridge, MA: Harvard University Press.

Dueck, Byron. 2013. *Musical Intimacies & Indigenous Imaginaries: Aboriginal Music in Public Performance*. Oxford: Oxford University Press.

Duffy, Timothy. 2002. *Music Makers: Portraits and Songs from the Roots of America*. Athens, GA: Hill Street Press (contains CD).

Dunaway, David King. 2008. *How Can I Keep from Singing: Pete Seeger*. Revised ed. New York: Villard/Random House.

Dunaway, David King, and Molly Beer. 2010. *Singing Out: An Oral History of America's Folk Music Revivals*. Oxford: Oxford University Press.

Dylan, Bob. 2004. *Chronicles, Volume 1*. New York: Simon & Schuster.

Epstein, Dena J. 1977. *Sinful Tunes and Spirituals: Black Folk Music to the Civil War*. Urbana: University of Illinois Press.

Filene, Benjamin. 2000. *Romancing the Folk: Public Memory and American Roots Music*. Chapel Hill: University of North Carolina Press.

Finson, Jon W. 1994. *The Voices that Are Gone: Themes in 19th Century American Popular Song*. New York: Oxford University Press.

Fong-Torres, Ben. 1991. *Hickory Wind: The Life and Times of Gram Parsons*. New York: Pocket Books.

Fowke, Edith, and Joe Glazer. 1993. *Songs of Work and Protest: 100 Favorite Songs of American Workers*. New York: Dover Publications.

Fowke, Edith, with Jay Rahn. 1994. *A Family Heritage: The Story and Songs of LaRena Clark*. Calgary: University of Calgary Press.

Garon, Paul, and Gene Tomko. 2006. *What's the Use of Walking if There's a Freight Train Going Your Way? Black Hoboes & Their Songs*. Chicago: Charles H. Kerr.

Garon, Paul, and Beth Garon. 1992. *Woman with Guitar: Memphis Minnie's Blues*. New York: Da Capo Press.

Gellert, Lawrence. 1936. *Me and My Captain: Chain Gang Negro Songs of Protest*. New York: American Music League.

Gellert, Lawrence. 1939. *Negro Songs of Protest Collected by Lawrence Gellert*. New York: Hours Press.

Gibson, Bob, and Carol Bender. 2001. *I Come for to Sing: The Stops along the Way of a Folk Music Legend*. Naperville, IL: Kingston Korner, Inc.

Glassie, Henry, Edward D. Ives, and John F. Szwed. 1979. *Folksongs and Their Makers*. Bowling Green, OH: Bowling Green University Popular Press.

Goldsmith, Peter D. 1998. *Making People's Music: Moe Asch and Folkways Records*. Washington, DC: Smithsonian Institution Press.

Gordon, Robert, and Bruce Nemerov, eds. 2005. *Lost Delta Found: Rediscovering the Fisk University-Library of Congress Cohoma County Study, 1941–1942*. Nashville: Vanderbilt University Press.

Gough, Peter. 2015. *Sounds of the New Deal: The Federal Music Project in the West*. Urbana: University of Illinois Press.

Graham, Sandra Jean. 2018. *Spirituals and the Birth of the Black Entertainment Industry*. Urbana: University of Illinois Press.

Gray, Michael. 2009. *Hand Me My Travelin' Shoes: In Search of Blind Willie McTell*. Chicago: Chicago Review Press.

Green, Archie. 1972. *Only a Miner: Studies in Recorded Coal-Mining Songs*. Urbana: University of Illinois Press.

Green, Archie, ed. 1993. *Songs about Work: Essays in Occupational Culture for Richard A. Reuss*. Bloomington, IN: Folklore Institute, Indiana University.

Green, Paula Hathaway-Anderson. 2002. *A Hot-Bed of Musicians: Traditional Music in the Upper New River Valley Whitetop Region*. Knoxville: the University of Tennessee Press.

Green, Victor R. A. 2004. *Singing Ambivalence: American Immigrants between Old and New, 1830–1930*. Kent, OH: Kent State University Press.

Greene, Kevin D. 2018. *The Invention and Reinvention of Big Bill Broonzy*. Chapel Hill: University of North Carolina Press.

Greenaway, John. 1953. *American Folksongs of Protest*. Philadelphia: University of Pennsylvania Press.

Gudgeon, Chris. 1993. *An Unfinished Conversation: The Life and Music of Stan Rogers*. Toronto: Viking.

Gura, Philip F., and James F. Bollman. 1999. *America's Instrument: The Banjo in the Nineteenth Century*. Chapel Hill: The University of North Carolina Press.

Gurza, Agustin, with Jonathan Clark and Chris Strachwitz. 2012. *The Arhoolie Foundation's Collection of Mexicana and Mexican American Recordings*. Los Angeles: UCLA Chicano Studies Research Center.

Gussow, Adam. 2017. *Beyond the Crossroads: The Devil and the Blues Tradition*. Chapel Hill: The University of North Carolina Press.

Gustavson, Kent. 2011. *Blind but Now I See: The Biography of Music Legend Doc Watson*. New York: Sumach Red Books.

Guthman, Jonathan. 2015. *Strangers Below: Primitive Baptists and Americana Culture*. Chapel Hill: The University of North Carolina Press.

Guthrie, Woody. 1977. *Bound for Glory: 101 Woody Guthrie Songs, Including All the Songs from Bound for Glory*. New York: TRO.

Hadju, David. 2001. *Positively 4th Street: The Life and Times of Joan Baez, Bob Dylan, Mimi Baez Farina and Richard Farina*. New York: North Point Press.

Haigh, Chris. 2009. *The Fiddle Handbook*. New York: Backbeat Books.

Halker, Clark D. 1991. *For Democracy, Workers and God: Labor Song-Poems and Labor Protest, 1865–1895*. Urbana: University of Illinois Press.

Harris, Craig. 2018. *Bluegrass, Newgrass, Old-Time, and Americana Music*. Gretna, LA: Pelican Music Publishing Company Inc.

Harrison, Daphne Duval. 1988. *Black Pearls: Blues Queens of the 1920's*. New Brunswick, NJ: Rutgers University Press.

Hast, Dorothy E., and Stanley Scott. 2004. *Music in Ireland*. New York: Oxford University Press.

Havens, Richie, with Steve Davidowitz. 1999. *They Can't Hide Us Anymore*. New York: Avon Books.

Hawes, Bess Lomax. 2008. *Sing It Pretty: A Memoir*. Urbana: University of Illinois Press.

Heilbut, Anthony. 1985. *The Gospel Sound: Good News and Bad Times*. Updated and revised ed. New York: Limelight Books.

Heller, Paul. A. 2011. *History of the Banjo: Frank Converse's Banjo Reminiscences*. Barre, VT: no publisher listed.

Herrick-Sobek, Maria. 1993. *Northward Bound: The Mexican Immigrant Experience in Ballad and Song*. Bloomington: Indiana University Press.

Hill, Michael. 2017. *The Mariposa Folk Festival: A History*. Toronto: Dundurn.

Honey, Michael K. 2013. *Sharecropper's Troubadour: John L. Handcox, the Southern Tenant Farmers' Union and the African American Song Tradition*. New York: Palgrave Macmillan.

Huber, Patrick. 2008. *Linthead Stomp: The Creation of Country Music in the Piedmont South*. Chapel Hill: The University of North Carolina Press.

Hughes, Charles L. 2015. *Country Soul: Making Music and Making Race in the American South*. Chapel Hill: The University of North Carolina Press.

Iglauer, Bruce, and Patrick A. Roberts. 2018. *Bitten By the Blues: The Alligator Records Story*. Chicago: University of Chicago Press.

Igliori, Paola. 1994. *Stickman: John Trudell*. New York: Inanout Press.

Isserman, Maurice. 1987. *If I Had a Hammer: The Death of the Old Left and the Birth of the New Left*. New York: Basic Books.

Ives, Edward D. 1964. *Larry Gorman: The Man Who Made the Songs*. Bloomington: University of Indiana Folklore Series, Number 19.

Ives, Edward D. 1978. *Joe Scott: The Woodsman Songster*. Urbana: University of Illinois Press.

Jackson, Bruce. 1999. *Wake Up Old Dead Man: Hard Labor and the Southern Blues*. Athens, GA: University of Georgia Press.

Jackson, Jerome A. 2004. *Singing in My Soul: Black Gospel Music in a Secular Age*. Chapel Hill: The University of North Carolina Press.

Jacobsen, Kristina M. 2018. *The Sound of Navajo Country: Music, Language and Dine Belonging*. Chapel Hill: The University of North Carolina Press.

Jamison, Phil. 2015. *Hoedowns, Reels and Frolics: Roots and Branches of Southern Appalachian Dance*. Urbana: University of Illinois Press.

Jarnow, Jesse. 2018. *Wasn't That a Time: The Weavers, The Blacklist, and the Battle for the Soul of America*. New York: Da Capo Press.

Jennings, Nicholas. 1997. *Before the Gold Rush: Flashbacks to the Dawn of the Canadian Sound*. Toronto: Viking Canada.

Jennings, Nicholas. 2017. *Lightfoot*. Toronto: Viking.

Jones, Michael L. 2014. *Louisville Jug Band Music: From Earl McDonald to the National Jubilee*. Charleston: S. C. History Press.

Jones-Bamman, Richard. 2017. *Building New banjos for an Old-Time World*. Urbana: University of Illinois Press.

Katonah Museum of Art. 2003. *The Birth of the Banjo*. Katonah, New York: Katonah Museum of Art.

Klein, Joe. 1980. *Woody Guthrie: A Life*. New York: Ballantine Books.

Koken, Walt. 2017. *Fire on the Mountain: An American Odyssey*. Kennett Square, PA: Mudthumper Music.

Kornbluh, Joyce. 1962. *Rebel Voices: An IWW Anthology*. Ann Arbor: University of Michigan Press.

Kort, Michele. 2002. *The Music and Passion of Laura Nyro: Soul Picnic*. New York: St. Martin's Press.

Kruth, John. 2017. *A Friend of the Devil: The Glorification of the Outlaw in Song from Robin Hood to Rap*. Milwaukee, WI: Backbeat Books.

Kun, Josh. 2005. *Audiotopia Music, Race and America*. Berkeley: University of California Press.

Kutukas, Judy. 1995. *The Long War: The Intellectual People's Front and Anti-Stalinism, 1930–1940*. Durham, NC: Duke University Press.

La Chapelle, Peter. 2007. *Proud to Be an Okie: Cultural Politics, Country Music, and Migration to Southern California*. Berkeley: University of California Press.

Lauterbach, Preston. 2015. *Beale Street Dynasty: Sex, Song and the Struggle for the Soul of Memphis*. New York: W. W. Norton and Company.

Lead Belly, with musical transcriptions by Harry Lewman. 1998. *Lead Belly: No Stranger to the Blues*. New York: TRO, Folkways Music Publishers.

Leech, Jeanette. 2011. *Seasons They Change: The Story of Acid and Psychedelic Folk*. London: Outline Press.

Lieberman, Robbie. 1998. *My Song Is My Weapon: People's Songs, American Communism, and the Politics of Culture, 1930–1950*. Urbana: University of Illinois Press.

Linn, Karen. 1991. *That Half-Barbaric Twang: The Banjo in American Popular Culture*. Urbana: University of Illinois Press.

Lomax, Alan. 2003. *Selected Writings, 1934–1997*. Edited by Ronald Cohen. New York: Routledge.

Lomax, Alan. 1993. *The Land Where the Blues Began*. New York: Pantheon Books.

Lomax, Alan, Woody Guthrie, and Pete Seeger. 1967. *Hard Hitting Songs for Hard-Hit People*. New York: Oak Publications.

Lomax, John and Alan Lomax. 1936. *Negro Folk Songs as Sung by Lead Belly*. New York: Macmillan Company.

Lornell, Kip. 2012. *Exploring American Folk Music: Ethnic, Grassroots and Regional Traditions in the United States*. 3rd ed. Jackson: University of Mississippi Press.

Lovell, John Jr. 1972. *The Forge and the Flame: The Story of How the Afro-American Spiritual Was Hammered Out*. New York: Macmillan.

Lowenthal, Steve. 2014. *Dance of Death: The Life of John Fahey, American Guitarist*. Chicago: Chicago Review Press.

Macmahon, Bernard, and Allison McGourty with Elijah Wald. 2017. *American Epic: The Companion Book to the PBS Series*. New York: Touchstone.

Madrid, Alejandro L., ed. 2011. *Transnational Encounters: Music and Performance at the U.S.-Mexico Border*. Oxford: Oxford University Press.

Mahal, Taj, with Stephen Foehr. 2001. *Taj Mahal: Autobiography of a Bluesman*. London: Sanctuary Publishing Limited.

Malkoski, Paul. 2012. *The Denver Folk Music Tradition: An Unplugged History, from Harry tuft to Swallow Hill and Beyond*. Charleston, SC: History Press.

Marcus, Greil. 1997. *The Weird Old America: The World of Bob Dylan's Basement Tapes*. New York: Henry Holt and Co.

Marovich, Robert M. 2015. *A City Called Heaven: Chicago and the Birth of Gospel Music*. Urbana: University of Illinois Press.

Mazow, Leo G., ed. 2005. *Picturing the Banjo*. University Park: Pennsylvania State University Press.

McAllister, Marvin. 2011. *Whiting Up: Whiteface Minstrels & Stage Europeans in African-American Performances*. Chapel Hill: The University of North Carolina Press.

McEuen, John. 2018. *The Life I've Picked: A Banjo Player's Nitty Gritty Journey*. Chicago: Chicago Review Press.

McGarrigle, Anna, and Jane McGarrigle. 2013. *Mountain City Girls: The McGarricle Family Album*. Toronto: Random House Canada.

McGinley, Paige A. 2014. *Staging the Blues: From Tent Shows to Tourism*. Durham, NC: Duke University Press.

McLauchlan, Murray. 1998. *Getting Out of Here Alive: The Ballad of Murray McLauchlan*. Toronto: Viking.

McLucas, Anne Dhu. 2010. *The Musical Ear: Oral Tradition in the USA*. Surrey, UK: Ashgate.

Metting, Fred. 1999. *The Unbroken Circle: Tradition and Innovation in the Music of Ry Cooder and Taj Mahal*. Lanham, NJ: Scarecrow Press.

Miller, Karl Hagstrom. 2010. *Segregating Sound: Inventing Folk and Pop Music in the Age of Jim Crow*. Durham, NC: Duke University Press.

Mitchell, Gillian. 2007. *The North American Folk Revival: Nation and Identity in the United States and Canada, 1945–1980*. London: Routledge.

Morton, David C., with Charles K. Wolfe. 1991. *DeFord Bailey: A Black Star in Early Country Music*. Knoxville: The University of Tennessee Press.

Nathan, Hans. 1962. *Dan Emmett and the Rise of Early Negro Minstrelsy*. Norman: University of Oklahoma Press.

Near, Holly. 1990. *Fire in the Rain ... Singer in the Storm: An Autobiography*. New York: William Morrow.

Odum, Howard W., and Guy B. Johnson. 1926. *Negro Workaday Songs*. Chapel Hill: The University of North Carolina Press.

Ohrlin, Glenn. 1989. *The Hell-Bound Train: A Cowboy Songbook*. Urbana: University of Illinois Press.

Oliver, Paul. 1993. *Meaning in the Blues*. 2nd ed. Cambridge: University of Cambridge.

Oliver, Paul. 2001. *Yonder Come the Blues: The Evolution of a Genre*. Note: This is actually three books bound as one. They are Oliver's *Savannah Syncopators: African*

*Retentions in the Blues*, Tony Russell's *Blacks, Whites and Blues*, and Robert M. W. Dixon, John Godrich, and Howard Rye's *Recording the Blues* (reprint of 1990 books). Cambridge: Cambridge University Press.

Palieri, Rick. 2003. *The Road Is My Mistress: Tales of a Roustabout Songster*. Hinesburg, VT: Koza Productions.

Paredes, Americo. 1976. *A Texas-Mexican Cancionero: Folksongs of the Lower Border*. Urbana: University of Illinois Press.

Parrish, Lydia. 1992. *Slave Songs of the Georgia Sea Islands*. 2nd ed. Foreword by Art Rosenbaum. Athens: University of Georgia Press.

Perea, John-Carlos. 2014. *Intertribal Native American Music in the United States*. New York: Oxford University Press.

Peterson, Richard A. 1997. *Creating Country Music, Fabricating Authenticity*. Chicago: The University of Chicago Press.

Petrus, Stephen, and Ronald D. Cohen. 2015. *Folk City: New York and the American Folk Revival*. Oxford: Oxford University Press.

Porterfield, Nolan. 1996. *Last Cavalier: The Life and Times of John A Lomax*. Urbana: University of Illinois Press.

Pratt, Ray. 1990. *Rhythm and Resistance: The Political Uses of American Popular Music*. Washington, DC: Smithsonian Institution Press.

Quigley, Colin. 1995. *Music from the Heart: Compositions of a Folk Fiddler*. Athens: University of Georgia Press.

Radcliffe, Philip R. 2011. *Mississippi John Hurt: His Life, His Times, His Music*. Jackson: University of Mississippi Press.

Raffi. 1999. *The Life of a Children's Troubadour*. Vancouver: Homeland Press.

Ragland, Cathy. 2009. *Musica Nortena: Mexican Migrants Creating a Nation between Nations*. Philadelphia, PA: Temple University Press.

Ramsey, Frederic Jr. 1960. *Been Here and Gone*. New Brunswick, NJ: Rutgers University Press.

Reid, Jan. 2004. *The Improbably Rise of Redneck Rock*. New ed. Austin: University of Texas Press.

Reuss, Richard A., and JoAnne *American Folk Music and Left-Wing Politics, 1927–1957*. Lanham, MD: Scarecrow Press.

Rickaby, Franz, with Gretchen Dykstra and James P. Leary. 2017. *Pinery Boys: Songs and Songcatching in the Lumberjack Era*. Madison: University of Wisconsin Press.

Riddington, Robin, and Jillian Riddington. 2006. *When You Sing It Now, Just Like New: First Nation Poetics, Voices and Representations*. Lincoln: University of Nebraska Press.

Riesman, Bob. 2011. *The Life and Times of Big Bill Broonzy*. Chicago: University of Chicago Press.

Robb, J. Donald. 1980. *Hispanic Folk Music of Old New Mexico and the Southwest: A Self-Portrait of a People*. Norman: University of Oklahoma Press.

Robinson, Earl with Eric A. Gordon. 1998. *Ballad of an American: The Autobiography of Earl Robinson*. Lanham, MD: Scarecrow Press.

Robinson, Tiny, and John Reynolds, eds. 2008. *Lead Belly: A Life in Pictures*. Gottingen, Germany: Steidl.

Rocigno, Vincent J., and William F. Danaher. 2004. *The Voice of Southern Labor: Radio, Music and Textile Strikes, 1919–1934*. Minneapolis: University of Minnesota Press.

Romalis, Shelly. 1989. *Pistol Packin' Mama: Aunt Moly and the Politics of Folksong*. Urbana: University of Illinois Press.

Rooney, Jim. 1974. *Bossmen: Bill Monroe and Muddy Waters*. New York: Da Capo Press.

Rooney, Jim. 2014. *In it for the Long Run: A Musical Odyssey*. Urbana: University of Illinois Press.

Rosenberg, Neil, ed. 1993. *Transforming Tradition: Folk Music Revivals Examined*. Urbana: University of Illinois Press.

Rosenberg, Neil. 2005. *Bluegrass: A History*. Urbana: University of Illinois Press.

Rosenberg, Neil. 2018. *Bluegrass Generation: A Memoir*. Urbana: University of Illinois Press.

Rosenbaum, Art. 1983. *Folk Visions & Voices: Traditional Music 7 Song in North Georgia*. Athens: University of Georgia Press.

Rowe, Mike. 1975. *Chicago Blues: The City & the Music*. New York: Da Capo Press.

Russell, Tony. 2010. *Country Music Originals: The Legends and the Lost*. Oxford: Oxford University Press.

Sandberg, Larry, and Dick Weissman. 1989. *The Folk Music Sourcebook*. Revised ed. New York: Da Capo Press.

Saviano, Tamara. 2016. *Without Getting Killed or Caught: The Life and Music of Guy Clark*. College Station: Texas A&M University Press,

Sawin, Patricia. 2004. *Listening for a Life: A Dialogic Ethnography of Bessie Eldreth through her Songs and Stories*. Logan: Utah State University Press.

Sapozknik, Henry. 1999. *Klezmer: Jewish Music from Old World to Our World*. New York: Schirmer Trade Books.

Scales, Christopher A. 2010. *Recording Culture: Powwow Music and the Aboriginal Recording Industry on the Northern Plains*. Durham, NC: Duke University Press.

Schreyer, Lowell. 2007. *The Banjo Entertainers: Roots to Ragtime*. Mankato, MN: Minnesota Heritage Publishing.

Schwartz, Ellen. 1988. *Born a Woman: Seven Canadian Women Singer Songwriters*. Winlaw, BC: Polestar Press.

Scott Berretta, Ed. 2012. *The Conscience of the Folk Revival: The Words of Israel "Izzy" Young."* Lanham, Md. Scarecrow Press.

Seeger, Peggy. 2017. *First Time Ever: A Memoir*. London: Faber & Faber.

Seeger, Pete. 1993. *Where Have All the Flowers Gone: A Singer's Stories, Songs, Seeds, Robberies*. Bethlehem, PA: Sing Out Corporation.

Seeger, Pete, and Bob Reiser. 1985. *Carry It On! A History in Song and Picture of the Working Men and Women of America*. New York: Simon & Schuster.

Seemann, Charlie. 2016. *The Real Singing Cowboys*. Guildford, CT: Two Dot.

Shelton, Robert. 1986. *No Direction Home: The Life and Music of Bob Dylan*. New York: William Morrow.

Slobin, Mark, ed. 2002. *American Klezmer: Its Roots and Offshoots*. Berkeley: University of California Press.

Smith, Craig. 2007. *Sing My Whole Life Long: Jenny Vincent's Life in Folk Music and Activism*. Albuquerque: University of New Mexico Press.

Smith, Richard D. 2000. *Can't You Hear Me Callin: The Life of Bill Monroe*. Boston: Little Brown & Co.

Stanley, Dr. Ralph, with Eddie Dean. 2009. *Man of Constant Sorrow: My Life and Times*. New York: Gotham Books.

Stimeling, Travis D. 2011. *Cosmic Cowboys and New Hicks: The Countercultural Sounds of Austin's Progressive Country Music Scene*. Oxford: Oxford University Press.

Stern, Lewis M. 2016. *Dwight Diller: West Virginia Mountain Musician*. Jefferson, NC: McFarland and Company, Publishers.

Strong, Martin G. 2010. *The Great Folk Discography, Volume 1: Pioneers & Early Legends*. Edinburgh: Polygon Books.

Strong, Martin G. 2011. *The Great Folk Discography, Volume 2: The Next Generation*. Edinburgh: Polygon Books.

Surdam, Maia A. 2014. *Chris Plata: From Fields to Stage*. Madison: Wisconsin Historical Society Press.

Szwed, John. 2010. *Alan Lomax: The Man Who Recorded the World*. New York: Penguin Books.

Taft, Michael. 2005. *Talkin' to Myself: Blues Lyrics, 1921–1942*. New York: Routledge.

Terry, Jill, and Neil A. Wynn, ed. 2012. *Transatlantic Roots Music: Folk, Blues and National Identities*. Jackson: University Press of Mississippi.

Thompson, Katrina Dyonne. 2014. *Ring Shout, Wheel About: The Racial Politics of Music and dance in American Slavery*. Urbana: University of Illinois Press.

Tilling, Robert, Compiler. 2010. *"Oh, What a Beautiful City": A Tribute to the Reverend Gary Davis (1896–1972)*. Pacific, MO: Mel Bay Publications.

Tisserand, Michael. 1998. *The Kingdom of Zydeco*. New York: Arcade Publishing.

Titon, Jeff Todd. 1977. *Early Downhome Blues: A Cultural Analysis*. Chapel Hill: The University of North Carolina Press.

Titon, Jeff Todd. 2001. *Old-Time Kentucky Fiddle Tunes*. Lexington: University of Kentucky Press.

Tooze, Sandra B. 1997. *Muddy Waters: The Mojo Man*. Toronto: ECW Press.

Turino, Thomas. 2008. *Music as Social Life: The Politics of Participation*. Chicago: The University of Chicago Press.

Tyson, Ian. 2011. *The Long Trail: My Life in the West*. Toronto: Vintage Canada.

Unterberger, Richie. 2002. *Turn! Turn! Turn! The 60's Folk-Rock Revolution*. San Francisco: Backbeat Books.

Unterberger, Richie. 2003. *Eight Miles High: Folk-Rock's Flight from Height Ashbury to Woodstock*. San Francisco: Backbeat Books.

Van Der Merwe. 1989. *Origins of the Popular Style: The Antecedents of Twentieth Century Popular Music*. Oxford: Clarendon Press.

Vandy, Greg, with Daniel Person. 2016. *26 Songs in 30 Days: Woody Guthrie's Columbia River Songs and the Planned Promised Land in the Pacific Northwest*. Seattle: Sasquatch Books.

Van Ronk. 2004. *Dave with Elijah Wald. The Mayor of MacDougal Street: A Memoir*. New York: Da Capo Press.

Von Schmidt, Eric, and Jim Rooney. 1979. *Baby Let Me Follow You Down: The Illustrated Story of the Cambridge Folk Years*. Garden City, NY: Anchor Press.

Wade, Stephen. 2012. *The Beautiful Music All around Us: Field Recordings and the American Experience*. Urbana: University of Illinois Press. Note: The hardback book includes a CD, which is essential listening to understand the musical context that Wade is discussing.

Wald, Elijah. 1998. *Narcorrido: A Journey into the Music of Drugs, Guns and Guerrillas*. New York: HarperCollins.

Wald, Elijah. 2000. *Josh White Society Blues*. Amherst: University of Massachusetts Press.

Wald, Elijah. 2001. *Escaping the Delta: Robert Johnson and the Invention of the Blues*. New York: Amistad/HarperCollins.

Wald, Elijah. 2015. *Dylan Goes Electric: Newport, Seeger, Dylan, and the Night that Split the Sixties*. New York: HarperCollins.

Wald, Elijah, and John Junkerman. 1999. *River of Song: A Musical Journey Down the Mississippi*. New York, ST: Martin's Press.

Wardlow, Gayle Dean. 1998. *Chasin' the Devil's Music: Searching for the Blues*. San Francisco: Miller Freeman Books.

Warner, Andrea. 2018. *Buffy Ste Marie: The Authorized Biography*. Vancouver: Greystone Books.

Waterman, Dick. 2003. *Between Midnight and Day: The Last Unpublished Blues Archive*. New York: Thunder's Mouth Press.

Webb, Robert Lloyd. 1984. *Ring the Banjar! The Banjo in America from Folklore to Factory*. Anaheim Hills, CA: Centerstream Publishing.

Weissman, Dick. 2005. *Which Side Are You On? An Inside History of the Folk Music Revival in America*. New York: Continuum.

Weissman, Dick. 2010. *Talkin' 'Bout a Revolution: Music and Social Change in America*. New York: Backbeat Books.

Weissman, Dick. 2014. *100 Books Every Folk Music Fan Should Own*. Lanham, MD: Rowman & Littlefield.

Weissman, Dick. 2017. *Understanding the Music Business: Real World Insights*. 2nd ed. New York: Routledge.

Wheeler, Bill Edd. 2018. *Hotter than a Pepper Sprout: A Hillbilly Poet's Journey from Appalachia to Yale to Writing Hits for Elvis, Johnny Cash & More*. No address: Published by BMG.

White, John I. 1975. *Git along Little Dogies! Songs and Songwriters of the American West.* Urbana: University of Illinois Press.

Wilburn, Gene. 1998. *Northern Journey 2: A Guide to Canadian Folk Music on CD.* Teeswater, ON: Reference Press.

Wilkinson, Alex. 2009. *The Protest Singer: An Intimate Portrait of Pete Seeger.* New York: Vintage Books.

Wilgus, D. K. 1959. *Anglo-American Folksong Scholarship.* New Brunswick, NJ: Rutgers University Press.

Willens, Doris. 1988. *Lonesome Traveler: The Life of Lee Hays.* New York: W. W. Norton & Company.

Williams, Dar. 2017. *What I Found in a Thousand Towns.* New York: Basic Books.

Williams, Justin A., and Katherine Williams, eds. 2017. *The Singer-Songwriter Handbook.* New York: Bloomsbury Academic.

Willis, Barry. 1997. *America's Music: Bluegrass, A History of Bluegrass Music in the Words of Its Pioneers.* Franktown, CO: Pine Valley Music.

Winans, Robert, ed. 2018. *Banjo Roots and Branches.* Urbana: University of Illinois Press.

Wolfe, Charles. 1997. *Devils Box: Masters of Southern Fiddling.* Nashville: Vanderbilt University Press.

Wolfe, Charles, and Kip Lornell. 1992. *The Life and Legend of Lead Belly.* New York: HarperCollins.

Wolliver, Robbie. 1986. *Hoot, A 25-Year History of the Greenwich Village Music Scene.* New York: St Martin's Press.

Yang, Mina. 2008. *California Polyphony: Ethnic Voices, Musical Crossroads.* Urbana: University of Illinois Press.

Zack, Ian. 2015. *Say No to the Devil: The Life and Musical Genius of Reverend Gary Davis.* Chicago: University of Chicago Press.

Zimmerman, Lee David. 2019. *Americana Music: Voices, Visionaries & Pioneers of an Honest Sound.* College Station: Texas A&M University Press.

Zwonitzer, Mark, with Charles Hirshberg. 2002. *Will You Miss Me When I'm Gone? The Carter Family and Their Legacy of American Music.* New York: Simon & Schuster.

# Index